DIVERSE VO
TORT I

Diverse Voices

Series Editors: **Se-shauna Wheatle**, Durham University and
Jonathan Herring, University of Oxford

As law faculties, academics and students realise that their reading lists are
'pale, male and stale', this series gives readers an opportunity to hear
voices that have so often been silenced. It presents a ground-breaking new
platform for debating and understanding the impact of the law on different
marginalised groups and critiquing the law from the
perspective of these groups.

Out now in the series

Diverse Voices in Public Law
Edited by **Se-shauna Wheatle** and **Elizabeth O'Loughlin**

Advisory board

Sharon Cowan, University of Edinburgh
Fiona de Londras, University of Birmingham
Didi Herman, University of Kent
Anna Lawson, University of Leeds
Ambreena Manji, Cardiff University
Stu Marvel, Emory University
Roger Masterman, Durham University
Alex Sharpe, Keele University
Iyiola Solanke, University of Leeds

Find out more at
bristoluniversitypress.co.uk/diverse-voices

DIVERSE VOICES IN TORT LAW

Edited by
Kirsty Horsey

BRISTOL
UNIVERSITY
PRESS

First published in Great Britain in 2024 by

Bristol University Press
University of Bristol
1–9 Old Park Hill
Bristol
BS2 8BB
UK
t: +44 (0)117 374 6645
e: bup-info@bristol.ac.uk

Details of international sales and distribution partners are available at bristoluniversitypress.co.uk

Chapter 9 was supported by the University of Essex's open access fund.

British Library Cataloguing in Publication Data
A catalogue record for this book is available from the British Library

ISBN 978-1-5292-3160-1 hardcover
ISBN 978-1-5292-3166-3 paperback
ISBN 978-1-5292-3162-5 ePub
ISBN 978-1-5292-3163-2 ePdf

Cover design: Nicky Borowiec
Front cover image: Alamy/imageBROKER.com
Bristol University Press uses environmentally responsible print partners.
Printed and bound in Great Britain by CPI Group (UK) Ltd, Croydon, CR0 4YY

FSC
www.fsc.org
MIX
Paper | Supporting
responsible forestry
FSC® C013604

I have enjoyed teaching tort for many years. My enthusiasm for the subject – including its idiosyncrasies and inconsistencies – as well as a critical understanding of its failings and limitations, can be credited to many of those who taught and inspired me, some of whom I later went on to teach alongside: Alan Thomson, Joanne Conaghan, John Wightman and Wade Mansell. Teaching, sharing an office and discussing cases and more over cups of tea or glasses of wine with Erika Rackley in our early careers cemented the passion, as has co-writing a tort textbook with her – the one we always wish we had as students – biannually since 2009. This book is dedicated to them all.

Contents

Series Editors' Preface

Law is dominated by a select range of actors: the wealthy, the white, the male and the enabled. Their prevalence among those who appear before the courts, whether as litigants or legal representatives, and those who judge the cases, is inescapable.

This is true in much academic discourse too. The privileged dominate the practice of law; the law reports; and the professorati. *Diverse Voices* is an attempt to engage with a wider range of voices and perspectives than are typically encountered within the legal academy and legal studies. What are the stories which are not told in traditional law courses? Whose values are permitted and who is ignored? Who is rendered visible and who subjected to the legal gaze? Who is controlled and who is empowered by the law?

Inevitably this series will not capture all the voices that need to be heard. It cannot capture the depth of nuance that a deep intersectional analysis requires. What the series does do is to disrupt the dominant discourse, to highlight those marginalised, silenced or misrepresented by the law. It seeks to start a listening process and begin a journey. It is certainly not the last word or the final destination. It is a beginning.

Table of Cases

England and Wales, Scotland and Northern Ireland

AAA v Unilever [2018] EWCA Civ 1532

A and B (by C, their mother and next friend) v A (Health and Social Services Trust) [2011] NICA 28

AB v Southwest Water Services Ltd [1993] QB 507

AB v XY [1917] SC 15

ABC v WH & Whillock [2015] EWHC 2687 (QB)

ABK v KDT & FGH [2013] EWHC 1192 (QB)

Adams v Cape Industries plc [1990] Ch 433

AH(unt) v AB [2009] EWCA Civ 1092

Airedale NHS Trust v Bland [1993] 2 WLR 316

Ajinomoto Sweeteners Europe SAS v Asda Stores Ltd [2009] EWHC 1717

Alcock v Chief Constable of South Yorkshire Police [1992] 1 AC 310

Appleton v Garrett [1996] PIQR P1 QB

ARB v IVF Hammersmith Ltd and Anor [2017] EWHC 2438 (QB)

ARB v IVF Hammersmith Ltd and Anor [2018] EWCA Civ 2803

Ashby v White 1703 2 Ld Raym 938

Ashley v Chief Constable of Sussex Police [2008] UKHL 25

Attorney General of Trinidad and Tobago v Ramanoop [2005] UKPC 15

Attorney-General's Reference (No.3 of 2003) [2004] EWCA Crim 868

AVB v TDD [2014] EWHC 1442

Bailey v Ministry of Defence [2008] EWCA Civ 883

Bamford v Turnley [1862] EWHC Exch J63

Banca Nazionale del Lavoro SPA v Playboy Club London Ltd [2018] UKSC 43

Banks v Ablex Ltd [2005] ICR 819

Barber v Somerset CC [2002] EWCA Civ 76

Barber v Somerset CC [2004] UKHL 13

Blyth v Birmingham Waterworks Co [1843–60] All ER Rep 478

Bolam v Friern Hospital Management Committee [1957] 1 WLR 583

Bourgoin SA v Ministry of Agriculture, Fisheries and Food [1986] QB 716

Broom v Ritchie & Co (1904) 12 SLT 205

Brown v Bower and Anor [2017] EWHC 2637

Bukovsky v CPS [2017] EWCA Civ 1529

Burstein v Times Newspapers Ltd [2000] EWCA Civ 338

European Court of Human Rights and Court of Justice of the European Union

Other jurisdictions

Notes on Contributors

Haim Abraham is Lecturer in Laws at UCL. His main research and teaching interests include tort law, private law theory, liability of public actors and authorities, and gender and sexuality law. His work has been published in peer-reviewed journals, such as the *Oxford Journal of Legal Studies*, *Law & Social Inquiry*, and the *American University Journal of Gender, Social Policy, and the Law*, as well as in professional and popular blogs such as 'EJIL! Talk', 'Lawfare' and 'Just Security', and has been cited by the Supreme Court of Israel. His forthcoming book, *Tort Liability in Warfare* (OUP), examines states' moral and legal obligations to compensate non-combatants who suffered wrongful losses during warfare and terrorism activities, using theoretical, doctrinal and empirical lenses.

Dimitris Akrivos is Lecturer in Criminology and a member of the Sex, Gender and Sexualities Research Group at the University of Surrey. His research interests lie at the intersection of criminology, law and media ethics, with a particular focus on issues of gender, sexuality and social harm.

Alexandros Antoniou is Lecturer in Media Law at the University of Essex and he researches communications law and intellectual property asset management. His work in these areas has been published in leading journals, including *The Journal of Media Law*, *Communications Law* and the *Journal of Intellectual Property Law and Practice*. He is a legal correspondent for the Council of Europe's European Audiovisual Observatory and a Fellow of the Higher Education Academy.

Eliza Bond supervises the Equity paper at the University of Cambridge. She started pupillage at Twenty Essex in September 2023. She is particularly interested in the law of tort and how equity operates in the commercial context.

Rita D'Alton-Harrison is Professor of Law teaching at Royal Holloway, University of London whose specialist subjects are tort, medical law, criminal litigation and practice, civil litigation and practice and advocacy. Rita is also a qualified solicitor, author and legal education trainer and adviser. Rita has been teaching in higher education for over 21 years both on undergraduate and postgraduate professional courses and is a Senior Fellow of the Higher Education Academy.

Iain Frame is Lecturer in Law at the University of Kent. His research interests span the law of obligations as well as, more specifically, issues of corporate governance and the relationship between law and the monetary system, specifically the monetary and banking systems of England and Scotland during the 18th and 19th centuries.

Jodi Gardner is the Brian Coote Chair of Private Law at the University of Auckland and an Adjunct Senior Research Fellow at the Centre for Banking & Finance Law, National University of Singapore. Her research focuses on the intersection between private law and social policy, analysing the impact of legal doctrines on inequality and vulnerability.

Nikki Godden-Rasul is Senior Lecturer in Law at Newcastle University. Her research expertise is in sexual violence, law and justice, as well as gender, visual culture and legal education. She focuses on justice from the perspectives of survivors and alternative responses to the criminal legal system, such as tort law, restorative justice and transformative justice. She is co-organiser of the Gender Research Group at Newcastle University and the Abolition Feminism for Ending Sexual Violence Collective, and is on the editorial board of *Feminist Legal Studies*.

Kirsty Horsey is Professor of Law at the University of Kent, where she has taught tort for many years. Her research interests lie primarily in the regulation of surrogacy, other forms of assisted human reproduction and genetic technologies. She is particularly interested in where these areas overlap and intersect with issues in family law, especially the concept of legal parenthood. She also researches within the law of tort, in particular those obligations based on 'relationship', assumptions of responsibility and/or imbalances of power.

Emily Jackson is Professor of Law at the London School of Economics and Political Science, where she teaches medical law. She is particularly interested in the regulation of reproductive technologies, assisted dying and the pharmaceutical industry. Emily has been a Member and then Deputy Chair of the Human Fertilisation and Embryology Authority (2003–12) and a Judicial Appointments Commissioner (2014–17).

Julie McCandless is Senior Lecturer in Law at the University of Kent, where she teaches and researches in the fields of family and healthcare law. Her current research is a socio-legal exploration of birth registration law and exclusion. She co-directs the Research Centre for Sexuality, Race and Gender Justice and is on the Editorial Board for the peer-reviewed open-access journal, *feminists@law*.

Colin Murray is Professor of Law and Democracy at Newcastle University. His research addresses pressing challenges within the UK's constitutional order, from prisoner disenfranchisement and the right to vote, to the role of civil liability in post-conflict and post-imperial litigation in the UK courts, to the human rights implications of special counter-terrorism powers and the implications of Brexit for Northern Ireland. He served as a Specialist Adviser to the Select Committee on the Draft Prisoner Voting Bill in 2013.

Aislinn O'Connell is Senior Lecturer in Law at Royal Holloway University of London. She researches a range of topics around intellectual property rights, digital rights, technology-based abuse and legal regulation of online harms. She has a particular interest in the gendered aspects of online abuse.

Craig Purshouse is Senior Lecturer in Law at the University of Liverpool. His research interests are in torts, private law theory and medical law.

Introduction: Why Recognising Diversity in Tort Law Matters

Kirsty Horsey

Tort law is, and will likely remain, a dynamic and ever-changing area of law. It is never static. Whether or not they are framed as such, tort law issues pervade the daily news, nationally and internationally. Because of this, conversations and debates over the dinner table or in bars regularly cover what are, in reality, tortious issues, which generate often heated debate even among people who usually agree with each other. One recent example might include discussions over whether and, if so, to what extent, Prince Harry and Meghan Markle are entitled to have aspects of their private life remain private. When an individual shares so much about their life, their views and the way they experience their treatment by their family and other institutions – including the press – does any private sphere remain?[1] Another example concerns the collective conduct of the Metropolitan Police Service in its failure to root out so-called 'rotten apples' or to stamp out institutional racism[2] – should conduct by its individual officers

---

[1] Compare, for example, Caitlin Moran, 'Why I'm still Team Harry' *The Times* 9 January 2023, who writes: 'Harry's revelations about his own life make up a minuscule percentage of all the thousands of stories other people have told about him', with the view of Dominic Ponsford, who suggests that 'Prince Harry has not only breached the privacy of his family members but also significantly undermined his own future right to privacy' ('Prince Harry waves goodbye to privacy with book revelations' *Press Gazette* 6 January 2023). See also *HRH The Duchess of Sussex v Associated Newspapers Ltd* [2021].

[2] Consider, inter alia, *R v Couzens (Wayne)* [2021], following the abduction and murder of Sarah Everard by a serving police officer; the report of Baroness Casey of Blackstock into conduct in the Metropolitan Police Service (MPS) more generally (The Baroness Casey Review, 2023); the conviction in January 2023 of PC David Carrick for 49 sexual offences, including rape, against 12 women (see June Kelly, Claire Ellison and Judith Burns, 'David Carrick: The serial rapist and abuser in a police uniform' *BBC News* 16 January 2023) and The Stephen Lawrence Inquiry: Report of an Inquiry by Sir William Macpherson of Cluny Cm 4262-1, 1999, commissioned following major failings by the MPS in its investigation

give rise to liability against the police service generally in respect of harms suffered by women or those in marginalised groups?[3] The Grenfell Tower fire provides a further example. If it is established the fire was caused or worsened by direct result of negligence and/or misfeasance in relation to building permissions, construction, design and manufacture,[4] then, as well as residents injured or killed in the tragedy, should those who attempted to help them be compensated in respect of both physical and psychiatric injuries they suffered?[5] And what about where the law itself fails? Should tort law step in to address failures in the criminal law, especially in relation to sexual violence, including image-based sexual abuse?[6]

Critical legal education in the UK gained ground from the 1970s onwards,[7] later including scholarship highlighting the politics and power relationships of and within tort law.[8] This critical movement highlighted the extent to which tort law privileged the already privileged and the gendered nature of much of tort law.[9] Overall, however, this critical work did little to impact the core of mainstream tort education.[10] In the field of tort law, particularly in textbooks aimed at university students rather than more abstract or advanced theoretical

---

of the racist murder of the Black teenager Stephen Lawrence in April 1993 and leading to a finding that the MPS is 'institutionally racist'.

3   See Vikram Dodd, 'Met officers charged over Wayne Couzens WhatsApp group named' *The Guardian* 21 February 2022; Emma Guy, 'How deep does misogyny run in the Met?' *EachOther* 25 January 2023.

4   See Robert Booth, 'Grenfell bereaved and survivors bring multimillion pound case to High Court' *The Guardian* 6 July 2021; Martina Lees and Harry Yorke, 'Michael Gove: We are to blame on Grenfell' *The Times* 29 January 2023.

5   See Tristan Kirk, '999 crews sue in £1m claim over Grenfell Tower trauma' *Evening Standard* 19 August 2020; Thomas Kingsley, 'Dozen Grenfell firefighters diagnosed with terminal cancer' *The Independent* 14 January 2023.

6   See Kirsty Horsey and Erika Rackley, 'Tort Law' in Rosemary Auchmuty (ed), *Great Debates in Gender and Law* (Palgrave Macmillan, 2018) 13–24.

7   See, for example, the work of Duncan Kennedy, including 'Legal Education as Training for Hierarchy' in David Kairys (ed), *The Politics of Law: A Progressive Critique* (Pantheon Books, 1982) 54–78; *Legal Education and the Reproduction of Hierarchy: A Polemic Against the System: A Critical Edition* (New York University Press, 2004). In the UK, notable texts include Ian Grigg-Spall and Paddy Ireland (eds), *The Critical Lawyer's Handbook* (Pluto Press, 1992).

8   Allan Hutchinson and Derek Morgan, 'The Canengusian Connection: The Kaleidoscope of Tort Theory' (1984) 22 *Osgoode Hall Law Journal* 69–113; Joanne Conaghan and Wade Mansell, *The Wrongs of Tort* (Pluto Press, 1993; 1998).

9   Conaghan and Mansell, ibid.; Joanne Conaghan went on to write extensively on gender and tort, including inter alia 'Tort Law and the Feminist Critique of Reason' in Anne Bottomley (ed), *Feminist Perspectives on the Foundational Subjects of Law* (Routledge-Cavendish, 1996) 47–68; 'Gendered Harms and the Law of Tort: Remedying (Sexual) Harassment' (1996) 16(3) *Oxford Journal of Legal Studies* 407–43; 'Law, Harm and Redress: A Feminist Perspective' (2002) 22(3) *Legal Studies* 319–39; 'Tort Law and Feminist Critique' (2003) 56(1) *Current Legal Problems* 175–209.

10   Though some of those who studied tort in these times have clearly absorbed the critical sentiment and as a result there is, in my co-written (with Erika Rackley) textbook *Tort Law* (currently 8th edn, Oxford University Press, 2023), at least one leading text on the market that incorporates critical perspectives into mainstream tort education.

scholarship, most texts – especially those more 'longstanding' and 'revered' (and notably written by male academics) – have tended to be largely immune from such critiques.[11] Though some notable tort textbooks (and textbooks generally) are now written by women,[12] many of these are 'new' in the marketplace and in terms of content, contain only very brief, if any, discussion of diverse perspectives in the field. Similarly, though women's voices are also represented in tort law scholarship beyond textbook level, academic tort publications also tend to be dominated by white British (male) perspectives. Scant attention is paid in most mainstream texts to the gendered nature of harm as defined in tort law,[13] and the same can be said of social class, sexual orientation, gender identity, able-ness[14] and 'race'.[15]

In recent years, there has been a general move in legal education towards recognising both the inequalities perpetuated by the law and the increased diversity of the students to whom we teach it, many of whom aspire to be the lawyers of the future. Vitally, the 'Whiteness' of English common law – and its foundations in empire – have been highlighted. Attempts to 'decolonise' law curriculums have increased, in efforts to highlight how some legal rules stem

---

[11] For example, Nicholas McBride and Roderick Bagshaw, *Tort Law* (6th edn, Pearson, 2018); Simon Deakin and Zoe Adams, *Markesinis & Deakin's Tort Law* (8th edn, Oxford University Press, 2019); James Goudkamp and Donal Nolan, *Winfield & Jolowicz on Tort* (20th edn, Sweet and Maxwell, 2020); Andrew Tettenborn, *Clerk & Lindsell on Torts* (23rd edn, Sweet and Maxwell, 2022); Ken Oliphant and Donal Nolan, *Lunney & Oliphant's Tort Law: Text and Materials* (7th edn, Oxford University Press, 2023). Law has been resistant generally to the incorporation and reflection of alternative perspectives – as highlighted in Erika Rackley and Rosemary Auchmuty, 'The Case for Feminist Legal History' (2020) 40(4) *Oxford Journal of Legal Studies* 878–904.

[12] For example, Rachel Mulheron, *Principles of Tort Law* (2nd edn, Cambridge University Press, 2020); Paula Giliker, *Tort* (7th edn, Sweet and Maxwell, 2021); Sarah Green and Jodi Gardner, *Tort Law* (Red Globe Press, 2021); Jenny Steele, *Tort Law: Text, Cases, and Materials* (5th edn, Oxford University Press, 2022); Horsey and Rackley, *Tort Law*.

[13] As well as Conaghan (see note 9), other scholars have highlighted the gendered nature of tort law (see, for example, Patricia Peppin, 'A Feminist Challenge to Tort Law' in Bottomley, *Feminist Perspectives*; Sally Sheldon, 'Rethinking the *Bolam* Test' in Sally Sheldon and Michael Thomson (eds), *Feminist Perspectives on Health Care Law* (Routledge-Cavendish, 1998) 15–32; chapters in Janice Richardson and Erika Rackley (eds), *Feminist Perspectives on Tort Law* (Routledge, 2012); Horsey and Rackley, 'Tort Law'), but this perspective rarely permeates traditional textbooks.

[14] Though disability is 'part' of tort law, because of the way tort must deal with disabling injuries caused by the fault of others, it is not itself a lens through which tort is usually viewed. Nor does tort law cover the full spectrum of the causes of disability, or even injury, hence there have been calls for total reform of tort in relation to negligently caused personal injury, such as by Patrick Atiyah in *The Damages Lottery* (Hart Publishing, 1999).

[15] 'Race' issues in tort have been better highlighted in the US context; see, for example, Martha Chamallas and Jennifer B. Wriggins, *The Measure of Injury: Race, Gender and Tort Law* (New York University Press, 2010).

from and replicate historical forms of power and domination.[16] Publications like *The Critical Legal Pocketbook* continue the critical legal tradition in seeking to provide students with the 'tools' with which to interrogate law's dominant and subterranean structures.[17]

And yet still the teaching of tort law has remained relatively unchanged. Tort law textbooks – and teaching (for the two enjoy a symbiotic relationship) – cover the usual core topics such as negligence, defamation, nuisance, trespass to the person and so on, omitting the perspectives that challenge this framing. Moreover, most tort (text)books (like judgments) present topics with a gloss of neutrality, which fails to reflect the impact of disparities in power and privilege that underlie tort law decisions: both those between individuals and/or between individuals and the state.[18]

This textbook is different. And deliberately so. In creating a tort law text that features marginalised or excluded perspectives and voices, our joint purpose – as editor and contributors – is to strengthen the argument that these should be viewed as part of the standard curriculum and discourse: that they are necessary inclusions for anyone seeking to truly understand tort. Everyone who studies law should be able to relate to it, by seeing their lives and experiences reflected. In that vein, this book introduces readers, including those studying tort for the first time, to a range of underexplored perspectives on some of the main topics and themes of tort law, and amplifies voices that remain underrepresented in the field.

We may ask why this matters. It occurs to me that it probably matters in the same way that judicial (lack of) diversity matters: particular judges bring their experience and worldview to their decisions, which, though supposedly objective and based on existing law, leads them to consider or interpret aspects of the law in different ways.[19] So too students should be better acquainted with the real impact

---

[16] See Suhraiya Jivraj, 'Decolonizing the Academy – Between a Rock and a Hard Place' (2020) 22(4) *Interventions* 552–73, and 'Towards Anti-racist Legal Pedagogy: A Resource' Project report (2020) (available at https://kar.kent.ac.uk/82763/1/82763_Towards-Anti-racist-Legal-Pedagogy-A-Resource.pdf).

[17] Illan rua Wall, Freya Middleton, Sahar Shah and CLAW (eds), *The Critical Legal Pocketbook* (Counterpress, 2021).

[18] Again, I hope, Horsey and Rackley's *Tort Law* is a notable exception. Additionally, it should be remembered, the cases that make it to the pages of a tort law textbook, or onto a tort course syllabus, are the tip of a very big iceberg. Many more cases under the surface of tort fail, or are settled, so are never even considered by a judge.

[19] See, for example, Erika Rackley, *Women, Judging and the Judiciary: From Difference to Diversity* (Routledge, 2012); Erika Rackley, 'Rethinking Judicial Diversity' in Ulrike Schultz and Gisela Shaw (eds), *Gender and Judging* (Oñati International Series in Law and Society, Hart Publishing, 2013) 6.3; Rosemary Hunter, 'More than Just a Different Face? Judicial Diversity and Decision-making' (2015) 68(1) *Current Legal Problems* 119–41. Also, as identified by the authors of the Public Law work in this series, '[g]ender disparity in scholarly influence, measured both in gendered publication patterns and differential citations of academic work, has been widely documented in the social sciences, and is also reflected in course syllabi' (Se-shauna Wheatle and Elizabeth A. O'Loughlin (eds), *Diverse Perspectives on Public Law* (Bristol University Press, 2023) 1.

of tort law – and the assumptions on which its principles rest – on people's lived experiences and should be helped to understand how these experiences relate to the tort law topics that they study. In bringing this to the fore it is hoped that at least some will use this knowledge as a pillar on which to build the foundations of their legal (or other) careers, and the pursuit of social justice.

After all, tort law (like most areas of law) affects 'real people' and their lives, often with catastrophic effect. This point is illustrated in the introductory chapter to Horsey and Rackley's *Tort Law*, in a discussion about 'the humanity of tort law':

> At the heart of every tort case – indeed of all the cases you'll encounter throughout your studies – are real people and real-life situations. As Master McCloud acknowledged in *Ovu v London Underground Ltd* [2021], a case involving the duty of care owed to the claimants under the Occupiers Liability Act 1984,
>
>> With most things in the Law, cases have a triangular character, such that what is at once personal or private between the parties becomes, in the panopticon of the court, both a legal and a public matter. The relatively abstract nature of the law with which this case deals should not detract from the fact that at the heart of this case is the loss of a life of a young man, whose family is bereaved, after he fell to his death at a London Underground station (at [1]).
>
> It is sometimes easy to forget, in our rush to skip to the end – to find the decision or ratio – or to understand the *judge's* reasoning, the humanity around which tort law revolves. In so doing, we risk downplaying or instrumentalising the human story: the individuals, with families and friends, who have experienced (and often are continuing to experience) often upsetting, sometimes tragic, occasionally criminal, events or sets of circumstances which lead to the case coming to court in the first place.[20]

Much of the substance of tort law is judicially created and developed. Because of this, it is inevitably shaped by the political and policy understandings of the times, and by responses to events that occur (consider the impact of the Hillsborough Stadium disaster on the law of negligently inflicted psychiatric harm, for example). It is unfortunate, therefore, that many tort law students are not introduced to the historical, political and other contexts within which judicial decisions in tort cases are made, nor to ideas about judicial (lack of) diversity and the effect this can/may have had on the development of the law. Though judges judge objectively and according to the law, and they must find or decipher that law from precedent or by statutory interpretation, there is a wide and growing understanding that background, privilege and even gender of judges hearing cases

---

[20] Horsey and Rackley, *Tort Law*, 24–25.

can make a difference to the way tort claims are initially framed and ultimately decided.[21] Often claimants must fight an uphill battle against more powerful – in terms of wealth, status and privilege – defendants. Because of this, this collection covers a range of tort law topics, or subtopics (for example, one aspect of the rules of duty of care within negligence) in a way that encourages students to consider the impact of tort law's rules on those (often) already disadvantaged or marginalised within contemporary society.

In addition to highlighting the non-neutrality of tort law, and its personal, real-life content and context, this collection includes chapters written by those who are often underrepresented in the field, in an effort to include a diversity not only of topic coverage and perspectives, but of voices. As such, the majority of the chapters that follow are written by women, racialised or minoritised or LGBTQ+ persons, with a significant number of the chapters being contributed by early career scholars, from a wide range of institutions. The deliberate welcoming of both diverse topics and interpretations, alongside diverse voices, is intended to help students gain and develop further critical understanding of the goals of tort, whether they are achieved (and if so, who for, and at what cost), or whether tort law serves to perpetuate existing inequalities and division. By including a wider range of voices and views within a core tort law text, we hope to provide a useful resource for those seeking to engage with more critical and diverse perspectives on tort.

Detailed synopsis

In most tort texts, foundational concepts (including negligence, trespass to the person [personal] torts, land torts including trespass to land and nuisance, economic torts and defamation) are covered to varying extents. While the tort of negligence usually dominates the page count – it is by far the 'biggest' tort and there are many rules to cover, often governing different situations in which negligence may occur, and the limitations placed on certain claimants in those situations – texts will usually also cover at least some of the more recent or 'bespoke' torts: including consumer protection torts, occupiers' liability, employers' liability, breach of statutory duty, misfeasance in public office or the relatively new tort of misuse of personal information.

Similarly, the coverage of this collection is not universal, though across the chapters it considers a variety of torts. It does this with an explicit focus on the impact of tort law norms from diverse critical and marginalised perspectives. As well as highlighting the role of core torts in maintaining or perpetuating

---

[21] This is why various Feminist Judgments projects have been initiated, in which actual judgments are reimagined by feminist scholars, revealing the practical manifestation of a lack of judicial diversity, and that who a judge is matters – beginning with the groundbreaking collection by Rosemary Hunter, Clare McGlynn and Erika Rackley (eds), *Feminist Judgments: From Theory to Practice* (Hart Publishing, 2010), and later extending to other jurisdictions and collections.

existing societal hierarchies and inequalities, it amplifies underrepresented voices to provide new and diverse critical perspectives on other current tort-related issues, including but not limited to sexual violence, reproductive autonomy, the effects of environmental pollution and the impact of medical devices. It takes a scholarly approach and contributes to the wider tort literature, while also being accessible to students on undergraduate and postgraduate tort law modules.

The collection is curated into three parts: the first contains chapters which cover core aspects of the tort of negligence. The second part consists of chapters relating to negligence, focused on in-depth examination of specific types of harm – reproductive and environmental – and the law's response to these. The third part considers other torts and tortious principles, including liability under the Consumer Protection Act, misfeasance in public office, defamation and the trespass to the person torts.

In Part I, Underexplored Ideas Within the Core of Negligence, some aspects of the law of negligence are given close critical examination. First, Nikki Godden-Rasul and Craig Murray's chapter, 'Negligence and the Vulnerable Subject: Public Bodies and the Duty of Care', considers whether and in what circumstances public bodies can be liable in negligence, with an analysis of the limits and radical potential of public authorities' duties of care to hold the state to account for harms suffered by those who are most marginalised in society. In particular, they analyse the conception of the subject underpinning the tortious construction of the relationship between the state and individuals. Invoking literature that calls for the placing of a vulnerable human subject at the centre of law, politics and ethics, they argue that there has been little consideration given to whether there has been a shift in the conception of the subject to whom duties of care are owed and any invocations of vulnerability. This oversight is more significant, they contend, when research identifying an increasingly prominent role of vulnerability in the context of human rights is considered, given the close – though contested – relationship between tort law and human rights in relation to public bodies' liability.

In his chapter 'The Politics of Pure Economic Loss', Craig Purshouse discusses the underlying and unspoken politics of the limits placed on recovery of pure economic loss in negligence. He considers how social class is reflected in the development or extension of the law relating to duty of care for pure economic loss caused by negligent actions or services and how – despite initial appearances to the contrary – some decisions that may at first have looked to be exceptions to the privileging of general neoliberal principles in most pure economic loss cases, and to represent the protection of vulnerable/weaker claimants from lower social class, can on closer examination be seen to be consistent with the neoliberal political ideology that was at its height in the 1980s and 1990s.

Haim Abraham's chapter, 'Queering the Reasonable Person', looks at the inimitable concept of the reasonable man or person and seeks to uncover what might be learned about this legal construct from a queer theory perspective. He explains how critiques of the 'reasonable man', through which tort claims are considered via a male lens only, led to the origins of the 'reasonable person', but shows that this development is not enough: other critical lenses show that individuals who do not share the expected qualities of the 'personified reasonable man' (such as class, Whiteness and straightness), become vulnerable. He argues that this means that such individuals are unlikely to be able to successfully claim against defendants who the reasonable man represents, while as defendants to claims themselves they are more likely to be found liable, having been unable to live up to the 'reasonable' standard expected of them. He goes on to explore what queer theory reveals about the reasonable man, arguing that, as a legal standard, the reasonable person is a queer standard and that it is this very character that continues to place LGBTQ+ individuals at risk in tort law.

In Part II, How Negligence Norms Respond to Particular Harms, Julie McCandless and Kirsty Horsey first consider how the law responds to 'reproductive harms' caused by negligence, before Iain Frame looks at the use of negligence as a response to environmental harm, pollution and degradation caused by multinational corporations. In their chapter 'Reproductive Harm, Social Justice and Tort Law: Rethinking "Wrongful Birth" and "Wrongful Life" Claims', McCandless and Horsey analyse how judges have developed the tort of negligence in the context of professional/clinical liability claims for harms associated with (unwanted) reproduction. They argue that the judicial development of tort law in this area has failed to adequately and consistently protect the interests that claimants have in their reproductive autonomy, as well as the realities of care and structural disadvantage, particularly in relation to gender, 'race' and disability, thereby failing to secure social justice.

Iain Frame's chapter, 'Coded Copper, Toxic Water. Multinational Corporations, Environmental Degradation and Tort Law' explains how, across national borders, diverse communities and individuals of the 'Global South' contend with environmental pollution and degradation and human rights violations, and how, as they do so, they confront the might of some of the world's largest multinational corporations. This chapter focuses on the use of the tort of negligence as a weapon in this battle, where the issue is whether a parent company owes a duty of care to those harmed by the actions or omissions of its subsidiaries, as a means of escaping the limits on corporate veil lifting elsewhere in law. Frame situates this discussion in the context of early 21st century capitalism by engaging with Katharina Pistor's work, which identifies how assets (for example, copper mined in Zambia) become capital. For that to happen the assets must be 'coded in law' to channel benefits to the asset owner and to shift costs and risks on to those who are left vulnerable to harm by the manipulation of those assets. As Pistor shows, fashioning such distributional outcomes relies on the institutions of private law. Frame takes this one step further by considering the work done by lawyers and judges to protect those left vulnerable.

In Part III, Diverse Voices Elsewhere in Tort, there are chapters considering product liability under the Consumer Protection Act 1987 (Emily Jackson), malicious prosecution and misfeasance in public office (Rita D'Alton-Harrison), defamation (Alexandros Antoniou and Dimitris Akrivos), the trespass to the person torts (Eliza Bond and Jodi Gardner) and image-based sexual abuse (Aislinn O'Connell).

Emily Jackson's chapter, 'Product Liability, Medical Devices and Harm to Women's Bodies' considers liability in tort for faulty medical devices. She contends that, in recent years, women have been disproportionately affected by a series of scandals involving faulty medical devices, including (but not limited to) PIP breast implants, the *Essure* permanent contraceptive device and vaginal mesh. As a result, she argues that well known defects in the product liability regime in the UK leave more women than men without a remedy when they are injured by medical devices. Female patients injured by medical devices are also disproportionately affected by what the Cumberlege Review referred to as 'the widespread and wholly unacceptable labelling of so many symptoms as "normal" and attributable to "women's problems"'.[22] Jackson's fear is that an ineffective product liability regime does not drive improvements in the safety of medical devices, but rather makes it more likely that defective devices will continue to be inserted into women's bodies.

In looking at the torts of malicious prosecution and misfeasance in public office, in 'The Tortious Response to Police Power, Misconduct and Abuse', Rita D'Alton Harrison considers the perceived tension between principles of 'public interest' in unmasking abuses of power and the public policy principle that allows the use of a wide judicial discretion to protect certain public office holders. She argues that this dichotomy serves to both aid and bar remedies in this area of law, becoming of particular concern where the behaviour of the public office holder is alleged to involve malice targeted at specific underrepresented groups that can be said to amount to dishonesty, bad faith and/or illegality. Her chapter examines whether microstructural factors such as damages based on perceptions of morality of conduct, ill-defined terms and the use of control tests with high thresholds serve to constrain the utility of this tort for certain marginalised groups, particularly when considered against the limits of the criminal offence of misconduct and the tort of negligence.

In 'Homosexuality, Defamatory Meaning and Reputational Injury in English Law', Alexandros Antoniou and Dimitris Akrivos take on the might of the tort of defamation, critically analysing English defamation law's treatment of false imputations of homosexuality (before and after the 2013 libel reforms) and considering the extent to which, if at all, reputational harm for being misidentified as gay or lesbian should be legally recognised. Their chapter first discusses the meaning of reputation to explain what defamation law is meant to protect, before going on to analyse the elements of the tort and the point at which a false description of another as gay or lesbian acquires defamatory

---

[22] Julia Cumberlege, Sir Cyril Chantler and Simon Whale, First Do No Harm: The Report of the Independent Medicines and Medical Devices Safety Review, IMMDS, 2020, para 1.18.

status. The chapter then juxtaposes judicial treatment of false statements of homosexuality as defamatory with scholarly work examining whether false imputations of homosexuality should retain defamatory meaning, especially in the context of the current legal environment and the societal progress of the gay rights movement.

In their chapter, 'Rethinking "Negligence" in "Medical Negligence": Can Trespass to the Person Torts Help Protect Autonomy?', Eliza Bond and Jodi Gardner analyse how intentional torts to the person (the 'trespass torts') have taken a back seat in English tort law and argue that this exacerbates pre-existing inequalities. They explain how the 'staggering march of negligence' has largely obviated the need for many claimants to rely on such torts, and the perceived criminal stigma surrounding the torts of battery and assault may have further contributed to their demise. They contend that these developments are unfortunate, as the intentional torts could have an important role in vindicating claimants' right to be free from interference without the need to show that the defendant has fallen below a required standard of care. They illustrate this in the context of informed consent and other cases that have highlighted that such vindication is particularly important for parties whose rights can so often be overlooked or undermined by the courts. They argue that the loss-based paradigm of negligence, its inability to protect autonomy interests and its struggle to accommodate non-conventional forms of damage, prompts questions about its appropriateness in these contexts, where the focus should be on protecting the rights of (rather than harms to) the claimant and not the reasonableness of the defendant.

Finally, in 'Image-based Sexual Abuse and Gendered Conceptions of Harm in Tort', Aislinn O'Connell examines the spectrum of actions which encompass image-based sexual abuse – the making, taking and sharing of intimate images without consent – and the lack of a framework in tort law that enables victim-survivors of such abuse to obtain remedies for this deliberate and harmful violation of their most intimate self. She argues that image-based sexual abuse falls uncomfortably into a lacuna in the provisions of tort law, falling outside of intentional interference with the person, often failing to fit the parameters of intentional infliction of emotional distress, not reaching the high threshold for the duty of care in freestanding psychiatric injury, skirting around the requirements of defamation, and struggling to fall within the tort of misuse of private information, especially where the person creating or sharing the images cannot be identified. Overall, despite the potential for clear and manifest harm, image-based sexual abuse fails to fall squarely within a single tortious cause of action, leaving claimants struggling to find a suitable avenue for redress. O'Connell contends that this magnifies the difficulty that (often-female) victim-survivors face, increasing barriers to obtaining a remedy, not least through cost, and exacerbates harms along intersectional identity lines, leaving marginalised communities at a greater risk of harm. The chapter explores the inadequacies of tort law as it stands for remedying a prevalent, but often hidden, and gendered, form of harm.

Collectively, the authors in this collection identify aspects of tort law where existing principles tend to fail or to hinder certain claimants achieving (social) justice. They highlight issues where recognition of the diversity – and specificity – of tort law claimants may make a difference to the expected outcome of a tort claim, which also illustrates how tort law's privileging of White, masculine and heteronormative norms have filtered down into tort law principles as they have developed through the common law. Paying more attention to difference, diversity and the human aspect of both the nature of claims and the way tort law frames harm and limits claimants may enable tort to better respond to vulnerability, particularly that created and maintained by the state and its institutions. Similarly, diversifying the judiciary may assist in allowing individualised human vulnerabilities and expectations to be foregrounded in tort, which *could* operate as a vehicle for social justice, rather than a barrier to claimants.

PART I

Underexplored Ideas Within the Core of Negligence

2

Negligence and the Vulnerable Subject: Public Bodies and the Duty of Care

Nikki Godden-Rasul and Colin Murray

Introduction

This chapter explores the conception of the subject within negligence law in England and Wales and the extent to which it aligns with the conception operating in human rights law. The development of positive obligations under the European Convention on Human Rights (ECHR) highlights the shifts in the conception of the subject in human rights law, providing a powerful contrast to the original emphasis of the Convention on preventing state interference with rights. The related area of negligence liability addresses duties of care where failures to act by organs of the state have led to harm being caused. In the human rights context, expansions of positive obligations under the ECHR have been accompanied by increasing references to the vulnerability of the human subject.[1] However, there has been no parallel expansion in public authority liability in the negligence context and little evident judicial engagement with the concept of vulnerability in such cases.

Nevertheless, Carl Stychin has argued that paying attention to vulnerability in the context of public authority liability could bring doctrinal coherence to this body of case law and offers a more ethical way to determine whether a duty of care should be imposed, but he did not see significant traces of this approach in England and Wales.[2] It has long been there at the margins; in *X (Minors) v*

---

[1] Lourdes Peroni and Alexandra Timmer, 'Vulnerable Groups: The Promise of an Emerging Concept in European Human Rights Convention Law' (2013) 11(1) *International Journal of Constitutional Law* 1056.

[2] Carl F. Stychin, 'The Vulnerable Subject of Negligence Law' (2012) 8(3) *International Journal of Law in Context* 337.

Bedfordshire County Council, Lord Browne-Wilkinson referred in passing to 'the cases where a common law duty of care has been sought to be imposed upon the police (in seeking to protect vulnerable members of society from wrongs done to them by others)'.[3] In the Australian High Court, Jane Stapleton identifies the 'golden thread' of negligence law as protecting the vulnerable, which has enabled new claims to be recognised while also limiting the scope of liability in a morally defensible way.[4] Continuing these conversations, this chapter draws on the extensive body of literature on the inherent vulnerability of human beings to analyse English and Welsh case law on duty of care where public authorities have failed to act to prevent harm. It starts by setting out the critiques of the liberal legal subject before exploring vulnerability scholarship. The chapter then considers how the liabilities of public authorities have been reshaped in recent decades, and to what extent there is engagement with the concept of vulnerability. We finally reflect on the relationship between the developments in human rights and tort law, explaining how the partial displacement of negligence liability can be connected to the conception of the subject in tort: while there are shifts in the nature of the human at the heart of human rights to accommodate vulnerability, in tort law the traditional liberal subject remains firmly grounded.

The subject(s) of tort law and human rights

Critiques of the liberal legal subject

There is extensive scholarship, led by feminists, outlining and critiquing the key features of the liberal legal person: 'rational, autonomous, self-contained, self-possessed, self-sufficient and formally equal before the law'.[5] This person is the subject of tort law; a person who is separate from others and their social context which are potential threats to their bounded and isolated autonomous self.[6] As such, Joanne Conaghan says tort law emphasises personal responsibility over caring for others and reflects a negative account of freedom – that is, freedom from interference by others.[7] In addition, despite an outward appearance of neutrality, the liberal legal subject embodies the experiences and worldviews of White, able-bodied men dominating positions of power and authority, and (re) produces structural hierarchies of gender, 'race', class and other intersecting social

---

3   *X (Minors) v Bedfordshire County Council* [1995] 2 AC 633, 751.
4   Jane Stapleton, 'The Golden Thread at the Heart of Tort Law: Protection of the Vulnerable' (2003) 24 *Australian Bar Review* 135.
5   Rosemary Hunter, 'Contesting the Dominant Paradigm: Feminist Critiques of Liberal Legalism' in Margaret Davies and E. Munro Vanessa (eds), *The Ashgate Research Companion to Feminist Legal Theory* (Ashgate, 2013) 13.
6   Joanne Conaghan, 'Tort Law and Feminist Critique' (2003) 56(1) *Current Legal Problems* 175, 199–200.
7   ibid.

relations. For example, the masculine qualities of the 'reasonable person' who, by and large, sets the standard of care in negligence have been exposed.[8] Martha Chamallas and Linda K. Kerber, moreover, show the types of harm recognised as actionable 'damage' in negligence are ones more commonly associated with men's lives compared to women's lives.[9] Consequently, women and other marginalised groups have been negatively impacted by tort law's 'deep cognitive structures' of bias and discrimination.[10]

This liberal subject's prominence within tort law has implications for the ethical questions which condition the responsibilities which it imposes.[11] As Stychin explains, tort law has 'privileged an autonomous subject of rights which pre-exists the responsibilities that come with relating to others'.[12] But relations to others based on care and dependency, and through structures of social relations,[13] often have greater significance for those who are less privileged in society. Some lives – typically women's lives – are more bound up with caring for others, and some being cared for by others. Furthermore, feminists have theorised the self as co-constituted by its relations with others and society.[14] Members of social groups whose lives are shaped by disadvantage, discrimination and violence[15] cannot meaningfully separate themselves from the social context. This approach to understanding human life is at odds with the liberal subject whose focus is on personal responsibility and being protected from external interferences.

This same liberal legal subject has also dominated human rights law, generating the same sharp criticisms. Despite the appearance of universality which guarantees certain rights to every human being, it is a particular kind of human being which has informed the nature, content and scope of such rights. Based on a bounded, self-reliant, self-possessive subject, human rights law, including the ECHR, has long been primarily concerned with negative freedom. It relies on the assumption that individual rights will not be violated if people are protected from interference

---

8   Joanne Conaghan, 'Tort Law and the Feminist Critique of Reason' in Anne Bottomley (ed), *Feminist Perspectives on the Foundational Subjects of Law* (Cavendish, 1996) 47–68. See also Haim Abraham, Chapter 4, this volume.

9   Martha Chamallas and Linda K. Kerber, 'Women, Mothers, and the Law of Fright: A History' (1990) 88(4) *Michigan Law Review* 814.

10   Martha Chamallas, 'The Architecture of Bias: Deep Structures in Tort Law' (1988) 146 *University of Pennsylvania Law Review* 463; and Martha Chamallas and Jennifer Wriggins, *The Measure of Injury: Race, Gender and Tort Law* (New York University Press, 2010).

11   Peter Cane, *The Anatomy of Tort Law* (Hart, 1997) 181.

12   Stychin, 'The Vulnerable Subject', 351.

13   ibid.

14   Jennifer Nedelsky, *Law's Relations: A Relational Theory of Self, Autonomy, and Law* (Oxford University Press, 2011). See also Martha Chamallas, 'Race and Tort Law' in Khiara Bridges, Devon Carbado and Emily Houh (eds), *Oxford Handbook on Race and the Law* (Oxford University Press, forthcoming).

15   ibid.

by the state.[16] However, social inequalities and injustices mean that marginalised and oppressed groups will not be able to rely upon rights which are protected by this approach.[17] Instead, Sandra Fredman argues, there must be 'a positive duty on the State to ensure the provision of a range of options, of public goods and the framework within which human relationships can flourish'.[18]

The common conception of the human subject underpinning tort law and human rights law can be exposed by looking at the case law on positive obligations on public authorities, which has the potential to challenge the traditional liberal approach to the subject and negative freedom. In tort law there has been extensive judicial and academic deliberation as to the circumstances in which, if any, public authorities should owe a person a duty of care in negligence to prevent harm or to prevent harm being caused by a third party. Similar questions have been raised in relation to human rights and the extent of positive obligations on state bodies to prevent or to respond to abuse by a third party. However, different answers have been given in each context. Public bodies' duties of care in negligence have been limited to a greater extent than human rights liability. The European Court of Human Rights (ECtHR) has gradually extended positive duties,[19] recognising that 'the protection of human rights requires the state to take appropriate measures to safeguard these rights from violation by others'.[20] It is easy to see that some may argue that public authorities should have greater responsibility under public law as opposed to in private law obligations. What is of interest here is less the debates about whether tort liability should mirror human rights liability[21] and more about what these different judicial discourses say about the human subject. In extending positive obligations, Lourdes Peroni and Alexandra Timmer have identified the Strasbourg court as paying greater attention to the vulnerability of certain rights holders.[22] The significance of this, Corina Heri argues, is that the role of vulnerability has the potential to transform the framework and operation of human rights.[23] In the context of tort law, Stychin argues that using vulnerability as a basis to determine duty of care issues

---

[16] Jill Marshall, 'A Right to Personal Autonomy at the European Court of Human Rights' (2008) *European Human Rights Law Review* 337, 340.

[17] ibid.

[18] Sandra Fredman, *Human Rights Transformed: Positive Rights and Positive Duties* (Oxford University Press, 2008) 18.

[19] Alastair Mowbray, *The Development of Positive Obligations under the European Convention on Human Rights by the European Court of Human Rights* (Hart, 2004).

[20] Piet Hein van Kempen, 'Four Concepts of Security – A Human Rights Perspective' (2013) 13(1) *Human Rights Law Review* 1, 16.

[21] See Donal Nolan, 'Negligence and Human Rights Law: The Case for Separate Development' (2013) 76(2) *Modern Law Review* 286; and Achas K. Burin, 'The Positive Duty of Prevention in the Common Law and the Convention' (2019) 40(2) *Legal Studies* 209.

[22] Peroni and Timmer, 'Vulnerable Groups', 1062.

[23] Corina Heri, *Responsive Human Rights: Vulnerability, Ill-treatment and the ECtHR* (Hart, 2021) 187.

in negligence can provide a more ethically sound way of making judgments about our responsibilities and duties of care in law to others.[24] To better understand the prospects for reshaping the subject of tort law and human rights, the next section turns to the scholarship on vulnerability.

Vulnerability discourse

A conception of human beings as inherently vulnerable has been developing across different disciplines. Vulnerability is a 'universal' and 'constant' aspect of the human condition, Martha Fineman explains, because human beings are always at risk of illness, injury or harm from our corporeal condition, environment or institutions.[25] As such, the sources of vulnerability, and the nature and extent, can change over time and depend on social and political contexts.[26] For Susan Dodds, giving due attention to vulnerability can recast 'citizens' ethical relations from a conception of 'independent actors carving out realms of right against each other and the state, to one of mutually-dependent and vulnerably-exposed beings whose capacities to develop as subjects are directly and indirectly mediated by the conditions around them'.[27] So understood, the vulnerable subject is at odds with the liberal individual whose freedom and integrity are secured by preventing interference by others and the state.

There are, however, multiple conceptions of vulnerability, and different scholars focus on different aspects of the vulnerable subject or have different purposes for highlighting vulnerability. For example, Judith Butler emphasises how the social and political construction and positioning of certain groups can render them particularly vulnerable or shape their experience of vulnerability,[28] whereas Jo Bridgeman highlights humans' relational vulnerabilities – that is, the worry, distress and harm that our love and care for others can cause.[29] Butler argues that the idea of human vulnerability should provide the basis for a non-violent ethics and politics, but she is sceptical as to whether the state can provide an appropriate response to vulnerability.[30] In comparison, Fineman argues that the vulnerable human should be centred in law and politics to demand and create a more responsive and responsible state, to work toward a renewed vision of substantive equality.[31] While Fineman pits the autonomous subject against the

---

[24]   Stychin, 'The Vulnerable Subject'.
[25]   Martha A. Fineman, 'The Vulnerable Subject: Anchoring Equality in the Human Condition' (2008) 20 *Yale Journal of Law & Feminism* 1, 1.
[26]   Catriona Mackenzie, Wendy Rogers and Susan Dodds, *Vulnerability: New Essays in Ethics and Feminist Philosophy* (Oxford University Press, 2014) 7–9.
[27]   Susan Dodds, 'Depending on Care: Recognition of Vulnerability and the Social Contribution of Care Provision' (2007) 21(9) *Bioethics* 500, 502.
[28]   Judith Butler, *Precarious Life* (Verso, 2004).
[29]   Jo Bridgeman, 'Relational Vulnerability, Care and Dependency' in Julie Wallbank and Jonathan Herring (eds), *Vulnerabilities, Care and Family Law* (Routledge, 2014) 201.
[30]   See Judith Butler, *Frames of War: When is Life Grievable?* (Verso, 2009).
[31]   Fineman, 'The Vulnerable Subject', 2.

vulnerable one, others, such as Catriona Mackenzie, Wendy Rogers and Susan Dodds, see human beings as both vulnerable and autonomous, and argue that an account of vulnerability must explain how people can be protected from harm and at the same time have their capacities for autonomy promoted.[32]

In addition to inconsistencies, theories of human vulnerability raise potential problems. Recognising a person or group as vulnerable can be used to justify paternalism and could compound vulnerability rather than identifying ways to enhance autonomy and freedom.[33] It has been used to explain the need to increase surveillance of particular groups, stigmatising and demeaning them, rather than addressing injustices and inequalities.[34] Moreover, situating particular groups as vulnerable could reify their vulnerabilities and increase the risk of abuse.[35] Indeed, in some areas of law – such as human rights law and family law – the concept of vulnerability has been increasingly invoked to identify and create groups of vulnerable persons.[36] In this way, group members can be seen to lack autonomy, as being 'other' to the norm of the autonomous liberal individual,[37] rather than vulnerability being a universal feature of being human. However, while there are potential issues with the concept of vulnerability, it brings with it possibilities for understanding what a state's legal responsibilities should be and for what harms a state or public body should be accountable. This is particularly the case in relation to positive obligations because the traditional liberal subject relies primarily on a negative conception of freedom whereas a vulnerable subject requires positive actions, provisions of services and (re)allocation of resources to secure freedom. The next section focuses on when public authorities have a duty to act to prevent harm in negligence, to what extent vulnerability features in the case law and the conception of the subject underpinning this jurisprudence.

Duty of care, positive obligations and public authorities in England and Wales

No liability for failing to confer a benefit

In general, in negligence law, positive acts causing direct harm attract liability but there is no duty to undertake positive actions to prevent harm to another,

---

32 Mackenzie, Rogers and Dodds, *Vulnerability*, 15–16.
33 See Michael C. Dunn, Isabel C.H. Clare and Anthony J. Holland, 'To Empower or to Protect? Constructing the "Vulnerable Adult" in English Law and Public Policy' (2008) 28(2) *Legal Studies* 234; and Mackenzie, Rogers and Dodds, *Vulnerability*.
34 Shelley Bielefeld, 'Cashless Welfare Transfers for "Vulnerable" Welfare Recipients: Law, Ethics and Vulnerability' (2018) 26(1) *Feminist Legal Studies* 1.
35 Ann V. Murphy, '"Reality Check": Rethinking the Ethics of Vulnerability' in Renée J. Heberle and Victoria Grace (eds), *Theorizing Sexual Violence* (Taylor & Francis, 2009) 55.
36 Alison Diduck, 'Autonomy and Vulnerability in Family Law' in Julie Wallbank and Jonathan Herring (eds), *Vulnerabilities, Care and Family Law* (Routledge, 2013) 95.
37 ibid.

unless there are particular exceptional circumstances.[38] This applies equally to private individuals and public bodies.[39] The main reason for this, as explained by Lord Hoffmann in *Stovin v Wise*, is that 'it is less of an invasion of an individual's freedom for the law to require him to consider the safety of others in his actions than to impose on him a duty to rescue or protect'.[40] However, public bodies are in a different position to individuals, as Stelios Tofaris and Sandy Steel explain:

> a private individual's freedom arguably has *intrinsic* value in so far as her having freedom to do various things contributes to her having an autonomous life. By contrast, the value of the state's freedom is purely instrumental: the state's freedom is valuable only in so far as it contributes to the fulfilment of its proper functions.[41]

Understood in this way, the extent to which public bodies should have private law positive duties to prevent harm being caused to an individual depends largely on the view one has of the 'proper functions' of the public bodies and the relationship between the state and the individual. On the whole, the approach in negligence is one which follows a negative freedom approach and a traditional liberal conception of the subject. As explained by Lord Toulson in *Michael v Chief Constable of South Wales*:

> it is a feature of our system of government that many areas of life are subject to forms of state control [sic] ... To compile a comprehensive list would be virtually impossible, because the systems designed to protect the public from harm of one kind or another are so extensive. It does not follow from the setting up of a protective system from public resources that if it fails to achieve its purpose, through organisational defects or fault on the part of an individual, the public at large should bear the additional burden of compensating a victim for harm caused by the actions of a third party for whose behaviour the state is not responsible.[42]

This approach presents public bodies as only being responsible for harm they have directly caused or in specific circumstances in which they are in a position

---

[38] *Robinson v Chief Constable of West Yorkshire Police* [2018] UKSC 4, para 34 (Lord Reed), quoting Stelios Tofaris and Sandy Steel, 'Negligence Liability for Omissions and the Police' (2016) 75(1) *Cambridge Law Journal* 128. For example, in *Home Office v Dorset Yacht Co Ltd* [1970] AC 1004; 2 WLR 1140 there was a duty of care owed by officers for the property damage caused by escaped 'Borstal boys' because the officers were in a position of supervision and control.

[39] *Robinson v Chief Constable of West Yorkshire Police* [2018] UKSC 4.

[40] [1996] AC 923 (HL), 943.

[41] Stelios Tofaris and Sandy Steel, *Police Liability in Negligence for Failure to Prevent Crime: Time to Rethink* (2014) 6. University of Cambridge Faculty of Law Research Paper No 39/2014.

[42] [2015] UKSC 2, paras 113–14.

to defend individuals from harms which come from other sources. It has been phrased more starkly: public bodies should not be liable for 'failing to confer a benefit', even where it is one they have a legislative power or duty to provide.[43] Put this way, it is clear that the jurisprudence does not recognise the state as contributing to or sustaining the patterns of violence and harms in people's lives, and with it to the creation of vulnerabilities.

Underpinning a longstanding judicial aversion to public authority liability in negligence, and particularly the imposition of positive obligations, are policy-based reasons suggesting that liability would interfere with the 'proper functions' of public bodies. The main reasons typically given are that liability will lead to 'defensive' practices being adopted; that floodgates could be opened to large numbers of claims given that negligent in/action of a public body could cause harm to a vast number of people; and that paying compensation claims would reduce public funds being spent on core functions.[44] The policy arguments *for* imposing duties of care – such as the raising of standards, the loss-spreading effects and concerns of distributive justice, and the protection of vulnerable groups – have typically been sidelined or wholly ignored by judges.[45] However, in more recent case law there has been judicial recognition that there are policy reasons which support positive obligations on public bodies in some circumstances. Rather than acting on this by weighing up competing policy considerations, the judicial trend has been to rely on legal principles as the primary basis for determining whether or not a duty of care is owed by a public body.[46]

Focusing more on the legal principles, at least on the face of recent judgments, there has been greater consideration paid to whether cases fall within the exceptions to the general rule that there is no liability for omissions or where a third party has caused harm. Particularly prominent in the case law is whether or not there is an 'assumption of responsibility' on the part of the public body

---

[43]   For example, see *Gorringe v Calderdale MBC* [2004] 1 WLR 1057, para 32 (Lord Hoffmann); *N and Another v Poole Borough Council v AIRE Centre and Others* [2019] UKSC 25, para 28 (Lord Reed). This language is typically used to sidestep the issues with trying to distinguish acts and omissions, with the idea that it is easier to distinguish between causing an injury or making things worse (misfeasance) and failing to benefit or failing to protect (nonfeasance). See, for example, Allan Beever, *Rediscovering the Law of Negligence* (Hart, 2007) 211.

[44]   For example, see *Hill v Chief Constable of West Yorkshire Police* [1989] AC 53, para 63; *Commissioner of Police for the Metropolis v DSD and Another* [2018] UKSC 11, para 132 (Lord Hughes).

[45]   Kirsty Horsey, 'Police Negligence, Invisible Immunity and Disadvantaged Claimants' in Janice Richardson and Erika Rackley (eds), *Feminist Perspectives on Tort Law* (Routledge, 2012) 80.

[46]   In *N and Another v Poole Borough Council v AIRE Centre and Others* [2019] UKSC 25, para 74 (Lord Reed) discredited *X (Minors) v Bedfordshire* as the decision relied on policy-based reasoning to deny a duty of care, concluding that courts should not primarily rely on policy. In relation to the duty of care generally, see *Robinson v Chief Constable of West Yorkshire Police* [2018] UKSC 4; and Stelios Tofaris, 'Duty of Care in Negligence: A Return to Orthodoxy?' (2018) 77(3) *Cambridge Law Journal* 454.

to prevent the harm.[47] This was a key question in *N and Another v Poole Borough Council v AIRE Centre and Others*[48] in which the local authority housed a mother and two children, one of whom is disabled, next to a family known for antisocial behaviour and who physically and verbally abused them and harassed them. Eventually, the mother and children were rehoused but argued that they had suffered physical and psychological harm from the harassment and abuse, which was a result of a breach of a duty of care owed by the council when carrying out its functions in relation to child protection and housing. The Supreme Court held that there was no duty arising from the authority carrying out its legislative functions, and that the council had not done anything specific to take responsibility for preventing the harm, and the claimant had not done anything to rely on the local authority.[49]

The case law has thus developed to incentivise public authorities to *avoid* assumptions of responsibility, even where harms directly connected with their specific public function are at issue. This is evident in *Michael v Chief Constable of South Wales*[50] in which the Supreme Court held that the police had done nothing to assume responsibility to act with reasonable care when responding to Joanna Michael's 999 call for help as her ex-partner was trying to kill her, and there is no general duty upon the police towards a person who they are aware, or ought to be aware, is subject to threats of physical harm. In adopting this position, the Supreme Court had to downplay the significance of the call handler asking Joanna Michael whether she could lock the house and to remain contactable to avoid generating an impression that she should remain in the property.[51] This decision, it must be emphasised, was as to whether these issues should even proceed to a full hearing with regard to negligence; the majority were content to establish that there was no real possibility of success without the facts having been fully ventilated. Requiring a public body to do 'something more' on which the claimant can demonstrate reliance to establish a duty of care shows a very narrow interpretation of exceptions to the general rule that there are no positive duties to act.[52] Indeed, as Donal Nolan points out, it has become very difficult to find examples of a public authority doing something 'voluntary' that is outside of their statutory responsibilities to raise an assumption of responsibility.[53] It rests

---

47   *N and Another v Poole Borough Council v AIRE Centre and Others* [2019] UKSC 25, paras 68–9 and 73 (Lord Reed), interpreting case law decisions based on whether or not there was an assumption of responsibility.

48   [2019] UKSC 25.

49   Following in particular *Gorringe v Calderdale MBC* [2004] 1 WLR 1057 and *Hedley Byrne & Co Ltd v Heller & Partners Ltd* [1964] AC 465.

50   [2015] UKSC 2.

51   ibid., para 138 (Lord Toulson).

52   For a recent example applying the principles from *Robinson*, *Poole* and *Michael* see *DFX v Coventry City Council* [2021] EWHC 1382 (QB), discussed later.

53   Donal Nolan, 'The Liability of Public Authorities for Failing to Confer Benefits' (2011) 127(2) *Law Quarterly Review* 260, 283.

on a view that public bodies are there to 'confer benefits' on individuals and are not implicated in the ways that people are harmed, even where they have foresight of likely harms.

While a formalist approach has been taken to determine public bodies' duties of care (or lack thereof), Tom Cornford argues that the phrase 'assumption of responsibility' is empty of clear meaning and is being used to mask the policy reasons underpinning judicial decision-making.[54] Indeed, Lord Hoffmann has acknowledged that:

> the phrase 'assumption of responsibility' is simply a slogan for the court to conclude that a duty of care is owed by the defendant. That is to say, the concept does not comprise a self-contained 'working' formula which can be applied to the facts of any case, at the outset, to yield a just solution.[55]

Even in *Robinson v Chief Constable of West Yorkshire Police*, Lord Mance said that '[i]t would be unrealistic to suggest that, when recognising and developing an established category of the duty of care, the courts are not influenced by policy considerations'.[56] Therefore, despite the efforts of some of the senior judiciary, policy concerns evidently continue to play a significant role in determining public bodies' negligence liability, and specifically policy reasons against liability. As the Supreme Court has generally disavowed explicit reliance upon public policy justifications in negligence,[57] there has been little opportunity to consider policy reasons which could justify the imposition of positive duties on public authorities. Furthermore, many of the public policy arguments against liability are not based on empirical evidence and, as Kirsty Horsey argues, have 'negative practical implications on society as a whole as well as for already vulnerable or disadvantaged individuals or groups'.[58] But as policy is not being explicitly considered, the Supreme Court has shut down ways to raise these concerns.

The (near) absence of vulnerability discourse in tort

There is little recognition of or use of the concept of vulnerability in the case law on public bodies and duty of care. In the pivotal case of *Stovin v Wise*, Lord Nicholls emphasised in his dissenting judgment that road users are 'vulnerable. They are dependent on highway authorities fulfilling their

---

[54] Tom Cornford, 'Liability for Failure to Exercise Child Protection Powers' (2022) 38 *Professional Negligence* 84, 89–90.

[55] *Customs and Excise Commissioners v Barclays Bank plc* [2006] UKHL 28, para 35.

[56] [2018] UKSC 4, para 48.

[57] *N and Another v Poole Borough Council v AIRE Centre and Others* [2019] UKSC 25, para 74 (Lord Reed).

[58] Horsey, 'Police Negligence', 81.

statutory responsibilities'.[59] This was one of the key features which, to him, made it fair, just and reasonable to impose a duty on the county council to act reasonably to exercise a statutory power (under the Highways Act 1980, section 79) to remove obstructions which could otherwise cause foreseeable harm.[60] However, this was not enough to persuade the majority that a statutory power should give rise to a duty of care. Another notable use of 'vulnerability' is in the cases of *X (Minors) v Bedfordshire County Council*[61] and *D v East Berkshire Community Health NHS Trust*,[62] which involved liabilities of public bodies in relation to child protection. In *X v Bedfordshire* the House of Lords held that there was no duty of care owed by local authority staff to children when making decisions about their welfare because it was not 'fair, just and reasonable' on policy grounds, including the potential for defensive practices and constraints on their autonomy in meeting considerable demands with limited resources.[63] This was despite a recognition that children are 'weaker members of society' in need of protection.[64]

Although in *X* the fact that children are a vulnerable group made no difference to duties of care, in *D v East Berkshire* the Court of Appeal held that a duty of care could be owed to children as a vulnerable group in society but not to parents negligently accused of child abuse by a local authority. This is because there could be a conflict in the interests of the parents and children if a duty was owed to both. The court continued: *X v Bedfordshire* could not survive the Human Rights Act 1998 because the policy reasons against negligence liability have been undercut by human rights liability, so it must be 'fair, just, and reasonable' to impose a duty on public authorities carrying out their child protection functions. However, as discussed earlier, in *N and Another v Poole Borough Council v AIRE Centre and Others*, the Supreme Court held that there is no general duty owed by local authorities to act to prevent harm to children; it is only when a case falls within the exceptions that a duty of care can be owed, such as if the local authority assumes responsibility. In the Court of Appeal, which came to the same decision that there was no duty of care but for different reasons, Irwin LJ explained that:

> society places a high emphasis on protecting vulnerable people, particularly vulnerable children. However, the essence of the common law answer to this problem is that it is not effective, or just, to do so

---

[59]   [1996] AC 923 (HL), 939.

[60]   ibid.

[61]   [1995] 2 AC 633.

[62]   [2003] EWCA Civ 1151.

[63]   *X (Minors) v Bedfordshire County Council* [1995] 2 AC 633, 749 (Lord Browne-Wilkinson).

[64]   ibid., 751 (Lord Browne-Wilkinson). The reference to 'weaker members of society' is not necessarily the same as a vulnerable group, but it indicates a potential recognition of vulnerability.

by singling out one agency of the state for tortious liability as against the others.[65]

There are some cases, however, where, typically due to an assumption of responsibility, a duty of care is owed by a public body to prevent harm which is not caused by their own actions and the claimant has been in a vulnerable position. For example, in *Phelps v Hillingdon* the House of Lords held that a local authority could be vicariously liable for harm caused by negligence of an educational psychologist who owed a duty of care to children when diagnosing specific learning difficulties.[66] In his concurring judgment, Lord Nicholls highlighted that 'the child was very dependent upon on [sic] the expert's assessment. The child was in a singularly vulnerable position'.[67] However, this did not factor significantly in the reasoning of the other Law Lords and does not seem to have impacted the decision. Rather, it is the professional relationship which is significant as there is no potential conflict between the professional's duty to the claimants and the authority carrying out its statutory duties. The professional relationship in this context is analogous to medical professionals, for example, who do owe patients a duty of care (for which, if breached, the relevant National Health Service Trust can be vicariously liable).[68] And yet, the professional relationship in the context of public authority services for children and vulnerable adults is not sufficient to establish a duty of care.

In *Reeves v Commissioner of Police for the Metropolis* the House of Lords held that the police can owe a duty to take reasonable care to prevent individuals being detained from harming themselves where there is or ought to be knowledge of mental vulnerability, because the police are in a particular position of responsibility relative to the claimant.[69] By contrast, although *Kent v Griffiths* denied a general duty of care on the part of the emergency services, the Court focused on the specific relationship established during a call to the ambulance service.[70] Broad statements of public duty have been treated as insufficient to establish an assumption of responsibility by the emergency services, but a focus 'on a particular individual and a particular individual's welfare' can provide the necessary basis in certain cases.[71] This narrow focus on the specific relationship at issue is not based on the wider context of the responsibility of the public body or of human vulnerabilities. Indeed, in *Darby v Richmond upon Thames London Borough Council*[72] it was made clear that if a local authority is aware of a person's

---

65   *CN v Poole BC* [2017] EWCA Civ 2185, para 98 (Irwin LJ).
66   *Phelps v Hillingdon LBC* [2001] 2 AC 619.
67   ibid., 666.
68   *Darnley v Croydon Health Services NHS Trust* [2018] UKSC 50.
69   [1999] 3 WLR 363.
70   [2000] 2 All ER 474.
71   *Sherratt v Chief Constable of Greater Manchester Police* [2018] EWHC 1746 (QB), para 83 (King J).
72   [2015] EWHC 909. See also *X v Hounslow London Borough Council* [2009] PTSR 1158, and *Mitchell v Glasgow City Council* [2009] AC 874.

vulnerability, this does not necessarily give rise to an assumption of responsibility that the authority will act to protect that person from harm, even where that harm is foreseeable.

It should be no surprise then that there are also cases where the claimant has been in a vulnerable position or is part of an identifiable vulnerable group, but no duty of care has been found, for lack of an assumption of responsibility or otherwise. Sad illustrations of this are *Smith v Chief Constable of Sussex Police*[73] and *Michael v Chief Constable of South Wales*.[74] Both cases involved victims of domestic violence and the question as to the circumstances in which, if any, the police would owe a duty of care to protect such an individual from harm by a third party. There is considerable evidence attesting to the high prevalence of domestic abuse, including for members of LGBTQ+ communities (as in *Smith*),[75] and of historic and contemporary state inaction which has contributed to perpetuating gender, sexual and other inequalities.[76] Despite the police being aware of the threat and knowledge of the person who made it in both cases, in neither case was a duty of care established. In *Smith* there was greater reliance on *Hill v Chief Constable of West Yorkshire Police*,[77] that imposing a duty of care on the police in relation to crime prevention would interfere with their functions: as Lord Hope explained, '[w]e must be careful not to allow ourselves to be persuaded by the shortcomings of the police in individual cases to undermine that principle. ... [T]he interests of the wider community must prevail over those of the individual'.[78] There was no acknowledgement of the countervailing prospect of negative impacts on the wider community of domestic violence victims (and the particular context of LGBTQ+ domestic violence at issue in the case) of not imposing a duty.[79] In *Michael*, the broader domestic violence context and concerns around policing and gender injustices was brought to the fore by the interveners, Liberty and Refuge. Indeed, Bowen QC, acting for the interveners, argued that:

> liability should attach to a negligent act or omission where the police are aware of a serious and special risk of physical harm to the person in respect of an individual or the member of an identifiable

---

73   [2008] UKHL 50 (heard with *Van Colle v Chief Constable of Hertfordshire Police* [2008] UKHL 50).
74   [2015] UKSC 2.
75   Rebecca Barnes and Catherine Donovan, 'Domestic Violence in Lesbian, Gay, Bisexual and/ or Transgender Relationships' in Nancy Lombard (ed), *The Routledge Handbook of Gender and Violence* (Routledge, 2018) 67.
76   See Katy Barrow-Grint, Jacqueline Sebire, Jackie Turton and Ruth Weir, *Policing Domestic Abuse: Risk, Policy, and Practice* (Routledge, 2022).
77   [1989] AC 53.
78   *Van Colle; Smith* [2008] UKHL 50, para 75.
79   For a discussion of the 'race-' and class-based dimensions of police inaction and limited negligence liability see Chamallas, 'Race and Tort Law'.

and delineated class, 'special' meaning that the person concerned is particularly vulnerable to the risk in question.[80]

However, the concept of vulnerability was not engaged by the majority who, in Lord Toulson's view, could see no good reasons for any exception to the general rule that the police owe no duty of care to members of the public. Nor was it engaged by Lady Hale or Lord Kerr, dissenting, arguing that there was a proximate relationship between Joanna Michael and the police sufficient to establish a duty of care.[81]

In relation to public authorities and duty of care, then, there has been very little use of the concept of vulnerability. Where the language of vulnerability is used it is to identify a particular group as vulnerable (or a particular person as a member of a vulnerable group) rather than reflecting an understanding that vulnerability is a feature of being human. Moreover, the identification of a person as particularly vulnerable has little or no bearing on whether or not the public authority owes that person a duty of care. The liberal legal subject who is privileged and benefits from social hierarchies, yet is apparently socially and relationally isolated, remains at the centre of negligence. As there is potentially human rights liability in these circumstances, the next part explores the overlaps and divergences between negligence and human rights in relation to positive obligations on public authorities, and the role vulnerability plays in shaping these trajectories.

Negligence and human rights liability

Interlocking jurisprudence, diverging subjects

The pronounced lack of judicial engagement with vulnerability in the context of negligence contrasts with the increasing reliance upon related ideas in the human rights context. The human rights obligations of public authorities are being shaped by judicial recognition of the duties that these bodies owe towards individuals. This shift started at the ECtHR, where from the 1990s onwards judges made use of the language of vulnerability to emphasise the importance of the authorities' duties to protect human rights, particularly in the case of marginalised groups.[82] These invocations of vulnerability were in many cases significant, with one prominent series of cases conceptualising widespread police failings with regard to domestic violence and sexual offences as breaches

---

[80]   This is based on Lord Bingham's 'liability principle' set out in his dissent in *Van Colle; Smith*.

[81]   *Michael v Chief Constable of South Wales* [2015] UKSC 2, para 187 (Lady Hale); para 184 (Lord Kerr). Given the trend away from reliance on policy, this could have been a strategic move as the judgments could have the potential to be more convincing if framed squarely within legal principles.

[82]   *Osman v United Kingdom* (1998) 29 EHRR 245.

of positive obligations under Articles 3 and 8 ECHR.[83] But they were also somewhat haphazard. The Court was not articulating an overarching departure from the liberal subject as the bearer of human rights, but enough judges were drawing upon ideas of vulnerability to address some of the evident shortcomings of this approach.

Responding to these shifts at Strasbourg, some judges in the UK's domestic jurisdictions have embraced positive obligations, even as public authority liability in tort has become subject to more constraints in the judgments considered earlier. This shift is illustrated in *Commissioner of Police for the Metropolis v DSD*,[84] an action brought by two of the victims of the serial rapist John Worboys in relation to severe shortcomings in the police investigation which had allowed his crimes to continue. The catalogue of police errors was not subject to much dispute by the time the proceedings reached the UK Supreme Court; at issue instead was whether, because of these failings, the police had breached the positive obligations that they owed to Worboys' victims. Lord Kerr led the majority in recognising that Strasbourg case law had developed to the extent that 'states have a positive obligation inherent in Articles 3 and 8 ECHR to enact criminal-law provisions, effectively punishing rape and to apply them in practice through effective investigation and prosecution'.[85] The key question was whether the claimants had to establish serious systemic failings, on the basis that mere operational failings would be insufficient as a basis for establishing liability. For the majority there was little value in trying to pull apart different elements of the state's duty; what mattered was that there was an investigative duty with regard to rape and the court's role was to assess whether any failings were sufficiently serious to breach the positive obligation in light of the seriousness of the resultant harm to the victims.[86]

The theoretical underpinnings of these positive obligations remain under-articulated; for Lord Neuberger, for example, it sufficed that there was a 'clear and consistent' line of Strasbourg authority and there would need to be good reason for the Supreme Court to depart from it.[87] True that may be, but it is not an effort to explain positive obligations; neither Strasbourg nor UK Supreme Court judges have sought to invite accusations of naked judicial activism on the basis that they are openly reconceptualising the subject of human rights law. But such decisions demonstrate how notions of vulnerability, or at least a heightened awareness of the limitations of the liberal subject, are influencing how these courts approach positive obligations.

This development has brought with it concerns that extensions of positive obligations make too little allowance for the public policy concerns which are so

---

83   See *MC v Bulgaria* (2005) 40 EHRR 20 and *Rumor v Italy* [2014] ECHR 557.
84   *Commissioner of Police for the Metropolis v DSD and Another* [2018] UKSC 11.
85   ibid., para 18 (Lord Kerr).
86   ibid., para 58 (Lord Kerr); para 92 (Lord Neuberger).
87   ibid., para 91.

dominant within negligence. Lord Mance, in his judgment in *DSD*, expressed his concern that there is less detailed analysis of the implications of extending positive duties on the police in human rights law than in the extensive body of related tort cases.[88] He found much in common with Lord Hughes, who regarded the majority's approach to positive obligations as insufficiently attentive towards the liability constraints imposed in tort. As a result, he foresaw that *DSD* would 'inhibit the robust operation of police work, and divert resources from current inquiries; it would be detrimental, not a spur, to law enforcement'.[89] It is inaccurate, however, to present the majority's conclusion – that the catalogue of egregious policing failures to investigate serious harm caused by a third party amounted to a breach of the state's positive obligations in this case – as neglecting such concerns. Lord Kerr explicitly addressed the issue, concluding that the scope of the positive duty was narrow enough that it would be unlikely to 'herald an avalanche of claims', precisely because 'only obvious and significant shortcomings in the conduct of the police and prosecutorial investigation will give rise to the possibility of a claim'.[90]

Human rights and negligence now provide alternative causes of action in many cases, but inherent in judgments like *DSD* is that the nature of the subjects of negligence and human rights law – the person to whom duties are owed – are becoming distinct. The liberal legal subject, so embedded in tort, is no longer the touchstone in many human rights cases. This emergent distinction could be regarded as inherent in the private and individualistic nature of tort law compared to the public function of human rights law.[91] As Lord Brown mused in *Van Colle; Smith*, 'Where civil actions are designed essentially to compensate claimants for their losses, Convention claims are intended rather to uphold minimum human rights standards and to vindicate those rights'.[92] Judges have furthermore maintained that it is not always necessary for causes of action to align precisely because parliament has authorised claims under the Human Rights Act 1998.[93] The majority in *DSD* evidently considered that they enjoyed more latitude to recognise public authority duties under the 1998 Act, especially when following Strasbourg's lead, by comparison to negligence.[94] Even before the Supreme Court reached this position in *DSD*, it is perhaps unsurprising that, having spent well over 100 paragraphs coming to the conclusion that the negligence claim could be struck out in *Michael*, Lord Toulson accepted that 'what the call

---

[88]   ibid., para 142.

[89]   ibid., para 132.

[90]   ibid., para 53 and para 72. See also para 92 (Lord Neuberger).

[91]   ibid., para 97 (Lord Neuberger); paras 68–70 (Lord Kerr); *Michael v Chief Constable of South Wales* [2015] UKSC 2, paras 123–8 (Lord Toulson). See Nolan, 'Negligence and Human Rights Law', 21.

[92]   [2008] UKHL 50, para 138.

[93]   ibid., para 138 (Lord Brown); *X (Minors) v Bedfordshire County Council* [1995] 2 AC 633 751 (Lord Browne-Wilkinson).

[94]   *Commissioner of Police for the Metropolis v DSD and Another* [2018] UKSC 11, para 97 (Lord Neuberger).

handler ought to have made of the 999 call in all the circumstances is properly a matter for investigation at a trial' under an Article 2 claim under the Human Rights Act within a scant few sentences.[95] Indeed, the fact that human rights actions are being permitted to proceed to full hearing in such cases might account for the lack of engagement with vulnerability in negligence cases before the UK Supreme Court; positive obligations negate any pressure for concomitant developments in tort.

Uncertainty in current trends

The extension of positive obligations and the resultant divergences between negligence and human rights in the realm of public authority liability might nonetheless be more significant in theory than practice. The extent to which human rights law and negligence now provide for overlapping causes of action where public authorities are accused of failing to fulfil their duties is illustrated by the case of *DFX v Coventry City Council*,[96] which involved a challenge to the failures of the council's social services department to initiate care proceedings for a group of siblings subject to abuse and neglect. These facts gave rise to both a negligence action and a human rights action grounded in the council's positive obligations under Article 3 ECHR. From the outset, Lambert J acknowledged that the requirements which would need to be addressed under each of these actions would be different. The negligence claim was that the council was vicariously liable for the negligent actions of the social workers, who owed a duty of care to the claimants as they assumed responsibility to take reasonable care to protect them and breached this by failing to initiate care proceedings when evidence demonstrated parental neglect and abuse. For the human rights action, by contrast:

> the Claimants assert that they were exposed to a real and immediate risk of sexual harm of which the Defendant was or ought to have been aware, together with a failure by the Defendant to take reasonable available measures which could have had a real prospect of altering the outcome or mitigating the harm.[97]

These claims might be conceptually distinct, but the *DFX* judgment illustrates that the different conception of the legal subject in tort and human rights law might not necessarily have a pronounced impact on case outcomes:

> for the purpose of the human rights claim the claimants need not establish the existence of a duty of care owed to the claimants, and the

---

[95]   *Michael v Chief Constable of South Wales* [2015] UKSC 2, para 139.
[96]   *DFX v Coventry City Council* [2021] EWHC 1382 (QB).
[97]   ibid., para 11.

causation requirement is different, the claim is not without its own particular difficulties, not least that it was commenced many years after the expiry of the limitation period for such actions.[98]

These hurdles ultimately became much more significant for the High Court's rejection of the claim than any theoretical advantages enjoyed by the claimants in relation to their human rights action. The positive obligations claim rested on whether the claimants were exposed to a 'real and immediate risk' of abuse which could be connected to 'operational failures' by the council, standard tests derived from Strasbourg's positive obligations case law (even though this is not discussed in the judgment).[99] But in assessing the scope of the operational duty test, the case defaulted back to negligence standards: 'it is common ground between the parties that the standard demanded for the performance of the operational duty is one of reasonableness'.[100] All roads, in this case, led back to tort's tests. Likewise, in the case of *HXA*, also concerning the potential liabilities of a council for social services' failures to use child protection powers, Stacey J dismissed appeals against the strike out of the claims. Drawing on *DFX*, she concluded that, in relation to tort, 'the principles established by *Poole*, *Robinson* and *Michael*' dominated omissions liability in cases like this, and meant that there was no prospect that the case law was developing in the claimants' favour.[101] Before the Court of Appeal, the local authorities insisted that it could not be said that 'the general denial of a claim in negligence deprives the professionals involved of any meaningful responsibility', in large part because there 'remains the option of a claim under the Human Rights Act'.[102]

All of this suggests that efforts to channel such claims away from negligence are in the ascendant, but they are yet to become completely dominant. The Court of Appeal in *HXA* ultimately accepted the appeals against Stacey J's judgment on the basis that:

> this is still an evolving area of the law in which it will only be through careful and incremental development of principles through decisions reached after full trials on the evidence that it will become clear where precisely the line is to be drawn between those cases where there has been an assumption of responsibility and those where there has not.[103]

Negligence has yet to be fully closed off in these cases, and it is difficult to argue that, in reaching this decision, considerations of the vulnerability of the claimants

---

[98]   ibid., para 11.
[99]   See *MC v Bulgaria* (2005) 40 EHRR 20 and *Osman v United Kingdom* (1998) 29 EHRR 245.
[100]   ibid., para 24.
[101]   *HXA v Surrey County Council* [2021] EWHC 2974 (QB), para 76.
[102]   *HXA v Surrey County Council* [2022] EWCA Civ 1196, para 82.
[103]   ibid., para 105 (Baker LJ).

were not prominent in the judges' minds, even if the term was never used. Baker LJ, after all, emphasised that the reason that these cases needed consideration at full hearing was that 'there is a very wide range of circumstances in which the social services department of a local authority may become involved in the lives of children in its area who are or are at risk of being abused or neglected'.[104]

Different conceptions of the subject are thus coming to underpin distinct developments in negligence and human rights, particularly in the divide which is opening up between the UK Supreme Court's decisions in *Poole*, *Robinson* and *Michael*, in the former regard, and *DSD* in the latter. But it would be simplistic to conclude that a highly developed account of vulnerability underpins the human rights jurisprudence or that some judges are not alive to conceptions of the vulnerable subject in negligence. Some of the concerns over the scale of the departure from tort standards inherent in the development of positive obligations in *DSD* expressed by Lord Hughes and Lord Mance are therefore overblown. The recognition of the significance of vulnerable groups is, nonetheless, more developed in human rights jurisprudence. This reconceptualisation of the subject is yet to be general or transformative, even in the context of positive human rights obligations, but this would certainly appear to be the more fertile seedbed for future developments.

Conclusion

This chapter has highlighted the limitations to accounts of vulnerability operative in tort law in England and Wales where public authority liability is at issue. This jurisprudence has all but bypassed vulnerability, notwithstanding the role it has played in other common law jurisdictions,[105] and the extent to which it could be said to be at work in human rights cases, particularly in relation to developments in positive obligations.[106] These developments are interconnected. The UK Supreme Court has gradually channelled litigation against public authorities away from tort and into Human Rights Act claims, to the point at which there is a better prospect of establishing liability through the latter avenue. Two decades of developments, however, could easily be thrown into reverse. Although eventually withdrawn in June 2023, Clause 5 of the Conservative government's Bill of Rights Bill set out to circumscribe the impact of positive obligations on public authorities, seeking to prevent domestic courts from keeping pace with developments at Strasbourg and to introduce factors intended to restrict existent positive obligations. Such proposals address a symptom, not the cause, of the government's concern, but that is not to say similar proposals will not be introduced again in future. Human Rights Act litigation over positive obligations

---

104   ibid.
105   Stychin, 'The Vulnerable Subject'.
106   Peroni and Timmer, 'Vulnerable Groups'.

has expanded precisely because of the more developed (although far from fully developed) conception of vulnerability within ECtHR jurisprudence. Such a blunt statutory intervention could well divert the flow of litigation back towards tort, and in doing so reinvigorate discussion of vulnerability in this context. The potential of vulnerability to reshape our conception of the public sector's liabilities towards the public it serves is unlikely to be so easily constrained.

3

The Politics of Pure Economic Loss

Craig Purshouse

Setting the scene: one principle and two difficult cases

Writing in a collection commemorating the 50th anniversary of *Hedley Byrne & Co Ltd v Heller & Partners Ltd*,[1] Kit Barker noted that the 'progressive social welfare assumptions that prevailed in the age of *Hedley Byrne* ... are being questioned in more exigent, conservative times'.[2] The case inspired debates about the 'proper balance between contractarian, free-market ideology on the one hand, and interventionist regulatory welfarism', on the other.[3] This seems to imply that an expansive law on recovery for pure economic loss under *Hedley Byrne* reflects a progressive political agenda. With respect to Barker, in this chapter I want to challenge this idea. Instead, I maintain, aspects of this area of law might be a result of a clash between two policies, namely freedom of contract and encouraging property markets, that reflect a (neo)liberal political agenda. To do this, let me begin by setting out the principle and two recalcitrant cases in its application.

The principle in Hedley Byrne

The general rule in negligence is that a defendant owes no duty of care to avoid negligently causing the claimant to suffer purely economic loss.[4] To illustrate,

---

[1] [1964] AC 465.
[2] Kit Barker, '*Hedley Byrne v Heller*: Issues at the Beginning of the Twenty-First Century' in Kit Barker, Ross Grantham and Warren Swain (eds), *The Law of Misstatements: 50 Years on from Hedley Byrne* (Hart, 2017) 5.
[3] ibid., 6.
[4] *Caparo Industries plc v Dickman* [1990] 2 AC 605, 618 (Lord Bridge).

consider pure economic loss caused by acquiring defective property. If I carelessly knock over your laptop and smash the screen, I will have damaged your property. If, instead, I carelessly knocked over the laptop before you purchased it so that you buy it with a smashed screen, I have not damaged your property. Instead, you have acquired defective property and this loss is considered purely economic in nature (the cost of having the screen repaired or buying a working laptop). No duty of care is owed in negligence to avoid causing this type of loss.[5] Instead, you should bring an action in contract law against the seller for supplying these faulty goods. Consider, too, what is often called relational economic loss. This is purely financial loss related to damage to a third party's person or property. If A lends B a laptop so that B can complete a business deal and the laptop is carelessly smashed by C, B will lose money if they cannot complete the deal because of C's negligence. C will owe A a duty of care to avoid causing damage to A's property (in this case, the laptop), but will not owe B a duty of care. This is because B has only suffered pure economic loss (the lost business deal) caused by damage to property belonging to another (A).[6]

There is, however, a significant exception to this general rule on the irrecoverability of pure economic loss in negligence in the form of the principle in *Hedley Byrne*. Originally applying only to negligent misstatements, this principle, extended by later case law, is now said to be the 'rationalisation or technique adopted by English law to provide a remedy for the recovery of damages in respect of economic loss caused by the negligent performance of services'.[7]

In *Hedley Byrne*, the appellants were advertising agents who had placed orders with a company, Easipower Ltd. Under the terms of the advertising order, Hedley Byrne was personally liable for the costs of the adverts. They asked their bankers to inquire into Easipower's financial stability and their bankers duly made inquiries of the respondents, Heller, who were Easipower's bankers. Heller gave references but stipulated that these were 'without responsibility'. Relying on the references, the appellants placed the orders. It later turned out that Easipower was not actually creditworthy and the claimants lost £17,000, the cost of the adverts. They brought a claim in negligence against Heller alleging that the references were carelessly prepared.

The appellants lost their case in the House of Lords as no duty of care arose on these facts, not least because of the disclaimer of liability. The House of Lords considered, albeit obiter, when a duty of care to avoid causing pure economic loss would arise in negligence. Their Lordships held that for a duty of care to avoid causing financial loss to exist there must be:

---

[5] *D & F Estates Ltd v Church Commissioners for England* [1989] 1 AC 177 and *Murphy v Brentwood DC* [1991] 1 AC 398.

[6] *Cattle v The Stockton Waterworks Co* (1875) LR 10 QB 453; *Leigh & Sullivan Ltd v Aliakmon Shipping Co Ltd ('The Aliakmon')* [1986] 1 AC 785; *Spartan Steel & Alloys Ltd v Martin and Co (Contractors) Ltd* [1973] 1 QB 27.

[7] *Williams v Natural Life Health Foods Ltd* [1998] 1 WLR 830, 835 (Lord Steyn).

1. A special relationship between the claimant and defendant.
2. A voluntary undertaking or assumption of responsibility by the defendant for a statement they have made to the claimant.
3. Reasonable reliance upon the statement by the claimant.

This principle allowed recovery for pure economic loss in cases of negligent misstatements and was extended in *Henderson v Merrett Syndicates Ltd* to encompass negligent services in order to allow rich investors in the Lloyd's of London insurance market to sue careless underwriting and management agents.[8] Recent Supreme Court decisions have confirmed that the concept of a voluntary 'assumption of responsibility' is the foundation of liability for pure economic loss.[9]

And yet the criticisms of this area of law have been relentless. The quality of appellate reasoning following *Hedley Byrne* is said to be 'abysmal'.[10] Judges are accused of relying on 'conceptual veils'[11] that obscure the rational development of the law, resulting in a pattern of decisions that are 'complex, uncertain and anomalous'.[12] Specifically, the courts appear to have been inconsistent in their interpretations of 'voluntary assumption of responsibility'. Does it involve agreeing to legal liability, agreeing to perform a task or something else?[13] There is also debate about whether a voluntary agreement is actually required, or whether the duty is imposed by law.[14]

The justice of allowing recovery for pure economic loss in negligence has also been questioned. In his commentary on *Hedley Byrne*, Tony Weir notes:

> a glance at the plaintiffs in this line of cases reveals that their claims to redress are not indisputably high. They made bad business deals, having taken only a free opinion before hazarding their wealth in the hope of profit, no part of which, had it eventuated, would they have transferred to the honest person whom they now seek to saddle with their loss. The defectiveness of a system which refuses in such cases to sever the risk of loss from the chance of profit is not obvious.[15]

---

8   [1995] 2 AC 145.

9   *Steel v NRAM Ltd* [2018] UKSC 13, 24 (Lord Wilson); *Banca Nazionale del Lavoro SPA v Playboy Club London Ltd* [2018] UKSC 43, 7 (Lord Sumption).

10   David Campbell, 'The Curious Incident of the Dog that did Bark in the Night-Time: What Mischief does *Hedley Byrne v Heller* Correct?' in Kit Barker, Ross Grantham and Warren Swain (eds), *The Law of Misstatements: 50 Years on from Hedley Byrne* (Hart, 2017) 131.

11   Kit Barker, 'Unreliable Assumptions in the Modern Law of Negligence' (1993) 109(3) *Law Quarterly Review* 461, 484.

12   Jane Stapleton, 'Duty of Care and Economic Loss: A Wider Agenda' (1991) 107 *Law Quarterly Review* 249, 258–9.

13   See Barker, 'Unreliable Assumptions', and Donal Nolan, 'Assumption of Responsibility: Four Questions' (2019) 72 *Current Legal Problems* 123.

14   See *Smith v Eric S Bush* [1990] 1 AC 831, 862 (Lord Griffith).

15   J.A. Weir, 'Liability for Syntax' (1963) 21(2) *Cambridge Law Journal* 216, 218.

Weir suggests that the claimants in *Hedley Byrne* could have paid a credit reference agency and the law could have held that it is only reasonable to rely on a word that one has bought (and, thus, that the law of contract is a more appropriate regime for the resolution of such disputes). He states, '[a] free tip is relevantly distinguishable from remunerated opinion, as social practice shows; the guest thanks the hostess, but the hostess chides the cook'.[16]

Recently, the principle has been defended in some quarters. Donal Nolan has developed a robust argument that assumption of responsibility involves A taking on a job or task for B.[17] Writing extrajudicially, Lord Sales' view is that the 'central unifying feature' of the 'core category of case' where the principle applies is:

> that the parties had a relationship in which it was open to the defendant
> to have bargained in respect of the risk involved in taking on a task for
> the claimant, in a context in which the defendant invited the claimant
> to rely on the due performance of the task.[18]

Both Nolan and Lord Sales believe the principle can be justified in such cases. These rationalisations go some way to explain a great number of the cases that have followed *Hedley Byrne*, but two landmark cases in particular stand out as significant exceptions: *Smith v Eric S Bush*[19] and *White v Jones*.[20] Few of *Hedley Byrne*'s defenders even attempt to encompass these cases within any rationalisations of the principle, with Lord Steyn in *Williams v Natural Life Health Foods Ltd* conceding that they were 'decided on special facts'.[21] It is therefore worth providing an overview of these recalcitrant decisions.

Smith v Bush

In *Smith v Eric S Bush* the claimant, Mrs Smith, had purchased her home with the help of a mortgage from a building society. Following standard practice, she paid the building society for a valuation report who in turn instructed the defendant firm of surveyors to carry out a visual inspection. This was carried out negligently: the surveyor had noticed that two chimney breasts had been removed but failed to check whether the chimneys were adequately supported.

---

16   ibid., 219. See also Campbell, 'The Curious Incident', 125 and Jane Stapleton, *Three Essays on Torts* (Oxford University Press, 2021) 56.
17   Nolan, 'Assumption of Responsibility'.
18   Lord Sales, 'Pure Economic Loss in the Law of Tort: The History and Theory of Assumption of Responsibility' The Annual Tort Law Research Group Lecture, 26 September 2022 (available at https://www.supremecourt.uk/docs/pure-economic-loss-in-the-law-of-tort-lord-sales.pdf).
19   [1990] 1 AC 831.
20   [1995] 2 AC 207.
21   [1998] 1 WLR 830, 837.

The valuation report subsequently said that no essential repairs were necessary. When the chimneys later collapsed, Mrs Smith suffered significant financial losses. Unable to sue the building society with whom she had contracted (it had done nothing wrong), she instead sought to bring a claim against the surveyors in negligence (with whom she had no contract – they had been instructed by the building society). Both the mortgage application form and the valuation report contained a disclaimer of liability for the accuracy of the report covering both the building society and the valuer. The claimant was also informed that the report was not a structural survey and though she was supplied with a copy of it, she was advised to also obtain independent professional advice.

Anyone with a passing acquaintance with this area of law might believe that Mrs Smith's claim would be rejected. After all, a key passage from Lord Reid's speech in *Hedley Byrne* had held that disclaimers can negate any assumption of responsibility:

> A reasonable man, knowing that he was being trusted or that his skill and judgment were being relied on, would, I think, have three courses open to him. He could keep silent or decline to give the information or advice sought: or he could give an answer with a clear qualification that he accepted no responsibility for it or that it was given without that reflection or inquiry which a careful answer would require: or he could simply answer without any such qualification.[22]

On this view, it was only in the latter situation where a defendant would have assumed responsibility. Such comments notwithstanding, the House of Lords in *Smith* held that a disclaimer of liability by the valuer was a notice within the meaning of the Unfair Contract Terms Act 1977. Such a clause would be ineffective by virtue of section 2(2) of the 1977 Act unless it satisfied the requirement of reasonableness provided by section 11(3), and the House of Lords found that it would not be fair and reasonable to allow the valuer to rely on such a disclaimer to exclude his liability to the mortgagor for the accuracy of the valuation. Lord Griffiths believed that there were several matters to be considered in such cases:

1. Were the parties of equal bargaining power?
2. Would it have been reasonably practicable to obtain the advice from an alternative source taking into account considerations of costs and time?
3. How difficult is the task being undertaken for which liability is being excluded?
4. What are the practical consequences of the decision on the question of 'reasonableness'?[23]

---

[22]   [1964] AC 465, 486.
[23]   [1990] 1 AC 831, 858.

Mrs Smith was behaving in the same way as other purchasers of 'modest' homes (including by not seeking an independent valuation at her own expense) and so, for their lordships, the defendant was held to have assumed responsibility to her and her reliance on the report was reasonable, even with the disclaimer.

White v Jones

The claimants in *White* were the two daughters of one Mr Barrett. After the daughters had become estranged from their father, he cut them out of his will. Following a later reconciliation, Mr Barrett instructed the defendant solicitor, Mr Jones, to prepare a new will. These instructions were not acted upon before Mr Barratt died, meaning that the old will remained valid, and the claimants inherited nothing. The daughters brought a claim in negligence against the defendant solicitor for the money that they would have inherited under the new will.

Like *Smith*, this claim seems hard to rationalise under the *Hedley Byrne* principle. As John Murphy states, the idea that the solicitor assumed responsibility to the daughters is 'a rather fanciful one'.[24] The solicitor had never made a statement or even supplied a service to the daughters, so it is hard to see how the defendant could have assumed responsibility *to them*. Solicitors' duties are to their clients. Similarly, there was no indication that the daughters knew that these changes to the will were taking place, let alone reasonably relied upon the solicitor to implement them. It is also notable that the daughters had not lost any money but had merely failed to make an economic gain. Despite this, the House of Lords, by a 3:2 majority, held that the defendant had assumed responsibility to the beneficiaries and therefore owed them a duty of care. Lord Goff thought it served justice to allow the claimants to succeed. He mentioned the 'extraordinary fact' that if a duty was not recognised then 'the only persons who might have a valid claim (that is, the testator and his estate) have suffered no loss, and the only person who has suffered a loss (that is, the disappointed beneficiary) has no claim' (as they did not have a contract with the solicitors).[25] This supposedly meant that there was 'a lacuna in the law which needs to be filled'.[26]

---

[24] John Murphy, 'Judicial Gap-Filling in the Law of Torts and the Rule of Law' in Jodi Gardner, Amy Goymour, Janet O'Sullivan and Sarah Worthington (eds), *Politics, Policy and Private Law* (Hart, 2023) 87–104.

[25] [1995] 2 AC 207, 259.

[26] [1995] 2 AC 207, 260. For criticisms of this idea see Joanne Conaghan and Wade Mansell, *The Wrongs of Tort* (2nd edn, Pluto Press, 1998) 30; and Judith Skillen and James Lee, '*White v Jones*: A Legacy of the Search for Principle' in Brian Sloan (ed), *Landmark Cases in Succession Law* (Hart, 2019) 109, 130–1.

The problem defined

These two cases are difficult to reconcile with the principle in *Hedley Byrne*. Their collective result is that defendants can not only assume responsibility to someone even if they explicitly state that they are not doing so, but also that they can assume responsibility to someone they have had no contact with whatsoever. In contrast to many other landmark pure economic loss decisions, the claimants in *Smith* and *White* initially seem worthy candidates for one's sympathy. Indeed, these cases, while often regarded as unprincipled, are rarely attacked as unjust in the same way as cases involving rich investors, such as *Henderson*. The claimants in *Smith* and *White* were not commercial parties and reasons of justice appeared to animate the judges in both cases to adapt or extend the law.

Jane Stapleton has explained these cases on the basis that the claimants were vulnerable and the threat of indeterminate liability was absent.[27] In an attack on *Henderson*, David Campbell said, 'it would be preposterous to maintain that the claimants in those cases were, or in the typical *Hedley Byrne* case are, "vulnerable" or anything other than contractually competent'.[28] Vulnerability appears to be a characteristic, supposedly common in *Smith* and *White*, that could justify negligence's protection of financial interests. These two cases therefore raise difficulties. First, they complicate any attempted rationalisation of the principle in *Hedley Byrne*. It is hard to see how they fit within the principle itself, without it being stretched so far to include other cases where a duty of care has been denied.[29] Second, for those who oppose all recovery for pure economic loss in negligence, they raise the prospect of treating sympathetic claimants in a callous way by sending them home empty-handed.

The first point does not concern me in this chapter. Most academic and judicial opinion accepts these cases are unprincipled. My focus is on the second point. Like David Campbell, Nicholas McBride and Tony Weir,[30] I am of the view that recovery of pure economic loss in negligence is difficult to justify. I will not reiterate their arguments here and, instead, consider these cases from a different perspective. Upon closer inspection, *Smith* and *White* could be explained as clashes between contrasting legal policies: freedom of contract and enabling markets in property. Examination of these policies indicates that they are not politically neutral and are consistent with a neoliberal zeitgeist that was dominant, at the very least, in the late 1980s and 1990s when *Smith* and *White* were decided. This political analysis challenges the idea that these cases are progressive ones or necessarily about protecting the vulnerable. If my arguments are accepted, these

---

27 Jane Stapleton, *Three Essays on Torts* (Oxford University Press, 2021) 63.

28 Campbell, 'The Curious Incident', 125.

29 Such as *Banca Nazionale del Lavoro SPA v Playboy Club London Ltd* [2018] UKSC 43, which has a similar structure to *White* but where a duty of care was denied.

30 Campbell, 'The Curious Incident'; Nicholas McBride, *The Humanity of Private Law – Part 1: The Explanation* (Hart, 2019) 235; Weir, 'Liability for Syntax'.

decisions should attract a lot less sympathy and should therefore not stand in the way of the repeal of the principle in *Hedley Byrne*. Although other scholars have made connections between tort law and neoliberalism,[31] there is very little research specifically on neoliberalism and the law of pure economic loss in negligence: this chapter therefore brings a new perspective to the academic literature on this topic by analysing these cases through this political lens.

Something that should be emphasised at the very outset is that my argument is *not* that judges mechanically apply neoliberal ideology. Rather, it is the much more modest claim that neoliberal thinking represents the ideology of the age, and these cases are arguably consistent with it. We cannot peer inside the judges' minds to find out what motivated them to decide *Smith* and *White* and judges rarely trumpet that they are deciding a case based on political ideology.[32] On this basis, neoliberalism may be *one factor* in the development of modern tort law generally and these cases in particular.

Neoliberalism and legal policy

Neoliberalism: an overview

In 1951 the economist Milton Friedman discussed A.V. Dicey's idea that legislation reflects public opinion but that there is about a 20-year time lag. This is because 'men legislate on the basis of the philosophy they imbibed in their youth'.[33] He said: '[m]en may deviate in emphasis from basic social values and beliefs but few can hold a thoroughly different philosophy, can fail to be infected by the intellectual air they breathe. By the standards of nineteenth century individualism, we are all of us collectivists in smaller or greater measure.'[34]

Despite this, Friedman was hopeful that neoliberalism was capable of 'capturing the enthusiasm of men of good-will everywhere, and thereby becoming the major current of opinion'.[35] In many respects, his hopes were realised. Since he wrote those words, neoliberalism has been said to be 'hegemonic as a mode of discourse'[36] and 'governs as sophisticated common sense'.[37] It has 'come to shape

---

[31] Dan Priel, 'Torts, Rights, and Right-Wing Ideology' (2011) 19(1) *Torts Law Journal* 1; Annette Morris, 'Tort and Neo-liberalism' in Kit Barker, Karen Fairweather and Ross Grantham (eds), *Private Law in the 21st Century* (Hart, 2017) 503.

[32] Though for some examples see John Murphy, *The Province and Politics of the Economic Torts* (Hart, 2022) 230–43.

[33] Milton Friedman, 'Neo-Liberalism and its Prospects' in Larry Ebenstein (ed), *The Indispensable Milton Friedman: Essays on Politics and Economics* (Regnery Publishing, 2012) 4.

[34] ibid.

[35] ibid., 9.

[36] David Harvey, *A Brief History of Neoliberalism* (Oxford University Press, 2007) 3.

[37] Wendy Brown, *Undoing the Demos: Neoliberalism's Stealth Revolution* (Zone Books, 2015) 35. See also Corinne Blalock, 'Neoliberalism and the Crisis of Legal Theory' (2015) 77(4) *Law and Contemporary Problems* 71, 85.

not only elite opinions and beliefs, but also the normative fabric of everyday life itself'.[38] Like classical liberalism or laissez-faire, neoliberalism perceives free markets as the best way to distribute goods, but it is said to differ from classical liberalism in an important way.

According to Friedman (regarded, along with Friedrich Hayek, as the leading intellectual of the movement), 19th century laissez-faire 'assigned almost no role to the state other than the maintenance of order and the enforcement of contracts'.[39] By taking such a limited role, it 'underestimated the danger that private individuals could through agreement and combination usurp power and effectively limit the freedom of other individuals'.[40] Neoliberalism differs from traditional laissez-faire economics by recognising that there are 'important positive functions that must be performed by the state'.[41] The state's role is to 'police the system, establish conditions favorable to competition and prevent monopoly, provide a stable monetary framework, and relieve acute misery and distress'.[42]

I do not trace the history of neoliberalism here as this has taken place elsewhere.[43] Likewise, I do not focus on the niceties of the different schools, such as the Austrian School associated with Hayek and the Chicago School associated with Friedman (though the influence of the Chicago School with the law and economics movement is discussed later in this chapter).[44] That said, some key features are worth noting. Neoliberalism promotes 'strong private property rights, free markets, and free trade'[45] and favours deregulation, privatisation and the dismantling of the welfare state.[46] To do this, it emphasises the 'compelling and seductive ideals'[47] of individual freedom and choice.

---

[38]   Nick Srnicek and Alex Williams, *Inventing the Future: Postcapitalism and a World Without Work* (Verso, 2016) 64.

[39]   Friedman, 'Neo-Liberalism', 6.

[40]   ibid.

[41]   ibid., 7. See also John Gray, *False Dawn: The Delusions of Global Capitalism* (revised edition, Granta, 2009) 17; Naomi Klein, *The Shock Doctrine* (Penguin, 2008) 15; Robert Knox, 'Law, Neoliberalism and the Constitution of Political Subjectivity' in Honor Brabazon (ed), *Neoliberal Legality: Understanding the Role of the Law in the Neoliberal Project* (Routledge, 2017) 92, 93.

[42]   Friedman, 'Neo-Liberalism', 7. See also Robert Nozick's discussion of the 'night-watchman state' of the classical liberal theory that is limited to the functions of 'protecting all of its citizens against violence, theft, and fraud, and to the enforcement of contracts, and so on'. Robert Nozick, *Anarchy, State, and Utopia* (Basic Books, 1974) 26.

[43]   See William Davies, *The Limits of Neoliberalism* (Sage, 2017) and Harvey, *A Brief History*.

[44]   Florence Sutcliffe-Braithwaite, Aled Davies and Ben Jackson, 'Introduction: A Neoliberal Age?' in Aled Davies, Ben Jackson and Florence Sutcliffe-Braithwaite (eds), *The Neoliberal Age? Britain Since the 1970s* (UCL Press, 2021) 3.

[45]   Harvey, *A Brief History*, 2.

[46]   Blalock, 'Neoliberalism and the Crisis', 83.

[47]   Harvey, *A Brief History*, 5.

Neoliberalism as a ruling class project

David Harvey maintains that we can interpret neoliberalism in two different ways: 'either as a *utopian* project to realise a theoretical design for the reorganisation of international capitalism or as a *political* project to re-establish the conditions for capital accumulation and to restore the power of economic elites'.[48] He believes that the second interpretation has been dominant. For this reason, neoliberalism is sometimes seen, as Vicente Navarro states, as the dominant classes' response 'to the considerable gains achieved by the working and peasant classes between the end of World War II and the mid-1970s'.[49] Class is not a stable category and so neoliberalism has 'not necessarily meant the restoration of economic power to the same people'.[50] It has allowed different categories of people to amass huge amounts of capital and power, such as the CEOs of large corporations.[51] The fact that the constitution of the upper class has changed does not detract from a class analysis. Existing holders of capital tend to fare well under 'free markets'. The Duke of Westminster will not be found sleeping on a cardboard box any time soon.

Neoliberalism and the judiciary

Being passed by elected politicians who espouse particular political views, the neoliberal nature of individual pieces of legislation may not be difficult to decipher. Such inferences are somewhat more complicated with the judge-made common law. It would be naïve to believe that judges alone are immune from being influenced by prevailing political moods, particularly in an area of law that is rife with indeterminacy and requires them to make value choices such as torts.[52] John Griffith long ago argued in *The Politics of the Judiciary* that judges, as a result of their shared backgrounds – mostly private school and Oxbridge educated middle-aged White men who have spent years in well-remunerated careers at the Bar – have 'acquired a strikingly homogenous collection of attitudes, beliefs

---

[48] ibid., 19. See also Honor Brabazon, 'Introduction' in Honor Brabazon (ed), *Neoliberal Legality: Understanding the Role of the Law in the Neoliberal Project* (Routledge, 2017) 1; and Ntina Tzouvala, 'Continuity and Rupture in Restraining the Right to Strike' in the same collection at 119.

[49] Vicente Navarro, 'Neoliberalism as a Class Ideology; Or, the Political Causes of the Growth of Inequalities' (2007) 37(1) *International Journal of Health Services* 47, 53.

[50] Harvey, *A Brief History*, 31.

[51] Klein, *The Shock Doctrine*, 57. See also Gérard Duménil and Dominique Lévy, 'Costs and Benefits of Neoliberalism: A Class Analysis' (2001) 8 *Review of International Political Economy* 578, 580.

[52] See Conaghan and Mansell, *The Wrongs of Tort*, 2-3; David Kairys, 'Introduction' in David Kairys (ed), *The Politics of Law: A Progressive Critique* (3rd edn, Basic Books, 1998) 4; John Murphy, 'Contemporary Tort Theory and Tort Law's Evolution' (2019) 32(2) *Canadian Journal of Law & Jurisprudence* 413.

and principles, which to them represent the public interest'.[53] As members of the establishment and ruling class,[54] there will be circumstances where they see the prevailing ideological zeitgeist that benefits their class as 'common sense' when making policy choices in tort cases. Perhaps this might explain some of the judicial sympathy for businessmen who have made bad deals. While such a thesis is intuitively attractive, judges have diverse views about the best policy for the law to adopt.[55] And numerous counterexamples can be found of judges acting in the interests of workers over capital.

It is worth illustrating some of these political tensions in tort law. In *The Province and Politics of the Economic Torts*, John Murphy discusses a sizeable range of factors that left their imprint on the development of the intentional economic torts, particularly in the 19th and 20th centuries. He demonstrates that many of these developments 'can best be understood as reflective of a (then) prevailing ideology or public sentiment'[56] and the political convictions of judges, including a commitment to individualism, faith in competitive markets and hostility to trade unionism.[57] The same period, however, also saw judges increase the circumstances in which employers would be liable in negligence to their employees.[58] More recently, we might find judges expressing neoliberal sentiments, such as that patients in the National Health Service should be regarded as 'consumers'.[59] But, equally, we can also find judges in tort cases praising citizens who take on 'the big battalions of ... industry'[60] or developing the law on causation to compensate victims of industrial disease.[61]

My argument, then, is not that judges have been mechanically applying a political ideology that favours fellow members of the ruling class. The influences on tort law are multifarious and so the 'ideological zeitgeist'[62] is but one factor among many. Instead, I want to argue that a clash between two important legal policies played an important role in the decisions in *Smith* and *White* and that these principles reflected the ideological mood of the time the cases were decided.

---

53 J.A.G. Griffith, *The Politics of the Judiciary* (5th edn, Fontana, 2010) 295.

54 Terry Eagleton, *Why Marx Was Right* (2nd edn, Yale University Press, 2018) 175.

55 See Craig Purshouse, 'Utilitarianism as Tort Theory: Countering the Caricature' (2018) 38 *Legal Studies* 24.

56 John Murphy, *The Province and Politics of the Economic Torts* (Hart, 2022) 223.

57 ibid., 230–43.

58 See *Wilsons & Clyde Coal Co Ltd v English* [1938] AC 57.

59 *Montgomery v Lanarkshire Health Board (Scotland)* [2015] UKSC 11, 75 (Lords Kerr and Reed). See Craig Purshouse, 'The Impatient Patient and the Unreceptive Receptionist: *Darnley v Croydon Health Services NHS Trust*' (2019) 27(2) *Medical Law Review* 318; and Emily Jackson, 'Challenging the Comparison in *Montgomery* Between Patients and "Consumers Exercising Choices"' (2021) 29(4) *Medical Law Review* 595.

60 *Ferguson v British Gas plc* [2009] EWCA Civ 46, 1 (Jacobs LJ), in a harassment case.

61 *Fairchild v Glenhaven Funeral Services Ltd and Others* [2003] 1 AC 32.

62 To use the phrasing of Murphy, 'Contemporary Tort Theory', 416.

Some disclaimers

Some further disclaimers are in order. Neoliberalism is a contested term. Some scholars, such as David Edgerton, have argued that we should dispense with it altogether.[63] He maintains that as a catch-all it 'misses key elements of radical changes that have been visited on the UK since the 1980s'.[64] Others have disputed whether there is, in fact, any distinction between neoliberalism and classical liberalism. Gary Gerstle, for example, states that '[m]arkets need structure in order to operate freely. This principle was as intrinsic to classical liberalism as it has been to neoliberalism'.[65] For him, the 'neo' in neoliberalism is less about distinguishing neoliberalism from classical liberalism than it is about distinguishing it from modern liberalism, which had often been associated with forms of social democracy.[66]

For some, the neoliberal project has died or is dying.[67] Harbingers of its demise are not hard to find. A non-exhaustive list might include: the 2008 financial crisis, the rise of populist politicians such as Jeremy Corbyn and Bernie Sanders (on the left) and Donald Trump, Boris Johnson and Giorgia Meloni (on the right), Brexit (on some interpretations)[68] and the COVID-19 pandemic.[69] For William Davies and Nicholas Gane, 'the number of apparently countervailing tendencies within and against neoliberalism is also growing'.[70] Despite this, neoliberal policies have been harder to shake off and seem to be with us for the foreseeable future.

The force of these critiques does not really affect my arguments. Nothing would be lost if we labelled the prevailing zeitgeist as just plain classical liberal or laissez-faire rather than *neo*liberal (indeed, I am persuaded by Gerstle's point). And if we are presently in a transition point, or even if neoliberalism is now dead, it may affect arguments about the present or future ideology underpinning tort law, but that is an argument for a different piece. It was at its height when the cases I am focusing on were decided in the late 1980s and mid-1990s. With

---

63   David Edgerton, 'What Came Between New Liberalism and Neoliberalism? Rethinking Keynesianism, the Welfare State and Social Democracy' in Aled Davies, Ben Jackson and Florence Sutcliffe-Braithwaite (eds), *The Neoliberal Age? Britain Since the 1970s* (UCL Press, 2021) 31.

64   ibid.

65   Gary Gerstle, *The Rise and Fall of the Neoliberal Order: America and the World in the Free Market Era* (Oxford University Press, 2022) 6.

66   ibid., 6–7.

67   ibid., 293.

68   See Perry Anderson, *Ever Closer Union? Europe in the West* (Verso, 2021), chapter 4.

69   See Adam Tooze, 'Has Covid ended the neoliberal era?' *The Guardian* 2 September 2021 (available at https://www.theguardian.com/news/2021/sep/02/covid-and-the-crisis-of-neoliberalism).

70   William Davies and Nicholas Gane, 'Post Neoliberalism? An Introduction' (2021) 38(6) *Theory Culture & Society* 3, 4.

this in mind, we can now discuss how *Smith* and *White* might reflect clashing neoliberal legal policies.

Freedom of contract and encouraging property markets

The idea that freedom of contract and encouraging the markets in property are two important legal policies is well-established. Writing extrajudicially, Lord Sales has said '[t]he existing common law supplies a basic stock of general moral principles, revolving around core values of the protection of property, promotion of promise-keeping and enforcement of reasonable behavioural social standards'.[71]

Jodi Gardner states that '[t]he primacy of freedom of contract has been the dominant value in the philosophy of contract law, the common law and, until relatively recently, statute law'.[72] This is the idea that 'men of full age and competent understanding shall have the utmost liberty in contracting'.[73] An important policy of the law is that it gives 'legal force to the risk allocations agreed between the contracting parties'.[74] Inroads have been made into the principle by, among other things, consumer protection legislation.[75] In *The Rise and Fall of Freedom of Contract*, P.S. Atiyah charted the principle's decline since its Victorian high point.[76] The book was published in 1979, the year that Margaret Thatcher was elected as prime minister, and its decline does not seem to have been permanent. In a later essay, Atiyah acknowledged that 'Freedom of Contract seems to have been re-established as the ideology of the common law, in accordance with the views of the New Right'.[77] It was also seen as important in later cases. For example, in *Photo Production Ltd Respondents v Securicor Transport Ltd*, decided in 1980, Lord Wilberforce held, 'in commercial matters generally … there is everything to be said … for leaving the parties free to apportion the risks as they think fit and for respecting their decisions'.[78] In a 2001 extrajudicial speech, Lord Bingham declared that the law should act 'as the handmaid of commerce and not as an adversary, a fetter or an irritant'.[79] We can therefore

---

[71] Sir Philip Sales, 'The Common Law: Context and Method' (2019) 135 *Law Quarterly Review* 47, 54.

[72] Jodi Gardner, *The Future of High-Cost Credit: Rethinking Payday Lending* (Hart, 2022) 42.

[73] *Printing and Numerical Registering Co v Sampson* (1875) LR 19 Eq 462, 465 (Sir George Jessell MR).

[74] Stapleton, *Three Essays*, 35.

[75] Such as the Unfair Contract Terms Act 1977. See Gardner, *Future of High-Cost Credit*, chapter 3.

[76] P.S. Atiyah, *The Rise and Fall of Freedom of Contract* (Oxford University Press, 1979).

[77] P.S. Atiyah, 'Freedom of Contract and the New Right' in *Essays on Contract* (Oxford University Press, 1990) 365.

[78] [1980] AC 827, 843.

[79] Lord Bingham, 'The Law as the Handmaid of Commerce' Sixteenth Sultan Azlan Shah Law Lecture, 5 September 2001 (available at https://www.sultanazlanshah.com/pdf/2004%20 Book%201/SAS_Lecture_16.pdf).

conclude that, although freedom of contract is not an absolute value, promoting it is an important legal policy. This often explains the reluctance of the courts to impose duties of care to avoid causing pure economic loss in negligence as doing so can undermine the parties' freedom to structure their relationships under contract.[80]

Additionally, we might consider a second legal policy to be the encouragement of markets in property by treating real property as an exchangeable commodity. According to Lord Upjohn in *National Provincial Bank Ltd v Ainsworth*, '[i]t has been the policy of the law for over a hundred years to simplify and facilitate transactions in real property'.[81] This view is supported by the arguments of Lorna Fox O'Mahony. She contends that land law's 'core doctrinal commitments to certainty, autonomous individualism, and efficiency were reinforced by legislative policies in [the Law of Property Act] 1925 and again in the Land Registration Act 2002, geared towards a political agenda to facilitate the flow of money through real property transactions'.[82] She also maintains that the 1925 legislation favoured strong trump rights in order to 'promote the pro-purchaser agenda to make land a more marketable commodity and to encourage people with capital ("property insiders") to invest in land as freely as they would in stocks and shares'.[83] This 'set the scene for the emergence, much later in the century, of the paradigm of owned housing as investment, and subsequently for the re-construction of home ownership as a vehicle for capital accumulation and de-cumulation'.[84]

I have argued elsewhere that a plausible explanation of tort law is that judges aim to arrive at decisions that have the best consequences, but will have different views about what outcome is best and also the relative weight they attribute to the importance of certainty and following precedent, on the one hand, and fair results in individual cases, regardless of the dictates of strict doctrine, on the other.[85] In what follows, I argue that *Smith* and *White* can be seen as cases where there is a clash between two different mid-level legal policies: freedom of contract and promoting property markets. Both are seen by the judiciary as policies that will lead to good outcomes. But freedom of contract can sometimes give way to the latter and vice versa.[86] The fact that different judges might have different

---

[80]   Stapleton, *Three Essays*, 35.

[81]   [1965] AC 1175, 1233.

[82]   Lorna Fox O'Mahony, 'Property Outsiders and the Hidden Politics of Doctrinalism' (2014) 67(1) *Current Legal Problems* 409, 421.

[83]   ibid.

[84]   ibid.

[85]   Purshouse, 'Utilitarianism as Tort Theory', 34.

[86]   This would be in keeping with the views of Nicholas McBride, *Humanity of Private Law*, 124, where he ranks the secondary goods of 'home' and 'private property' above the tertiary good of 'contract law'. For a critique of this theory see Craig Purshouse, 'Flourishing Under Private Law? A Critique of McBride's Explanatory Theory' (2021) 34(1) *Canadian Journal of Law & Jurisprudence* 239.

views on the correct balance between these two values can sometimes account for the seemingly anomalous nature of tort doctrine in this area.[87] These legal policies are not politically neutral, though. Despite being of a much older vintage, they are consistent with the neoliberal zeitgeist that was at its height when *Smith* and *White* were decided.

Smith, White and neoliberalism

Encouraging property ownership

A key plank in Margaret Thatcher's privatisation drive was the sale of council houses. Intended to capture the votes of people who were eligible to rent their homes from their local council, the policy enabled council tenants to purchase their homes at hugely discounted rates.[88] The thinking behind the policy was that council tenants, after buying their homes, would begin to identify as bourgeoisie homeowners and then switch their votes to the Conservatives. Traditionally, council estate tenants would not have voted Conservative as it would not have been in their economic self-interest to do so, but Thatcher 'was convinced that if they could be brought into the market, they would start to identify with the interests of the wealthier people who opposed redistribution'.[89] The policy resulted in 'a chronic shortage of affordable housing, increased the burden of household debt, and cemented council housing as a residual form of tenure for the poorest members of society'.[90] In addition to 'right to buy', there has also been broader financialisation of the property market that has been detrimental to working people. According to research by Johnna Montgomerie and Mirjam Büdenbender, this has resulted in:

> wealth gains for a select group who bought at the right time and the right place and dire consequences for those who buy the wrong house, at the wrong price or in the wrong place – at best, they look forward to years of indebtedness, possibly negative equity and, at worst, bankruptcy or homelessness.[91]

---

[87] For a discussion of anomalies in tort law see John Murphy, 'Anomalies in Tort Law: A Cause for Concern?' (2023) 86(4) *Modern Law Review* 872.

[88] Selina Todd, *We the People: The Rise and Fall of the Working Class 1910–2010* (John Murray, 2015) 319; Klein, *The Shock Doctrine*, 135; Aled Davies, '"Right to Buy": The Development of a Conservative Housing Policy, 1945–1980' (2013) 27(4) *Contemporary British History* 421, 421.

[89] Klein, ibid.

[90] Davies, 'Development of a Conservative Housing Policy', 422.

[91] Johnna Montgomerie and Mirjam Büdenbender, 'Round the Houses: Homeownership and Failures of Asset-Based Welfare in the United Kingdom' (2015) 20(3) *New Political Economy* 386, 401.

Smith should be viewed in this context. Decided towards the end of Thatcher's term in office, it is in keeping with a general policy to encourage people to purchase homes and wider trends to treat property as an exchangeable commodity. If surveyors were not made to compensate purchasers for losses they suffered because of careless valuations, then many purchasers would feel obliged to pay for their own additional valuations, rather than relying upon ones produced for building societies. This might price out people on lower incomes from buying their homes, who might not be able to afford such upfront costs. Awareness of these issues, albeit not necessarily expressed in an approving manner, can be found in the speech of Lord Templeman:

> The public are exhorted to purchase their homes and cannot find houses to rent … In these circumstances it is not fair and reasonable for building societies and valuers to agree together to impose on purchasers the risk of loss arising as a result of incompetence or carelessness on the part of valuers.[92]

The decision in *Smith* can therefore be seen as an example of the law treating home ownership as being of fundamental importance and of judges willing to discard freedom of contract to encourage people to enter the property market.

Inheritance

Recall that in *White*, the majority were willing to reshape the *Hedley Byrne* principle for reasons of practical justice. It is worth excavating some of the assumptions underpinning this decision. Positioning himself in opposition to the 'strict lawyer' who 'may well react by saying that the present claim can lie only in contract',[93] Lord Goff believed that the 'strong impulse for practical justice'[94] meant that the case should succeed, notwithstanding the difficulty of holding that the solicitor had assumed responsibility to the claimants. He claimed that the injustice of denying the claim was 'reinforced' if:

> one considers the importance of legacies in a society which recognises (subject only to the incidence of inheritance tax, and statutory requirements for provision for near relatives) the right of citizens to leave their assets to whom they please, and in which, as a result, legacies can be of great importance to individual citizens.[95]

---

[92]   [1990] 1 AC 831, 854.
[93]   [1995] 2 AC 207, 261.
[94]   [1995] 2 AC 207, 260.
[95]   [1995] 2 AC 207, 260.

At first sight, inheritance might seem the antithesis of a neoliberal ideology. If neoliberal clichés are to be believed, free markets allow the talented and hard working to rise and the lazy and feckless to fall.[96] Those providing a useful or desirable service are rewarded. Inherited wealth passing down the generations should be contrary to the dynamism of free markets. Yet, as Stuart Hall has argued, '[e]conomically, neo-liberalism's foundations lay in the right of free men … to dispose of their property as they see fit'.[97] Neoliberalism would support people being able to pass on their wealth through generations rather than having it be distributed by the state. Remember, too, that neoliberalism is a system for the restoration of class power. Although ordinary people do, of course, receive bequests, inheritance is an important way in which power and resources can be kept with economic elites.

No less a figure than Milton Friedman has defended inheritance. Any distinction between 'inequality in personal endowments and in property, and between inequalities arising from inherited wealth and from acquired wealth' was said to be 'untenable'.[98] For him:

> it seems illogical to say that a man is entitled to what he has produced by personal capacities or to the produce of the wealth he has accumulated, but that he is not entitled to pass any wealth on to his children; to say that a man may use his income for riotous living but may not give it to his heirs. Surely, the latter is one way to use what he has produced.[99]

Promoting inheritance is therefore consistent with a neoliberal ideology. Furthermore, Lord Goff, in his paean to the importance of inheritance, said that it was 'very often the only opportunity for a citizen to acquire a significant capital sum; or to inherit a house, so providing a secure roof over the heads of himself and his family; or to make special provision for his or her old age'.[100] Like *Smith*, *White* can therefore be seen as a decision that places a high value on people being able to enter the property market.

The decisions therefore reflect the courts departing from freedom of contract to prioritise markets in property. One neoliberal policy can give way to another.

Tensions

As already indicated, my aim in this chapter is to show how *Smith* and *White* might be consistent with a neoliberal ideology that is reflected in legal policy. It

---

[96] See Jo Littler, *Against Meritocracy: Culture, Power and the Myths of Mobility* (Routledge, 2018).

[97] Stuart Hall, 'The Neo-Liberal Revolution' (2011) 25(6) *Cultural Studies* 705, 709.

[98] Milton Friedman with Rose Friedman, *Capitalism and Freedom* (first published 1962; University of Chicago Press, 2002) 164.

[99] ibid.

[100] [1995] 2 AC 207, 260.

is not to show that judges blindly follow the neoliberal zeitgeist. As such, there are points of tension with both decisions that are worth considering.

Defective property

It is instructive to compare *Smith* with *Murphy v Brentwood DC*.[101] In the latter case the House of Lords denied that a duty of care was owed to a claimant who suffered pure economic loss after acquiring a house built on faulty foundations negligently approved by the defendant local authority. How might this be squared with *Smith*? Surely, if *Smith* elevates a neoliberal ethos, by encouraging home purchases, then *Murphy* disproves the thesis by leaving the house purchaser empty-handed? The cases do seem hard to distinguish, if one ignores the flimsy basis of 'assumption of responsibility'.

Indeed, commentators have been sceptical about the methods of distinguishing the cases. For Sarah Green and Paul Davies, '[i]t seems odd that a negligent builder cannot be liable for economic loss in tort, yet surveyors and architects who negligently give bad advice to a purchaser about the property can be so liable'.[102] Jane Stapleton raises the idea that the distinction may be a regressive one. For her, there is no reason why the risks of defective building construction should be 'channelled to professional advisers and away from builders' especially when this 'would most disadvantage those at the modest end of the market (for example, home improvements) who typically rely on expert builders and do not engage the costly services of professional advisers'.[103]

Yet this need not be inconsistent with the underlying politics of *Smith*. *Murphy* does not discourage people from *purchasing* houses, whereas, if *Smith* were decided the opposite way, it would. A person's upfront costs when purchasing a house are unaffected by *Murphy* – it is, after all, concerned with *hidden* defects – whereas if *Smith* were decided differently, people would have to pay for their own surveys. In such circumstances, people might choose to rent. The result of all this is that people are encouraged to purchase property only to be lumbered with extortionate costs when they discover, for example, that it is clad in flammable material.[104] The developers are free to move on to their next project unencumbered by the need to compensate the purchaser. What could be more neoliberal than that?

A more persuasive way of explaining the cases is that, in both, the judges see freedom of contract and promoting property markets as important considerations

---

[101] [1991] 1 AC 398.

[102] Sarah Green and Paul Davies, ' "Pure Economic Loss" and Defective Buildings' in Andrew Robertson and Michael Tilbury (eds), *Divergences in Private Law* (Hart, 2016) 58.

[103] Stapleton, 'Duty of Care and Economic Loss', 282.

[104] Anonymous, 'Cladding crisis: "We are saddled with unsellable worthless homes"' *BBC* 13 January 2022 (available at https://www.bbc.co.uk/news/uk-england-beds-bucks-herts-59972062).

but arrived at different conclusions as to the correct balance in the individual cases.[105] Numerous factors affect judicial reasoning and so the different outcomes in these cases need not necessarily render them inconsistent with the prevalent neoliberal zeitgeist of the time. It is just that there is diversity of judicial opinion about the weight given to each factor in the individual case.

Modest amounts

Another point of tension is that *Smith* and *White* are both couched in terms that do not favour the rich. *Obiter dicta* in *Smith* limited it to the 'dwelling house of modest value'.[106] Lord Griffith thought the result would be different with 'industrial property, large blocks of flats or very expensive houses'[107] where purchasers would be expected to pay for their own surveys. The approach was adopted in *Scullion v Bank of Scotland plc (trading as Colleys)*,[108] where the Court of Appeal distinguished *Smith* and held that it was not reasonable to rely on a building society valuation when purchasing a buy-to-let property. Instead, one should obtain one's own advice. For Lord Neuberger: 'people who buy properties to let are as a class likely to be richer and more commercially astute than people who buy to occupy. People who buy to let can therefore be regarded as more likely to obtain, and more able to afford, an independent valuation or survey.'[109] He also noted that 'the buy-to-let market was undeveloped in so far as it involved individuals'[110] when *Smith* was decided, so evidence that most people relied upon building society surveys would not apply to this class of purchaser.

Similarly, in *White*, Lord Goff emphasised that the defendant was employed by a high street firm of solicitors, saying that it was where a testator 'instructs a small firm of solicitors that mistakes of this kind are most likely to occur, with the result that it tends to be people of modest means, who need the money so badly, who suffer'.[111] Inheritance is not only of value to those receiving vast country estates.

These points, however, can be countered. Mistakes can be made by expensive estate solicitors. And purchasers of expensive homes, commercial property and buy-to-let property do not need the same encouragement to enter the property market as those purchasing modest homes. Again, it may just come down to different judicial views about the weight given to each policy in the individual case. A judge in one case might believe encouraging a person to enter the property market outweighs freedom of contract but a judge in another case

---

[105] Purshouse, 'Utilitarianism as Tort Theory', 24.
[106] [1990] 1 AC 831, 859 (Lord Griffith).
[107] ibid.
[108] [2011] 1 WLR 3212.
[109] ibid., [49].
[110] ibid., [50].
[111] [1995] 2 AC 207, 260.

might not. It does not mean that the underlying assumptions are not neoliberal in nature.

Law and economics

Neoliberalism is often associated with the economic analysis of law. The economics department of the University of Chicago was not only the home of Friedman and Hayek and the training ground for the Chilean economic advisors to Pinochet's military junta (the so-called 'Chicago Boys'), but leading lights of the law and economics movement, such as Ronald Coase and Richard Posner, held posts there.[112] For law and economics scholars, the reasoning in tort cases disguises the real underlying economic forces that influence the outcomes. Tort law is seen as complementing the market in efficiently allocating society's resources to maximise wealth. Wealth is maximised when resources are in the hands of those who value them the most, and judges deciding tort cases have an important role to play by ensuring that resources (broadly defined) are not destroyed in economically inefficient ways.[113] This theory of law is sometimes associated with neoliberalism. According to Nicolás Perrone, '[n]eoliberal legality can be understood as the laws that articulate the purposes of wealth maximisation and internal social order, and more importantly, that provide only certain means to achieve these goals'.[114]

One point of tension is that the economic analysis of tort law could be utilised to reject all claims for pure economic loss. Negligently inflicted pure economic loss might involve private loss but there is no destruction of social wealth – it is mostly just transferred from one person to another. For example, if A destroys B's bridge with the result that C's bakery loses customers, this might be a private loss for C but will not necessarily involve an overall social cost as the customers can buy bread from D. The money that C would have made would be transferred to D, involving no overall loss of wealth in society.[115] If this is accepted, then it might be hard to maintain my argument about *Smith* and *White*. After all, if the leading legal theory of the Chicago School would deny recovery in those cases, then how can they be described as neoliberal? Further support for this comes from the fact that David Campbell, perhaps the finest economic analyst working on English law, uses such a framework in his tour de force attack on *Hedley Byrne* liability. He describes the policy behind *Hedley Byrne* as 'economically irrational,

---

[112] See Ross Emmett (ed), *The Elgar Companion to the Chicago School of Economics* (Edward Elgar, 2010).

[113] McBride, *Humanity of Private Law*, 7–11.

[114] Nicolás Perrone 'Neoliberalism and Economic Sovereignty: Property, Contracts, and Foreign Investment Relations' in Honor Brabazon (ed), *Neoliberal Legality: Understanding the Role of the Law in the Neoliberal Project* (Routledge, 2017) 43.

[115] See William Bishop, 'Economic Loss in Tort' (1982) 2(1) *Oxford Journal of Legal Studies* 1, 4–6.

and it is for this reason that it is morally wrong and the law of the attempt to give it effect is absurd'.[116] He believes that 'there appears to be no good general reason not to use the law of contract to determine the extent of the legal protection of reliance on others' statements'.[117] James Goudkamp and John Murphy also see *White* as posing a challenge for the economic analysis of law, maintaining that the theory would prevent recovery in that case.[118]

Despite this, an economic analysis, while sceptical of liability for pure economic loss *generally*, need not cast off all such pockets of liability. Just as there are variations in neoliberalism, so there are with the economic school. William Bishop, in an article predating *Smith* and *White*, provided an economic analysis of the law on recovery for pure economic loss in negligence.[119] While he maintained that the law would generally not impose a duty of care for pure economic loss as it involves no social cost, he did think that certain negligent misrepresentation cases might be justified on economic grounds. Citing *Ross v Caunters*,[120] a case with similar facts to *White*, Bishop argued that, at first sight, a lack of liability appears to involve no social cost, the loss of inheritance to the claimant is balanced out by the gain to the beneficiary who gained because of a carelessly drafted will. But this account leaves out the impact of the decision on future testators:

> If a testator cannot rely on the advice of his solicitor he will come to regard as unreliable the legal mechanisms available to control his property at death. He will be induced either to spend more of his wealth before death or to transfer more of it before death. Since both courses of action are available now it must be the case that the testator values them less highly than he would value a reliable testamentary law. So the solicitor's action does induce real social cost and not merely a transfer.[121]

This might indicate that a 'Chicago School' economic approach could arrive at the same conclusion as the judges did in *White*. If so, economic analysis does not render these cases inconsistent with a neoliberal ideology.

Conclusion: a progressive agenda?

This chapter has examined the politics of two difficult cases on the recovery of pure economic loss in negligence. Many scholars have questioned cases that

---

116 Campbell, 'The Curious Incident', 132.
117 ibid., 113.
118 James Goudkamp and John Murphy, 'The Failure of Universal Tort Theories' (2016) 21(2) *Legal Theory* 47, 64–5.
119 Bishop, 'Economic Loss in Tort'.
120 [1980] Ch 297.
121 Bishop, 'Economic Loss in Tort', 28–29.

have allowed experienced commercial parties to rely on the assistance of tort law when they make bad investment decisions. Against this backdrop, the 'vulnerable' claimants in *Smith* and *White* have attracted a more sympathetic response. In this chapter, I have argued that these cases, in promoting property markets (or people entering them through inheritance), are consistent with the neoliberal political zeitgeist that was at its height around the time they were decided and can be explained by different judges arriving at different conclusions regarding the correct balance between these two important legal policies. If my arguments are accepted, then *Smith* and *White* should not be seen as 'progressive' cases. For those who do not support (neo)liberal economic policies, these decisions should not attract less sympathy than they currently do.

I nailed my colours to the mast earlier in this chapter in opposing recovery for pure economic loss in negligence. Like Nicholas McBride and others, I believe that *Hedley Byrne* 'goes well beyond what is needed to protect claimants who were too legally unaware to know that the provision of a peppercorn would have made the defendant's promise to take care in performing some task for the claimant contractually binding'[122] and would favour its repeal. If one does not wish to go that far, then Donal Nolan and Lord Sales' recent proposals have much merit. Whichever route is chosen, *Smith* and *White* should not, for those opposed to neoliberalism, stand in the way of a more rational development of the law.

Acknowledgements

I would like to thank Jodi Gardner, John Fanning, Kirsty Horsey and the anonymous reviewers for helpful comments on an earlier version of this chapter.

---

[122] McBride, *Humanity of Private Law*, 237.

4

Queering the Reasonable Person

Haim Abraham

Introduction

In his description of various personifications of the legal standard of 'objective reasonableness', Lord Reed refers to different 'passengers' on the Clapham omnibus, from which two groups emerge: the gender-specific reasonable man, and gender-neutral individuals, such as the 'right-thinking member of society', 'officious bystander', 'reasonable parent' and the 'fair-minded observer':

> The Clapham omnibus has many passengers. The most venerable is the reasonable man, who was born during the reign of Victoria but remains in vigorous health. Amongst the other passengers are the right-thinking member of society, familiar from the law of defamation, the officious bystander, the reasonable parent, the reasonable landlord, and the fair-minded and informed observer, all of whom have had season tickets for many years. The horse-drawn bus between Knightsbridge and Clapham, which Lord Bowen is thought to have had in mind, was real enough. But its most famous passenger, and the others I have mentioned, are legal fictions.[1]

By not clearly distinguishing between these groups, Lord Reed appears to use the 'reasonable man' and 'reasonable person' interchangeably, continuing two centuries of conceptual flexibility.[2] Yet, given that feminist critique of the standard in the late 20th century led to the general adoption of the gender-neutral term of the reasonable *person*, Lord Reed's use of the reasonable *man* is telling,

---

[1] *Healthcare at Home Ltd v The Common Services Agency* [2014] UKSC 49, paras 1–2 (Lord Reed).
[2] See, for example, *Blyth v Birmingham Waterworks Co* [1843–60] All ER Rep 478, 480.

especially as he is the 'most venerable'. The purpose of this chapter is to begin to uncover what might be learned about this reasonable man and his fellow omnibus passengers from a queer theory perspective.

Critical lenses, such as feminist and critical race theories, have been employed extensively to analyse the reasonable man as the legal standard and the way in which it is used. Generally, the reasonable man/person is held to be objective and neutral,[3] not reflecting any actual person but rather representing a means of demarcating the limits of acceptable conduct. However, by implementing critical lenses, scholars have demonstrated that even if the standard of the reasonable man/person is objective in the sense that it does not adopt the approach of one party to litigation, it is hardly a neutral standard. Based on the description of the reasonable man as a commuter, garden mower and magazines taker,[4] scholars noted that he is middle class.[5] Furthermore, some have suggested that the reasonable person is also White and straight.[6] These suggestions are based on an examination of the way in which the 'reasonable person' was used in the late 19th and early 20th centuries. One such example is that it was held to be defamatory to attribute Blackness to White individuals.[7] Another example is that the reasonable person was used to justify a defence from criminal liability in instances where heterosexual men attacked homosexual men following sexual advances.[8]

Consequently, scholars have argued that real individuals, who do not share the qualities of the personified reasonable man, become vulnerable. They are unlikely to be able to succeed in bringing claims against the people who the reasonable

---

[3] *Nettleship v Weston* [1971] 2 QB 691, 702.

[4] *Nomikos Papatonakis v Australian Telecommunications Commission* [1985] HCA 3, para 36; *McQuire v Western Morning News Co* [1900–03] All ER Rep 673, 674; Lucinda M. Finley, 'A Break in the Silence: Including Women's Issues in a Torts Course' (1989) 1 *Yale Journal of Law and Feminism* 41, 58 [citing Guido Calabresi, *Ideals, Beliefs and Attitudes in the Law* (1985)].

[5] Mayo Moran, *Rethinking the Reasonable Person: An Egalitarian Reconstruction of the Objective Standard* (Oxford University Press, 2003) 132; Elizabeth Handsley, 'The Reasonable Man: Two Case Studies' (1996) 1 *Sister in Law* 52, 59. Simon Stern pointed out to me in a conversation that in Victorian times the phrase 'man on the Clapham omnibus' indeed had such connotations. Indeed, examples of literature of the time describes the man who takes this bus as 'an active man, rather tall, rather shabby, and dressed in the customary black suit of London middle-class life … He might have been a lecturer, or a town-traveller for some firm, or a newspaper reporter, or any one of fifty things else' (John Berwick Harwood, *Lord Ulswater* [ii, Richard Bentley, 1867] 78).

[6] Handsley, 'The Reasonable Man', 59; Lawrence McNamara, *Reputation and Defamation* (Oxford University Press, 2007) 193.

[7] *Strauder v West Virginia* 100 US 303 (1880), 306; *Flood v News & Courier Co* 50 SE 637 (SC, 1905), 639.

[8] Christina Pei-Lin Chen, 'Provocation's Privileged Desire: The Provocation Doctrine, Homosexual Panic, and the Non-Violent Unwanted Sexual Advance Defense' (2000) 10(1) *Cornell Journal of Law and Public Policy* 195; Cynthia Lee and Peter Kar Yu Kwan, 'The Trans Panic Defense: Heteronormativity and the Murder of Transgender Women' (2014) 66 *Hastings Law Journal* 77.

man represents, while as defendants to claims they are more likely to be held to a higher standard and as such more likely to be found liable.[9] These critiques are illuminating, but they are not particularly queer, nor do they exhaust all that queer theory can reveal about the reasonable man and the reasonable person. In fact, there appears to be no scholarly work that examines the reasonable person through queer theory.[10]

This chapter begins filling this gap in the literature. I start by offering a short gloss of queer theory. This theory is apprehensive of definitions and categories due to a concern that through them heterosexuality and heteronormativity are framed as natural and normal, thus creating a structural hierarchy of domination and subordination of queer individuals and sexuality. I will then argue that despite existing critiques, the reasonable person – as a legal standard – is compliant with queer theory and can be queer-friendly, as it is a flexible standard that can take up a range of contents. The reasonable person does not necessarily conform to a particular identity, nor does it necessarily construct a particular identity. Yet, I will illustrate that the flexible character of the reasonable person places LGBTQ+ individuals at risk, for two primary reasons. First, past (and current) applications and personifications of the reasonable person into a White, middle class, cisgender, heteronormative man raise others' standard of care while limiting the ability to hold 'reasonable men' liable. Second, the move from reasonable man to reasonable person, even if it signals a deep(er) commitment to inclusivity, does not mean that this objective standard now has a fixed meaning or grounds gender-neutral norms. One of its core features is its ability to take on a wide range of meanings, making the concept uncertain and in flux. Consequently, there is a risk that judges will read into the reasonable person views and norms that subordinate and marginalise LGBTQ+ individuals. I will rely on issues relating to conversion 'therapy', defamation and privacy to demonstrate these risks. The chapter concludes by noting that a possible resolution to the risks the reasonable man creates for LGBTQ+ individuals could be alleviated to a degree by diversifying the judiciary, as they are the puppeteers while the reasonable person is merely the puppet.

---

[9] Martha Chamallas, 'Social Justice Tort Theory' (2021) 14 *Journal of Tort Law* 309, 324; Handsley, 'The Reasonable Man', 70; Moran, *Rethinking the Reasonable Person* 86, 128. The different attitudes towards claimants and defendants that are based on binary sex/gender distinctions could suggest in theory that women and minorities might be held to a lower standard in some instances as opposed to men, but it appears that there are no clear trends where this possibility was established.

[10] That said, queer theory has been deployed to analyse other legal issues. See, for example: Brenda Cossman, 'Queering Queer Legal Studies: An Unreconstructed Ode to Eve Sedgwick (and Others)' (2019) 6 *Critical Analysis of Law* 23, 23 [footnotes 1–4, for instance]; Marc Mason, Steven Vaughan and Benjamin Weil, 'The Possible Forms of Professionalism: Credibility and the Performance of Queer Sexualities Among Barristers in England and Wales' (2023) 50 *Journal of Law and Society* 77, 78–9 [and footnotes there].

It should be noted that this chapter is not intended to exhaust all of what can be learned about the reasonable person through a queer theory lens. Rather, its purpose is to make an exploratory theoretical intervention, raise some concerns and suggest some preliminary solutions – all from a theoretical perspective. Inquiries that go beyond this scope, such as empirical and doctrinal analyses, will be reserved for another time.

Defining the definition-resistant

To undertake the task of analysing the reasonable man through a queer theory perspective, it should first be clarified exactly what queer theory is. However, this is no easy task. Queer theory means different things to different people.[11] This is not to say that queer theory lacks conceptual coherence so that it cannot be unified under a single definition. Nor does it mean that no one ever attempted to articulate a taxonomy of the different views relating to queer theory. Instead, the multiplicity of meanings is one of the theory's core features. I will not attempt to unify or clarify all queer theory in this chapter, but I will build on what I view as the core features of the theory.

The first feature to mention and unpack is queer theory's resistance to definitions.[12] This resistance is not solely grounded in anarchist or libertarian beliefs. Rather, queer theories peek behind definitions to identify the underlying hierarchical structures that require and enforce definitions. These structures are made, not set, and the inequality they produce is what drives the desire to resist definitions, as they are seen as one of the vehicles through which hierarchical structures are perpetuated. By resisting definitions, it might be possible to undo or undermine this self-sustaining cycle.

The second feature of queer theory is its awareness of relationships of domination and subordination. Queer theory does not engage with, or resist, botanical classifications, for example. It has no quarrel with the distinction between apples and oranges, or with the classification of tomatoes as fruit or vegetable. In contrast, it is concerned with structures that empower some and

---

11   Generally see: Robert Leckey and Kim Brooks, 'Introduction' in Robert Leckey and Kim Brooks (eds), *Queer Theory: Law, Culture, Empire* (Routledge, 2011); Siobhan B. Somerville, 'Introduction' in Siobhan B. Somerville (ed), *The Cambridge Companion to Queer Studies* (Cambridge University Press, 2020); Steven Seidman, 'Queer-Ing Sociology, Sociologizing Queer Theory: An Introduction' (1994) 12(2) *Sociological Theory* 166; Michael Warner, 'Introduction: Fear of a Queer Planet' (1991) 29 *Social Text* 3; Lauren Berlant and Michael Warner, 'Guest Column: What Does Queer Theory Teach Us about X?' (1995) 110(3) *PMLA* 343.

12   Eden Sarid, 'A Queer Analysis of Intellectual Property' (2022) 2022(1) *Wisconsin Law Review* 91, 94; Cossman, 'Queering Queer Legal Studies', 27; Annamarie Jagose, *Queer Theory: An Introduction* (New York University Press, 1996) 1.

disenfranchise others.[13] Concepts like 'normal' and 'abnormal' or 'moral' and 'immoral' are quintessential examples, as they are used to explain, justify and perpetuate the existence of rights and protection of interests of some while excluding others.

The third feature of queer theory is its particular interest in power dynamics that regulate and relate to sexuality.[14] Whereas feminist theory explores power dynamics between sexes and between genders, and a key component of critical race theory engages power dynamics from the perspective of ethnicity, queer theory investigates this question through a sexuality focus. It is only concerned with good and bad apples when these terms are used metaphorically to describe the degree to which individuals conform to society's norms of acceptable heterosexual conduct. In doing so, it uncovers how heterosexuality usurps and maintains power, and enforces its standards on others by rendering anyone who departs from these norms into a deviant with fewer rights and weakened protections. Sexuality is viewed as something that is structured and performed, and queer theory seeks to disentangle what is deemed by convention as a natural relationship between sex, gender and desire.[15]

I will now turn to analyse how these features of queer theory – resistance to definitions, focus on power dynamics and concern with social norms relating to sexuality – shed light on the reasonable man/person.

What's queer about the reasonable person?

The reasonable person standard is an elusive standard. It is supposed to be intuitive and familiar, as well as objective. It is not the product of the beliefs and views of a single party to litigation, but rather the shared beliefs and views a court considers all of us to have. Through the lens of this reasonable person, the court determines what will be considered negligent, defamatory and foreseeable, to name a few of the many uses the reasonable person has.

But how do judges cast actual content into this idea of the reasonable person? In the context of determining what might be considered negligent, there is some attempt of identifying reasonableness using (quasi) mathematical calculations using the Hand formula. The standard of care, that is, determining what conduct is reasonable, is determined in relation to the marginal costs of making an activity safer vis-à-vis the magnitude of loss times its probability of materialising.

---

13   Cossman, 'Queering Queer Legal Studies', 37; Somerville, 'Introduction', 2; Keguro Macharia, 'Queer Writing, Queer Politics: Working across Difference' in Siobhan B. Somerville (ed), *The Cambridge Companion to Queer Studies* (Cambridge University Press, 2020) 40.

14   Kadji Amin, 'Genealogies of Queer Theory' in Siobhan B. Somerville (ed), *The Cambridge Companion to Queer Studies* (Cambridge University Press, 2020) 17, 20–1.

15   Michel Foucault, *The History of Sexuality, Vol I: An Introduction* (Patheon Books, 1978); Judith Butler, *Bodies That Matter: On the Discursive Limits of 'Sex'* (Routledge, 2011); Mason, Vaughan and Weil, 'The Possible Forms of Professionalism', 6–7.

Individuals are required to take precautions to the extent the marginal costs of doing so will not be greater than the magnitude of loss times its probability of materialising.[16] For instance, if I decided to place a potted plant outside my window, my costs of securing it to ensure it does not fall off on windy or rainy days is marginal (the cost of a few zip ties), whereas were it to fall on someone's head (and that's a real possibility), the costs could be considerable. So, for me to act reasonably, I must take precautions up to the point at which their cost would be equal to those that would be incurred by the accident materialising. If I don't secure my plant or refrain from placing it outside my window altogether, and it falls on someone's head, I acted in breach of the standard of care, that is, unreasonably.

While this approach is used to some degree, it is not the sole approach used to determine what is and ought to be considered negligent,[17] and it is not used in other contexts in which the reasonable person standard is employed, such as determining what is defamatory. Instead, it seems that judges import extra-legal standards to fill the reasonable person with relevant content, turning the extra-legal norms into legal ones.[18] For example, to determine which statements might lower a person's standing in society, judges do not engage in empirical surveys or make calculations about which standard will maximise social welfare. They use what they know and think about society to reach a conclusion about what they deem the reasonable person knows and believes. Put differently, in some instances judges identify what is 'reasonable' as they have some form of judicial notice about what the intuitive and shared understandings are about the society we live in.[19]

It is therefore clear that the reasonable person standard is 'objective', but 'objectivity' has a meaning that is a legal term of art. When something is said to be objective it conveys the idea that it represents the viewpoint of the law, which is not deduced by the particular views or abilities of any party to litigation. The claimant's and the defendant's perspective and abilities do not constitute what the standard is or ought to be. That is why, for instance, in *Nettleship*, a learner driver who hit a lamp-post that resulted in breaking her instructor's kneecap was held to be liable. The court held the standard of care to be that of an experienced

---

[16] See, for example: *United States v Carroll Towing Co* 159 F2d 169 (2d Cir 1947); Robert Cooter and Thomas Ulen, *Law & Economics* (5th edn, Pearson/Addison Wesley, 2008) 349–53; Richard Posner, 'A Theory of Negligence' (1972) 1 *Journal of Legal Studies* 29, 32; William M. Landes and Richard A. Posner, 'The Positive Economic Theory of Tort Law' (1981) 15 *Georgia Law Review* 851, 877; Steven Shavell, *Foundations of Economic Analysis of Law* (Belknap Press of Harvard University Press, 2004) 182–9.

[17] See the discussion in Gary T. Schwartz, 'The Myth of the Ford Pinto Case' (1991) 43 *Rutgers Law Review* 1013.

[18] John Gardner, *Torts and Other Wrongs* (Oxford University Press, 2019) 273.

[19] *Donoghue v Stevenson* [1932] AC 562; Gardner, *Torts and Other Wrongs*, 287; John C.P. Goldberg and Benjamin C. Zipursky, *Recognizing Wrongs* (Belknap Press, 2020) 234.

driver, not because of the fact that the claimant was one but because that is what the law requires.[20]

Nevertheless, given the impact of judges' views and opinions on what the reasonable man/person would deem to be, do or believe, it is important to stress that it is not a standard that is 'objective' in the sense that it is free of biases or based on empirical studies. Rather, it is a legal standard that is fluid and sponge-like. It is a sufficiently defined concept to be conceived of independently from other concepts, such as proportionality or authority, but it can absorb any content judges attribute to it. As John Gardner argues:

> [t]he reasonable person embodies no particular standard of justification, not even a socially prevailing standard. But there is no denying the appeal, for the law, of fudging the issue, conflating the reasonable with the socially acceptable … the law may end up containing the reasonable person, recasting him so that (depending on the legal context) he stands for a particular standard of justification, or a particular approach to justification, rather than for justification simpliciter.[21]

In this sense, the reasonable person can be said to be coherent with queer theory, and in this respect it can be queer-friendly. It is an inherently definition-resistant standard. If taken as is, without its personification and contextualisation, the reasonable person is a form of articulating and locating reasons. It is only when the reasonable person is given personal attributes, or is limited to reflect a particular set of views, that it transforms from a definition-resistant fluid standard into a fixed heteronormative male one.

The perils of contingent standards

Queer theory's resistance to definitions should not be confused with a view that all definitions are problematic. The need for resistance arises in relation to those definitions that are used to create and perpetuate structures of domination and subordination, while justifying these structures as natural, necessary or positive. Queer theory will not adopt and admonish content-fluid norms simply because they are more openly defined. What must be examined is how these standards are used. Definition-resistance can be a double-edged sword, as it allows for inclusivity and change but it does not limit what could be included and what could be changed.

---

[20] It is interesting to note the language used by the court here disregards the plaintiff's gender and refers to hypothetical parties and the reasonable drivers as male: 'The learner driver may be doing his best, but his incompetent best is not good enough. He must drive in as good a manner as a driver of skill, experience and care' (*Nettleship v Weston* [1971] 2 QB 691, 699).

[21] Gardner, *Torts and Other Wrongs*, 289.

The 'reasonable person' is a clear example of such risks, as it can take up any content and change over time, the standard can maintain prejudice and biases just as much as it can support inclusivity and scientific knowledge. Even if in some instances the reasonable person set inclusive and scientific views as legal standards, it does not mean that a similar view will be held in another instance.

The risk of bias is the first challenge that the reasonable person's inherent flexibility creates for LGBTQ+ parties to litigation. Given that studies have found the reasonable person to offer greater protection to White, straight, middle-class men and those who fit their norms,[22] it is not surprising that some LGBTQ+ individuals are deterred from bringing claims or are prompted to settle.[23] Were the reasonable person historically more inclusive of LGBTQ+ individuals, or if there was some additional reassurance that existing interpretations of it would not be replaced by detrimental ones, perhaps these concerns could be mitigated.[24]

A further issue relates to the hierarchical structures of domination and subordination that the personification and use of the reasonable person standard into the reasonable man create and maintain. By relying on the reasonable person, the law seems to invoke some intuitive and shared understanding about our society.[25] Holding X to be reasonable is, therefore, a predictable and unavoidable conclusion. Maintaining that this standard is objective seems to suggest that it is in line with the rule of law, and can be relied on to be consistent between cases and over time. A queer analysis suggests that none of these understandings should be adopted at face value.

Consider the assumptions of predictability and unavoidability. In identifying the shared social values upon which the reasonable person is concretised, judges are not engaging in a sociological or anthropological study. Rather, judges use their understanding based on their experiences to identify what they hold to constitute common sense and judicial notice that displace logic and analysis.[26] Moreover,

---

[22]   Chamallas, 'Social Justice Tort Theory', 313; Chen, 'Provocation's Privileged Desire'; Lee and Kwan, 'The Trans Panic Defense'; Handsley, 'The Reasonable Man', 70; Moran, *Rethinking the Reasonable Person*, 86, 128.

[23]   Eden Sarid, 'Revisiting Drag Queens' Intellectual Property Norms' (unpublished manuscript).

[24]   In some ways, this risk of bias is familiar to LGBTQ+ individuals as it is one that arises in the perpetual ritual of coming out. Eve Sedgwick articulates the oppressive nature of the closet as setting heterosexuality as the default sexuality, homosexuality as a secret, and consequently sexuality is a practice that involves discovery that is inherent and continual (Eve Kosofsky Sedgwick, *Epistemology of the Closet* [updated edn with a new preface, University of California Press, 2008] 67–8). Indeed, the sexuality of parties to litigation might be irrelevant, yet, following Sedgwick's arguments, finding out individuals' sexualities could occur regardless. As sexual minorities continue to encounter explicit and implicit biases upon discovery of their sexuality, the fear of similar negative treatment by the courts is not unfounded.

[25]   *Donoghue v Stevenson* [1932] AC 562, 11; Gardner, *Torts and Other Wrongs*, 287; Goldberg and Zipursky, *Recognizing Wrongs*, 234.

[26]   Moran, *Rethinking the Reasonable Person*, 78–9, 158; Joanne Conaghan and Wade Mansell, *The Wrongs of Tort Law* (2nd edn, Pluto Press, 1999) 53. For such effect in the context of tort liability during warfare see Haim Abraham, 'Tort Liability, Combatant Activities, and the Question of Over-Deterrence' (2022) 47(3) *Law & Social Inquiry* 885.

expert evidence and testimony could be rejected in favour of the judge's own view of what is and ought to be reasonable.[27] As Lord Radcliffe observed in *Davis Contractors Ltd v Fareham Urban District Council*: '[t]he spokesman of the fair and reasonable man, who represents after all no more than the anthropomorphic conception of justice, is and must be the court itself'.[28] So viewed, judges transform their subjective understandings into objective legal standards, normalise their views and maintain that their views are the only legally (and perhaps socially) acceptable views. Apart from the constraints of binding precedent, which can be distinguished, it is difficult to say that individuals are able to clearly predict what content judges will prescribe to the reasonable person.

At this stage some may argue that in England and Wales there are no clear tort cases in which the reasonable person standard was applied in a way that explicitly subordinates or marginalises LGBTQ+ individuals.[29] While this observation appears valid, it does not make the risks posed by the reasonable person less concerning for LGBTQ+ individuals. Some issues have not yet been settled by existing case law, and there is potential there that a reasonable person standard would be articulated in a way that subordinates and marginalises LGBTQ+ individuals. Moreover, in some cases judges' approaches to sexuality implicitly reinforces structures that are detrimental to LGBTQ+ individuals.

Take conversion 'therapy' as an example of a yet unsettled matter for which queer theory can shed light on potential risks. Conversion 'therapy' is a process by which individuals attempt to change others' sexual orientation through various intrusive and non-intrusive practices, which have been proven to be ineffective and dangerous, causing physical and mental injuries.[30] Assume that Ben, a gay

---

27   Mary Eberts, 'New Facts for Old: Observations on the Judicial Process' in Richard Devlin (ed), *Canadian Perspectives on Legal Theory* (Emond Montgomery Publications, 1991) 475.

28   *Davis Contractors Ltd v Fareham Urban District Council* [1956] AC 696, 728.

29   That said, there are jurisdictions in which it is either unclear whether an attribution of homosexuality could be regarded as defamatory, or that such attribution is regarded as defamatory. The US would be one example of a jurisdiction in which attributing homosexuality may or may not be defamatory. See: Haven Ward, 'I'm Not Gay, M'Kay: Should Falsely Calling Someone a Homosexual Be Defamatory?' (2010) 44 *Georgia Law Review* 739, 752–7. Israel is an example of a jurisdiction in which an attribution of homosexuality is still regarded as defamatory, although in a minority of cases this approach has been rejected [For the general rule see: *CivC (Tel Aviv) 20174/94 Amsalem v Klein* (Nevo, 20/06/1995); For its rejection see: *CivC (Tel Aviv) 56910-09-17 Zinger v Medical Technological Corp Ltd* (Nevo, 05/07/2020)]. See also Alexandros Antoniou and Dimitris Akrivos, Chapter 9, this volume.

30   Jack Drescher and others, 'The Growing Regulation of Conversion Therapy' (2016) 102(2) *Journal of Medical Regulation* 7; Ariel Shidlo and Michael Schroeder, 'Changing Sexual Orientation: A Consumers' Report' (2002) 33(3) *Professional Psychology: Research and Practice* 249, 254–5; United Nations General Assembly, 'Practices of So-Called "Conversion Therapy": Report of the Independent Expert on Protection Against Violence and Discrimination Based on Sexual Orientation and Gender Identity' (2020) A/HRC/44/53 (available at https://documents-dds-ny.un.org/doc/UNDOC/GEN/G20/108/68/PDF/G2010868.pdf?OpenElement).

18-year-old man, was pressured by his family to undertake conversion 'therapy', by the end of which his sexual orientation did not change, but he developed chronic depression. Could he attempt to find a remedy for his psychiatric injury through tort law?[31] There are preliminary questions that should be considered, such as whether Ben is emotionally and financially willing and able to subject his experience to the scrutiny of office holders who may well hold the same views and beliefs as those who have inflicted his injuries. For the purpose of this chapter, I will not engage with these questions further, rather, I focus on how a judge might use the reasonable man in a claim such as this. Two uses arise: to determine what the expected standard of care in such contexts is, and to identify what injuries could be foreseeable. The outcome of these investigations is not predetermined or limited, as the reasonable man can take on any view. It is as possible for a judge to decide that the reasonable man can engage in conversion 'therapy' and should not foresee possible psychiatric injuries as it is for a judge to reach the opposite conclusions.[32]

Were the reasonable person to adopt male heteronormative qualities, as it has in the past,[33] then a court would be unlikely to find conversion 'therapy' inherently tortious. The analysis could resemble the following. Seeking therapy and advice from professionals and faith leaders on a wide range of issues would be deemed as a common fact of life. If something is a common fact, it is usually considered normal and reasonable. Consequently, for the heteronormative reasonable man, there is nothing problematic per se with conversion 'therapy', as it no different to other forms of advice.

This is the genius of branding conversion 'therapy' as a form of therapy – legally there is nothing inherently wrong with therapy. Whereas prevailing medical advice deems conversion 'therapy' ineffective and dangerous generally,[34] the heteronormative reasonable man would only deem it as a breach of the relevant standard of care if the treatment itself was not up to par. The procedure is not inherently wrongful. The fact that there is no equivalent 'therapy' to convert heterosexuals to homosexuals means that LGBTQ+ individuals who seek redress for conversion 'therapy' injuries face both the ordinary uncertainty regarding judges' interpretation of the reasonable man, and the uncertainty of lack of precedent.

---

[31] For a comprehensive analysis of the issue see Craig Purshouse and Ilias Trispiotis, 'Is "Conversion Therapy" Tortious?' (2022) 42(1) *Legal Studies* 23.

[32] ibid., 36.

[33] Chamallas, 'Social Justice Tort Theory', 313; Chen, 'Provocation's Privileged Desire'; Lee and Kwan, 'The Trans Panic Defense'; Handsley, 'The Reasonable Man', 70; Moran, *Rethinking the Reasonable Person*, 86, 128.

[34] Jen Christensen, 'Conversion Therapy is Harmful to LGBTQ People and Costs Society as a Whole, Study Says' *CNN* 7 March 2022 (available at https://edition.cnn.com/2022/03/07/health/conversion-therapy-personal-and-financial-harm/index.html).

Furthermore, the concretisation of reasonableness creates and maintains a hierarchical structure of domination and subordination. It is worth repeating that studies have found that the reasonable person is often framed as the reasonable man, who is White, middle class and heterosexual.[35] He and his views are deemed socially acceptable and warranted, and are protected by the sphere of normality that he symbolises and defines. As all others are evaluated against the reasonable man, they are subordinated to this imagined reasonable person and are abnormal in comparison to it.

A helpful example in this context could be found in the tort of defamation, the basic meaning of which is often ascertained using the test Lord Atkin laid down in the case of *Sim v Stretch*: 'Would the words tend to lower the plaintiff in the estimation of right-thinking members of society generally?'[36] The term 'right-thinking members of society' is not fundamentally different to the reasonable man.[37] It gives voice and legitimises the views and beliefs of some, while excluding others. However, as 'right-thinking members of society' is used in the particular context of defamation, it has an additional implication of setting a social hierarchy. The right-thinking members of society are not merely a tool to identify how people should behave, but also to determine what is the social value of different attributes. A personal trait can lower someone's standing because it is, in the eyes of the law, bad or lesser than the qualities that normal individuals possess.

The risks faced by LGBTQ+ individuals by the 'right-thinking members of society' test is demonstrated by the *Cowan v Bennett* case, in which the defendant repeatedly referred to the claimant as 'the gay painter' in weekly professional network meetings when he was not.[38] Sheriff McGowan held that these comments did not cause other members of the network to think that the claimant was gay.[39] He also held that even if the comments had such effect, imputing homosexuality cannot be considered as causing reputational harm – normally:

> An imputation of homosexuality cannot generally be regarded as calculated (i.e. likely) to harm the reputation of a person, save perhaps in very special circumstances. As Mr McPhate put it, times have

---

35 Chamallas, 'Social Justice Tort Theory', 313; Chen, 'Provocation's Privileged Desire'; Lee and Kwan, 'The Trans Panic Defense'; Handsley, 'The Reasonable Man', 70; Moran, *Rethinking the Reasonable Person*, 86, 128.

36 *Sim v Stretch* [1936] 2 All ER 1237, 1240. Also see: Paul Mitchell, 'Malice in Defamation' (1998) 114 *Law Quarterly Review* 639, 646.

37 This much can be deduced from *Healthcare at Home Ltd v The Common Services Agency* [2014] UKSC 49, paras 1–2 (Lord Reed). Similar arguments have been made by Hilary Young, 'But Names Won't Necessarily Hurt Me: Considering the Effect of Disparaging Statements on Reputation' (2011) 37 *Queen's Law Journal* 1, 6–7; Michele Mangini, 'Is the Reasonable Person a Person of Virtue?' (2020) 26(2) *Res Publica* 157, 162.

38 *Cowan v Bennett* [2012] 11 WLUK 94, paras 8, 15 (Sheriff McGowan).

39 ibid., para 105.

moved on. Homosexuality is not illegal. On the contrary, the rights of homosexuals are widely protected by the law. There are many people in public life in Scotland and the UK who are openly homosexual.[40]

An analysis of Sheriff McGowan's ruling suggests that there are two caveats to the general rule. One, there might be circumstances in which an imputation of homosexuality could be defamatory even in current society. Sheriff McGowan does not articulate what these circumstances might be. However, we can surmise what might constitute such circumstances. For LGBTQ+ individuals, any social value and standing that the law prescribes to them depends on the degree to which they lead heteronormative lives – have monogamous relationships with one spouse, raise kids and have an ordinary middle-class job – and are accepted by (the mostly-heterosexual) society.[41] Yet, this is not the lived reality of many LGBTQ+ individuals, as well as many other non-heteronormative individuals, for whom the use of the term 'right-thinking members of society' is marginalising and alienating. It depicts all others as irrational, perhaps even immoral, and at the very best as holding fundamentally mistaken views that should be dismissed and disregarded. Heteronormativity is the default standard, against which 'right-thinking' is evaluated and to which homosexuality is subordinated. As a result, it seems likely that an imputation of homosexuality could be considered defamatory in instances in which homosexual and heterosexual lives, views and norms diverge.

Two, Sheriff McGowan implicitly argues that if societal views regarding LGBTQ+ individuals change, an imputation of being LGBTQ+ could once again be defamatory. Both 'right-thinking members of society' and the reasonable person are flexible standards. They have institutionalised biases in the past, and all that Sheriff McGowan does is to highlight that they can do so again.

Sex, scandals, outing and doxing

After ten years of a complicated and volatile same-sex relationship, one party (let's call him 'C') decided he had enough and ended it. His ex-partner (whom we can refer to as 'D') refuses to accept the break-up, and sends his former lover emails upon emails, pleading, begging and threatening – all seeking to get back together. When his efforts bear no fruit, D decides the only way to get C's attention and affection is by creating a blog, depicting his story of their relationship, and sharing information about C's bisexuality, exploits in sex and dating websites and apps, past romantic relationships, family relationships, occupation, finance, health, intimate details about their sexual history, and photos from their relationship. C has no interest in having this information shared by D in this fashion, easily

---

[40] ibid., para 107.

[41] Yuvraj Joshi, 'Respectable Queerness' (2012) 43(2) *Columbia Human Rights Law Review* 349.

accessible to all through a simple search on the internet. So, C brings a tort claim against D, arguing D's misuse of private information, asking for an injunction ordering D to take the blog down and to refrain from further publications, and seeking damages for the distress caused.

The events I am depicting here are the facts of *BVC v EWF*,[42] but they are also the story of many others who unwillingly had intimate details and pictures shared online (a phenomenon termed as 'doxing' or 'revenge porn'), or had their sexual orientation outed. As *BVC v EWF* illustrates, the dichotomy between private/public is another area in which we can see how judges use the standard of the reasonable person. In this context, as in many others, the standard is not used in its neutral sponge-like form, but instead it is concretised and takes on a form of a reasonable heterosexual man. To fully appreciate this point, consider the following paragraphs of Judge Parkes QC's ruling:

> The information disclosed on the Defendant's website was information which became known to the Defendant because he was in an intimate relationship with the Claimant over a period of years … The central information disclosed by the Defendant, on which everything else depends, is the information about the Claimant's sexuality and sexual behaviour. Information of that sort, together with information about his mental and physical health, finances and private and family life, is at the core of the values which Art.8 protects … In my judgment it makes no difference whatever if (as the Defendant maintains, but the Claimant denies) a number of his and the Claimant's friends and family did in fact know of their relationship, or if (as I think is accepted) the Claimant's identity as a person seeking a certain sort of sexual partner on the internet will have been known to users of such websites. Even if the information were much more widely available than even the Defendant contends, the question would be not whether the information was generally accessible but whether the remedy of injunction would serve a useful purpose … Much of the information disclosed in the Defendant's website concerns private matters other than the Claimant's sexual life; but even if it concerned his sexuality alone, the Claimant would be entitled to ask that such information should not be disclosed more widely than to the fairly narrow coterie which (even on the Defendant's case) is aware of it. On the facts of this case, an injunction would plainly serve a useful purpose.[43]

Several key observations can be made in this context. First, information about sex and sexuality is, by default, a secret. Secondly, individuals can choose to share this

---

[42]   *BVC v EWF* [2019] EWHC 2506 (QB).

[43]   ibid., paras 136–7.

secret, but, by and large, they get to choose whether to share it and with whom. Thirdly, even if the secret is out, it is never fully out – it always remains a secret in relation to all those who did not learn about the secret through its 'owner'. These observations are held to stem from the perspective of 'what a reasonable person of ordinary sensibilities would feel if placed in the same position as the Claimant and faced with the same publicity'.[44] Judge Parkes QC's ruling is reflective of how judges' approach to sexuality could implicitly reinforce structures that are detrimental to LGBTQ+ individuals.

For the purposes of this chapter, I will set aside questions about whether the reasonable person should expect privacy and control over information that they created online and via apps. User agreements, which are likely read almost exclusively by privacy scholars, can and do contain terms that allow websites and apps to store personal data and even send it to third parties for commercial gain. But even if the reasonable person of this day and age should not be held to have read and understood hundreds of pages of the complicated legal jargon of standard form contracts, the frequency and scope of doxing and data breaches could suggest that the reasonable person should foresee the possibility their online data could be stored, spread and even leaked.[45] Instead, I will focus on the framing of sex and sexuality as, naturally and by default, a secret.

In her impactful and insightful monograph *Epistemology of the Closet*, Eve Kosofsky Sedgwick masterfully depicts what the closet is and why it is so taxing and problematic for LGBTQ+ individuals:

> Even at an individual level, there are remarkably few of even the most openly gay people who are not deliberately in the closet with someone personally or economically or institutionally important to them. Furthermore, the deadly elasticity of heterosexist presumption means that, like Wendy in Peter Pan, people find new walls springing up around them even as they drowse: every encounter with a new classful of students, to say nothing of a new boss, social worker, loan officer, landlord, doctor, erects new closets whose fraught and characteristic laws of optics and physics exact from at least gay people new surveys, new calculations, new draughts and requisitions of secrecy

---

[44]   ibid., para 135.

[45]   Janet Burns, 'Report says Grindr exposed millions of users' private data, messages, locations' *Forbes* 29 March 2018 (available at https://www.forbes.com/sites/janetwburns/2018/03/29/report-says-grindr-exposed-millions-of-users-private-data-messages-locations/); Zak Doffman, 'Ashley Madison hack returns to "haunt" its victims: 32 million users now watch and wait' *Forbes* 1 February 2020 (available at https://www.forbes.com/sites/zakdoffman/2020/02/01/ashley-madison-hack-returns-to-haunt-its-victims-32-million-users-now-have-to-watch-and-wait/); Adam Forrest, 'Facebook fined $5bn for "inappropriate" sharing of personal data' *The Independent* 12 July 2019 (available at https://www.independent.co.uk/news/world/americas/facebook-data-privacy-scandal-settlement-cambridge-analytica-court-a9003106.html).

or disclosure. … there can be few gay people, however courageous and forthright by habit, however fortunate in the support of their immediate communities, in whose lives the closet is not still a shaping presence.[46]

The closet, as Sedgwick portrays it, is a constant daily experience for LGBTQ+ individuals. Heterosexuality (and in many respects heteronormativity as well) is presumed.[47] You are straight until proven otherwise. Being in the closet is a forced status.[48] It is necessarily a secret that every individual decides whether to share and with whom. Alongside this automatic assumption of heterosexuality comes the continuous fact of coming out. People don't find out somebody is straight, they do find out that someone is gay, lesbian, bisexual, transgender, two-spirited and so on. Coming out is taxing not only because it is a perpetual task, but also because with it there is always a fear of discrimination, rejection and violence. Sedgwick's description of the closet as 'the defining structure for gay oppression in this century'[49] is powerfully accurate and succinct. By constituting sexuality as a secret, and homosexuality as the only necessarily secret identity,[50] other distinctions follow, such as normal/abnormal, good/bad and honourable/shameful.

In *BVC v EWF*, Judge Parkes QC merely continues this long practice of closeting LGBTQ+ sexuality and identity. He held sex and sexuality to be at the core of what is considered private, or in other words – secret.[51] Whether or not the claimant was in fact out as a bisexual man was irrelevant. What mattered was that it is the claimant's choice to whom his sexual orientation is disclosed, keeping his sexuality a secret from all but a 'fairly narrow coterie'.[52] What Judge Parkes QC failed to capture is that based on this approach, the claimant's coterie – as well as that of all LGBTQ+ individuals – necessarily is and will be narrow. It only includes those people with whom the secret sexuality is shared, and not one person further. The results of *BVC v EWF* might be justified on a variety of grounds, but the approach to sex and sexuality in it reaffirms and reproduces the forced default closeting of LGBTQ+ individuals.

An additional question arises when the notion of 'disclosure' is evaluated based on heteronormative and queer standards. Andrew Gilden argues that the approach

---

[46]   Sedgwick, *Epistemology of the Closet*, 67–8.
[47]   Also see: Nicholas A. Guittar, 'The Meaning of Coming Out: From Self-Affirmation to Full Disclosure' (2013) 9(3) *Qualitative Sociology Review* 168, 168–9, 174–5.
[48]   Steven Seidman, *Beyond the Closet: The Transformation of Gay and Lesbian Life* (Routledge, 2004) 4.
[49]   Sedgwick, *Epistemology of the Closet*, 71.
[50]   As Sedgwick argues: 'by the end of the nineteenth century, when it had become fully current … that knowledge meant sexual knowledge, and secrets sexual secrets, there had in fact developed one particular sexuality that was distinctively constituted as secrecy' (ibid., 73).
[51]   *BVC v EWF* [2019] EWHC 2506 (QB), para 136.
[52]   ibid., para 137.

taken in several US jurisdictions' laws regulating revenge porn are unfavourable to the LGBTQ+ community, as they stipulate that 'if you show your body to anyone but your spouse or committed significant other, then it becomes available for all to see'.[53] As the LGBTQ+ community uses apps with intimate content, Gilden asserts that these revenge porn laws make LGBTQ+ individuals susceptible to misuse of this information with no expectation of privacy. This argument is true more broadly. If in *BVC v EWF* the claimant had a profile in a dating or sex app or website, it would be very difficult to support the claim that his sexuality is only known to a 'fairly narrow coterie' that he is aware of. Rather, this information could be available to a wide range of individuals whom even the claimant in *BVC v EWF* may or may not have known of. Consequently, it would be harder for him to assert control, through privacy, over information regarding his sexuality. Abstracting from the particularities of this case, assuming that LGBTQ+ individuals are more likely to supply intimate content online than heterosexuals, it becomes apparent that tortious protection of privacy likely offers a lesser degree of protection to LGBTQ+ individuals. Even if all matters regarding sexuality will be deemed a private matter by default, community practices would mean that tort will offer privacy protection to LGBTQ+ individuals in a far fewer number of cases than heterosexuals.

For transgender members of the LGBTQ+ community, and transwomen in particular, the closet creates a further unique vulnerability, as the reasonable person could deem information on their sex and gender as inherently public, and so not warranting protection. Lesbians, gays and bisexuals seem to have a level of protection as sexuality is seen as inherently private and disclosure requires a positive act to some degree. A transgender person's identity could become visible when they begin living in accordance with their non-biological gender. Whereas LGBQ+s need to come out of the closet and their sexuality is protected by privacy otherwise, transgenders' sex and sexuality are not as private as it could be deduced from visual references of nonconformity.[54] The closet might be a tool of oppression for the LGBTQ+ community, but it sets the benchmark for having the power to control information about individuals' sex and sexuality. Consequently, not having the ability to rely on the assumption of a closeted space, transgender individuals' sex and sexuality can become a spectacle, with reduced legal protection against sharing of information. The disparity in legal power is troubling of itself, but it is particularly concerning given that due to the reduced legal powers to protect private information, transgender people are exposed to greater risks of discrimination, rejection and violence.

---

[53] Andrew Gilden, 'Are you sure you know what revenge porn is?' *Wired* 6 October 2022 (available at https://www.wired.com/story/revenge-porn-platforms-grindr-queerness/).

[54] See Kirsty Horsey and Emily Jackson, 'The Human Fertilisation and Embryology Act 1990 and Non-Traditional Families' (2023) 86(6) *Modern Law Review* 1472–88.

The discussion in this section demonstrates how the reasonable man has a significant role in constituting the hierarchical structures of sexual identities and the power dynamics between them. LGBTQ+ identity remains a secret that only few have the right to tell. The reasonable man will only extend the protection that is granted through his normality to those individuals who comply with his traits and the rights that he would expect to enjoy. But, as LGBTQ+ individuals are defined in opposition to the straight reasonable man, the burden of proof of being the same – of being as worthy – is placed on all those who wish to have and exercise legal rights.

Conclusion: Resisting the reasonable man

Pulling together the different threads of this chapter reveals a complex understanding of the reasonable person from a queer theory perspective. As an abstract legal principle, it is queer, or at least queer-friendly, given its flexibility in assuming multiple contents. In this sense, it is aligned with one of queer theory's core features of being definition-resistant. It does not necessarily conform to a particular identity, nor does it necessarily construct a particular identity. The reasonable person is simply the mechanism through which extra-legal standards and views become legal ones.

However, from its inception and to a large extent to this day, in the process of concretisation and personification of the reasonable person, it lost the fluid qualities of an abstract standard, and instead emerged a much more fixed, identity-specific reasonable man. This man is middle class, White, heterosexual and heteronormative.[55] Through him, social hierarchies are maintained by setting him and his qualities as the benchmark of being right and enjoying the protection of having rights. The reasonable man replicates and reinforces the conception of homosexuality as abnormal and secretive. Consequently, during legal proceedings, LGBTQ+ individuals are closeted by default, forcing another experience of coming out while facing the constant uncertainty of the reasonable person standard. It is, therefore, no surprise that the reasonable person can deter LGBTQ+ individuals from litigation, as it is interpreted through prisms of marginalisation and subordination. While over time the reasonable man became more inclusive and tolerant, the interpretation and application of the reasonable man standard results in structures that are far from ideal for those who are not middle class, White, heterosexual men.

Throughout this chapter, I have demonstrated that the reasonable person has no inherent qualities, just those attributed to (mostly) him by judges. It seems plausible that one possible solution to the risks the reasonable person poses to sexual minorities could be diversifying the judiciary, who shape the reasonable

---

[55]   Chamallas, 'Social Justice Tort Theory', 313; Chen, 'Provocation's Privileged Desire'; Lee and Kwan, 'The Trans Panic Defense'; Handsley, 'The Reasonable Man', 70; Moran, *Rethinking the Reasonable Person*, 86, 128.

person standard. My suggestions here are not meant to be conclusive of the arguments that could be made in this context. Rather, I want to point out the potential that diversification of the judiciary has to challenging hegemonic views and traditional power structures' control over what ought to be considered 'reasonable', by integrating the lived experiences of minorities into the process of adjudication.[56] As such, while a more diverse judicial body cannot guarantee that the problems raised in this chapter will be resolved, it promotes the possibility that more viewpoints will be incorporated into the reasonable person – bringing it closer to its true fluid character. Put differently, a more diverse judiciary can assist in ensuring that the reasonable person is indeed a person and not a man in a third-person gender-neutral trench coat disguise.

Statistics from England and Wales show that there is much room for change in terms of the diversity of the bench. As of 1 April 2021, 66 per cent of judges were men and 91 per cent were White.[57] The same year, men represented only 49 per cent of England and Wales's population,[58] and, while data for 2021 does not appear to be publicly available, in 2019 White individuals accounted for 85 per cent of the population of England and Wales.[59] While data on sexual orientation does not exist, it appears that women and minorities are underrepresented in the judiciary.

Some critiques could be raised against my proposition. For instance, it might be argued that there is no need to diversify the composition of the judiciary but rather to educate judges, as diversity in a deep sense can be achieved through diversity of thought, not by merely diversity of backgrounds.[60] In addition, it could be argued that even if the judiciary's background is diversified, the culture

---

[56] See Nigel G. Fielding, 'Judges and Their Work' (2011) 20(1) *Social & Legal Studies* 97, 101; Erika Rackley, 'Judicial Diversity, the Woman Judge, and Fairy Tale Endings' (2007) 27(1) *Legal Studies* 74, 76–7; Kate Malleson, 'Rethinking the Merit Principle in Judicial Selection' (2006) 33(1) *Journal of Law and Society* 126, 140.

[57] Ministry of Justice, 'Diversity of the judiciary: Legal professions, new appointments and current post-holders – 2021 Statistics' *GOV.UK* 15 July 2021 (available at https://www.gov.uk/government/statistics/diversity-of-the-judiciary-2021-statistics/diversity-of-the-judiciary-2021-statistics-report). The statistics are more striking in the Supreme Court, which as of November 2022 is 100 per cent White, and 92 per cent male. There is no official data on judges' sexualities, but there are two who are openly gay and one who is openly transgender. Frances Bleach, 'History of LGBT+ representation in the UK Judiciary' *CIPA* 12 February 2021 (available at https://www.cipa.org.uk/diversity-inclusion/history-of-lgbt-representation-in-the-uk-judiciary/).

[58] Office for National Statistics, 'Population and household estimates, England and Wales: Census 2021' *Office for National Statistics* 28 June 2022 (available at https://www.ons.gov.uk/peoplepopulationandcommunity/populationandmigration/populationestimates/bulletins/populationandhouseholdestimatesenglandandwales/census2021).

[59] Office for National Statistics, 'Population estimates by ethnic group and religion, England and Wales: 2019' *Office for National Statistics* 16 December 2021 (available at https://www.ons.gov.uk/peoplepopulationandcommunity/populationandmigration/populationestimates/articles/populationestimatesbyethnicgroupandreligionenglandandwales/2019).

[60] Rackley, 'Judicial Diversity', 91.

and views of office holders continue to reflect White male beliefs and sensibilities, thus failing to disrupt and change existing patterns of oppression.[61]

These are valid criticisms, and indeed diversifying the backgrounds of judicial office holders is meant to be a means of introducing different perspectives and lived experiences to an institution that is largely homogenous. That said, to learn about the perspectives of 'others' is entirely different from living the experience of being an 'other'; from fearing that you will be outed, be discriminated against and attacked. Diversification efforts should not be exclusive of one another, but inclusive. Diversifying judicial appointments can achieve both goals, as judges of minority backgrounds could introduce different perspectives into the interpretation and operation of existing doctrines, as well as assist in formal and informal education of the judiciary on the lived experiences of minorities.

This chapter illustrates the significance of using queer theory to analyse tort law and theory. Queer theory challenges orthodox concepts and doctrines, prompting us to be aware of structural marginalisation and oppression through making certain sexual practices and sexualities normal and reasonable, and others abnormal and unreasonable. It demonstrates the need to ask questions about all the passengers on the Clapham omnibus, even the most venerable ones. Some of the questions were asked here, others are yet to be explored.

Acknowledgements

I thank Kirsty Horsey, Karen Nokes, Craig Purshouse, Eden Sarid, Steven Vaughan and the anonymous reviewers for their helpful comments and suggestions on earlier drafts.

---

[61]   Fielding, 'Judges and Their Work', 101.

PART II

How Negligence Norms Respond
to Particular Harms

5

Reproductive Harm, Social Justice and Tort Law: Rethinking 'Wrongful Birth' and 'Wrongful Life' Claims

Julie McCandless and Kirsty Horsey

Introduction

In this chapter we consider how developments in reproductive medicine and technology – from sterilisation techniques to preconception and prenatal testing, advice and prescribing, to medically assisted conception techniques such as in vitro fertilisation (IVF) – have brought new issues to bear on traditional tort law principles, by taking a closer look at what we call 'reproductive torts'. In doing so, we consider the following themes separately, but also the relationship between them. First, the idea of reproductive harm – what is it, who does it affect and who should pay for it when it occurs? Second, social justice and reproduction, particularly in relation to structural inequalities relating to gender, 'race', class and disability. Third, tort law's response, considering specifically its purpose and development and the extent to which it can address reproductive harm and issues of social justice.

These issues are interesting, and should concern us, because, in the first place, feminist legal analysis has long shown that tort law has struggled with acknowledging and compensating gendered harms.[1] And reproduction is a highly gendered activity. Reproductive harm is also not a straightforward personal injury, at least in the context of how tort law has developed. Reproductive negligence *may* result in physical harm, but it may not, or, even if it does, the more significant issue is often the reproductive repercussion and the impact that has on a person's life – their desire

---

[1] See, for example, Joanne Conaghan, 'Gendered Harms and the Law of Tort: Remedying (Sexual) Harassment' (1996) 16(3) *Oxford Journal of Legal Studies* 407; and 'Law, Harm and Redress: A Feminist Perspective' (2002) 22(3) *Legal Studies* 319.

to have a child, not to have a child, to have a particular child or to avoid having a particular child.[2] All are issues of life self-direction or personal autonomy.

As well as autonomy, these issues further relate to social justice concerns. For example, if people are not compensated for negligence which results in the birth of a child that they did not intend to have, statistically speaking it will be women who shoulder the costs and burden of raising that child; thus creating and maintaining gender injustice. Injustice relating to disability, 'race' and class are also important, as we shall see. The main question to consider is how good tort law is (or is not) at dealing with wider injustices in society and, specifically, the tort of negligence, which relies on individual people – in our case, patients – to bring individual claims against those at fault (that is, healthcare professionals) for causing the harm that they have suffered. This chapter interrogates whether this focus on individual professional liability, combined with the retrospective nature of tort law and its emphasis on individualised compensation (corrective justice), dooms tort law as an ineffective means of ameliorating societal injustice. Or, might we be more hopeful on that front, and point also to tort law's role in distributive justice in this context?

'Reproductive torts' and professional liability

What do we mean by 'reproductive torts'? This is an important question, as we clearly do not mean all reproductive mishaps. People have always sought to control their reproductive lives; whether as individuals or in conjunction with others, from sexual partners, to friends and experts who may offer 'advice'.[3] However, when 'mistakes' happen – a missed contraceptive pill, a carelessly put on condom or a miscalculation over an ovulation cycle – 'injured' parties – such as the woman who ends up pregnant, or those who end up as parents when they did not want to be – do not generally have recourse in tort law, and there are good reasons for this. The corrective and/or distributive impulses of tort law are not necessarily well served by imposing liability in these circumstances; and a great deal of harm to social relations may also occur. Moreover, most people simply would not have the necessary resources to pay for their negligence.

Instead, this chapter considers what happens when professionals are involved in procedures that affect our fertility or reproductive capacity or autonomy.

---

[2] For the framing of reproductive negligence in this three-pronged way, see Dov Fox, 'Reproductive Negligence' (2017) 117(1) *Columbia Law Review* 149.

[3] To be clear, we are not concerned with *intentional* injury here – including non-consensual sex/rape but also things like 'stealthing', or tampering with a person's contraceptive device, whether that's a pill, a condom or something else. We are also not talking about reproductive injury from things like environmental toxins, for which states and corporations often escape liability and arguably should be held accountable (see further Khiara Bridges, 'Beyond Torts: Reproductive Wrongs and the State' (2021) 121(3) *Columbia Law Review* 1017. For an account of environmental pollution affecting claimants, though not specifically about reproductive harm, see Iain Frame, Chapter 6, this volume).

Typically, these will be healthcare professionals, but sometimes related technical professionals such as embryologists in a fertility clinic, or a technician responsible for medical testing or keeping storage freezers working. Developments in reproductive medicine, such as contraceptive and sterilisation techniques, prenatal testing and prescribing, and medically assisted conception, have brought new issues to bear on tort law in terms of professional liability. As we know, all healthcare professionals owe their patients a duty of care not to be negligent in the provision of treatment – but how far does this extend?

Like all other branches of medicine, reproductive medicine is not without risk. Properly informed patients are aware of this and should have opportunities to make decisions based on an evaluation of such risks in relation to their own personal circumstances.[4] That aspect of autonomy is, however, not our focus here. Instead, when we consider reproductive negligence in this chapter, we mean negligently performed treatment. For example, an incorrectly performed sterilisation; a doctor failing to order the proper tests when a pregnant woman presents with symptoms of rubella or seeks genetic testing for a certain condition; or when results are read incorrectly; or the wrong sperm or embryo is used in fertility treatment. Patients *do not* consent to these negligent errors and in cases where the legal rules of breach and causation are also satisfied, a patient *should* be able to claim damages against a negligent practitioner (with the employer being vicariously liable). But as we will see, claiming for damages is not always straightforward in the reproductive context.

If reproductive harms are not well recognised by tort law, we then face several questions – first, whether they should be, in terms of the tort of negligence incrementally developing.[5] Second, if so, what damages should be recoverable, and whether the answer to this should be any different in the context of publicly funded National Health Service (NHS) treatment, as compared to treatment in the private healthcare sector – which raises different considerations of risk-spreading due to the profit-making dimension of treatment provision. Third, if not, how else should we hold negligent professionals accountable, improve clinical standards and respond to the harms and social injustice experienced by patients and their families in the aftermath of negligently provided treatment? A significant issue underpinning all these questions is that our current tort system relies on individual fault, but claimants will be compensated through professional insurance, the premiums for which are paid for either via policy holders (or policies held by their employer), or in the case of a public health service like the NHS, ultimately

---

4   *Montgomery v Lanarkshire Health Board* (Scotland) [2015] UKSC 11. For an interesting critical analysis of the impact of this case on the principle of consent in healthcare law, see T.T. Arvind and Aisling McMahon, 'Responsiveness and the Role of Rights in Medical Law: Lessons from *Montgomery*' (2020) 28(3) *Medical Law Review* 445.

5   As we were reminded in *Robinson v Chief Constable of West Yorkshire Police* [2018] UKSC 4, the proper role of the 'Caparo test' is to assist with this incremental development (*Caparo Industries plc v Dickman* [1990] 2 AC 605, 617–18).

through general taxation.[6] Does this do anything to improve standards, or help clinicians to perform to the best of their ability? Does it properly distribute risk and societal resources? What does this redistribution say about the society we live in or aspire to live in, and how does it relate to social justice aims? It is these questions that this chapter addresses in the specific context of reproductive harm.

In thinking about these questions, it is helpful to bear in mind this quote from the Law Commission report on injuries to unborn children which prefaced the Congenital Disabilities Act 1976: 'Law is an artefact and, if social justice requires that there should be a remedy given for a wrong, then logic should not stand in the way. A measure of damages could be artificially constructed.'[7] We like what this quote says about law: that it is an artefact – that is, a thing made by humans. We all know this, but when it comes to the common law, rules of precedent, or traditions of legal theory and philosophy, the law sometimes takes on its own persona as a pregiven entity or dogma that we cannot alter, interpret or reinterpret. What we really wanted to emphasise with this quote is the way it brings attention to social justice, wrongs and the need for a remedy – and that if the current logic of the law does not provide a remedy when social justice has been wronged, damages could – and we might argue *should* – be 'artificially' constructed – or just constructed! In the context of negligence (factually) causing congenital disabilities, damages have been facilitated through legislative means to overcome certain doctrinal impediments.[8] This also provides us with food for thought when it comes to reproductive negligence and what we should focus on: should our focus be on reworking the logic of tort law to better encompass reproductive harm and social justice related issues? Or would a different legal measure, such as legislation, be preferable? Obviously, this reflects the enduring debate on whether judges, parliament or the executive should develop rules in response to changing norms and new issues. The idea of what legal change is needed will be returned to at the end of this chapter. For now, we will spend some time illustrating exactly what we see are the current problems with the existing law.

The tort of clinical negligence – reproductive challenges

As indicated earlier, tort law, and clinical negligence specifically, has been heavily criticised in terms of its ability to protect patients and improve professional standards (its deterrent function), as well as the difficulties patients face in bringing and establishing claims (its corrective function).[9] We know, for example,

---

[6] For a wider critique on the role of fault in clinical negligence see Ian Kennedy, 'Clinical Negligence Reform is an Ethical and Financial Necessity' *Prospect* 9 August 2021.

[7] Law Commission, Report on Injuries to Unborn Children No 60 Cmnd 5709, 1974, para 89.

[8] Congenital Disabilities Act 1976.

[9] For a helpful critical consideration of the ethical imperatives for compensating for clinical negligence through tort law, see Shaun Pattinson, *Medical Law and Ethics* (6th edn, Sweet & Maxwell, 2020).

that the medical profession itself set the 'standard' for breach, with the courts showing a firm reluctance to interfere with the 'reasonable doctor' test (the *Bolam* test);[10] although things may be shifting on this front, especially in relation to patient decision-making, with a move towards recognising the value of properly informed consent.[11] Further difficulties arise from the complexity of proving both legal and factual causation, as there may be several different factors leading to a patient's injury, illness or death.[12]

However, while issues of breach and/or causation usually form the backdrop for critical discussions pertaining to clinical negligence, in the context of reproductive torts, they have not been the main challenges: indeed, breach and causation are often clearly established in terms of legal principle. Instead, what we see are issues around the conceptualisation of legal 'harm' as well as policy considerations being used to prevent claims succeeding. So, rather than the breach and causation requirements, it is the application of the 'fair, just and reasonable' factor from *Caparo* which stands in the way of the tort of negligence developing incrementally and responsively to those who experience reproductive harm. Another issue relating to duty of care comes into play when we consider harms that do not directly affect the patient, where duty is straightforward, but affect their child. Does a doctor's duty of care extend to children born following negligent treatment? Additionally, there are questions about the *scope* of a doctor's duty: does it relate only to a condition tested for or does it relate to all conditions that a child is born with?

In considering these doctrinal questions, it is important to keep in mind what we want the law to *do*, because that will influence how we think it should develop. Is it about determining our own lives, our autonomy? The idea of reproductive self-determination, planning or decision-making? One of the reasons why medical and technological developments relating to reproduction are interesting is that they often make 'choices' very explicit, as well as sometimes introducing new choices and options: Do I want to have a child now? Do I want to stop having children? Do I want *this* child? Children and families are increasingly seen as being 'planned' rather than just 'happening'. Of course, this is an oversimplification that fails to capture the reality that rationality is not always the main motivation underpinning reproductive decision-making and that people can have their reproductive hopes and 'choices' hugely restricted.[13] Moreover,

---

10   *Bolam v Friern Hospital Management Committee* [1957] 1 WLR 583.

11   *Chester v Afshar* [2004] UKHL 41; *Montgomery v Lanarkshire Health Board* (Scotland) [2015] UKSC 11.

12   *Wilsher v Essex Area Health Authority* [1988] AC 1074 – notwithstanding inroads made into medical causation by courts applying the concept of 'material contribution to harm' in some cases: *Bailey v Ministry of Defence* [2008] EWCA Civ 883; *Williams v The Bermuda Hospitals Board* [2016] UKPC 4.

13   See further Carol Sanger, 'The Lopsided Harms of Reproductive Negligence' (2018) 118(1) *Columbia Law Review* 29. This article is discussed in detail in the conclusion of this chapter.

reproductive medicine is far from certain, particularly in terms of explaining failed reproduction, which we often have very little control over. However, the ability – or need – to make reproductive decisions, and to be explicit about choices that might otherwise have gone unsaid or simply not have been possible before the development of various reproductive technologies, from reliable medical contraception to IVF, has arguably reshaped notions of reproductive autonomy and decision-making. 'Family planning' is actively encouraged by governments and policy makers, and citizens who do so are regarded as 'responsible'. However, is responding to the desire to control our reproductive lives, or reproductive autonomy, all that tort law should seek to achieve? Or, if we consider the wider aims of reproductive justice, which are that people not only have control over their bodies, but also access to the resources that they need, to include resources to parent and care for their children,[14] should it have wider social justice aims? How can tort law, focused as it is on individuals who suffer 'injury', at the hands of those at fault, play a role in the wider distribution of societal resources?[15]

Naming the reproductive torts

To help us answer some of these questions, we now turn to 'wrongful birth' and 'wrongful life' claims in negligence.[16] Before doing so, we should acknowledge that there are terminological difficulties attached to such claims. As Harvey Teff states:

> [t]hese labels are unfortunate not least in their bizarre, even macabre, overtones. One is not instinctively attracted to the cause of someone who appears to be impugning life itself. ... [T]he terms are neither

---

[14] Loretta Ross and Rickie Sollinger, *Reproductive Justice: An Introduction* (University of California Press, 2017).

[15] For our purposes, a comparison with ideas that come from critical disability studies is useful. Disability activists and critical disability scholars are critical of depictions of disability in law – as something tragic, to be pitied, as making a person less than whole. This is reflected in the 'wrongful birth' and 'wrongful life' cases involving disability, which we discuss later. A different approach might be to use the social model of disability – which looks at barriers faced in society – to frame the narrative in the legal case, rather than purely the medical model which sees disabled persons as in need of 'fixing' and therefore, in our sense, in need of compensation. In terms of tort law, there is certainly room for improvement in how disabled persons and their lives are narrated and, importantly, responded to. The need to do so clearly relates to social justice ambitions for society, both for the individuals involved in litigation, but also wider discourses and material realities.

[16] There is another growing subset of related cases, not covered in this chapter, which some commentators call 'loss of genetic affinity' claims. These are cases where, for example, the wrong gamete or embryo is used in a woman's fertility treatment, depriving her or her partner of the genetic connection to their child. See, for example, Vera Lucia Raposo, 'Wrongful Genetic Connection: Neither Blood of my Blood, Nor Flesh of my Flesh' (2020) 23(2) *Medicine, Healthcare and Philosophy* 309; and Bond and Gardner, Chapter 10, this volume.

immediately intelligible nor readily distinguishable from each other
… they conceal a host of different legal and social implications,
depending both on the circumstances leading up to the birth and on
its consequences.[17]

He concludes that the terms are 'potentially a source of considerable confusion'.[18] We agree, but believe that what is important here is that the terms are highly emotive in conveying not only that a wrong has been done to the claimant, but also that 'pregnancy', 'birth', 'conception' or even 'life' itself can quite simply be 'wrong', in and of themselves. Some of the difficulties these labels cause are illustrated as we work through the following sections. That said, it is difficult to know what to replace the terms with: what we discuss are 'personal injuries', but not as tort law has hitherto understood personal injury. Should we use something more generic like 'reproductive torts', as this chapter suggests? Or does this fail to encompass significant differences between potential causes of action? Conversely, with more specific labels like 'pregnancy' or 'prenatal' torts, do we become overly preoccupied with differences relating to whether the defendant's negligence caused the child's injuries, conception or birth? Another idea is 'wrongful suffering', which, rather than making assertions about the value of a birth or a life itself, shifts the focus to the experience of the claimant, and what they have suffered. But how would that square with trying to frame disability or care in a more positive way? There are no clear answers, which is why, for now, we continue to use the standard terms adopted in the literature.

Wrongful birth

We use 'wrongful birth' as an umbrella term to include two distinct types of claim from adults following reproductive negligence: 'wrongful pregnancy' and 'wrongful conception'. In them, parents seek compensation for an unplanned birth and child, where clinical negligence has led to the child being born. 'Wrongful pregnancy' claims arise where the parent(s) sought medical treatment in order *not* to conceive at all, such as a sterilisation procedure, which is then performed negligently. In these cases, parents have a child that they actively sought treatment to avoid having. 'Wrongful conception' claims occur when the parent(s) may well have been trying to conceive, but medical negligence means that their reproductive plans have been frustrated. For example, negligent prenatal testing or advice might mean that a woman is not properly informed of a particular risk of her child developing a certain condition or illness which, had she known about, she may have chosen to end the pregnancy. Alternatively, there may be a mistake in the gametes or embryos used in someone's fertility

---

[17]   Harvey Teff, 'The Action for "Wrongful Life" in England and the United States' (1985) 34(3) *International & Comparative Law Quarterly* 423, 425.

[18]   ibid.

treatment – for example with patient(s) who have used preimplantation genetic diagnosis (PGD) to screen embryos for a particular genetic trait that they have a family history of and wish to avoid.[19] Instead of implanting an embryo that does not have the tested-for genetic trait, an embryo with the genetic trait could be mistakenly implanted and a child with the associated condition, which the parent(s) sought to avoid, may be born.

These claims have proved controversial, because, despite satisfying the usual principles of liability, and despite compensation once being available in English law, over the past two decades the courts have refused to award full compensation in relation to the child's upbringing, reflecting a deliberate change in (judicial) policy. Additionally, some exceptions have been created, which are interesting as they only come into play when a child is born with a disability, or when a parent has a disability.

Wrongful pregnancy

In 2000, the House of Lords delivered an important ruling: *McFarlane v Tayside Health Board*.[20] In this decision, their Lordships – all male at this time, and all reasonably affluent – reversed nearly two prior decades of case law whereby parents had been able to recover not only the costs associated with the pain and distress of an unwanted pregnancy and birth following a negligent sterilisation procedure, but also the cost of the child's upbringing.[21] Prior to *McFarlane*, upbringing (or maintenance) costs were recoverable because they satisfied the usual principles of negligence: that is, they are reasonably foreseeable damage caused by a breach of a duty of care. In other words, it is reasonably foreseeable that if a clinician performs a sterilisation procedure negligently, a child, all of whom come with upbringing costs, may be born.[22] On what basis then, did their Lordships refuse to compensate the McFarlanes – who sought the sterilisation of Mrs McFarlane precisely because they felt they could not cope financially (and likely emotionally and physically) with a further child – reversing twenty odd years of case law?[23]

---

[19]   The UK has a comprehensive regulatory framework for embryo screening, with the authorised use of PGD limited to scenarios where there is a 'significant risk' of 'serious' illness, physical or mental disability or other medical condition – see Human Fertilisation and Embryology Act 1990 (as amended), Schedule 2, s 1ZA.

[20]   [2000] 2 AC 59.

[21]   See, in particular, *Scuriaga v Powell* [1979] 123 SJ 406, approved in *Emeh v Kensington and Chelsea and Westminster Area Health Authority* [1984] 3 All ER 1044.

[22]   This is explained clearly by the (as she then was) Rt Hon Lady Justice Hale DBE in 'The Value of Life and the Cost of Living - Damages for Wrongful Birth' (2001) 7(5) *British Actuarial Journal* 747. She also critiques the highly gendered impact of this decision and others that followed: that is, the particular impact on women as they go through pregnancy and birth, and then are statistically most likely to be a child's primary carer.

[23]   Note that the decision was not universally welcomed. Kirby J in the Australian case *Cattanach v Melchior* [2003] HCA 38 (where the majority of the High Court permitted the recovery of

You might expect that for something so significant to tort law – the reversing of well-established legal principle – we would be able to point to coherent and principled reasoning. Many scholars have tried, all concluding that we cannot.[24] Instead, *McFarlane* is an example of a case where the judges disagree on separate points, but somehow reach the same conclusion (that upbringing costs should not be recoverable), all for very different reasons.[25] These include the idea that such a cost is 'pure economic loss', only compensable in tort in very specific circumstances;[26] that the benefits of having a child outweigh the harms; that paying upbringing costs would leave parents overcompensated; and that recovery would go against the opinion of the 'reasonable man'[27] that a (healthy) child is a 'blessing'.[28] Undoubtedly, much of this reasoning rests on assumptions, highly generalised and selective experiences of parenting, and is based on particular worldviews – all dressed up as a policy-based exception to established legal principle. Distributive justice concerns were also raised, on the reasoning that it would be unfair for society – through the NHS – to pay for the raising of the parents' child; the converse of which, of course, is that the costs of raising a child should be privatised and absorbed by the family, rather than society at large. This is a view of distributive justice that is blind to, in particular, the gender and class dimensions of further privatising the costs of the care of children born following negligence.[29] It is regrettable that none of their Lordships acknowledged either the gendered dimension of their decision, nor the greater impact it would have on less affluent families in society, such as the McFarlanes.

McFarlane has been an influential case, with later judges regarding it as important precedent not only for wrongful birth, but also wrongful life claims, as well as, for example, in a contract law dispute, where a fertility clinic used a man's previously stored sperm to inseminate his ex-partner without his consent.[30] It has also been influential in other common law jurisdictions. But it has also been heavily

---

maintenance damages) considered that *McFarlane* went well beyond the merely unconventional and was 'arbitrary and unjust'.

24   See, for example, Laura Hoyano, 'Misconceptions about Wrongful Conception' (2002) 65(6) *Modern Law Review* 883; Anne Morris, 'Another Fine Mess … the Aftermath of *McFarlane* and the Decision in *Rees v Darlington Memorial Hospital NHS Trust*' (2004) 20 *Professional Negligence* 2; Cressida Auckland and Imogen Goold, 'Offsetting Damages in Wrongful Conception and Birth Cases: A Way through the Post-McFarlane Mire' (2022) 138 *Law Quarterly Review* 407.

25   See further Rosamund Scott, 'Reconsidering "Wrongful Life" in England After Thirty Years: Legislative Mistakes and Unjustifiable Anomalies' (2013) 72(1) *Cambridge Law Journal* 115.

26   Arising and developed from *Hedley Byrne & Co Ltd v Heller & Partners Ltd* [1964] AC 465.

27   See Haim Abraham, Chapter 4, this volume, for a queer critique of the reasonable man, or person.

28   See Nicolette Priaulx, 'Joy to the World! A (Healthy) Child Is Born! Reconceptualizing Harm in Wrongful Conception' (2016) 13(1) *Social & Legal Studies* 5.

29   See Nicolette Priaulx, 'Damages for the "Unwanted" Child: Time for a Rethink?' (2005) 73(4) *Medico-Legal Journal* 152.

30   *ARB v IVF Hammersmith and Anor* [2018] EWCA Civ 2803, discussed later.

criticised, in relation to the previously mentioned gender and class dimensions, and also for its undermining of the legal coherency of negligence.[31] Given these criticisms, it is perhaps not surprising that in order to lessen the impact of the decision, subsequent case law quickly established two exceptions to the exception (to established legal principle) in *McFarlane*.

First, in *Parkinson v St James and Seacroft University Hospital NHS Trust*,[32] the Court of Appeal decided that parents are entitled to recover for *additional* costs associated with the upbringing of a disabled child, when the child's birth follows negligent sterilisation treatment. Brenda Hale was on the Court of Appeal bench in this case, and her discomfort with the *McFarlane* decision is very clear in the case report. Second, in *Rees v Darlington Memorial Hospital NHS Trust*,[33] the House of Lords declined to overrule the decision that damages could not be awarded for the upbringing costs of a healthy child – likely because *McFarlane* was a majority decision from only three years earlier. Instead (by a slim majority) they decided that a case brought by Karina Rees, a disabled mother of a healthy child, could be distinguished from *McFarlane*. While full damages were still denied for the birth of a healthy child, a judicially invented 'conventional sum' of £15,000 was awarded to Ms Rees as a way of acknowledging that she, who was blind and had sought sterilisation as she did not want a child that she felt she could not cope with, had suffered a wrongful interference with her reproductive autonomy.

This idea of a 'conventional award' goes against many of the principles of tort law. It might be argued that perhaps it goes some way to recognising that a wrong was done, and maybe it was a useful way of recognising a 'reproductive injury' that is to do with something more intangible like autonomy, rather than physical or psychiatric injury in the traditional sense. However, in the context of full damages (the upbringing costs that would otherwise have been recoverable 'but for' the policy exception created by the House of Lords in *McFarlane*), £15,000 seems rather meagre. This is particularly true in the light of modern healthcare ethics, which place a very high value on patient autonomy.[34] The question, therefore, is whether a higher sum would have made the situation better, or if only full damages would suffice?

It is also useful to reflect on whether the two 'disability exceptions' here can be justified. Arguably, the Court of Appeal in *Parkinson* went as far as it could under the restrictive precedent created by the *McFarlane* ruling, with the judgment perhaps acknowledging the reality that it often costs more to care for a disabled child given the ableist society we live in and shrinking welfare and other public

---

[31] See, for example, Hoyano, 'Misconceptions about Wrongful Conception', and Morris, 'Another Fine Mess'.

[32] [2001] EWCA Civ 530.

[33] [2003] UKHL 52.

[34] For a discussion of this and whether this dominance is or can be translated into law, see Sheila McLean, *Autonomy, Consent and the Law* (Taylor & Francis, 2009).

supports.[35] But what about the House of Lords in *Rees*? Should they have been braver in overruling *McFarlane*, rather than creating a further disability-based exception? Would this have better responded to the demands of justice, rather than prioritising legal rules like precedent?[36]

When we look more closely at *Rees*, we start to see more clearly what the judges were actually uncomfortable with, which was perhaps less the thought of overruling a recent House of Lords bench, and more about the thought of the NHS compensating parents, some of whom may be relatively affluent, for the costs of raising healthy children. In other words, we come back to the supposedly common-sense logic of a healthy child being a 'blessing' that cannot constitute damage (while a disabled child can), despite the context of the claimant actively seeking medical treatment precisely to avoid having a child. Generally, the NHS pays a not insignificant amount to patients in compensation, with payments in the obstetric sector being particularly high. Yet paid they are, and as Nicolette Priaulx has argued, it is not clear why the NHS budget should determine the direction of tort law in this context, when in other areas it does not.[37] Or, if distinctions are to be made based on a child being healthy rather than disabled, why it should be the courts and not parliament who decide this. Indeed, if the courts were genuinely affronted by the thought of the NHS paying out full maintenance costs to affluent parents, why was it not seen as more appropriate to put a threshold on the recoverable costs, as opposed to prohibiting them entirely and only allowing for the 'extra' costs of a child's disability? We come back to the issue of disability later.

In terms of case law, what happened next? For many years, students would learn about the *McFarlane* decision, then the exceptions drawn from *Parkinson* and *Rees*, and that would be it. But since then, there have been some very interesting cases, in different contexts: namely fertility treatment and prenatal testing cases. These fall under the heading of 'wrongful conception', as opposed to wrongful pregnancy.

Wrongful conception

In the context of fertility treatment, *ARB v IVF Hammersmith*[38] is a useful case to consider. *ARB* involved a couple who started fertility treatment together, leading to the birth of one child, before storing their remaining embryos for future use. The couple then separated, but the woman, unbeknownst to her former male partner – who had since married a different partner – went back to the clinic

---

35 A critical disability studies approach would take this critique further and argue that rather than make individualised compensation payments, we should aim to change the wider support in society for disabled lives.

36 As *McFarlane* itself ironically had not done.

37 Priaulx, 'Damages for the "Unwanted" Child'.

38 *ARB v IVF Hammersmith and Anor* [2018] EWCA Civ 2803.

later to restart the fertility treatment, forging his signature on the relevant consent forms. She later sent him a text saying 'And by the way I'm pregnant. Baby due [in the summer]'.[39]

A daughter was born and the man (ARB) sued the clinic for breach of contract and claimed upbringing costs as part of the 'damage'. In the High Court judgment, Mr Justice Jay relied on *McFarlane* and *Rees* as providing a general policy exemption – transferrable to contract law – to providing damages for reasonably foreseeable harm in the context of a healthy child's upbringing costs.[40] An appeal by ARB on this point was subsequently dismissed by the Court of Appeal. Is this the correct outcome? Does the answer to this depend on how we conceptualise the harm experienced by ARB – was it simply a breach of his reproductive autonomy, or something more? Does the answer to that depend on whether the law regards him to be the legal father of the child, who must provide for her financially?[41] Or is that not the point? In other words, is the fact that ARB had his autonomy and reproductive control wrongly interfered with enough that he should have a remedy? If so, what should the remedy be?

This kind of questioning inevitably leads to more questions. Do differently situated claimants make us feel differently about what the 'just' outcome of a case might be? For example, we know from the case report that the McFarlanes already had four children and were – as many people are – concerned about the financial and emotional impact of having a further child. It is perhaps easy to sympathise with them and their circumstances and feel that they should be compensated. In contrast, we gain a picture of ARB being in significantly better-off financial circumstances, not least with the mention of private school fees for the children. Do differences in familial and financial circumstances influence whether we think a healthy child's upbringing costs should be fully recoverable, or whether there should be a standard amount, or whether the amount should differ relative to the affluence of the family – but perhaps not in the way tort has traditionally compensated, so that the wealthy get more, but that in cases of more need, the compensation is larger and vice versa? What about who the defendant is? In *ARB* it was a for-profit fertility clinic, not the NHS. This brings us back to the arguments about risk spreading and social utility, and whether that needs to be differently weighed in the context of private as opposed to publicly funded healthcare? Finally, what about the accountability of the clinic: it does seem that something quite wrong has happened here, so what should the remedy be, especially when the defendant has made a profit out of the negligent

---

[39] See *ARB v IVF Hammersmith Ltd and Anor* [2017] EWHC 2438 (QB), para 47.

[40] So, the policy exemption from tort moved across to contract, in the context where someone was paying for services. This move was expressly acknowledged by Jay J, ibid., 294 and 305–18.

[41] For a critical discussion of this issue in a cognate case, see Sally Sheldon, '*Evans v Amicus Healthcare, Hadley v Midland Fertility Services*: Revealing Cracks in the "Twin Pillars"?' (2012) 16(4) *Child and Family Law Quarterly* 437.

activity? Should they be held accountable directly to the 'victim' – a version of corrective justice; or should accountability here be more general, perhaps through professional regulation, and say the clinic receiving a fine from the sector regulator for poor practice? Would this be better for distributive justice, or would it miss the point?

A further, more recent, case to consider is *Khan v Meadows*, heard by the Supreme Court in 2021.[42] Ms Meadows was not trying to avoid having a child – she wanted a child, but when she became pregnant she discovered a family history of haemophilia and sought prenatal testing in order to find out if she was a carrier of the relevant gene, with a view to terminating her pregnancy if she was. Ms Meadows was negligently told by Dr Khan that she was not a carrier of the relevant gene, so she proceeded with her pregnancy. Her son was born with haemophilia, and also autism. The issue was the extent of damages she could claim for, under the 'disability exception'. Was it just the additional upbringing costs associated with her son's haemophilia, or the full costs of his care given his additional needs associated with autism? This question about the scope of Dr Khan's duty was important as the damages for the latter were set at £9 million, whereas the costs associated with the haemophilia only were set at £1.2 million. Ms Meadows' claim succeeded in the High Court, but in the Court of Appeal damages were reduced to £1.4 million, with the Supreme Court agreeing.

What was the more 'socially just' award out of this binary choice? It seems that for the Court of Appeal and the Supreme Court the issue was the 'risk' (or responsibility) the doctor had assumed, compared to the risks assumed by Ms Meadows:

> As to the apportionment of risk, the doctor would be liable for the risk of a mother giving birth to a child with haemophilia because there had been no foetal testing and consequent upon it no termination of the pregnancy. The mother would take the risks of all other potential difficulties of the pregnancy and birth both as to herself and to her child.[43]

On this view, Dr Khan had assumed the risk of not testing for the haemophilia gene, while Ms Meadows assumed all other risks in connection with going ahead with a pregnancy. In addition, it would be unfair to hold a doctor liable for something they had no role in testing for because the extent of the damages would be disproportionate to their responsibility. However, it might be argued that this prioritises one version of legal logic over the reality of people's lives. The other version is that adopted in the initial High Court judgment by Mrs Justice Yip, which was to accept that without (but for) the doctor's negligence,

---

[42] [2021] UKSC 21.
[43] *Khan v MNX* [2018] EWCA Civ 2609, para 26ii (Davies LJ).

Ms Meadows would have terminated her pregnancy and her son would not have been born. In other words, she would not be caring for a son with both haemophilia and autism.[44] Another legal concept that the judges could have used is the 'egg-shell skull' rule, which is that you take your victim as you find them. But perhaps that is tricky – the 'victim' in a wrongful conception claim is the parent, not the child – although of course they are bringing a claim for the child's benefit as well as their own, as they try to secure compensation to help with the child's upbringing. Another useful way to reason or analyse the 'damage' is to argue that tort law needs to go beyond recognising only 'parts' of us, and to contemplate the full human experience.[45] Ms Meadows' experience is that she is caring for a son with two very severe conditions. Only by taking account of both of those in the award of damages do we acknowledge her and her son's full humanity and experience.

Yet, this kind of thinking raises more questions. The first is about the framing of *Khan v Meadows*, and the case being brought by the mother rather than her son (or the mother and the son). Is it fair that he cannot bring a claim in his own right, if his mother can in the same circumstances? And, what about the general language of damage, loss, harm and injury? Is the traditional language of tort law useful when we talk about conditions that people are born with? This brings us full circle, back to the question of terminology and what to call these claims, and leads nicely to the question of 'wrongful life' claims.

Wrongful life

Wrongful life claims are claims not from the patients who were directly treated (the mother and/or father), but from the child(ren) born following negligent treatment. The damages would therefore be for life, as opposed to for the child's upbringing, which applies only to the child's minority. This makes them a potentially more powerful claim. In wrongful life claims, children typically seek compensation because they have been born with very severe disabilities. It is important to note that the doctor's negligence is not the direct cause of the disability, illness or condition in a wrongful life claim.[46] Instead, the issue is that the mother was not (properly) advised of the possibility of the child being born with the illness or disability – because of negligent prenatal testing,

---

[44] This is like the reasoning in *Chester v Afshar* [2004] UKHL 41, in the context of negligent treatment advice, where the 'damage' was the deprivation of a 'choice', and as a consequence, the defendant was liable for the full damages, even though their 'fault' may not have been proportionate.

[45] See for example, Nicolette Priaulx, 'Reproducing the Properties of Harms that Matter: The Normative Life of the Damage Concept in Negligence' (2017) 1 *Journal of Medical Law and Ethics* 1.

[46] This type of claim would fall under the Congenital Disabilities Act 1976.

advice or failure to do so[47] – and thus she was deprived of making an informed decision about continuing with the pregnancy, or to opt into treatment that may potentially have helped lessen the effects of the condition. Alternatively, there could be preconception negligence, as in *Toombes v Mitchell*,[48] which we consider later. In this case, the claimant's mother was negligently advised that taking folic acid was not necessary, with her daughter subsequently being born with spina bifida, which folic acid helps prevent.

Whether prenatal or preconception negligence, the nub of the wrongful life claim is that but for the defendant's negligence, the child would not have been born (and the damage suffered would have been avoided). Framing the claim in this way, we can see how the name 'wrongful life' has emerged. Interestingly, historically (that is, before the widespread use of the technologies that we have discussed here), in the US, wrongful life claims were also submitted by 'illegitimate' children, not against medical practitioners, but against their putative fathers.[49] No such case was successful, but they highlight a very interesting issue of societal injustice – the (supposed) stigma and shame of illegitimacy – as well as legal distinctions between 'legitimate' and 'illegitimate' children. For us, another important aspect of wrongful life claims is that that they can remove some stigma from a parent who prefers not to make a wrongful birth claim, worried that this somehow makes a statement that they did not want and do not love their child.[50]

Some more recent wrongful life claims have involved racial issues, rather than a child's disability or illness. For example, a couple (usually White), expects (or contracts with) a fertility clinic to provide them with sperm from a White donor, but sperm from a Black or other racially different donor is accidentally used. The children then suffer racial abuse, and a questioning of their family origins that they would not otherwise have suffered had they inherited their parents' White privilege. Should these children be able to claim from the careless fertility clinician, who, after all, made a profit from their wrongdoing? This is a difficult question that we will later return to. For now, we wonder if it would be better to frame these cases differently. Not as about 'wrongful life' – for it seems challenging to say that a child's life is wrongful because of the colour of their skin, given that it is not their skin that is the problem, but societal racism – but instead as 'the child is born and suffers because of the defendant's negligence', shifting the focus away from a 'wrongful life' to the negligent actions of the defendant and their role in the child's suffering. But this requires yet further terminological gymnastics.

---

47   In the UK, non-invasive prenatal testing is offered as routine, while more invasive testing like amniocentesis is offered if a certain risk threshold is established.

48   [2021] EWHC 3234.

49   For example, *Zepeda v Zepeda* 190 N.E.2d 849 (Ill. App. Ct. 1963).

50   This point is illustrated in *Toombes v Mitchell*, where the claimant's mother did not want to bring a wrongful birth claim precisely for this reason.

The framing of 'wrongful life' cases as some kind of value judgment between life and non-existence is one reason they have been considered controversial. But there are other reasons. Carol Sanger captures another here:'[T]ort reforms that might otherwise extend notions of liability for reproductive negligence may be seen as dangerous or unacceptable because of their explicit recognition that not all children are wanted and that people will take steps to prevent their births.'[51]

This relates to the idea that the development of reproductive technology and medicine has made reproductive decisions more explicit – whether to have children, when, how many and so forth. Part of these calculations is to consider, as Sanger suggests, that not all children are wanted (or a 'blessing'), and that people will take steps to prevent their birth. Though she is referring to termination of pregnancy (for whatever reason), we can also extend this critique to preconception testing of IVF embryos, for example. Nevertheless, this possibility of pregnancy termination has been very influential in the development of wrongful life claims. This of course says something about the value that we give – or rather do not – to the reproductive autonomy of women in society. There is still a huge amount of controversy over abortion and its permissibility.[52] Sanger goes on to analyse how the framing of reproductive autonomy as being about 'choice' has somewhat backfired on the feminist movement, in the sense that it paved the way for abortion to be framed in consumerist terms by its opponents. Or as a type of lifestyle choice for women, rather than a *right* or a *need*. Similar arguments are made in relation to technologies that allow for embryo selection or prenatal testing: or so-called 'designer babies'.

Pitched against this consumerist framing of reproductive choice is the sanctity of life discourse, so the idea that all life is precious, and that humanity should not decide who lives or dies, or rather, who does or does not come into existence. As well as these conservative impulses and critiques of wrongful life claims, some progressives have also been critical, mainly invoking reasons of disability and racial injustice, and questioning what the claims potentially say about disabled life, or racialised existence. Lydia X.Z. Brown, a critical disabilities scholar and activist, criticises the individualistic nature of wrongful life claims, arguing that they are a highly problematic legal tool designed to achieve compensation for one individual, rather than focusing on bigger societal issues and structures which would remove the need for the claim in the first place.[53] Similarly, Wendy Hensel analyses the impact of such claims on disabled persons and their experiences, and

---

51   Sanger, 'The Lopsided Harms', 46.

52   As illustrated in the US with the recent Supreme Court decision in *Dobbs v Jackson Women's Health Organization* No. 19-1392, 597 US (2022), which in overturning *Roe v Wade* 410 US 113 (1973) and *Planned Parenthood v Casey* 505 US 833 (1992), declared that the US Constitution did not provide a right to abortion.

53   Lydia X.Z. Brown, 'Legal Ableism, Interrupted: Developing Tort Law & Policy Alternatives to Wrongful Birth & Wrongful Life Claims' (2018) 38(2) *Disability Studies Quarterly*.

makes the argument that they should not be allowed because of the pejorative messages that they send about disability.[54]

So far, you will have noticed, we have only cited US literature on wrongful life. There is a reason for that, which is that different US states have different rules on whether or not wrongful life claims are permissible. Most states do not allow them, but some do, and they are permitted in some circumstances in others. This inevitably means there is a bit more to write about! In the UK context, the scholar who has written the most in-depth analysis of wrongful life claims is Rosamund Scott.[55] However, her substantive work was published a decade ago, reflecting the fact that wrongful life cases have been regarded as inadmissible since the English Court of Appeal decision in *McKay v Essex Health Authority*.[56]

Mary McKay was born with very severe disabilities, caused by the fact that her mother, Jacinta McKay, had contracted rubella during the early stages of pregnancy. Jacinta suspected she had rubella and visited a doctor about her symptoms. Negligence on the doctor's part meant the condition went undiagnosed and Jacinta was unable to make a properly informed decision about continuing with the pregnancy considering the risks. The judges gave several reasons for concluding that wrongful life claims should not be admissible. In these reasons, we see the spectre of the sanctity of life principle, when a severely disabled child is refused compensation that would help significantly to improve her quality of life, on the basis that her claim offends the sanctity of life. Another version of the framing reflects a determination that the costs for meeting Mary's care should come from her mother, family and general taxation (social security), rather than through the professional insurance of a negligent doctor.[57]

We can draw our own conclusions about how the judges believed resources should be attributed in society, and who should bear the responsibility of risk and the burdens of care but, unsurprisingly, none of their reasoning was so overtly political. Instead, they suggested, first, that it would be contrary to public policy for a doctor to owe a child a duty of care to ensure that s/he did not exist, as this would undermine the sanctity of human life. Second, they thought that it might result in doctors being under a duty to persuade pregnant women to have a termination. Third, they said that the law did not recognise being born as 'damage': life, however painful or disabled, is better than non-existence. Finally, they suggested damages could not be quantified, it being impossible to quantify the relative value of existence versus non-existence.

All aspects of this reasoning can be challenged. It is an equally valuable policy argument that 'a doctor has a duty to do their job properly so that their patient can make informed choices about whether or not to continue with a pregnancy',

---

54 Wendy F. Hensel, 'The Disabling Impact of Wrongful Birth and Wrongful Life Actions' (2005) 40 *Harvard Civil Rights – Civil Liabilities Law Review* 141.

55 Scott, 'Reconsidering "Wrongful Life" in England'.

56 [1984] 1 QB 1166 (CA).

57 Although note that tortious damages are much higher than social security/disability benefits.

which will ensure patients' trust. The idea that doctors would have a duty to persuade women to terminate pregnancies seems highly misplaced, as any such duty would be restricted merely to advising her of this option. This is how the principles of informed consent already operate, and it is very clear under the law that pregnant women must consent to a pregnancy termination. Again, it would merely be imposing a duty on doctors to do their job properly. The third reason is a value judgment and one that arguably none of us – especially those with relative good health and a daily existence free from severe pain or life-limiting illness – are qualified to make. Further, judges and policy makers make quantifications about life and disabilities all the time.[58] Was this then just a convenient excuse?

How convinced should we be by this reasoning? What does it say about who should bear the responsibility for reproductive (professional) negligence? Should society be left to pick up the tag? Individual families? Parents? Or would it be more appropriate for professional insurance to pay, or at least contribute? If we do instinctively think that wider society should bear the brunt of the costs, then given structural inequalities relating to health and disability, among other factors, a further question is whether tort 'helps' by raising awareness, testing private law and finding its faults and parameters, or 'hinders' wider civil society action by 'individualising' the damage, both in terms of the person who suffers and the element of 'fault'? In other words, is tort a distraction to wider societal change, or can it complement those efforts?

In 2013, Rosamund Scott asked whether the time had come to revise *McKay*, given developments in how courts had more recently developed the sanctity of life principle (in neonatal and other end of life decisions) as well as possibilities for wrongful life claims in the context of assisted reproduction under the Congenital Disabilities Act 1976, implemented before many current assisted conception techniques were developed.[59] Additionally, she built an argument for allowing wrongful life claims when the child's suffering reaches a certain threshold. However, there has been absolutely no change in the law in this area since *McKay*, and the reasoning in *McKay* has been followed in many other jurisdictions, with the effect of 'fossilising' the common law. There are some alternative models of legal reasoning, but not many. And where there have been successful cases, such as in France in the *Perruche* case,[60] legislative action has swiftly followed to bar future claims.[61] One example of a successful wrongful life claim is the Californian Supreme Court case of *Curlender v Bio-Science Laboratories*,[62] where

---

[58] See, for example, *Judicial College Guidelines for the Assessment of General Damages in Personal Injury Cases* (16th edn, Oxford University Press, 2021).

[59] Scott, 'Reconsidering "Wrongful Life" in England'.

[60] *"Perruche"* Cass Ass. Pl. 17 Nov. 2000, n° 99-13.701; Bulletin A. P. n° 9.

[61] It is interesting that this legislative action did not make compensation impossible, but instead brought about an administrative agency to administer compensation when gross negligence causing disabilities could be shown. See further Julia Field Costich, 'The *Perruche* Case and the Issue of Compensation for the Consequences of Medical Error' (2006) 78(1) *Health Policy* 8.

[62] [1980] 165 Cal.Rptr. 477, 106 Cal.App.3d 811.

a child recovered damages after negligent prenatal testing failed to detect that she had Tay-Sachs disease. In this case, the judges observed that the 'reality of the "wrongful life" concept is that such a plaintiff both exists and suffers due to the negligence of others'. So, a different way is possible. This leads us neatly to consider what might be called a recent 'revival' in wrongful life claims in the UK.

Reviving wrongful life claims, tort and social justice

Toombes v Mitchell,[63] mentioned earlier, starkly brings us back to the controversial role of pregnancy termination in wrongful life claims. Unlike *McKay*, which was about prenatal testing and advice, Caroline Toombes was given negligent advice about taking folic acid when she visited her GP to discuss family planning. Dr Mitchell advised it was not recommended and was up to her, when in fact it is medically recommended to take folic acid in advance of conception and at the start of pregnancy. Acting on this negligent advice, Caroline Toombes conceived and gave birth to Evie Toombes. Evie was born with a severe congenital defect caused by spinal tethering, causing her severe pain and significant debilitating conditions including double incontinence. Caroline Toombes did not want to bring a wrongful birth claim, for the reasons discussed earlier. Instead, Evie herself brought a wrongful life claim against the doctor.

In the *Toombes* judgment, emphasis was placed on the fact that there had been pre*conception* rather than pre*natal* negligence – in other words, no question of pregnancy termination arose. This being true, the focus that the High Court judge continued to place on the undesirability of doctors being under a duty to present pregnancy termination as an option to their patients was surprising and can be interpreted as ongoing judicial discomfort with traditional wrongful life claims. However, it was the pre*conception* distinction that allowed Evie Toombes' claim to succeed, on the basis that her case was framed not as between existence or no existence, but rather that as her mother would have delayed conception and taken folic acid for a few months, a different child would have been conceived at a different date, and one who was unlikely to have the spinal cord tethering. We do not know yet how much Evie's compensation award will be, but given the severity of her conditions, an award in the millions is likely, as was reported in the press.[64]

It is interesting how the media portrayed this case, and how they highlighted that Evie is a keen horse rider and show jumper and indeed competes professionally in both able bodied and para-Olympic competitions. She also campaigns for invisible disabilities,[65] with the motto 'find a way, not an

---

63   [2021] EWHC 3234.

64   For example, Laurence Dollimore, 'Spina bifida showjumper WINS landmark legal case over her "wrongful conception": Evie Toombes, 20, who sued her mother's GP claiming she should never have been born could win MILLIONS in damages' *Mail Online* 1 December 2021.

65   See, for example, her role as an ambassador for the Mintridge Foundation (available at https://www.mintridgefoundation.org.uk/mintridge-foundation/ambassador-evie-toombes).

excuse'[66] – which sits uneasily with wider disability justice activism, as it seems to individualise the challenges that disabled persons face in society and potentially sends the message that 'you just have to try harder'. Given how she has had to manage her condition, the equipment and support that is required, and how the professional show-jumping world is not readily accessible to her without the need for significant specialised support and equipment – which seemingly she herself must fund and secure[67] – we are not sure this motto encapsulates the wider concerns of social justice. As with *Khan* and *ARB*, which we have already discussed, it is valuable to reflect on this case, noting one's emotional reaction to it, and considering whether the outcome sits well in terms of social justice. *Toombes* is an effective contrast to a case like *McKay*, where Mary's condition was so debilitating that she simply would not have been able to present herself in the way Evie Toombes has been able to. That, of course, is fine – not all persons who are ill or disabled have the same life, and it is important that law and case reports acknowledge that. But equally, if Evie Toombes is entitled to damages, hers being the first successful wrongful life claim since *McKay* in the 1980s – what does that say about children in a similar situation to Mary McKay; should they not also be compensated?

Another wrongful life claim presented itself earlier in *A and B (by C, their mother and next friend) v A (Health and Social Services Trust)*,[68] heard in the Northern Irish High Court, then Court of Appeal. It is interesting for very different reasons from *Toombes*. A and B (the children, who were twins) were not born with severe disabilities. Instead, they were born with a different skin colour from their parents and each other when a fertility clinic negligently used sperm from the wrong donor in their mother's fertility treatment. The harm that the children were claiming for related not to physical injury, but rather to racist abuse and harassment that they had been subject to, as well as their relationship with their parents being questioned (that is, the assumption that their mother had had an extra-marital affair). *A and B* is difficult and controversial for several reasons.[69] It is very difficult, wrong and completely undesirable to say that being born a certain skin colour is a 'harm'. A person's skin colour is not the harm, racism is, and we all know it exists, and that people suffer deeply from it, just as people suffer from ableism, sexism and various other intersections of inequality and injustice. But should people be able to claim damages through the tort system for racism that occurs in part because of the negligent action of a doctor?

Via the Evie Toombes Foundation (available at https://foundation.evietoombespararider. com/).

[66] For example, as cited on the 'In Due Horse' site (available at https://www.induehorse.com/ lifestyle/the-evie-toombes-foundation/).

[67] We can see this in the explanation on 'In Due Horse' detailing what Evie's fundraising will go towards – namely a specialised medical facility and horse box.

[68] [2011] NICA 28.

[69] See Sally Sheldon, 'Is it a harm to be born with different skin colour to your parents?' *BioNews* (616) 18 July 2011.

A and B's claims were unsuccessful. In coming to this conclusion, the Northern Irish judges took an unhelpfully colour-blind approach to analysing the family's suffering. What would have been better would have been to acknowledge the damage done by the fertility clinic's negligence, and to put this in the context of wider societal and public responsibilities to ameliorate the impact of racism. In other words, to highlight the accountability of the negligent clinic, but also the wider role of the state.[70] Obviously, this is a difficult line to tread, as the legal claim rests on problematic assumptions around the genetic family, the privilege of Whiteness, as well as inheritability. There is also an important social justice question here, as to the extent to which systemic and structural issues in society like racism, sexism, ableism and so forth, are well addressed by tort law, relying as it does on individual fault, harm and recovery.[71] Can tort law be developed to take account of these collective issues, or, if you are really concerned about them, are you better off campaigning and taking action in other ways?

That said, the doctor/clinic *had* been negligent, and it feels right that they should be held accountable for negligent practices. Further, the family *did* suffer in terms of their reproductive plans being disrupted — their reproductive autonomy — and *then* because of this, having the legitimacy of their family questioned repeatedly, as well as experiencing racist abuse and harassment. Is it possible to (theoretically) allow the claim to acknowledge these issues, while at the same time, not also contributing to racialised social injustice?

Conclusion: What can tort law do?

The time has probably come for tort law to rid itself of the problematic labels attached to 'wrongful birth' and 'wrongful life' claims. But how? And what should we replace them with? Dov Fox suggests that, because current torts cannot and do not respond well to the nature of reproductive harm, we should replace these heads of loss with a new, broader tort of 'reproductive negligence'.[72] But what should this look like? He frames reproductive negligence as being about loss of control or choice. Understandably, this is an effort to pin the proposed tort to autonomy interests and rights.

This proposal has prompted some important critiques. Carol Sanger, for example, questions how the tort would be devised, and the extent to which it

---

70 As argued comprehensively by Julie McCandless in her rewritten feminist judgment on the case in Máiréad Enright, Julie McCandless and Aoife O'Donoghue (eds), *Northern/Irish Feminist Judgments: Judges' Troubles and the Gendered Politics of Identity* (Bloomsbury, 2017), chapter 30. Also see Marian Duggan's response to the rewritten judgment in the same volume and chapter.

71 See Patricia Williams' critical race theory critique of a similar wrongful life case in the US: 'The Value of Whiteness', *The Nation* 12 November 2014. See also Suzanne Lenon and Danielle Peers, '"Wrongful" Inheritance: Race, Disability and Sexuality in *Cramblett v Midwest Sperm Bank*' 25(2) *Feminist Legal Studies* 141.

72 Fox, 'Reproductive Negligence'.

considers the wider political context in which a tort of reproductive negligence would operate.[73] In doing so, she urges three main points of caution in relation to Fox's proposal. First, she urges caution with framing any tort of reproductive negligence as being about control and choice, for two reasons. The first is political, in terms of the rhetorical connotations of couching reproductive planning in the language of choice, given that this has allowed opponents of the abortion rights movement to attribute abortion with connotations of consumerism and self-satisfaction (as discussed earlier). The downside of a choice framework, therefore, is making something like having children (or not) seem selfish or self-serving. Second, Sanger asks whether choice accurately reflects what has been lost in these cases, which she alternatively frames as 'a loss of a hoped-for outcome' or disappointment. In other words, while we may all adopt the language of 'reproductive control' and 'family planning', real-life trajectories are marked by much more ambivalence and chance than we are often prepared to concede. And while faith in technology and invention may make us think we are in control,[74] we should not forget that in this context we are not concerned with failed technology, but lack of careful medical practice, which often comes down to *chance*. Sanger also questions whether parents would want to frame any action as being about loss of control, given that loss of control over a certain 'planned for child' can often become acceptance (of the child you do have).

The second of Sanger's three main criticisms relates to the gendered nature of the harms, which Fox discusses only in gender-neutral terms. Here, Sanger wonders whether the differences potentially experienced by women and men in understanding the nature of the harm involved are too crucial to leave undeveloped: so for example, the emotional harm of fertility-related stress and how this is experienced differently by women and men,[75] notwithstanding the different physical interventions that take place in treatment. She argues that we should acknowledge this gender dimension throughout the process of trying to ascertain the cause of action: even if it comes to be implemented in a gender-neutral way. So, for example, she says we must ask what is at stake when motherhood is denied – and try to understand this by looking at why women seek it in the first place: whether to meet social, emotional, spousal expectations; keep a relationship together; move it forward; experience pregnancy; pass on a family name, genes, closeness, love; the idea of what having a baby is thought to mean and so forth. We should also ask the same for fatherhood; and see how the answers may be different.

Finally, Sanger's third concern, which appeared in part in her concern about framing a reproductive negligence tort as being about 'choice', is about how reproductive torts, especially wrongful life claims, ultimately come to be about

---

[73] Sanger, 'The Lopsided Harms'.

[74] Though see Emily Jackson, Chapter 7, this volume.

[75] We must also extend this reasoning to trans and other gender non-conforming persons and their particular reproductive experiences and expectations.

abortion politics – we saw this clearly in *Toombes*. As she argues, the issue of abortion looms large: 'abortion suddenly seems to be about everything, and everything can quickly come to be about abortion'.[76] In other words, abortion can be seen as a cipher for a much wider political conversation around basic reproductive rights and access to decent reproductive and sexual healthcare.[77] The Northern Ireland *A and B* wrongful life case is a good example, with the original judges tying themselves in knots about duties being owed to fetuses (while being completely inattentive to the wider restrictions on abortion in the jurisdiction in place at the time of the case), as indeed is case law from English courts, with judges worried that to allow wrongful life claims would somehow mean imposing duties on doctors to recommend terminations – a complete straw man given that a woman must clearly consent to a termination under the law. Either way, Sanger encourages us to think about the wider political context in which doctrine develops, within which she regards a basic proposal for a tort of reproductive negligence as simply not up to the job, even as she is sympathetic to the aims of Fox's proposal.

Khiara Bridges is also sympathetic to Fox's aims, particularly as they relate to the harms imposed by negligent *private* actors – clinicians, fertility practitioners and so forth.[78] But in her reproductive justice critique of his proposed new tort, she introduces the harms that result when public actors impose, deprive and confound procreation and asks how *state*-inflicted harms in this domain compare to private actor-inflicted harms. Importantly, she urges us to reconsider the harms caused by private actors' reproductive negligence in light of inequality along 'race' and class lines. This brings us back to one of the broader themes of this chapter, which is whether tort law can help with wider social justice issues, rather than merely provide individualised corrective compensation. Bridges' point about analysing harms in light of societal inequality is a generative method for thinking about this possibility. Perhaps, when it comes to inequality, we should not confine our thinking to certain 'niche' areas of law, but all areas in a type of 'all hands on deck' approach to social justice.[79] We know, for example, that anti-discrimination and public sector equality duties have thus far failed to fully grasp or respond to the intersectional reality of people's lives.[80] Could tort law

---

[76] Sanger, 'The Lopsided Harms'.

[77] See, for example, the feminists@law Rapid Response collection (2022, 11(2)) responding to the decision in *Dobbs v Jackson*, and addressing the impact of the decision on issues beyond abortion.

[78] Bridges, 'Beyond Torts'.

[79] As argued for by Martha Chamallas, 'Social Justice Tort Theory' (2021) 14(2) *Journal of Tort Law* 309.

[80] On the former, see Kimberlé Crenshaw, 'Demarginalizing the Intersection of Race and Sex: A Black Feminist Critique of Antidiscrimination Doctrine, Feminist Theory and Antiracist Politics' (1989) 1 *University of Chicago Legal Forum* 139. On the Public Sector Equality Duty in the Equality Act 2004, see Simonetta Manfredi, Lucy Vickers and Kate Clayton-Hathway, 'The Public Sector Equality Duty: Enforcing Equality Rights Through Second-Generation Regulation' (2017) 47(3) *Industrial Law Journal* 365.

do any better, if we started to explicitly develop principles with social justice as a priority – in a way that collectivises, rather than privatises, responsibility for health and care, and recognises and values not only the suffering, but also the experiences, transitions and adjustments that people who are injured, and those who love and care for them make – without understating the need for societal resources, and indeed, society and the state's obligation to foster equality and resilience through the institutions, like law, that it propagates?

6

Coded Copper, Toxic Water. Multinational Corporations, Environmental Degradation and Tort Law

Iain Frame

Introduction

Bangladeshi and Pakistani garment workers fatally injured by unsafe factories; Chilean communities harmed by toxic sludge; Peruvian farmers vulnerable to flood risk; Nigerian farmland and fishing grounds damaged by oil spills; Zambian watercourses polluted by toxic emissions.[1] Diverse communities of the 'Global South' contend with environmental degradation and labour and human rights violations. As they do so they confront the world's largest multinational corporations (MNCs). This chapter focuses on the 2019 English case, *Lungowe v Vedanta*,[2] in which Zambian residents sued the then London-headquartered mining group, Vedanta Resources. Its task is to identify the role of tort law in the conflict between MNCs and those exposed to environmental degradation. It will do so by contrasting two types of legal work.

Katharina Pistor's *The Code of Capital* presents the idea of corporate lawyers 'coding' assets – such as the copper mined in Zambia – to turn these assets into wealth for the asset's owner.[3] This type of lawyering relates to tort law in that

---

[1] For information on lawsuits connected to these examples, see the Business and Human Rights Resource Centre website (available at www.business-humanrights.org/en/big-issues/corporate-legal-accountability).

[2] *Lungowe v Vedanta Resources plc* [2019] UKSC 20.

[3] Katharina Pistor, *The Code of Capital: How Law Creates Wealth and Inequality* (Princeton University Press, 2019).

these coding strategies deliberately challenge tort law's capacity to deter or to compensate. Tort law's limits combined with weak environmental regulation leave those harmed by MNCs without legal protection.

Yet *Lungowe*, and, before it, *Chandler*,[4] suggest a different role for tort law, one in which the tort of negligence becomes a site of distributional conflict.[5] To see that role, this chapter draws on the insights of two figures who have left their mark on realist and critical legal thinking: Wesley Hohfeld and Duncan Kennedy. With their insights at our service, the chapter turns to a second type of legal work – the work of strategic litigation and interpretation by public interest lawyers and sympathetic judges, a type of legal work exemplified by the judgments in *Chandler* and *Lungowe*.

The goals of tort law

To locate tort law in the conflicts between MNCs and those they harm, consider some of tort law's goals. Many scholars regard tort law as a means of deterring undesirable behaviour, a form of judge-made regulation where the threat of liability incentivises people to alter their conduct.[6] Other tort law scholars, however, question tort law's capacity to regulate future conduct. They do so by emphasising tort law's 'essence', which they claim unites a specific claimant and a specific defendant so that the claimant's recovery corresponds to the defendant's liability. Such a structure is backward looking since it seeks to correct past wrongs, transferring back to the claimant that which the defendant has wrongfully taken and must restore.[7] And because its structure is backward looking, tort law should not try to prevent future harms by deterring wrongs or incentivising conduct. Environmental and health and safety agencies more effectively pursue that objective.[8] Yet does weak enforcement not sometimes undermine the effectiveness of public regulation?[9] And regardless of the effectiveness of public regulation, how

---

[4] *Chandler v Cape plc* [2012] EWCA Civ 525.

[5] Private nuisance is the other area of tort law that claimants have deployed to challenge environmental degradation. See, for example, *Jalla v Shell International Trading and Shipping Co Ltd* [2023] UKSC 16. This chapter, however, focuses only on negligence.

[6] Steve Shavell, 'Liability for Harm versus Regulation for Safety' (1984) 13(2) *Journal of Legal Studies* 357. For scepticism about tort law's capacity to deter, see Douglas A. Kysar, 'The Public Life of Private Law: Tort Law as a Risk Regulation Mechanism' (2018) 9(1) *European Journal of Risk Regulation* 48.

[7] Ernest Weinrib, *The Idea of Private Law* (rev edn, Harvard University Press, 2012), discussing tort law in chapter 6, 'Negligence Liability'. For scepticism about reducing tort law to corrective justice, see Dan Priel, 'Structure, Function, and Tort Law' (2020) 13(1) *Journal of Tort Law* 31.

[8] T.T. Arvind and Joanna Gray, 'The Limits of Technocracy: Private Law's Future in the Regulatory State' in Kit Barker, Karen Fairweather and Ross Grantham (eds), *Private Law in the 21st Century* (Bloomsbury, 2017) 237.

[9] See Michael G. Faure, 'The Complementary Roles of Liability, Regulation and Insurance in Safety Management: Theory and Practice' (2014) 17(6) *Journal of Risk Research* 689, 694–5.

good is tort law at deterring or correcting wrongs?[10] To explore these questions, consider first copper mining in Zambia, and then Pistor's *The Code of Capital*.

Copper mining in Zambia

Zambia's economy has long been dependent on and vulnerable to swings in the price of copper.[11] The first copper mining in the British protectorate of Northern Rhodesia began in the 1920s only to stall soon after with the onset of the Great Depression. The sector recovered in the 1940s and 1950s under the control of US and South African based corporations. After Zambia's independence from the UK in 1964, the Zambian government started the process that culminated in the 1974 nationalisation of the country's mines under a single organisation, Zambia Consolidated Copper Mines (ZCCM). Yet the oil crisis of the 1970s led to a decline in demand for copper. Zambia initially borrowed from overseas creditors to offset the fall in revenues. However, the price of copper did not recover, ZCCM was starved of investment and Zambia found itself at the mercy of the World Bank and the International Monetary Fund.

In return for access to the World Bank's Highly Indebted Poor Countries initiative, in 1996 Zambia started the process of privatising ZCCM, doing so by breaking the conglomerate up and selling its assets as separate packages to international investors.[12] To entice investors, the World Bank helped Zambia draft the Investment Act 1995 and the Mines and Minerals Act 1995, which together created a low-tax, investor friendly legal framework.[13] Sufficiently enticed, in 2002 Anglo American invested in Konkola Copper Mines (KCM), the company which controls the Nchanga mine, one of the largest open-pit mines in Africa. Yet just two years later, Anglo American sold its controlling shareholding in KCM claiming that the still depressed price of copper made mining unprofitable.[14] Vedanta Resources – a company controlled by the Agarwal

---

[10]   See Kenneth S. Abraham, *The Liability Century* (Cambridge University Press, 2008), who notes that tort law 'probably is not terribly good at achieving any of its possible goals' (9).

[11]   Alastair Fraser, 'Introduction: Boom and Bust on the Zambian Copperbelt', and Miles Larmer, 'Historical Perspectives on Zambia's Mining Booms and Busts', both in Alastair Fraser and Miles Larmer (eds), *Zambia, Mining and Neoliberalism* (Oxford University Press, 2010) 1 and 31. See also Robert Liebenthal and Caesar Cheelo, 'The Boom-Bust Cycle of Global Copper Prices, Structural Change, and Industrial Development in Zambia' in John Page and Finn Tarp (eds), *Mining for Change* (Oxford University Press, 2020) 374; and John Lungu, 'Socio-Economic Change and Natural Resource Exploitation: A Case Study of the Zambian Copper Mining Industry' (2008) 25(5) *Development Southern Africa* 543.

[12]   Christopher S. Adam and Anthony M. Sompasa, 'The Economics of the Copper Price Boom in Zambia' in Fraser and Larmer, *Zambia, Mining and Neoliberalism*, 65.

[13]   For an overview of the legal framework, see Ndinawe Mtonga Ruppert et al, 'Law, Global Value Chains and Upgrading the Mining Industry: A Case Study of Zambia' (2021) 29(4) *African Journal of International and Comparative Law* 521, 530–1.

[14]   Adam and Sompasa, 'The Economics of the Copper Price Boom in Zambia', 66–7.

family, with large operations in India but headquartered in London – took its place, eventually owning 79.4 per cent of KCM's shares, the Zambian government owning the rest.[15] And then, in 2005, the price of copper soared. Other than in the immediate aftermath of the 2008 financial crisis, its price has remained high ever since, fueled by demand that has doubled over the period from the mid-1990s to 2019.[16] In the years ahead, demand for copper is expected to grow further given copper's contribution to laptops and smartphones,[17] construction projects and household goods, green technologies and electric cars.[18]

With the second largest reserve in Africa, and as the seventh largest producer in the world, Zambia will remain at the centre of demand for copper.[19] To meet this demand, mining companies like Vedanta Resources separate copper ore from the earth in which it is found, an operation which requires heavy machinery to blast and grind the earth, before mixing the copper ore with water and chemicals to separate the copper from unwanted rocks. If not carefully controlled, this process can lead to toxic waste contaminating the water that others use for drinking, cooking, cleaning, farming and fishing.[20] In the Zambian case *Nyasulu v KCM*, 2,000 claimants alleged that KCM's mining operation at Nchanga fell below the standard of care in common law negligence, causing water pollution which harmed their health and degraded their farmland.[21] The court found that KCM had acted with 'gross recklessness'[22] and with 'no regard for human, animal and plant life'.[23] It awarded the claimants approximately US$1.5 million in general and punitive damages 'to deter others who may discharge poisonous substances without diminishing their potency to cause harm'.[24] The judgment in *Nyasulu* was later upheld by the Zambian Supreme Court,[25] but the level of damages was reduced to 'virtually nothing'.[26] Yet even if

---

[15]   On Vedanta Resources' investment in KCM, see Samarendra Das and Miriam Rose, 'Copper Colonialism: British Miner Vedanta KCM and the Copper Loot of Zambia' Foil Vedanta report (2014) (available at http://www.foilvedanta.org/articles/copper-colonialism-foil-vedanta-zambia-report-launched/).

[16]   Linda Scott Jakobsson, 'Copper with a Cost: Human Rights and Environmental Risks in the Mineral Supply Chain of ICT: A Case Study from Zambia' Swedwatch Report No 94 (2019) (available at https://swedwatch.org/wp-content/uploads/2019/05/94_Zambia_190429_enk elsidor.pdf).

[17]   Copper is an excellent conductor of electricity, and for that reason is the largest metal component of smartphones.

[18]   Jakobsson, 'Copper with a Cost', 17.

[19]   Liebenthal and Cheelo, 'The Boom-Bust Cycle', 24.

[20]   Jakobsson, 'Copper with a Cost', 18.

[21]   *Nyasulu v KCM* [2011] ZMHC 86 J2.

[22]   ibid., J20.

[23]   ibid., J21.

[24]   ibid., J22.

[25]   *Nyasulu v Konkola Copper Mines plc* [2015] ZMSC 33.

[26]   John Vidal, 'I drank the water and ate the fish. We all did. The acid has damaged me permanently' *The Guardian* 1 August 2015 (available at https://www.theguardian.com/glo bal-development/2015/aug/01/zambia-vedanta-pollution-village-copper-mine).

the Zambian Supreme Court had not set aside the award of damages, many feared that KCM would 'not ultimately be good for the money'[27] because it 'may have insufficient resources to meet the claims'.[28] That fear prompted the claimants in *Lungowe* – who argue that the same Nchanga mine 'repeated[ly] discharge[d] ... toxic matter' into watercourses[29] – to turn to the English courts. Katharina Pistor's *The Code of Capital* explains why KCM's inability to compensate is far from unusual.

Pistor's *The Code of Capital*

The Code of Capital argues that an asset will become 'capital', and so generate wealth for its owner, when lawyers 'code' that asset. The asset might be part of the natural environment, like the copper found in Zambia; or it might be an intangible asset, like an idea or a promise. Pistor uses the term 'code' to name the process whereby lawyers combine parts of the law of contract and property law, collateral law and the law of trusts, corporate law and bankruptcy law to bestow legal attributes on the chosen asset. Her insight is that the asset's legal attributes make it capable of producing wealth for the asset owner. Four such attributes stand out: priority, durability, universality and convertibility. Priority privileges the asset holder's claim ahead of other claims, such as when collateral law gives the asset holder a security interest and when bankruptcy law ranks that claim ahead of the claims of unsecured creditors.[30] Durability extends the asset holder's claim to priority over time, doing so through trusts and corporate structures that insulate the asset and the revenue it generates from the claims of others.[31] Universality makes the asset holder's claims to priority and durability good against the whole world. And convertibility provides a type of insurance: it enables the asset holder to shift into state money even when 'they can no longer find private takers' for the asset.[32] Once an asset has been legally coded – once it has all or many of these legal attributes bestowed on it – 'it is fit for generating wealth for its holder'.[33]

How, then, do the corporate lawyers who serve MNCs legally code the copper mined in Zambia?[34] Space constraints prevent consideration of all four legal attributes with respect to copper. But given the work performed by the attribute

---

[27] *Lungowe & Others v Vedanta Resources plc & Anor* [2016] EWHC 975, 22.

[28] ibid., [24].

[29] *Lungowe v Vedanta Resources plc* [2019] UKSC 20, 1.

[30] Pistor, *The Code of Capital*, 13.

[31] ibid., 14.

[32] ibid., 13–15.

[33] ibid., 3.

[34] *The Code of Capital* focuses on the Global North. Yet Pistor's work prior to *The Code of Capital* was mostly about the Global South, and the implications of her argument in *The Code of Capital* apply also to countries 'on the periphery of global capitalism' (Katharina Pistor, 'Coding Capital: On the Power and Limits of (Private) Law: A Rejoinder' (2021) 30(2) *Social & Legal Studies* 317, 321).

of durability in the context of mining in Zambia, the next section focuses on the corporate structures which extend that durability.

Entity shielding and loss shifting

Until 2019, the shares of Vedanta Resources, a company incorporated in England, were listed on the London Stock Exchange and held by institutional and retail investors.[35] Vedanta Resources in turn owned shares in subsidiary companies incorporated in both its 'home' jurisdiction of England and in jurisdictions around the world – including KCM in Zambia. One of these subsidiaries (the India incorporated Sesa Sterlite) was in turn parent company to, and hence owned the shares of, several of its own subsidiaries. Why do lawyers create such corporate group structures? They may do so for tax purposes or to comply with the regulatory requirements of the jurisdictions in which the group operates.[36] Yet 'it is likely that the ability to asset partition – and therefore facilitate judgment-proofing and limiting the group's liability – is the largest benefit for businesses'.[37]

Asset partitioning or shielding builds on the separate legal personality of each entity within the corporate group. As distinct entities, each company alone is responsible for its actions and liable for its debts. By contrast, the entity's shareholders – whether another entity or outside investors – are not responsible for the company's actions nor are they liable for its debts. That distinction matters where a subsidiary within the group undertakes operations that entail risk, such as the risk of toxic discharge at the Nchanga mine. We have seen that local farmers harmed by this pollution successfully obtained judgment against KCM; we have also seen that KCM is unlikely to pay out much (if any) of this compensation. In these circumstances, claimants might turn to Vedanta Resources because the parent company will likely have the means to meet any judgment against it. But if claimants make that move, they will encounter the logic of separate legal personality and limited liability: it is the subsidiary and not the parent company that has caused the harm, hence it is the subsidiary and not the parent company that is liable to pay compensation. And it is this logic that shields the parent company's assets – including past revenues generated by the subsidiary and transferred to the parent – from the subsidiary's judgment creditors. That makes the group structure judgment-proof: the subsidiary is liable but is unable to pay; the parent can pay but is not liable.[38] And a judgment-proof group structure 'can

---

[35]   See Das and Rose, 'Copper Colonialism', 8, for a simplified overview of Vedanta Resources' corporate structure as of June 2013, and the same authors (at 26) for a list of Vedanta Resources' shareholders as of December 2013.

[36]   See Barnali Choudhury and Martin Petrin, *Corporate Duties to the Public* (Cambridge University Press, 2019) 96.

[37]   ibid.

[38]   On judgment-proofing, see Lynn M. LoPucki, 'The Death of Liability' (1996) 106(1) *Yale Law Journal* 1.

extend the life span of assets and asset pools'.[39] In short, it adds to the asset the legal attribute of durability.

Slade LJ in *Adams v Cape Industries plc* – a judgment to which we return later – said such a use of the corporate structure 'is inherent in [UK] corporate law'.[40] It follows that corporate lawyers may deliberately design group structures 'to capture the upside, while shifting the downside to others – including employees, tort creditors, and the public at large'.[41] Shifting the downside to others blunts the goals of tort law because it will 'under-produce compensation and deterrence'.[42] Entity shielding and loss shifting undermine deterrence because, if a defendant knows that they are shielded from liability, then any potential judgment will not serve as an effective means of altering the defendant's behaviour. And the strategies documented by Pistor restrict compensation because claimants such as those in *Nyasulu* do not receive that which must be resorted to them to correct past wrongs. Perhaps these limits to tort law account for the mere fleeting references to it in *The Code of Capital*: when it does feature it does so where tort creditors have a judgment in their favour but which they cannot enforce because the lawyers hired or employed by MNCs have made the corporate group judgment-proof.[43]

Roving capital

Given tort law's limits as a means of deterring or correcting wrongs, is environmental regulation an alternative to tort law? Insights from *The Code of Capital* explain why environmental regulation often fails as an alternative, at least in contexts like the mining sector in Zambia. In his review of *The Code of Capital*, Iagê Miola observes that countries such as Zambia lurch between two extremes: they are 'either a successful destination of transplants that harmonize the [laws] demanded by global capital', or global capital avoids the countries of the Global South because their legal systems do not offer 'good prospects for coding'.[44] Pistor reinforces that point when she tells us 'today's capital is of the roving kind; it has and needs no (physical) home and instead moves from place

---

[39] Pistor, *The Code of Capital*, 14.

[40] *Adams v Cape Industries plc* [1990] Ch 433, 544.

[41] Pistor, *The Code of Capital*, 59.

[42] Joshua Ulan Galperin and Douglas A. Kysar, 'Uncommon Law: Judging in the Anthropocene' in Jolene Lin and Douglas A. Kysar (eds), *Climate Change Litigation in the Asia Pacific* (Cambridge University Press, 2020, 15–37) (also available at https://papers.ssrn.com/sol3/papers.cfm?abstract_id=3650360. The quotation is at page 12 of the latter version).

[43] There are five references to tort law (or tort creditors) in *The Code of Capital*: two references in the context of entity shielding/loss shifting (55 and 59); two references in the context of conflict of laws (69 and 135); and one reference as part of a general discussion about the obstacles faced by 'would-be plaintiffs' when trying to access the courts (214).

[44] Iagê Z. Miola, '(De)coding Capital in the Periphery' (2021) 30 *Social & Legal Studies* 296, 299.

to place in search of new opportunities'.[45] States like Zambia participate in the process, subjecting themselves to regulatory competition as they design domestic laws to attract investors.[46]

We saw earlier that in the mid-1990s the World Bank encouraged Zambia to pass the Investment Act 1995 and the Mines and Minerals Act 1995. Both reflected a shift towards an 'investor friendly policy regime',[47] an aspect of which was later captured by the Zambian government's summary of its efforts to attract investment, specifically that '[i]nvestors face no restriction on the amount of interest, profit, dividends, management fees, technical fees and royalties' that they may distribute from Zambia to their jurisdiction of choice.[48] Development agreements between the Zambian state and MNCs provide the latter with further advantages, including: further reductions to their already low rate of corporation tax;[49] limitations to their exposure to fines and penalties under environmental laws;[50] and the Zambian state's assumption of responsibility for past environmental damage.[51]

Such investor-friendly policies are not unique to Zambia. In recent decades, across both the Global North and South, their adoption responds, on the one hand, to the fear that the government might alter laws and regulations to the detriment of investors.[52] On the other hand, their adoption coincided with a sense that government regulation via detailed rules backed by criminal sanctions – so-called top-down 'command-and-control' regulation – was and is sometimes ineffective and counterproductive.[53] From the 1990s, organisations like the World Bank consciously shifted to a different view of regulation, one which the academic literature associates with 'regulatory governance',[54] and which in Zambia took the form of what Dan Haglund calls 'the partnership approach

---

[45]   Pistor, *The Code of Capital*, 220.

[46]   See also Sol Picciotto, *Regulating Global Corporate Capitalism* (Cambridge University Press, 2011) 454; and Horst Eidenmüller, 'The Transnational Law Market, Regulatory Competition, and Transnational Corporations' (2011) 18(2) *Indiana Journal of Global Legal Studies* 707.

[47]   Lungu, 'Socio-Economic Change and Natural Resource Exploitation', 547.

[48]   Zambia Development Agency, *Zambia Review* (14th edn, Ministry of Commerce, Trade and Industry, 2013) 24. Quoted in Das and Rose, 'Copper Colonialism', 5.

[49]   Adam and Sompasa, 'The Economics of the Copper Price Boom in Zambia', 67–8.

[50]   'Management of Environmental Degradation Caused by Mining Activities in Zambia', Report of the Auditor General of the Republic of Zambia, July 2014, 16.

[51]   Lungu, 'Socio-Economic Change and Natural Resource Exploitation', 551–3; Joanna Lindahl, 'Environmental Impacts of Mining in Zambia: Towards Better Environmental Management and Sustainable Exploitation of Mineral Resources' SGU-rapport 2014:22 (Geological Survey of Sweden 2014) (available at http://resource.sgu.se/produkter/sgurapp/s1422-rapport.pdf).

[52]   See Navroz K. Dubash and Bronwen Morgan, 'Understanding the Rise of the Regulatory State of the South' (2012) 6(3) *Regulation & Governance* 261, 265.

[53]   Sol Picciotto, 'Regulation: Managing the Antinomies of Economic Vice and Virtue' (2017) 26(6) *Social & Legal Studies* 676, 679.

[54]   ibid., 680. For an example of the World Bank embracing these ideas, see World Bank, *Greening Industry: New Roles for Communities, Markets, and Governments* (Oxford University Press, 2000).

to regulating the mining sector'.[55] Regulators monitor their private-sector 'partners', persuading and negotiating in response to compliance problems. But otherwise, mining companies self-regulate through internal control systems, in-house compliance officers and corporate social responsibility initiatives.[56]

Yet as Penelope Simons and Audrey Macklin observe, self-regulatory regimes 'can be misleading because they tend to apply indicators of "success" that bear little relationship to the effects "on the ground"'.[57] Earlier we documented the impact 'on the ground' of water pollution for the farming community near the Nchanga mine. Consider now the challenges facing Zambia's environmental regulatory agency – Zambia Environmental Management Agency (ZEMA) and its predecessor, the Environment Council of Zambia (ECZ). In 2006 a report to Zambia's parliament concluded that 'ECZ was not well equipped, especially in terms of manpower, to carry out regular compliance visits'; the report then documented the problems encountered by ECZ as it tried to respond to pollution at KCM's Nchanga mine.[58] In 2014, a report by Zambia's Auditor General found that '[d]ue to lack of capacity and resources, most institutions including ZEMA ... were unable to carry out monitoring regularly and consistently as they are mandated';[59] like the earlier report, this report also documents examples of mining companies (including KCM) failing to comply with environmental laws, failures that 'ZEMA was unable to take any action against ... as ... the Development Agreement virtually gave the company immunity against any punitive measures by the Government and any of its agencies'.[60] As the court in *Nyasulu* observed, the Zambian regulator operates under 'difficult circumstances'.[61] Perhaps impossible circumstances: where self-regulation fails, the environment agency – gutted of the resources to deter – must sway MNCs deft at exploiting global regulatory competition.

From 'governance gap' to distributional conflict

Consider how the threads of the discussion so far may be brought together. In *The Code of Capital,* corporate lawyers code assets by bestowing upon them legal attributes that turn assets into a source of wealth for the asset's owner.

55   Dan Haglund, 'From Boom to Bust: Diversity and Regulation in Zambia's Privatized Copper Sector' in Fraser and Larmer, *Zambia, Mining and Neoliberalism,* 109.

56   See any of Vedanta's Sustainable Development Reports, which cover health and safety management, stakeholder engagement, human rights and environmental protection.

57   Penelope Simons and Audrey Macklin (eds), *The Governance Gap* (Oxford University Press, 2014) 12.

58   Report of the Committee on Energy, Environment and Tourism for the First Session of the Tenth National Assembly, appointed on 8 November 2006, 9–11.

59   'Management of Environmental Degradation Caused by Mining Activities in Zambia', Report of the Auditor General of the Republic of Zambia, July 2014, x.

60   ibid., 19.

61   *Nyasulu v KCM* [2011] ZMHC 86 J2, J22.

The copper mined in Zambia is one such asset, the extraction of which has polluted waterways to the detriment of local farmers. Yet when these farmers turn to tort law to remedy that harm, they find mining companies deploying corporate structures that shield wealth and limit liability – deployments that blunt tort law's capacity to deter or to correct wrongs. And if those harmed turn to environmental laws and regulatory agencies to police mining companies, they find exemptions from environmental laws to attract 'roving capital' and resource deprived regulatory agencies expected to 'partner' with the very MNCs that they are mandated to regulate.

It is no coincidence that Zambian farmers face these obstacles, for Pistor's analysis suggests that the obstacles which frustrate the farmers are from the opposite perspective the very legal attributes that advantage asset owners. The insight that advantages for some correspond to disadvantages for others invokes the work of Wesley Hohfeld.[62] To illustrate this correspondence, Hohfeld considers the relations between right and duty and between what he calls privilege and no-right. In his scheme, a *privilege* is a type of liberty and allows one party to act (or not) as they see fit even if another finds that decision objectionable; the other party has *no right* to a legal remedy in response to the exercise of the privilege. By contrast, if the party who objects holds a *right*, then they may call upon a legal remedy to curtail the objectionable conduct – in other words, the privilege to act or not act becomes a *duty* to accommodate the right of the party who objects.[63] Hohfeld's insight is that the right of one party must correspond to another's duty, just as a privilege must correspond to the absence of a legal remedy; as Joe Singer explains, 'correlatives express a single legal relation from the point of view of the two parties'.[64]

So, when scholars describe the effect of corporate structures and regulatory competition as a 'regulatory void',[65] 'zones of weak governance'[66] and 'a *governance gap*',[67] they capture the perspective of one side of a legal relation. Terms like 'gap', 'void' and 'zone' suggest a law-free space. And from the perspective of those harmed by the MNC, there is indeed a 'gap' or 'void' in the sense that they are without legal protection. Yet when viewed from the perspective of the MNC, this 'gap' or 'void' is, in Hohfeld's terminology, a privilege to act or not

---

[62] Anna Chadwick observes 'something Hohfeldian' in Pistor's effort in *The Code of Capital*. See Anna Chadwick 'Capital Without Capitalism? Or Capitalism Without Determinism?' (2021) 30(2) *Social & Legal Studies* 302, 304.

[63] Wesley Hohfeld, 'Some Fundamental Legal Conceptions as Applied in Legal Reasoning' (1913) 23(1) *Yale Law Journal* 16. For an insightful discussion of Hohfeld's framework, see Anna di Robilant and Talha Syed, 'Property's Building Blocks: Hohfeld in Europe and Beyond' (2020) (available at https://papers.ssrn.com/sol3/papers.cfm?abstract_id=3710102).

[64] Joseph William Singer, 'The Legal Rights Debate in Analytical Jurisprudence from Bentham to Hohfeld' (1982) 1982(6) *Wisconsin Law Review* 975, 987.

[65] Simons and Macklin, *The Governance Gap*, 17.

[66] ibid., 2, 16.

[67] ibid., 9, emphasis in original.

act as the MNC sees fit. That privilege grants the MNC permission to injure others, others who must then carry the burden of this legalised injury.[68]

As Duncan Kennedy suggests, it may be that few see 'rules of permission as ground rules at all, by contrast with rules of prohibition',[69] because the former may often be invisible, taken-for-granted common sense.[70] To illustrate the point, Kennedy adds '[w]ithin the category of legal permissions, perhaps the most invisible is the decision not to impose a duty to act on a person who is capable of preventing another's loss or injury or misfortune'.[71] With that point in mind, consider again the corporate structures that shield assets and limit liability. The logic of separate legal personality and limited liability entails that it is the subsidiary and not the parent company that has caused the harm, hence it is the subsidiary and not the parent company that is liable to pay compensation. Notice, however, that for such an arrangement to advantage the parent company, it relies not only on the logic of separate legal personality and limited liability, but also on those 'most invisible' of legal ground rules – that acts will be treated differently from failures to act to prevent 'another's loss or injury or misfortune'.[72] Suppose, for example, that the parent company has powers of control over the subsidiary and could use these to prevent the toxic discharges that pollute the waterways. In these circumstances, the corporate group's judgment-proofing strategy will only succeed provided the parent's failure to prevent such a discharge does not result in liability. The MNC benefits from, and those harmed by the discharge are burdened by, the assumption that omissions attract less liability than acts.[73] But that absence of liability, which from the perspective of those harmed may look like a gap, is from the perspective of the MNC a powerful legal advantage – one

---

68   On Hohfeld and company law, see Malcolm Rogge, 'Business, Human Rights, and the Jural Relations of Corporate Law: Interpreting the Global Economic System Through Wesley Hohfeld's Philosophy of Jural Relations', author's manuscript, forthcoming 2024. See also Pierre Schlag, 'Hohfeldian Analysis, Liberalism, and Adjudication (Some Tensions)' in Shyamkrishna Balganesh, Ted Sichelman and Henry E. Smith (eds), *Wesley Hohfeld A Century Later: Edited Work, Select Personal Papers, and Original Commentaries* (Cambridge University Press, 2022) 441.

69   Duncan Kennedy, 'The Stakes of Law, or Hale and Foucault!' (1991) 15(4) *Legal Studies Forum* 327, 333.

70   See also Dennis M. Davies and Karl Klare, 'Critical Legal Realism in a Nutshell', in Emilios Christodoulidis, Ruth Dukes and Marco Goldoni (eds), *Research Handbook on Critical Legal Theory* (Edward Elgar Publishing, 2019) 27.

71   Kennedy, 'The Stakes of Law', 334. A further example of a taken-for-granted ground rule is the recognition of the legal personality of a foreign corporation outside the jurisdiction of its incorporation. Without that recognition, a MNC would not be able to own shares in companies incorporated outside of its home jurisdiction. See Clair Quentin, 'Corporations, Comity and the "Revenue Rule": A Jurisprudence of Offshore' (2020) 8(3) *London Review of International Law* 399.

72   Kennedy, 'The Stakes of Law', 334.

73   See *Stovin v Wise* [1996] AC 923 (HL); and *Smith v Littlewoods Organisation Ltd* [1987] AC 241 (HL).

which allows it to choose not to act, and to be free from liability for any injury inflicted on others by that choice.

The rest of this chapter explores how *Lungowe* builds on *Chandler* to surmount some of these obstacles, including less visible obstacles such as the act/no act distinction.[74] Hohfeld's insight guides that exploration, for it both makes these obstacles visible and creates an opening to reassess tort law's contribution to the legal coding of assets. In *The Code of Capital*, tort creditors appear only when frustrated by corporate group structures that limit tort law's capacity to deter or to repair past wrongs. But under Hohfeld's guidance it becomes difficult to ignore the act/no act distinction as a legal device that empowers asset owners to sidestep responsibility for their failure to prevent harm to others. And once this privilege is visible, once we see that the advantages it confers on asset owners correspond to disadvantages for others, a further possible role for tort law, besides deterrence and corrective justice, presents itself: tort law's allocation of benefits and burdens make it a site of distributional conflict;[75] for that reason, tort law may be used 'as a tool in social justice struggle',[76] as a device to challenge taken-for-granted assumptions by asking of corporate structures and the act/no act distinction: why must these arrangements work to the advantage of MNCs and to the disadvantage of others?

'Strategic behavior in interpretation'

One way to see shifts in law's distribution of benefits and burdens is to follow Duncan Kennedy and view law 'as a medium in which one pursues a project'.[77] On such a view it is not the legal materials themselves that decide outcomes, but rather the deployment of these materials by lawyers and judges in pursuit of that project. Their project may be inspired by a 'sense of justice'[78] and an awareness that legal arrangements strike 'the wrong balance between two identifiable conflicting groups'.[79] Suppose that a group of 'public interest' lawyers conclude

---

[74] For an overview of tort litigation against MNCs in the UK courts over the past 25 years, see Richard Meeran, 'Perspectives on the Development and Significance of Tort Litigation against Multinational Parent Companies' in Richard Meeran (ed), *Human Rights Litigation Against Multinationals in Practice* (Cambridge University Press, 2021) 24. Richard Meeran is Head of the International Department at Leigh Day, the law firm that has brought almost all this litigation, including *Chandler* and *Lungowe*.

[75] Peter Cane, 'Distributive Justice and Tort Law' (2001) 4 *New Zealand Law Review* 401.

[76] Leslie Bender, 'Tort Law's Role as a Tool for Social Justice Struggle' (1998) 37(2) *Washburn Law Journal* 249. See also Anita Bernstein, '*Muss Es Sein?* Not Necessarily, Says Tort Law' (2004) 67(4) *Law and Contemporary Problems* 7.

[77] Duncan Kennedy, 'Freedom and Constraint in Adjudication: A Critical Phenomenology' (1986) 36(4) *Journal of Legal Education* 518, 526. This paper is also in Duncan Kennedy, *Legal Reasoning: Collected Essays* (The Davies Group Publishers, 2008) 11.

[78] ibid., 526.

[79] ibid., 519.

that corporate structures and the act/no act distinction do indeed strike the wrong balance between MNCs and those who live near the Nchanga mine. How might these lawyers assist the latter against that hostile legal regime?[80]

Public interest lawyers and sympathetic judges might try to destabilise that legal regime. They might do so either by showing that the initially taken-for-granted legal outcome is inaccurate and that the legal materials necessitate a different outcome; or by showing that the initially apprehended legal outcome is only one possible outcome among alternatives.[81] Kennedy calls this work 'strategic behavior in interpretation'.[82] It serves to 'create or undo determinacy'[83] and it draws upon the techniques of legal reasoning to do so – distinguishing and drawing analogies between cases, construing statutes broadly or narrowly, classifying issues as relevant to one body of doctrine rather than or as well as another. These techniques open up argumentative strategies because, in the words of Walter Wheeler Cook, legal norms 'are in the habit of hunting in pairs'.[84] Karl Llewellyn's insight that law 'speaks with a forked tongue' captures the same idea,[85] one that Llewellyn illustrates by presenting the canons of statutory interpretation as moves of 'thrust' versus 'parry'.[86] Kennedy's own work builds on legal realists like Llewellyn when matching stereotypical argument 'bites' with 'counter-bites' – for example: 'the defendant should have looked out for the plaintiff's interests' vs 'the plaintiff should have looked out for his own interests'; or 'people have a right to be secure from (this kind of) injury' vs 'people have a right to freedom of (this kind of) action'; and so on.[87] These interpretative strategies explain why lawyers and (or) judges inspired by a sense of social justice have scope to manoeuvre and manipulate, reconstruct and reframe the legal materials – the statutes, the case law, the doctrine – to displace that which had initially appeared as the common-sense understanding of the law. Their efforts will not always succeed.[88] But where someone has the time, resources and motivation to attempt to reinterpret the materials, then we cannot discount 'the possibility that legal work will destabilise the initial apprehension of what the legal materials require'.[89]

---

80 The account that follows is indebted to Joanne Conaghan, 'Celebrating Duncan Kennedy's Scholarship: A "Crit" Analysis of *DSD & NBV v Commissioner of Police for the Metropolis*' (2015) 5(4) *Transnational Legal Theory* 601.

81 Duncan Kennedy, 'A Left Phenomenological Alternative to the Hart/Kelsen Theory of Legal Interpretation' in Kennedy, *Legal Reasoning*, 153, 159.

82 ibid.

83 ibid.

84 Walter Wheeler Cook, 'Book Reviews' (1929) 38(3) *Yale Law Journal* 402, 406.

85 Karl N. Llewellyn, 'Some Realism About Realism – Responding to Dean Pound' (1931) 44(8) *Harvard Law Review* 1222, 1252.

86 Karl N. Llewellyn, 'Remarks on the Theory of Appellate Decision and the Rules or Canons about How Statutes Are to Be Construed' (1950) 3(3) *Vanderbilt Law Review* 395.

87 Duncan Kennedy, 'A Semiotics of Legal Argument' (1991) 42 *Syracuse Law Review* 75.

88 Kennedy, 'A Left Phenomenological Alternative', 160–1, 170.

89 ibid., 169.

One specific type of strategic behaviour in interpretation is legal work that deploys an exception to challenge the general rule that initially appears to cover the situation. We have already observed two such general rules: that the parent company is legally separate from the subsidiary company; and that the failure of one party to prevent a third party from harming another does not result in liability.[90] Yet both general rules are subject to exceptions. In company law, courts sometimes set aside separate legal personality when they 'lift the corporate veil', doing so because, for example, the facts indicate that the parent–subsidiary relationship is a sham.[91] And in tort law the courts sometimes draw on the exceptions identified by Lord Goff in *Smith v Littlewoods Organisation Ltd*[92] to impose liability on a person for failing to prevent harm to another, doing so where, for example, there is a special relationship between the defendant and the claimant either due to an assumption of responsibility by the defendant or due to the control exercised by the defendant. *Home Office v Dorset Yacht*[93] is a classic example of that exception: the Home Office had control over Borstal boys, that control gave rise to a 'special relationship' between the Home Office and third parties, and that special relationship placed responsibility with the Home Office for damage done by the Borstal trainees to one such third party, in this case the owner of a yacht.

When public interest lawyers and sympathetic judges do the work of strategic behaviour in interpretation, exceptions have the potential to serve as a 'parry' (in Llewellyn's terminology) to the 'thrust' of the general rule, a 'counter-bite' (in Kennedy's terminology) to the 'bite' of the initially taken-for-granted, self-evident interpretation of the situation. Recall, however, that the legal materials do not themselves decide outcomes. For an exception to destabilise the legal materials that initially appear to favour the MNC, the lawyers and judges who deploy that exception must make two strategic moves.[94] A strategic interpreter's first move is to decide how to frame the situation: should the situation be categorised as a matter of company law or tort law or some other area of law? That decision matters because sometimes the general rule is hard to shift and, moreover, the lawyers acting for the claimant will have limited time and resources.[95] Once our strategic interpreter decides how to frame the situation, they must then make a second move: their task now is to work on their argumentative strategy to develop as strong a legal argument as the materials, time constraints and resources allow. It is to these two moves and their contribution to *Chandler* that we now turn.

---

90   See *Stovin v Wise* [1996] AC 923 (HL); and *Smith v Littlewoods Organisation Ltd* [1987] AC 241 (HL).

91   For an overview of veil lifting, see Alan Dignam and John Lowry, *Company Law* (10th edn, Oxford University Press, 2018), chapter 3.

92   [1987] AC 241 (HL).

93   [1970] AC 1004; 2 WLR 1140.

94   I borrow these strategic moves from Conaghan, 'Celebrating Duncan Kennedy's Scholarship'.

95   Kennedy, 'A Left Phenomenological Alternative', 160–1, 170.

Chandler v Cape plc

Chandler is one of many cases dealing with the consequences of asbestos. Mr Chandler worked for Cape Building Products Ltd, a subsidiary of Cape plc. His job included stacking asbestos bricks and in 2007 he was diagnosed with the lung disease asbestosis. In the 1970s many of the employees of Cape's US subsidiary received the same diagnosis. In response, these employees successfully sued the US subsidiary, only to discover that it had no assets. So, in *Adams*, they sued the UK parent company,[96] a move that proved unsuccessful because of the general rule that we encountered earlier: it is the subsidiary and not the parent company that has caused the harm, hence it is the subsidiary and not the parent company that is liable to pay compensation. It is against this background that Mr Chandler sought compensation from Cape plc. His direct employer, Cape Building Products Ltd, was defunct and so could not pay him compensation. Its parent company, Cape plc, did have the financial means to pay him compensation, but claiming against it ran into the logic of separate legal personality: why should the parent company be held responsible for the actions of another legal entity?

Move 1: company law or tort law?

Mr Chandler's legal team set in motion their first strategic move when they asked: is this a company law case, or is it possible and favourable to cast the situation another way? Company law would only help the claimant if the court felt able to lift the corporate veil and set aside the separate legal personality of the parent company. But the shadow cast by *Adams* cautioned against veil piercing as a strategy. Not only did *Adams* refuse to lift the veil, it also stressed '[i]f a company chooses to arrange the affairs of its group in such a way that the business carried on in a particular foreign country is the business of its subsidiary and not its own, it is, in our judgment, entitled to do so', adding: '[n]either in this class of case nor in any other class of case is it open to this court to disregard [separate legal personality] merely because it considers it just so to do'.[97] Case law since *Adams* has confirmed this hostility to veil lifting, with the consequence that strategic interpretation that utilises veil piercing to parry the thrust of separate corporate personality will likely fail.[98]

Against that background, both Mr Chandler's legal team and Williams J in his judgment decided not to frame the case as a matter of company law, Williams J emphasising that 'this is not a case in which it would be appropriate to "pierce the corporate veil"'.[99] Instead, both turned to tort law and asked: did Cape plc owe

---

[96] *Adams v Cape Industries plc* [1990] Ch 433.

[97] ibid., 537.

[98] See *Prest v Petrodel Resources Ltd* [2013] 3 WLR 1; and *VTB Capital plc v Nutritek International Corp* [2012] EWCA Civ 808.

[99] *Chandler v Cape plc* [2011] EWHC 951 (QB), 66.

Mr Chandler a duty of care in negligence? So framing the situation set Williams J his task – to apply the *Caparo* 'three-stage test' to the facts before him.[100] But this was not an easy task. When discussing the genesis of the legal strategy that succeeded in *Chandler*, one of the lawyers involved later observed: '[t]he approach was canvassed with a senior Queen's Counsel and a retired appeal court judge, both of whom agreed that it was an interesting and novel idea that would never succeed'.[101] Why then did the strategy succeed? Answering this question takes us to Williams J's second strategic move: he set about fashioning a legal argument out of the materials of tort law.

Move 2: fashioning a strong legal argument

To fashion that argument, Williams J first considered *Connolly v The RTZ Corporation*.[102] Mr Connolly's cancer was caused by working in a uranium mine in Namibia while in the employment of an RTZ subsidiary. His claim failed because his action was time barred under the Limitation Act 1980. Even so, Wright J took a sympathetic view of the substance of his claim: although '[t]he situation would be an unusual one', 'in appropriate circumstances' the actions of a parent company could satisfy *Caparo* where the parent company takes responsibility for the health and safety of its subsidiary's employees.[103] Building on Wright J's remarks in *Connolly*, Williams J then turned to the *Caparo* test. He had to establish 'proximity', which in turn required countering the rule 'that generally the law imposes no duty upon a party to prevent a third party from causing damage to another'.[104] Could Williams J fashion a 'parry' from the exceptions that set limits to the 'thrust' of this general rule?

To fashion that parry, Williams J turned to *Smith v Littlewoods*[105] and the exception to the general rule that covers situations where the defendant has assumed responsibility for the wellbeing of the claimant or where the defendant has control over the third party.[106] Williams J had to establish that the facts of the case positioned it closer to this exception than the general rule. To that end,

---

[100] *Caparo Industries v Dickman* [1990] 2 AC 605. Under this test, a duty of care is established where (i) it's reasonably foreseeable that the defendant's conduct will cause harm; (ii) there is a relationship of proximity between the parties; and (iii) it's fair, just and reasonable to impose a duty. Note, however, that if Williams J had to determine the existence of a duty of care in negligence after 2018, he would need to consider *Robinson v Chief Constable of West Yorkshire Police* [2018] UKSC 4, where Lord Reed challenged the notion that *Caparo* established a 'test' for determining the existence of a duty of care, and instead invited the courts to develop the law 'incrementally and by analogy with established authorities' (21).

[101] See Meeran, 'Perspectives on the Development and Significance of Tort Litigation', 26.

[102] [1999] CLC 533.

[103] ibid, [1999] CLC 533.

[104] *Chandler v Cape plc* [2011] EWHC 951 (QB), 71.

[105] *Smith v Littlewoods Organisation Ltd* [1987] AC 241 (HL).

[106] *Chandler v Cape plc* [2011] EWHC 951 (QB), 71.

he observed: the parent company employed a medical officer with responsibility for the wellbeing of employees across the corporate group; it was the parent company, and 'not the individual subsidiary companies, which dictated policy in relation to health and safety issues'; and it was the parent company that '[a]t any stage … could have intervened and Cape Products would have bowed to its intervention'.[107] Williams J could then conclude that these facts 'established a sufficient degree of proximity between the Defendant and [Mr Chandler]';[108] that proximity demonstrated that Cape plc had assumed responsibility for the wellbeing of Cape Products' employees; and its failure to act to rectify the subsidiary's inadequate health and safety policy was a breach of its duty of care.

Will the exception to the general rule 'stick'? Or is it too 'out-of-the-ordinary'?

Did Williams J succeed at fashioning a strong legal argument? Could he get his 'position to stick'?[109] Would his position convince appellate judges with the power to reverse it? Would it 'convince the good faith observer struggling to understand what the law is'?[110] Or would it appear as too great a stretch, as a result that is too 'out-of-the-ordinary'?[111] Consider Cape plc's appeal against Williams J's judgment.[112] Since all parent companies exercise some control over subsidiaries, Cape argued that to support a finding that the parent had assumed responsibility, Williams J needed to identify those features of the relationship between Cape plc and Cape Products that 'were unusual or outwith'[113] the '[n]ormal incidents'[114] of parent-subsidiary relations – such as, for example, where 'the parent has absolute control of the subsidiary'.[115] Williams J had failed to identify such features. Did that make his position too out-of-the-ordinary?

Arden LJ rejected that conclusion. Rather than cast Williams J's approach as novel, Arden LJ positioned it in relation to established precedent, finding that Williams J was 'correct to hold that the analogous line of cases in negligence to the instant case is the line of authority on the duty of a person to intervene to prevent damages to another'.[116] She observed Lord Goff's exceptions in *Smith* and the responsibility imposed in *Dorset Yacht*.[117] She observed also the duty of care owed by an independent contractor to the employees of the employer.[118] And

---

[107] ibid., 75.
[108] ibid.
[109] Kennedy, 'Freedom and Constraint in Adjudication', 527.
[110] ibid., 529.
[111] ibid.
[112] *Chandler v Cape plc* [2012] EWCA Civ 525.
[113] ibid., [43].
[114] ibid., [44].
[115] ibid., [66].
[116] ibid., [63].
[117] ibid., [63] and [65].
[118] ibid., [65].

she observed, as had Williams J, *Connolly v The RTZ Corporation*, where Wright J indicated that in the right circumstances a parent may owe a duty of care to the employees of its subsidiary.[119] In contrast to this established line of analogous cases, Cape's legal team could not cite any authorities that directed the court to identify 'normal incidents of the relationship between parent and subsidiary company';[120] and Arden LJ added that such an approach should be rejected because 'the way in which groups of companies operate is very varied'.[121] She preferred to see the court's task as identifying whether the parent had 'relevant control of the subsidiary's business'[122] – an exercise she hoped to help future courts perform by setting out a four-part test to identify circumstances where such control may be present.[123] Instead of rejecting Williams J's approach as out-of-the-ordinary, then, Arden LJ helped it to 'stick' by attaching it to established legal authority. By so doing, she preserved it as part of the legal materials at the disposal of the lawyers representing residents of Zambia as they confronted Vedanta Resources.

Lungowe v Vedanta Resources

Recall that the legal materials themselves do not decide outcomes. That point holds for *Chandler* too; for it to influence future cases, lawyers and judges must decide how to interpret it. And *Chandler* presents those who read it with scope for competing interpretations. Isn't the search for control overinclusive, since almost all corporate groups include group-wide policies? And isn't the search for a duty of care equivalent to veil piercing by other means? But, then again, isn't *Chandler* distinguishable – and so of narrow application – given its unusual facts, in particular that the subsidiary carried out its business on the parent's land?[124] Yet even if confining *Chandler* to its facts is too narrow a reading, what about corporate groups where there is limited overlap between the parent and its subsidiaries?[125] Will parent companies not escape liability if they defer entirely to the subsidiary on matters of health and safety? Yet is the parent company's involvement ever negligible since those who act on behalf of the parent company decide on the design of the corporate group structure, decisions that consciously shield assets and limit liability?[126]

---

[119] ibid., [66]; *Connolly v The RTZ Corporation* [1999] CLC 533.

[120] *Chandler v Cape plc* [2012] EWCA Civ 525 [67].

[121] ibid.

[122] ibid., [46].

[123] ibid., [80].

[124] ibid., [7–8]. See also Christian Witting, 'The Corporate Group: System, Design and Responsibility' (2021) 80(3) *Cambridge Law Journal* 581, 605–6.

[125] Such as was the case in *Thompson v The Renwick Group plc* [2015] 2 BCC 855.

[126] Witting, 'The Corporate Group', 601–2.

It is because *Chandler* generated these competing interpretations that some commentators criticised it for unsettling 'clearly defined boundaries'[127] – such as between company law and tort law and between acts and omissions. Does this blurring of boundaries have 'the potential to open the floodgates?'[128] In response to that possibility it is worth reemphasising Hohfeld's insight: advantages for some entail disadvantages for others. Protecting boundaries protects those who benefit from corporate structures and from the act/no act distinction. Closing the floodgate 'implies that someone else is wallowing in a floodplain elsewhere'[129] – sometimes a toxic one. By litigating, Mr Chandler named the problem: why should those least able to bear injuries caused by the negligence of subsidiaries do so to the advantage of parent companies? By finding in favour of Mr Chandler, Williams J and Arden LJ chose to confront rather than deny this problem – and by so doing, they invited future claimants and defendants, lawyers and judges to grapple with the questions thereby unleashed. How then did they grapple with these questions in *Lungowe*?

Before considering how the court in *Lungowe* navigated competing interpretations of *Chandler*, note one key difference between the two cases. Even a cursory glance at the *Lungowe* judgments will show a dispute about the English court's jurisdiction to hear the claim.[130] That issue did not arise in *Chandler* because the parent company and the subsidiary company were both incorporated in England and the claimant was a resident of England. In *Lungowe*, by contrast, 1,826 residents of Zambia brought an action in England against Vedanta Resources (incorporated in England) and against KCM (incorporated in Zambia). Is an English court the proper forum, or should the dispute be heard in Zambia? Lord Briggs gave the judgment on behalf of the Supreme Court, concluding that the case could be heard in England. To reach that conclusion, one issue he had to consider was whether there was a 'real issue to be tried': did the claimant have an arguable case or could the claim against Vedanta be rejected without a trial?

Vedanta presented Lord Briggs with several opportunities to interpret the holding in *Chandler* narrowly and find that the claimant did not have an arguable case. He could have refused to broaden the scope of *Chandler* to cover groups beside employees, such as those affected by environmental pollution. But he rejected that invitation, reasoning that in *Chandler* 'the result would surely have been the same if the dust had escaped to neighbouring land where third parties worked, lived or enjoyed recreation'.[131] In addition, or alternatively, Lord Briggs

---

127 Martin Petrin, 'Assumption of Responsibility in Corporate Groups: *Chandler v Cape plc*' (2013) 76(3) *Modern Law Review* 603, 619.

128 ibid.

129 Ewan McGaughey, '*Donoghue v Salomon* in the High Court' (2011) 4 *Journal of Personal Injury Law* 249, 258.

130 *Lungowe & Others v Vedanta Resources plc & Anor* [2016] EWHC 975; *Lungowe v Vedanta Resources plc* [2017] EWCA Civ 1528; *Lungowe v Vedanta Resources plc* [2019] UKSC 20.

131 *Lungowe v Vedanta Resources plc* [2019] UKSC 20, 52.

could have taken a sympathetic view of Vedanta's main argument, that 'this was by no means a *Chandler* type of case' because, although *Chandler* happened to feature a parent company and its subsidiary, it did not establish the liability of parent companies in relation to the activities of their subsidiaries as a distinct category of negligence.[132] Since *Chandler* had not established that category of negligence, the issue before the court in *Lungowe* was whether to assert 'a new category of negligence liability'.[133] Surely, Vedanta argued, such 'a novel and controversial issue in common law negligence made it inherently unsuitable for summary determination' of the sort performed by the lower court. But Lord Briggs rejected that conclusion, preferring to find that 'for these purposes, there is nothing special or conclusive about the bare parent/subsidiary relationship'.[134]

From that finding, it was apparent to Lord Briggs 'that the general principles that determine whether A owes a duty of care to C in respect of harmful activities by B are not novel at all'.[135] They invoke *Dorset Yacht*[136] and ask whether the parent 'exercised a sufficiently high level of supervision and control of the activities' of the subsidiary. At this point, Lord Briggs could have insisted that the claimant fit their pleaded case into Arden LJ's four-part test in *Chandler*.[137] But instead Lord Briggs noted that Arden LJ herself had indicated that the situations she identified 'were no more than particular examples of circumstances in which a duty of care may affect the parent'.[138] In Lord Briggs' view, Arden LJ's four-part test had 'if anything imposed an unnecessary straightjacket'.[139] In a similar vein, Lord Briggs also chose not to follow Sales LJ's attempt in *AAA v Unilever*[140] to 'shoehorn' corporate group structures into 'specific categories', for '[t]here is no limit to the models of management and control which may be put in place within a multinational group of companies' – models which range from the parent company as 'passive investor' at one end of the spectrum to the corporate group as 'a single commercial undertaking' at the other end.[141]

By emphasising the spectrum of corporate structures, Lord Briggs pushed beyond *Chandler*, where there was considerable overlap between the operations of the parent and those of the subsidiary, to cover what Christian Witting calls 'indirect control'.[142] Such control may entail a duty of care where, for example, the parent supervises the subsidiary's management, or provides the subsidiary with defective advice, or takes steps to train the subsidiary's employees or holds itself

---

[132] ibid., [49].
[133] ibid.
[134] ibid., [54].
[135] ibid., [54].
[136] See *Home Office v Dorset Yacht Co Ltd* [1970] AC 1004; 2 WLR 1140.
[137] *Chandler v Cape plc* [2012] EWCA Civ 525, 80.
[138] *Lungowe v Vedanta Resources plc* [2019] UKSC 20, 56.
[139] ibid., [56].
[140] [2018] EWCA Civ 1532, 36.
[141] *Lungowe v Vedanta Resources plc* [2019] UKSC 20, 51.
[142] Witting, 'The Corporate Group', 606.

out as exercising responsibilities in its published materials.[143] The commitments found in such published materials, including commitments to corporate social responsibility, are conventionally understood as voluntary, in that the company will not incur liability if it fails to meet self-imposed standards. *Lungowe* sets the limits to that convention. In its 'Embedding Sustainability' report, Vedanta 'asserted its responsibility for the establishment of appropriate group-wide environmental control and sustainability standards, for their implementation throughout the group by training, and for their monitoring and enforcement'.[144] If at trial the claimants were to show that Vedanta had failed to implement these controls and standards, then Vedanta would have failed to fulfil its responsibilities and would have hence breached the duty of care it owes to the claimants. In the event of that happening, 'voluntary' corporate social responsibility commitments would turn into legally binding obligations.

Conclusion

In December 2020 the claimants in *Lungowe* reached an out-of-court settlement with Vedanta Resources and KCM – a common outcome if the case is not dismissed or discontinued at an earlier stage.[145] Why do parties settle in such circumstances? If one of the goals of tort law is to compensate those who have been wronged, an out-of-court settlement at least provides financial compensation.[146] And that compensation combined with the threat of litigation may 'provide a potentially powerful deterrent against MNC wrongdoing',[147] which, if true, helps to achieve a second of tort law's goals. Yet notice the consequences of settlement for tort law as a site of distributional conflict: the settlement turns the antagonism between corporate lawyers and public interest lawyers into a mutually agreeable bargain. The MNC and its lawyers settle because the payment of compensation today avoids a potentially larger payment tomorrow; by making that payment, the MNC also avoids the disclosure process and averts the threat of a disadvantageous precedent.[148] And the public interest lawyers will accept the settlement too because, from their perspective, the benefits of doing so outweigh the costs: they avoid an expensive, lengthy trial; that trial

---

143   Daniel Leader, 'Human Rights Litigation against Multinationals in Practice: Lessons from the United Kingdom' in Meeran, *Human Rights Litigation Against Multinationals in Practice*, 58, 68–9.

144   *Lungowe v Vedanta Resources plc* [2019] UKSC 20, 55.

145   Angela Lindt, 'Transnational Human Rights Litigation: A Means of Obtaining Effective Remedy Abroad?' (2020) 4(2) *Journal of Legal Anthropology* 57.

146   ibid., 58.

147   Richard Meeran, 'Tort Litigation Against Multinational Corporations for Violation of Human Rights: An Overview of the Position Outside the United States' (2011) 3(1) *City University of Hong Kong Law Review* 1, 24.

148   Stuart Kirsch, 'The Role of Law in Corporate Accountability' (2020) 4(2) *Journal of Legal Anthropology* 100, 102.

is worth avoiding because they might lose; they might lose because they will be up against an 'army of corporate lawyers';[149] and by avoiding defeat the public interest lawyers get paid, for if they do not recover their costs then they won't be able to represent future claimants against MNCs.[150]

Note, however, that '[l]egal cases that are pursued represent only the tip of the iceberg of the actual harm that is done';[151] settlements represent a small subset of those pursued; and of those pursued, *Chandler* is exceptional – it remains the only case to date in which at trial a parent company has been found by an English court to owe a duty of care to those harmed by a subsidiary. In sum, claimants such as Zambian farmers face 'formidable barriers to justice'.[152] These include the corporate structures in *The Code of Capital*; and, even if against the odds a claimant dislodges these structures enough to persuade a MNC to settle, that settlement is not the same as 'a determination of justice and search for truth'.[153] What happens when claimants seek that determination but public interest lawyers from the Global North wish to settle? Do the lawyers displace and disempower those whom they represent?[154]

Has this chapter produced a similar effect of displacement? Consider its structure. It began with residents of Bangladesh and Pakistan, Chile and Peru, Nigeria and Zambia as they confront environmental degradation and labour and human rights violations. It then focused on the environmental damage caused by KCM's Nchanga copper mine. But once this chapter had identified the legal obstacles faced by the residents of Zambia, it switched perspective, and did so by turning to the ideas of Hohfeld and Kennedy to analyse the public interest lawyers who use the materials of tort law to challenge MNCs. And once we made that move, the residents of Zambia were cast as 'victims' and then displaced by the technical terms of law. Our narrative turned to the courts of the Global North, to the 'strategic behavior in interpretation' of (mostly) White men; our worldview narrowed; as it did so, it fixed on the legal vocabulary of Williams J, Arden LJ and Lord Briggs; it celebrated the work of these judges as they turned the Zambian farmers' exposure to injury into a right to protection from harm. Yet when Zambian farmers reappear in this conclusion, they do so as a party to 'an exchange relationship where the "victim" sells her right and the corporate offender calculates risk',[155] expressed as the 'price' of settlement. Doesn't that

149   Lindt, 'Transnational Human Rights Litigation', 61.
150   ibid., 65–6.
151   Meeran, 'Perspectives on the Development and Significance of Tort Litigation', 57.
152   ibid.
153   Lindt, 'Transnational Human Rights Litigation', 73.
154   Andreas Fischer-Lescano, 'From Strategic Litigation to Juridical Action' in Miriam Saage-Maaß and others (eds), *Transnational Legal Activism in Global Value Chains: The Ali Enterprises Factory Fire and the Struggle for Justice* (Springer, 2021) 299; and Sarah Knuckey and others, 'Power in Human Rights Advocate and Rightsholder Relationships: Critiques, Reforms, and Challenges' (2020) 33 *Harvard Human Rights Journal* 1.
155   Grietje Baars, ' "It's not me, it's the corporation": the Value of Corporate Accountability in the Global Political Economy' (2016) 4(1) *London Review of International Law* 1, 28.

outcome permit the MNC to continue to injure others, provided it pays the cost of settlement on those rare occasions when strategic litigation forces a settlement?

If that conclusion is accurate, then it serves to emphasise the extent to which law today – including tort law – serves to 'code' assets like the copper mined in Zambia to the advantage of the shareholders of MNCs. Perhaps strategic litigation comes with too many costs and risks to ever prove truly effective at countering these advantages. Yet choosing not to litigate comes with its own costs and risks: for one, it gives the corporate lawyers who code assets greater scope to do as they please with the legal materials; for another, choosing not to litigate places on public regulators the burden of challenging the work of corporate lawyers, regulators who, as we have seen in the context of Zambia, have limited options when MNCs can pick and choose between jurisdictions.[156] And when, in response to weak regulatory enforcement, those harmed by corporate misconduct do choose to litigate, their engagement with the world of strategic litigation need not displace and disempower if '[l]awyers working and living in the Global North … engage with individuals and groups affected by corporate exploitation in solidarity, using their privileges in a way that is driven by the interests of the affected communities'.[157] At a minimum that engagement helps us to at least name the problem: look at your smartphone; ignore, if you can, its bright and distracting screen; if you dare, look inside; inside you'll find copper; that copper may come from Zambia; it also comes at a price, and it's this price which names our problem: what do we owe each other?

Acknowledgements

For comments and advice on a draft of this paper, I thank the KLS obligations discussion group: Tobias Barkley, Shaun McVeigh, Nick Piška, Clair Quentin, Geoffrey Samuel, John Wightman and Clare Williams. My thanks also to Kirsty Horsey and to the two anonymous reviewers. All errors remain my own.

---

[156] To be clear, public regulatory agencies can and often do challenge and remedy harms. But as the example of Zambia shows, regulatory agencies are not always successful at doing so.

[157] Miriam Saage-Maaß, 'Legal Interventions and Transnational Alliances in the Ali Enterprises Case: Struggles for Workers' Rights in Global Supply Chains', in Saage-Maaß, *Transnational Legal Activism in Global Value Chains*, 25, 54.

PART III

Diverse Voices Elsewhere in Tort

7

Product Liability, Medical Devices and Harm to Women's Bodies

Emily Jackson

Introduction

The purpose of this chapter is to consider the gendered implications of product liability claims for injuries caused by dangerous medical devices. In recent years, alarmingly large numbers of women have been injured in a series of scandals involving medical devices, including (but by no means limited to) Poly Implant Prothèse (PIP) breast implants, the Essure permanent contraceptive device and transvaginal mesh.[1] In addition, there is growing evidence that devices that are implanted into both male and female bodies, such as joint replacements and cardiac devices, fail more frequently in women than they do in men. As a result, women's health is more at risk, as evidenced by, first, that the 'number of medical devices subject to recalls or warnings in the UK has risen dramatically',[2] and, second, that the risk of harm from medical devices is serious: 'nearly half of medical-device alerts were related to devices that had a reasonable probability of causing serious adverse health consequences or death'.[3]

If women are more likely to be injured by medical devices, they are also more likely to want to seek compensation for injuries caused by medical devices.[4] Women will therefore be disproportionately affected by any defects in the

---

[1] Transvaginal mesh is a net-like medical device that is used to repair weakened or damaged tissue in a woman's bladder or pelvic area.

[2] Carl Heneghan, Matthew Thompson, M. Billingsley and Deborah Cohen, 'Medical-Device Recalls in the UK and the Device-Regulation Process: Retrospective Review of Safety Notices and Alerts' (2011) 1(1) *British Medical Journal Open* e000155.

[3] ibid., 4.

[4] In this chapter, I use the term 'women' to refer to people who were born biologically female. Most of the people who are injured by the devices discussed here are women.

product liability regime. An effective product liability regime could be said to give manufacturers an incentive to ensure that their products are as safe as possible, but the converse is also true. An ineffective product liability regime does not drive improvements in the safety of medical devices, rather it makes it more likely that dangerous devices will continue to be implanted into women's bodies. This is exacerbated by the fact that many women who are injured by medical devices will encounter what the Independent Medicines and Medical Devices Safety (IMMDS) Review referred to as 'the widespread and wholly unacceptable labelling of so many symptoms as "normal" and attributable to "women's problems"',[5] which in practice means that they are often dismissed, downplayed or ignored.

Of course, it could be argued that the most important issue raised by defective medical devices is the fact that it is possible to market products that will be implanted into people's bodies without first carrying out the sort of rigorous clinical trials that are required before a new medicine can receive a marketing authorisation. Although it is worth noting that medical device regulation in the UK is currently under revision,[6] devices can be approved for use through a much less demanding process, in which manufacturers merely have to establish that their device is 'substantially equivalent' to a device which is already in circulation, and have their product design certified by a 'notified body'. The 'substantial equivalence' test for new medical devices may itself have gendered implications: women have historically been excluded from clinical trials, so if new devices are approved because they are similar to older devices (which were not tested in women), then the greater risk of harm for women which results from previously inadequate testing will be reproduced for new devices.[7]

Of course, medical devices vary, and while the risks to patients from a tongue depressor or blood pressure monitor may be comparatively slight, the risks from devices that are implanted or inserted into patients' bodies are considerable. Indeed, it might be thought that implanted devices should be subject to even greater regulatory scrutiny than medicines, because if a patient has an adverse reaction to a medicine, she can stop taking it and throw the packet away, whereas if an implanted device fails, its removal may not be straightforward.

---

[5] Julia Cumberlege, Sir Cyril Chantler and Simon Whale, First Do No Harm: The Report of the Independent Medicines and Medical Devices Safety Review, IMMDS, 2020, para 1.18.

[6] At the time of writing, the Medicines and Medical Devices Act 2021 gives the Secretary of State for Health and Social Care wide powers to amend or supplement the provisions of the Medical Devices Regulations 2002, but new regulations have not been published. Following a consultation, the Medicines and Healthcare products Regulatory Agency (MHRA) has said that it will prepare new regulations which reclassify products such as certain implantable devices and strengthen and increase post-market surveillance requirements in order to improve incident monitoring, reporting and surveillance.

[7] Katrina Hutchison, 'Gender Bias in Medical Implant Design and Use: A Type of Moral Aggregation Problem?' (2019) 34(3) Hypatia 570–91.

Even if the best way to prevent inadequate medical devices from causing harm is to make sure that they cannot be marketed unless there is robust evidence of their safety and efficacy, it is also necessary to ensure that there is an effective product liability regime in place in order to compensate people who have been injured by defective medical devices, and to ensure that the companies which market inadequately-tested devices – often making vast profits as a result – are held responsible for the harm they have caused.

This chapter begins by pointing out a parallel between the 'male as default' approach to clinical trials, and tort law's claims to neutrality. It then sets out some of the ways in which medical devices are different from other consumer products that might cause harm. It then considers several examples of how the harm caused by medical devices disproportionately affects women, before highlighting some of the deficiencies of the system for compensating people who are injured by defective products. Finally, it concludes that recent acknowledgement that the clinical negligence system is in need of reform, while welcome, needs to be joined up with evidence from the Women's Health Strategy,[8] in order to ensure that tort law does not add to the injustice of a systemic failure to take women's health concerns seriously.

The 'male as default' model

Medicine has treated the male body as the 'norm' since the ancient Greeks. As Caroline Criado Perez has explained, medical textbooks continue to use male bodies in order to illustrate body parts which are shared by men and women.[9] Women's historical exclusion from clinical research means that much medical 'progress' has proceeded without sufficient understanding of how disease, and medical interventions to treat those diseases, affect women's bodies.[10] The systemic failure to recruit sufficient women to clinical trials, or to routinely carry out sex-specific analysis of a trial's results, means that medical products, including drugs and devices, are more likely to cause adverse effects when used by women.[11] Even when devices are designed for women's bodies only, they are often approved for use on the basis of inadequate information, for example,

---

8   Women's Health Strategy for England, Department of Health and Social Care, 2022 (available at: https://www.gov.uk/government/publications/womens-health-strategy-for-england/womens-health-strategy-for-england).

9   Caroline Criado Perez, *Invisible Women: Exposing Data Bias in a World Designed for Men* (Vintage, 2019).

10   Alison M. Kim, Candace M. Tingen and Teresa K. Woodruff, 'Sex Bias in Trials and Treatment Must End' (2010) 465(7299) *Nature* 688–9; Teresa K. Woodruff, 'Sex, Equity, and Science' (2014) 111(14) *Proceedings of the National Academy of Sciences* 5063–4; Ellen Pinnow, Naomi Herz, Nilsa Loyo-Berrios and Michelle Tarver, 'Enrollment and Monitoring of Women in Post-Approval Studies for Medical Devices Mandated by the Food and Drug Administration' (2014) 23(3) *Journal of Women's Health* 218–23.

11   Sanket S. Dhruva and Rita F. Redberg, 'Evaluating Sex Differences in Medical Device Clinical Trials: Time for Action' (2012) 307(11) *JAMA* 1145–6.

by relying on short-term safety data for devices which will be inside women's bodies for the rest of their lives.

This 'male by default' problem in device approval is mirrored by tort law's apparent neutrality and objectivity. As Joanne Conaghan has explained, the primary focus of feminist critiques of law 'is on how formally neutral legal criteria can operate to women's disadvantage'.[12] In the context of tort law, '[t]he picture that emerges is one of systematic, gender-based disadvantage, in stark contrast to traditional characterizations of tort as a formally neutral redistributive regime'.[13]

A feminist approach to product liability would therefore be 'sceptical of claims to objectivity'.[14] Patients who are injured by medical devices encounter statutory provisions and case law which look neutral and objective. In reality, however, the mechanisms through which injured patients can seek compensation from the manufacturers of defective products may not operate in an entirely neutral way.[15] Most obviously, in the context of product liability litigation, there is invariably an enormous power imbalance between the manufacturer and the injured patient. In addition to having 'better access to scientific studies, product development information, experts and lawyers',[16] the manufacturer will usually be much better able to bear (and spread) the costs of litigation. A person who suffers excruciating pain immediately after having a device inserted into her body will receive no compensation for her pain and suffering unless she is able to prove, on the balance of probabilities, that it was the device that caused her injuries. As is evident from the paucity of successful claims, this is by no means an easy task.

It could even be argued that a private law response to injuries caused by defective products is itself problematic,[17] because the inherent difficulties in bringing a claim (such as a lack of legal aid for what are likely to be very expensive proceedings) mean that only a minority of injured patients stand a chance of receiving compensation. If most injured patients are left without a remedy, then in addition to raising questions about access to justice, any deterrent effect of product liability litigation is likely to be weak. Where a widely used medical device causes harm to a significant percentage of its users, the characterisation of the claim for compensation as a 'private' case, between individual claimants and defendants, misses the public nature of systemic harm to patients.

---

[12]   Joanne Conaghan, 'Tort Law and Feminist Critique' (2003) 56 *Current Legal Problems* 175.
[13]   ibid.
[14]   Joanne Conaghan, 'Reassessing the Feminist Theoretical Project in Law' (2000) 27(3) *Journal of Law and Society* 351–85.
[15]   Joanne Conaghan, 'Law, Harm and Redress: A Feminist Perspective' (2002) 22(3) *Legal Studies* 319–39.
[16]   Leslie Bender, 'Overview of Feminist Torts Scholarship' (1992) 78 *Cornell Law Review* 575–96.
[17]   Joanne Conaghan and Wade Mansell, *The Wrongs of Tort* (Pluto, 1998).

What is special about medical devices?

There are hundreds of thousands of medical devices in use, in comparison to a few thousand medicines. There are also many different ways in which medical devices can fail. In addition to manufacturing faults, devices can fail as a result of long-term wear and tear, a lack of skill or experience in installation, inadequate patient selection or because the patient does not follow medical advice, perhaps by exercising vigorously soon after receiving a replacement joint, or failing to take medication to prevent blood clotting.

If clinical trials are not carried out before a device is marketed, defects will be discovered only after the device has been in use for some time. The inevitable consequence of not identifying adverse effects during clinical trials is that more patients will have been injured by the time the problem is identified.[18] This 'cycle of innovation, premature adoption, and subsequent discredit' results in unnecessary harm to patients, and could be prevented if data was collected systematically before a product is widely marketed.[19]

There are, however, several reasons why new medical devices are seldom subject to the sort of large-scale clinical trials which are the norm when testing new medicines. First, as Nassim Parvizi and Kent Woods explain, 'medical device safety and effectiveness are, in part, determined by the user's skill and patient selection',[20] so that 'training in the use of the medical device can substantially affect outcomes'.[21] If a trial is carried out 'before appropriate training and experience has been acquired, [it] may not reflect the true performance of the medical device investigated'.[22] A poor outcome could be the result of 'poorly mastered technique', rather than being indicative of a defect in the device itself.

Second, a blind trial would have to involve carrying out 'sham' procedures on patients in the control group, and these raise special ethical issues. Carrying out 'sham' surgery in a trial of transvaginal mesh would involve the control group undergoing an extremely invasive procedure with no possible clinical benefit. Third, it would be difficult, if not impossible, to blind both the physician and the patient. If a physician has to carry out an invasive procedure in order to place a device inside the patient's body, they will know what it is, and the patient too may be able to tell if a foreign object has been inserted into her body.

---

[18] John B. McKinlay, 'From "Promising Report" to "Standard Procedure": Seven Stages in the Career of a Medical Innovation' (1981) 59(3) *The Milbank Memorial Fund Quarterly. Health and Society* 374–411.

[19] L. Lewis Wall and Douglas Brown, 'The Perils of Commercially Driven Surgical Innovation' (2010) 202(1) *American Journal of Obstetrics and Gynecology* 30–e1.

[20] Nassim Parvizi and Kent Woods, 'Regulation of Medicines and Medical Devices: Contrasts and Similarities' (2014) 14(1) *Clinical Medicine* 6–12.

[21] ibid.

[22] Edmund A.M. Neugebauer et al, 'Specific Barriers to the Conduct of Randomised Clinical Trials on Medical Devices' (2017) 18 *Trials* 1–10.

Fourth, innovation in medical devices generally takes place through incremental modifications to the design of a product, so that 'by the time a clinical trial was complete the device may be onto a new iteration'.[23] It would therefore be impractical to repeat a full clinical trial every time a device's design is modified. Fifth, given that many implanted medical devices are intended to be in patients' bodies for the rest of their lives, it would be impracticable to delay approval until data was available from a trial that had tracked users over the whole lifetime of a medical device.[24] If an innovative new prosthetic hip could not be marketed until there was evidence of its safety after 50 years of use, it would only ever be possible to use 'old' and inevitably outdated products in treatment. Requiring clinical trials to run for several decades before a product is approved for use might also be said to be unnecessarily cautious: because medical devices are 'based on principles of engineering, rather than of chemistry and pharmacology', it is assumed that 'greater reliance can be placed on laboratory tests rather than clinical studies in patients'.[25]

But while clinical trials of devices may pose some additional obstacles, these are not necessarily insurmountable. For example, if an innovative product fulfilled an unmet patient need, '[l]imited access could be provided through temporary licences that restrict use to within clinical trials with long follow-up'.[26] In addition, patient registries would enable users to be tracked, so that robust evidence about safety and efficacy could continue to be gathered after the device has been approved for use.

In practice, however, current mechanisms for the follow-up of patients who have been implanted with medical devices is wholly inadequate. As the IMMDS Review explained:

> [t]he system does not know, so neither do we, just how many women have been treated for stress urinary incontinence and the repair of pelvic organ prolapse using polypropylene mesh. The system does not know, so neither do we, how many women have been cured of their incontinence, or been successfully treated for their prolapse – only then to experience a long list of life-changing conditions that include loss of sex life, chronic pain, infection, difficulty voiding, recurrent urinary incontinence, permanent nerve damage or damage to surrounding organs, haemorrhage, autoimmune disease and psychiatric injury.[27]

---

[23] Cumberlege, Chantler and Whale, First Do No Harm: The Report of the IMMDS Review, para 1.44.

[24] House of Commons Science and Technology Committee, Regulation of Medical Implants in the EU and UK Fifth Report, 2012.

[25] ibid.

[26] Carl Heneghan et al, 'Transvaginal Mesh Failure: Lessons for Regulation of Implantable Devices' (2017) 359 British Medical Journal j5515.

[27] Cumberlege, Chantler and Whale, First Do No Harm: The Report of the IMMDS Review.

There is a further important difference between defective medical devices and other defective products. Once a medicine, or another consumer product like a kettle, is found to be defective, it can be removed from the market. Efforts can be made to ensure that anyone who has already been prescribed the medicine or bought the kettle is told to stop using it. When evidence emerges that there is a risk of failure with an implanted medical device, it is not just those patients who have actually been injured by the device who might seek to make a claim against the manufacturer. Once a risk of failure has been identified in a class of devices, people whose implanted devices might in fact be working perfectly normally (and which might continue to do so) are likely to want to have the device removed, in order to eliminate the *risk* of failure and injury. As a result, claims for compensation for defective medical devices are not confined to people who have in fact been injured by the implanted device, but might also include anyone who is advised to have the device removed, or who chooses, because of the increased risk of failure, to undergo a removal procedure.

Discovery of a fault in an implantable device might therefore mean that thousands of patients, including those whose devices are, in fact, completely safe, might seek to have the device removed. Sometimes removal will be funded by the manufacturer, through a 'care and compensation package' agreed when the withdrawal of a device from the market is accompanied by advice that all patients should have it removed.[28] In the absence of this sort of agreement, however, removal may impose additional costs on the National Health Service (NHS).

Aside from the expense, removal will often involve an invasive procedure, which will cause additional pain and discomfort, as well as carrying risks of its own. In some cases, removal may not even be feasible. If tissue is intended to grow around an implantable device, as was the case with *Essure*, or if the device is intended to become 'permanently embedded into the surrounding tissue', as was the case with transvaginal mesh, removal might be impossible, or worse than the problem it is seeking to solve. Indeed, transvaginal mesh removal is so complex and difficult that there is a risk that 'the cure may often be less beneficial or worse than the original symptoms', and, as a result, there 'is a real danger of women being inappropriately counselled about the likely outcome of major mesh removal surgery'.[29] In addition, removal may not solve the problem: a recent study found that 'only 33% of women with pain complications have improved symptoms after urogynaecological mesh removal'.[30] In the case of some devices, including implantable cardioverter-defibrillators, patients may be in the invidious

---

[28]   Sonia Macleod and Christopher Hodges, *Redress Schemes for Personal Injury* (Hart Publishing, 2017) 597.

[29]   Natalie Pace et al, 'Symptomatic Improvement After Mesh Removal: A Prospective Longitudinal Study of Women with Urogynaecological Mesh Complications' (2021) 128(12) *British Journal of Obstetrics and Gynaecology* 2034–43.

[30]   ibid.

position of having to 'choose between risky removal ... or living with uncertainty of death due to a faulty device'.[31]

A further issue raised by the removal of faulty devices is that this will be possible only if all patients who have been fitted with the defective device are readily traceable. As we saw earlier, the absence of registries of patients means that 'we have limited ability to trace most patients in whom medical devices have been used (or implanted), so when problems or recalls occur, it can be impossible to know the magnitude of the problem'.[32] This lack of traceability in implanted medical devices is particularly shocking given that manufacturers of other potentially dangerous consumer products, like cars and tumble driers,[33] have systems in place to trace the owners of defective products quickly and efficiently.

Because removal may be required even if the device is working normally, defective devices thus expand the category of affected patients, so that potentially *everyone* who has had the device fitted will experience harm as a result. The IMMDS Review found that the list of medicines and devices where there were serious safety concerns was 'long', and gave six examples, five of which primarily affect women ('Essure (a contraceptive device), Roaccutane (a treatment for severe acne that can cause birth defects if used in pregnancy), PIP breast implants, cervical cancer vaccination, in utero exposure to hormones, valproate use in children').[34] If women are more likely than men to be fitted with implanted medical devices, any expansion of the group of patients who are harmed by defective devices, and subsequently let down by the product liability regime, will disproportionately affect women.

Medical device scandals and women's health

PIP breast implants

In March 2010, the Agence française de sécurité sanitaire des produits de santé discovered that the manufacturer PIP had filled most of its breast implants with cheap industrial silicone, as opposed to the medical grade silicone which it had specified in its product design, and which had been certified by TÜV Rheinland (a notified body) as being safe. This deliberate fraud was random: some implants contained medical silicone gel, while others contained a mixture of industrial and medical silicone, and others only industrial silicone. The substandard implants were more likely to rupture, and to cause infections.

---

[31] Sanket S. Dhruva and Rita F. Redberg, 'Medical Device Regulation: Time to Improve Performance' (2012) 9(7) *PLoS Med* e1001277.

[32] Carl Heneghan and Mathew Thompson, 'Rethinking Medical Device Regulation' (2012) 105(5) *Journal of the Royal Society of Medicine* 186–8.

[33] 'Whirlpool told to recall dryers in "unprecedented" government move' *BBC News* 12 June 2019.

[34] Cumberlege, Chantler and Whale, First Do No Harm: The Report of the IMMDS Review.

Before PIP's fraud was revealed, around 400,000 women worldwide had received PIP breast implants. Immediately afterwards, PIP filed for bankruptcy, and women tried to find other potential defendants, such as TÜV Rheinland. Although there was no problem with its certification of the original product design, TÜV Rheinland could have done more to monitor PIP's continued compliance, for example, by carrying out unannounced inspections. In fact, it notified PIP 11 days before its inspection visits, which enabled PIP to ensure it was using medical grade silicone when the visits occurred.[35] Although the European Court of Justice (CJEU) said 'the purpose of the notified body's involvement in the procedure relating to the EC declaration of conformity is to protect the end users of medical devices',[36] it held that the question of whether a notified body should be directly liable to end users was for the national courts. In France, some women's claims against TÜV Rheinland succeeded, while the German Federal Court of Justice held that TÜV Rheinland was not liable.[37]

In the UK, approximately 1,000 women began litigation against various clinics which had used PIP implants, and while most claims were resolved in favour of the women, this route was not open to the very substantial number of women whose clinics had since ceased trading.[38] If clinics, as well as manufacturers, can disappear, then this adds to the problem identified by Holly Jarman et al:

> If we add in the ability of supply chain actors to simply go bankrupt or otherwise disappear before incriminating data appears or punitive action is taken, as did PIP, then we have a system which could have been designed to help manufacturers avoid oversight.[39]

Safety concerns in relation to breast implants are by no means new, and have been raised since the mid-1970s.[40] Trilucent breast implants, which are filled with soybean oil and hence were perceived to be more 'natural' than silicone implants, were first marketed in 1995. Four years later, analysis of the implants indicated that they might cause harmful genotoxic effects, that is, that they might damage the genetic structure of cells. In 1999, the Medical Devices Agency (MDA, since amalgamated into the MHRA) asked the manufacturer voluntarily to withdraw Trilucent implants from the market.[41] After further investigations,

---

[35] Sonia Macleod and Sweta Chakraborty, *Pharmaceutical and Medical Device Safety: A Study in Public and Private Regulation* (Bloomsbury Publishing, 2019) 221.

[36] *Elisabeth Schmitt v TÜV Rheinland LGA Products GmbH* (2017) Case C-219/15.

[37] Macleod and Chakraborty, *Pharmaceutical and Medical Device Safety*, 232.

[38] ibid.

[39] Holly Jarman, Sarah Rozenblum and Tiffany J. Huang, 'Neither Protective Nor Harmonized: The Crossborder Regulation of Medical Devices in the EU' (2021) 16(1) *Health Economics, Policy and Law* 51–63.

[40] Macleod and Chakraborty, *Pharmaceutical and Medical Device Safety*, 223.

[41] Maged Rizkalla, R.N. Matthews and Christian Duncan, 'Trilucent Breast Implants: A 3 Year Series' (2001) 54(2) *British Journal of Plastic Surgery* 125–7.

the MDA issued a Hazard Notice, which recommended that the 5,000 women who had received Trilucent implants should have them removed, and, in the meantime, they should avoid becoming pregnant and breast feeding. Sonia Macleod and Sweta Chakraborty note that although some claims were started, no cases involving Trilucent implants were litigated, and '[l]itigation played no part in the detection of the safety signal, the ensuing regulatory action or in compensating affected individuals'.[42]

Mesh repairs

Stress urinary incontinence (SUI) and pelvic organ prolapse (POP) are common, occurring in as many as 30 to 50 per cent of women.[43] The size of this market means that a 'solution' to these embarrassing problems could be phenomenally profitable. Transvaginal mesh (TVM) repairs – modelled on the use of mesh in the treatment of hernias – were developed to fill this gap in the 1990s, but without robust evidence from clinical trials to establish their safety. In the UK, more than 100,000 women had mesh procedures for SUI between 2008 and 2017, and more than 27,000 women underwent a mesh procedure for POP.[44]

Hundreds of different mesh devices were developed – indeed Macleod and Chakraborty note that the 'sheer number of different products and manufacturers is remarkable'[45] – but within ten years it had become clear that around 30 per cent of mesh recipients suffered complications. Many adverse events following mesh surgery were serious, including pain (sometimes severe and chronic); recurrent infections; mobility issues; recurring or new incontinence/urinary frequency; recurring or new prolapse; haemorrhage; bowel issues, sometimes requiring colostomy and ileostomy surgery; erosion of mesh; sexual difficulties; autoimmune issues; psychological impacts; and death.[46]

For example, the 'ProteGen pubovaginal sling' was a polyester mesh impregnated with collagen which was implanted underneath the urethra and fixed in place with surgical screws.[47] Approval had been given on the basis that there had been a study in rats and the mesh was already used in cardiovascular grafting. The mesh had never been tried in human urological operations, or inserted into a vagina. It was, as Lewis and Brown point out, 'a disastrous marriage of two bad ideas

---

[42] Macleod and Chakraborty, *Pharmaceutical and Medical Device Safety*.

[43] Kim Keltie et al, 'Complications Following Vaginal Mesh Procedures for Stress Urinary Incontinence: An 8 Year Study of 92,246 Women' (2017) 7(1) *Scientific Reports* 1–9.

[44] Retrospective Review of Surgery for Urogynaecological Prolapse and Stress Urinary Incontinence using Tape or Mesh: Hospital Episode Statistics, Experimental Statistics, April 2008-March 2017, NHS Digital, 2018.

[45] Macleod and Chakraborty, *Pharmaceutical and Medical Device Safety*, 256.

[46] Cumberlege, Chantler and Whale, First Do No Harm: The Report of the IMMDS Review, para 5.2.

[47] Lewis Wall and Brown, 'The Perils of Commercially Driven Surgical Innovation'.

and produced catastrophic consequences in many patients'.[48] By the time it was recalled, 'the ProteGen Sling had not been the subject of a single randomised, controlled clinical trial published in a peer-reviewed journal'.[49]

Tension-free vaginal tape (TVT) was another type of mesh, which was rapidly approved in the US because of its 'substantial equivalence' to an existing product, and in the UK, the Safety and Efficacy Register of New Interventional Procedures (SERNIP), a forerunner of the National Institute for Health and Care Excellence (NICE), gave it an 'A' rating, solely on the basis of documentation submitted by the manufacturer, and without any evidence from clinical trials to back this up.[50] Indeed, research published in the *British Medical Journal* 'traced the family tree of 61 surgical mesh products to two original devices approved in 1985 and 1996. None had completed clinical trials at the time of approval'.[51]

Worldwide, hundreds of thousands of women were affected by TVM.[52] As Miriam Wiersma et al explain:

> TVM was marketed aggressively despite emerging evidence of the weakness of the research base and the association of TVM with adverse clinical outcomes, high rates of repeat surgery and high rates of adverse events including pain, bleeding, dyspareunia, urinary tract infections, organ perforation, and mesh exposure requiring corrective surgery.[53]

NHS England set up the Mesh Oversight Group in 2015, and following further investigations, a revision to the NICE guidelines recommended that mesh should only be used for research purposes for POP. In 2018, the government appointed Baroness Julia Cumberlege to chair the IMMDS Review, and it recommended that the use of vaginal mesh for SUI should be paused. This was accepted by the government and NHS, and implemented in July 2018, and subsequently extended to cover the use of vaginal mesh for POP.

Essure

Female sterilisation used to involve invasive surgery, such as tubal ligation. Essure was designed to be a minimally invasive alternative. It consists of two small metal coils, wrapped in fibres, which are inserted into each fallopian tube with

---

[48] ibid.

[49] ibid.

[50] Jonathan Gornall, 'How Mesh Became a Four Letter Word' (2018) 363 *British Medical Journal* k4137.

[51] International Consortium of Investigative Journalists (ICIJ), 'Medical devices harm patients worldwide as governments fail on safety: A global investigation reveals the rising human toll of lax controls and testing standards pushed by a booming industry' *ICIJ* 25 November 2018.

[52] Miriam Wiersma, Ian Kerridge and Wendy Lipworth, 'Transvaginal Mesh, Gender and the Ethics of Clinical Innovation' (2020) 50 *Internal Medicine Journal* 523–6.

[53] ibid. See also Keltie et al, 'Complications Following Vaginal Mesh Procedures'.

a catheter, and which induce the production of scar tissue which will block the fallopian tubes. Essure was marketed as a device which could be inserted in 15 minutes in a GP surgery,[54] with oral analgesics and minimal local anaesthesia, even though the package insert for Essure warned that women might experience '[m]ild to moderate pain during and immediately following the Essure placement procedure', and '[c]ramping, vaginal bleeding, nausea, vomiting, dizziness, lightheadedness, pelvic or back discomfort immediately after the procedure'. Non-randomised trials had been carried out, but these relied on short-term outcomes, and only 25 per cent of participants had been followed up after two years.

In fact, Essure led to extremely serious adverse effects, including chronic pelvic pain, bowel injury, persistent bleeding, nickel allergy and ectopic pregnancy.[55] A doctor who had removed nearly 500 Essure devices explained 'how the implant turned into a "calcified nail" inside the body', which led to 'devices having pierced through internal tissue and migrated into the abdomen'.[56] In the US, the Food and Drug Administration recorded eight deaths due to Essure. And because removing Essure was not straightforward, some women suffered additional harm from removal surgery, such as shards of metal being left behind, or having to undergo a full hysterectomy. Essure was withdrawn from sale in 2017, after more than one million women had been fitted with it.[57]

Higher failure rates of non-gendered devices

In addition to being injured by devices which are developed to address women's health problems, women are also injured more frequently by medical devices which are implanted into both men and women,[58] such as cardiac devices like pacemakers and implantable cardioverter-defibrillators.[59] Metal-on-metal hip replacements, in which metal is used for both the ball and the socket of the prosthetic hip joint, were thought to be likely to last a long time, and hence to have advantages over the previously used metal-on-polyethylene joints for younger patients. In fact, the harms caused by metal debris from wear were more

---

54 Hannah Devlin, 'Contraceptive implant surgically removed from thousands of women' *The Guardian* 25 November 2018.

55 Jennifer L. Carey et al, 'Drugs and Medical Devices: Adverse Events and the Impact on Women's Health' (2017) 29(1) *Clinical Therapeutics* 10–22.

56 Devlin, 'Contraceptive implant surgically removed from thousands of women'.

57 ICIJ, 'Medical devices harm patients worldwide as governments fail on safety'.

58 Katrina Hutchison and Wendy Rogers, 'Hips, Knees, and Hernia Mesh: When does Gender Matter in Surgery?' (2017) 10(1) *International Journal of Feminist Approaches to Bioethics* 148–74.

59 Katherine Moore et al, 'Sex Differences in Acute Complications of Cardiac Implantable Electronic Devices: Implications for Patient Safety' (2019) 8(2) *Journal of the American Heart Association* e010869; Mohamed Osama Mohamed et al, 'Trends of Sex Differences in Outcomes of Cardiac Electronic Device Implantations in the United States' (2020) 36(1) *Canadian Journal of Cardiology* 69–78.

dangerous than expected. Both men and women were affected, but, in line with the higher rates of failure in women of other orthopaedic devices,[60] the failure rate of metal-on-metal hips is higher in women than in men.[61]

The most important reason for 'evidence of worse outcomes for women from at least some types of implant failure' is, as we saw earlier, 'that the bodies, activities, and experiences of women patients are not adequately reflected in the design and clinical use of medical implants'.[62] If a device is to be implanted in men's and women's bodies, it is vital to take into account differences between their bodies at the design stage. In relation to prosthetic hips, for example, women's gait is different from men's; sexual intercourse places different stresses on women's joints,[63] and women's lower blood volume may mean that debris leads to higher metal ion concentrations. If differences like these are not taken into account when devices are designed, or if sex-based analysis of results is not carried out, increased failure rates in women are wholly predictable.[64]

Disbelieving women

In addition to women being more likely to be adversely affected by medical devices, they are also more likely to have their complaints ignored or trivialised. The IMMDS Review spelled this out:

> [P]atients – almost universally women – spoke in disbelief, sadness and anger about the manner in which they were treated by the clinicians they had reached out to for help. The words 'defensive', 'dismissive' and 'arrogant', cropped up with alarming frequency. They spoke of being 'gaslighted' and of not being believed ... Women, in reporting to us their extensive mesh complications, have spoken of excruciating chronic pain feeling like razors inside their body, damage to organs, the loss of mobility and sex life and depression and suicidal thoughts. Some clinicians' reactions ranged from '*it's all in your head*' to '*these are women's issues*' or '*it's that time of life*' wherein anything and everything

---

[60] Marco S. Caicedo et al, 'Females with Unexplained Joint Pain Following Total Joint Arthroplasty Exhibit a Higher Rate and Severity of Hypersensitivity to Implant Metals Compared with Males: Implications of Sex-Based Bioreactivity Differences' (2017) 99(8) *Journal of Bone and Joint Surgery* 621–8.

[61] Hutchison and Rogers, 'Hips, Knees, and Hernia Mesh'; Alison J. Smith, Paul Dieppe, Kelly Vernon, Martyn Porter and Ashley W. Blom, 'Failure Rates of Stemmed Metal-on-Metal Hip Replacements: Analysis of Data from the National Joint Registry of England and Wales' (2012) 379(9822) *The Lancet* 1199–204.

[62] Hutchison, 'Gender Bias in Medical Implant Design and Use'.

[63] Diane L. Dahm, 'Surgeons Rarely Discuss Sexual Activity with Patients After THA: A Survey of Members of the American Association of Hip and Knee Surgeons' (2004) 428 *Clinical Orthopaedics and Related Research* 237–40.

[64] Hutchison, 'Gender Bias in Medical Implant Design and Use'.

women suffer is perceived as a natural precursor to, part of, or a post-symptomatic phase of, the menopause.[65]

In an Australian context, Wiersma et al explain that:

[w]omen are also more likely to have their illness disregarded and their pain pathologised, or ignored. This in turn, has not only physical but also psychological consequences for women, who feel that their pain is downplayed or dismissed by medical professionals (and who may already be at higher risk of mental ill-health, depression and self-harm).[66]

In addition to the harm to individual women of not being believed, the dismissal of women's reports of adverse effects has wider safety implications for other patients, because it means that early indications that a product might not be safe are likely to be overlooked. If there is a delay in investigating reports of an adverse effect, this will translate into a delay in the recall of a dangerous product, and more patients will suffer injuries as a result. The direct consequence of telling mesh recipients who reported excruciating pain that it was in their heads, or just a symptom of menopause, was a delay in recognising the harms of transvaginal mesh, during which time many more women received mesh implants and experienced wholly preventable harm.

The deficiencies of the product liability regime in the UK

The Consumer Protection Act 1987 and its application

In the UK, Part I of the Consumer Protection Act (CPA) 1987 implemented an EU Directive which was intended to harmonise European product liability regimes through the introduction of a strict liability regime. The Act imposes strict liability on manufacturers and, in certain circumstances, suppliers for defective products which cause physical injury or property damage. In theory, not having to establish negligence should make it easier for claimants to receive compensation. In practice, with the caveat that it is impossible to know how many settlements are made 'in the shadow of the law',[67] the dearth of litigation under the Act has been striking.[68] As Macleod and Chakraborty explain, even

---

[65] Cumberlege, Chantler and Whale, First Do No Harm: The Report of the IMMDS Review, para 2.3.

[66] Wiersma et al, 'Transvaginal Mesh, Gender and the Ethics of Clinical Innovation'.

[67] Robert H. Mnookin and Lewis Kornhauser, 'Bargaining in the Shadow of the Law: The Case of Divorce' (1978) 88(5) *Yale Law Journal* 950.

[68] Duncan Fairgrieve, Geraint Howells and Marcus Pilgerstorfer, 'The Product Liability Directive: Time to get Soft?' (2013) 4(1) *Journal of European Tort Law* 1–33.

though 'the introduction of strict liability was intended to make it easier to claim compensation from manufacturers for injuries caused by products, this is rarely the outcome with medical products'.[69]

One difficulty is that, in the absence of legal aid, the factual issues in medical product liability claims tend to be so complex that litigation may be prohibitively expensive; indeed, even finding out if a case has a reasonable chance of success can itself be extremely expensive.[70] Class actions, brought on a 'no win no fee' basis, may make it easier for patients to claim, but given how few litigants have succeeded at trial, only patients with extremely strong claims might be likely to be offered contingency fee arrangements.

A further issue is that the fact a product has been withdrawn from the market on safety grounds does not necessarily mean that injured patients are likely to succeed in a product liability claim. Regulators must respond to evidence that there *could* be a *risk* of harm, perhaps because there is an early indication of a correlation between a device and an adverse effect. In contrast, product liability claims require the claimant to *prove*, on the balance of probabilities, that the product *caused* her injury. This is substantially more challenging than establishing that a product *might* no longer have a positive risk-benefit profile. As a result, a not uncommon scenario is that someone who thinks she has been harmed by an unsafe product – which may have been withdrawn on safety grounds – begins 'an adversarial process', thus incurring considerable legal costs, 'only to be told that they will not receive any answers in court, nor any compensation, because they cannot prove legal harm'.[71] As Macleod and Chakraborty put it, 'it is hard to imagine a less satisfactory process for attempting to resolve an issue'.[72]

There has been considerable criticism of the CPA and its implementation in relation to consumer products in general,[73] but there are also aspects of the Act which may pose particular problems for people seeking compensation for harm caused by medical devices. For example, the definition of 'defect' under section 3 of the Act is confusing and circular: 'there is a defect in a product for the purposes of this Part if the safety of the product is not such as persons generally are entitled to expect'. This is, as Jane Stapleton points out, unhelpful, because 'what a person is entitled to expect is the very question a definition of defect should be answering'.[74] In relation to implanted medical devices, no one who receives a breast implant or a replacement hip actually expects to be injured by it, so it could be said that consumers always expect 100 per cent safety. This is

---

[69] Macleod and Chakraborty, *Pharmaceutical and Medical Device Safety*.

[70] ibid., 265.

[71] ibid., 279.

[72] ibid.

[73] Fairgrieve et al, 'The Product Liability Directive'; Joe Thomson, *Delictual Liability* (5th edn, Bloomsbury, 2014); Donal Nolan, 'Strict Product Liability for Design Defects' (2018) 134(2) *Law Quarterly Review* 176–181.

[74] Jane Stapleton, *Product Liability* (Butterworths, 1994) 234.

not the question, however, which is instead what level of safety consumers are *entitled* to expect.

On the one hand, in *Boston Scientific Medizintechnik GmbH v AOK Sachsen-Anhalt – Die Gesundheitskasse (Boston Scientific)*,[75] the CJEU suggested that, in relation to life-saving medical devices, such as pacemakers and implantable cardioverter-defibrillators, 'in the light of their function and the particularly vulnerable situation of patients using such devices, the safety requirements for those devices which such patients are entitled to expect are particularly high'.[76] That meant that, it was 'of little consequence that it is accepted in specialist medical circles that it is not possible for a pacemaker or a cardioverter-defibrillator that has been implanted to be 100% safe'. Rather, '[i]n view of the life-threatening risk presented by a defective device, the patient may, in principle, reasonably expect the implanted device to have a failure rate of close to zero'.[77]

On the other hand, if some wear and tear and occasional failure of all devices is inevitable, how do we tell whether the device fails to meet the safety that persons generally are entitled to expect? In *Gee v Depuy International Limited*,[78] 312 claimants claimed to have suffered an adverse reaction to metal wear debris from their replacement hips. Andrews J held that because:

> [a]ll hip prostheses will eventually wear out and fail, if the patient survives long enough, and some will fail within 10 years: the natural propensity of a hip implant to fail therefore cannot be a 'defect', any more than the inevitable wear and tear that causes minute particles of debris to enter the patient's body. Otherwise all hip implants would be 'defective'.[79]

Although there is some tension between the reasoning in *Boston Scientific* and *Gee v Depuy*, it might be concluded that where a device's safety is a matter of life-and-death for the patient, a patient could reasonably expect that the device will be safe. But where some deterioration in the device over time is normal and to be expected, an expectation that this deterioration will not happen would not be reasonable.

Section 3(2) of the CPA sets out several factors which are relevant to what consumers generally are entitled to expect, including any warnings provided with the product, and what might reasonably be expected to be done with it. Section 3(2)(c) specifies that a product is not to be considered defective simply because a better product is subsequently put into circulation. Hence, a device

---

75 Case C-503/13, 504/13 [2015] 3 CMLR 173 (CJEU) AG§27.
76 ibid., [39].
77 ibid., [26].
78 [2018] EWHC 1208 (QB).
79 ibid., [96].

that has been superseded by a safer one does not thereby become defective for the purposes of the Act.

The case law appears to indicate that the benefits of the product, as well as the rigour of the regulatory process, might also be relevant to the question of whether a device is defective. In *Wilkes v DePuy International Ltd,*[80] a case in which an artificial hip fractured after three years, Hickinbottom J found that, '[g]iven that such a product will inevitably have some risks attached, ... any assessment of its safety will necessarily require the risks involved in use of that product to be balanced against its potential benefits including its potential utility'.[81] Moreover, he went on to say that:

> [c]ertainly, where every aspect of the product's design, manufacture and marketing has been the subject of the substantial scrutiny, by a regulatory body comprised of individuals selected for their experience and expertise in the product including its safety, on the basis of full information, and that body has assessed that the level of safety is acceptable, then it may be challenging for a claimant to prove that the level of safety that persons generally are entitled to expect is at a higher level.[82]

Although there has been very little litigation under the CPA in the UK, thus far claims have been brought by patients who have actually been harmed by devices. As we saw earlier, however, patients who have been fitted with devices which are subsequently found to cause problems in some users may be advised to have the device removed, or may choose to do so, even if their device is currently working normally. Whether or not such a device is 'defective' for the purposes of the EU's product liability Directive came before the CJEU in *Boston Scientific*, which involved two separate cases.

In the first case, two patients had been implanted with pacemakers, which were subject to a 'Dear Doctor' letter after the discovery of a safety fault which meant that their likelihood of failure was 17 to 20 times higher than normal. Replacement was recommended. In the second case, the patient had been fitted with an implantable cardioverter-defibrillator, which was also subject to a 'Dear Doctor' letter. In this case the fault could be addressed by deactivating its magnet mode, but the patient chose instead to have it removed. The question in both cases was whether these patients' devices were defective (the devices had been disposed of, so it was not possible to find out if they were actually defective). The CJEU found that they were, because they had 'abnormal potential for damage'

---

[80] [2016] EWHC 3096 (QB).

[81] ibid., [82].

[82] ibid., [100]. A point also illustrated by the Supreme Court in *Hastings v Finsbury Orthopaedics Ltd and Another (Scotland)* [2022] UKSC 19.

and, as a result, the removal operations amounted to personal injury for the purposes of the Directive.

It was not necessary to demonstrate that the patients' devices had the safety faults that had been identified in other devices, just that they belonged to a group or series of products which had a significantly higher than normal risk of such a fault. Of course, as Duncan Fairgrieve and Marcus Pilgerstorfer explain:

> [t]he Court's language of 'abnormality' ... only acquires meaning by virtue of a departure from 'normality'. Accordingly, determining whether the potential for damage in the index product departs from what is 'normal' necessarily requires comparing the product with comparators.[83]

Thus, for example, in the case of PIP breast implants containing industrial silicone, since normal breast implants do not contain industrial grade silicone, it could be argued that 'all breast implants manufactured by PIP have an abnormal potential to cause damage to women'.[84]

Even if an injured consumer is able to establish that the product was defective and that it caused her injury, that may not be the end of the story, because there are some defences available to the manufacturer under section 4 of the Act. For example, there is a defence if the defect was not present when the product was supplied. In another case involving failure of a prosthetic hip, *Piper v JRI Ltd*,[85] the Court of Appeal agreed with the first instance judge that, because the defendant manufacturer had subjected its product to a 'vigorous and meticulous process of work and inspection of the highest quality', the defect in the titanium alloy was likely to have occurred *after* the product was supplied.[86] Contributory negligence also applies, so if the patient fails to follow medical directions, her damages will be reduced according to the extent to which her injury was caused by her own conduct.

In addition, the time limits the CPA imposes on actions may pose particular issues for people who are injured by medical devices. Any claim must be brought within three years of the discovery of the damage or injury, with a longstop of ten years from when the product was first put into circulation. Devices like breast implants, *Essure* and vaginal mesh are intended to be in patients' bodies for the rest of their lives, and damage may take some time to become apparent. Yet ten years after each of these devices was first put into circulation, the possibility of

---

[83] Duncan Fairgrieve and Marcus Pilgerstorfer, 'European Product Liability after *Boston Scientific*: An Assessment of the Court's Judgment on Defect, Damage and Causation' (2017) 28(6) *European Business Law Review* 879–910.

[84] Barend Van Leeuwen and Paul Verbruggen, 'Resuscitating EU Product Liability Law' (2015) 23(5) *European Review of Private Law* 899–915.

[85] [2006] EWCA Civ 1344.

[86] ibid., para 22.

recovery under the CPA expires. In practice, therefore, only a small percentage of people who are affected by defective medical devices will be able to make a claim.

Certainly, the IMMDS Review admitted that 'litigation has, so far, not served our patient groups well'.[87] Women in other jurisdictions, such as Australia, have already won substantial class action claims against the manufacturers of transvaginal mesh. In the US, there have been 108,000 lawsuits claiming that transvaginal mesh caused pain, bleeding, infection, organ perforation and autoimmune problems. One of the largest transvaginal mesh settlements to date was US$830 million for 20,000 cases. Johnson & Johnson 'agreed to pay nearly $117 million to settle claims brought by the attorneys general of 41 US states and the District of Columbia that it deceptively marketed and advertised the products'.[88] Some individual women in the US have received tens of millions of dollars in compensation. In total, it is estimated that in the US 'mesh manufacturers have paid close to $8 billion in settlements'.[89]

Even in Scotland, there have been reports that Johnson & Johnson have paid out £50 million to women who claim to have been injured by mesh products (although the exact sum is confidential, and Johnson & Johnson have maintained that it is much less than this).[90] Such settlements do not necessarily involve any admission of liability, rather it is common for them to be made 'without prejudice to liability', and, despite the public health benefits of openness about dangerous products, 'subject to confidentiality agreements'.[91]

Mesh injuries: suing the NHS rather than mesh manufacturers

Difficulties in bringing an action under the CPA against the manufacturer of the device – perhaps because the manufacturer is no longer in business or the product has been in circulation for more than ten years – may mean that the only option is a negligence claim. For example, a woman might be able to bring a negligence action against the surgeon who implanted the device, either by claiming that they were negligent in carrying out a mesh repair, or that she was not given enough information about the risks of mesh, and any alternatives to it, in order to give informed consent.[92] The only case that has gone to trial so far is *Diamond v Royal Devon and Exeter NHS Foundation Trust*,[93] in which the surgeon was found to have breached his duty to provide the claimant with the

---

87 Cumberlege, Chantler and Whale, First Do No Harm: The Report of the IMMDS Review, para 33.
88 Clare Dyer, 'Mesh Implants: Women Launch Claims Against NHS Trusts and Surgeons for Failing to Warn of Risks' (2020) 369 *British Medical Journal* m2605.
89 Michelle Llamas, 'Transvaginal mesh lawsuits' *Drugwatch* 15 October 2021.
90 Dyer, 'Mesh Implants'.
91 Alexander C. Egilman et al, 'Confidentiality Orders and Public Interest in Drug and Medical Device Litigation' (2020) 180(2) *JAMA Internal Medicine* 292–9.
92 *Montgomery v Lanarkshire Health Board* [2015] UKSC 11.
93 [2019] EWCA Civ 585.

information she needed in order to give informed consent to a mesh repair, by failing to explain that it would make a future pregnancy risky. Despite this, the claimant's case failed, because she was unable to establish that, if she had been properly informed, she would have opted for a suture repair instead. The Court of Appeal declined to interfere with the judge's conclusion, 'that the "sad outcome" coloured and informed her view of what she would have done had she been appropriately warned'.[94]

In deciding that Ms Diamond would have opted for a mesh repair even if she had been properly warned that a subsequent pregnancy would be risky, the judge took into account that '[s]he was single at the time. A pregnancy was not within her immediate contemplation albeit that she had thought about having a child two years earlier with her ex-partner'.[95] He also found that 'it would have been irrational for her to opt for a suture repair; and I find that she is not a person who would act irrationally'. Even if a 39-year-old woman in Ms Diamond's position might be likely to have been influenced by the surgeon's 'strongest possible advice that she should have a mesh repair', her claim in her witness statement that '[t]he ability to have children has always been very important to me and I would not have wanted to be stripped of my womanhood in this way' looks like reasoning that many women would consider wholly rational.

There have been cases brought by women injured by mesh products which NHS trusts have chosen to settle. In the UK, the response to a Freedom of Information request revealed that in 2018–19 damages totalling £634,956 were paid to 16 women, and the following year, 11 claims were settled, with damages totalling £571,055.[96] (Before 2018, there were fewer than five cases each year.) In comparison to the damages paid out worldwide to mesh victims, these sums are modest, to say the least.

Conclusion

In December 2021, the House of Commons Health and Social Care Select Committee published a report on clinical negligence reform which found that:

> a costly and adversarial litigation system is evermore at odds with our understanding of how the NHS should respond to failures in care. England's system of clinical negligence stands in stark contrast to international best practice in terms of patient safety. In other countries,

---

[94] Per Nicola Davies LJ. For commentary see Joanna M. Manning, 'Oh What an Unholy Mesh! *Diamond v Royal Devon & Exeter NHS Foundation Trust* [2019] EWCA Civ 585' (2019) 27(3) *Medical Law Review* 519–29.

[95] *Diamond v Royal Devon & Exeter NHS Foundation Trust* [2017] EWHC 1495 (QB), 49 (HHJ Freedman).

[96] See https://resolution.nhs.uk/wp-content/uploads/2021/02/FOI_4926_Vaginal-mesh-implants.pdf

gains are made by careful system–wide analysis rather than an insistent search for individual error.[97]

Its central recommendation was therefore:

> that the NHS adopt a radically different system for compensating injured patients which moves away from a system based on apportioning blame and prioritises learning from mistakes. An independent administrative body should be made responsible for investigating cases and determining eligibility for compensation in the most serious cases.

A few months later, the Department of Health and Social Care published its Women's Health Strategy for England,[98] which accepted that too often women's voices were ignored (84 per cent of respondents to their survey had said that there had been instances in which they had not been listened to by healthcare professionals), and promised to 'improve the way in which the health and care system listens to women's voices, and boost health outcomes for women and girls'. It also accepted that 'historically the health and care system has been designed by men for men', and that the 'male as default' approach in clinical trials, training and policy development 'has led to gaps in our data and evidence base'.[99]

Some issues raised by medical devices were mentioned in the Women's Health Strategy, such as the need for conversations about pain relief before the fitting of an intrauterine contraceptive device. It also advocated the adoption of digital technologies (such as the Scan4Safety programme[100]) to record and track implanted medical devices in order to improve the safety and traceability of devices, including those used in women's health. There was also a commitment 'that health and care research which should, but does not, take into account sex-based differences does not receive public funding'.

Although the prospect of reform to the clinical negligence system is welcome and long overdue,[101] and taking women's health concerns seriously and addressing the consequences of the 'male as default' approach is self-evidently desirable, what is missing from these reports taken together is a recognition that defects in the clinical negligence system are supplemented by defects in the product liability regime, and that these disproportionately affect women. If medical devices

---

[97] House of Commons Health and Social Care Committee, NHS Litigation Reform: Thirteenth Report of Session, 2021–22.

[98] Women's Health Strategy for England.

[99] ibid.

[100] Scan4Safety (available at https://www.scan4safety.nhs.uk/).

[101] A strong and compelling case for reform was made more than 20 years ago in Department of Health, Learning from Bristol: The Department of Health's Response to the Report of the Public Inquiry into Children's Heart Surgery at the Bristol Royal Infirmary, 1984–1995 Cm 5363 2002.

are inadequately tested, especially on women, and if more women than men are implanted with devices, then any difficulty injured patients experience in bringing product liability claims will be magnified for women. It is disappointing that we do not seem to have made very much progress since Joan Steinman asked thirty years ago:

> [a]re there no medical products peculiarly for men? If there are, is it mere coincidence that they have not proven to be seriously harmful? I assume that if such products had caused widespread and serious harm, the injured would have sued; evidence of the problem would appear in the case reports. But it is not there. ... I strongly suspect that a disparity exists between the care invested in products for men and that invested in drugs and medical devices for women. One might say that I am overstating the problem because the troublesome products have been limited to a narrow category, to items that relate to women's reproductive and sexual functions and structures. But that is not a narrow category of products; such products are used by all of us, and millions of us use any given variety. Moreover, one has to wonder why the scientific community has placed so much emphasis on developing and marketing contraceptive drugs and devices for women, and so little emphasis on developing them for men. My own speculation is that it is because men ... don't want to mess with their own body chemistry or genitalia ... They would much prefer to let the women take the pills and the injections or have the foreign objects installed in them.[102]

---

[102] Joan E. Steinman, 'Women, Medical Care, and Mass Tort Litigation' (1992) 69(1) *Chicago-Kent Law Review* 409–29.

8

The Tortious Response to Police Power, Misconduct and Abuse

Rita D'Alton-Harrison

Introduction

This chapter considers two torts that are relevant to the area of police misconduct, namely the tort of malicious prosecution and the tort of misfeasance in public office. I explore the extent to which these torts are vital as acknowledgement that 'policing by consent' should not become a licence for serving police officers to inflict racial or sexual harm against members of the public. For the purposes of this chapter these two torts are collectively referred to as abuse of position of power torts. It is argued that in their current form these torts perpetuate some of the systematic problems involved in disciplining police officers and highlight how difficult it can be to obtain compensation when abuse of police power is alleged. This is of particular concern because police misconduct disproportionately affects those from marginalised groups, particularly women and those from minority ethnic backgrounds.

Several recent published reports[1] and criminal prosecutions[2] have highlighted the damage caused to the trust and confidence that members of the public place in the police service. Baroness Casey's interim report revealed a stark increase in the number of sexual misconduct allegations made against male police officers. Cases such as the 2021 prosecution of a serving police officer (Wayne Couzens)

---

[1] See, for example, Operation Hotton: Learning Report, Independent Office for Police Conduct, 2022; An Inspection of Vetting, Misconduct, and Misogyny in the Police Service, His Majesty's Inspectorate of Constabulary and Fire and Rescue Services, 2022; and the interim report of Baroness Casey of Blackstock into the Metropolitan Police's misconduct system, Analytical Report, The Baroness Casey Review, 2022.

[2] See, for example, *R v Couzens (Wayne)* [2021] Sentencing Remarks, para 19 (available at https://www.judiciary.uk/wp-content/uploads/2021/09/Wayne-Couzens-Sentencing-Remarks.pdf).

for the kidnap and murder of a female member of the public (Sarah Everard) revealed the extent to which a police officer can abuse the trust of a woman walking home at night. The conviction of David Carrick[3] in 2023 additionally shows us how police officers can use their status to prevent complainants coming forward to reveal abuse in domestic situations because they fear they will not be believed.

In the Metropolitan Police Service (MPS) alone there has been a sharp increase in reports of sexual misconduct, particularly in 2013 (78 reported cases) and again in 2018 (87 reported cases).[4] As Fulford LJ noted in his sentencing remarks in the case of *R v Couzens (Wayne)*: 'the police are in a unique position, which is essentially different from any other public servants. They have powers of coercion and control that are in an exceptional category.'[5]

Questions are raised as to just how pervasive misogyny is in the MPS,[6] and what can be done about it.[7] Similarly, ethnicity is known to be a factor that increases the likelihood of an individual being subjected to police misconduct either through the disproportionate use of force, unwarranted stop and search or mistreatment and death in police custody. The 2017 Lammy report found that there was an overrepresentation of Black and minority ethnic people in the criminal justice system.[8]

These statistics are concerning, especially when we consider the paucity of women and ethnic minority individuals serving in the police force. As of 31 March 2021 there were 135,301 full-time police officers working in the 43 police forces in England and Wales, of which 7.6 per cent were from a Black, mixed heritage, Asian or other minority ethnic group. Just 32.4 per cent were women.[9] In addition, Baroness Casey noted in her interim report into police misconduct that women and minority ethnic police officers were more likely to drop out of the police service before the end of their probationary period or face

---

3   PC David Carrick was convicted at Southwark Crown Court on 16 January 2023 after pleading guilty to 49 counts of sexual offences, including rape, against 12 separate complainants. He was later sentenced to a minimum 31 years in prison. See June Kelly, Claire Ellison and Judith Burns, 'David Carrick: The serial rapist and abuser in a police uniform' *BBC News* 16 January 2023.

4   See Tables CM 4 and PC 13–PC 16 in the Freedom of Information Request reference no 01.FOI.21.018992 (available at https://www.met.police.uk/foi-ai/metropolitan-police/disclosure-2021/july-2021/police-staff-accused-of-sexual-assaultharassment/).

5   *R v Couzens (Wayne)* [2021] Sentencing Remarks, para 19.

6   Emma Guy, 'How deep does misogyny run in the Met?' *EachOther* 25 January 2023.

7   Jonathan Freedland, 'What to do with a Met police that harbours rapists and murderers? Scrap it and start again' *The Guardian* 20 January 2023.

8   The Lammy Review: An Independent Review into the Treatment of, and Outcomes for, Black, Asian and Minority Ethnic Individuals in the Criminal Justice System, 2017.

9   Home Office National Statistics, Police Workforce, England and Wales: Second Edition, 31 March 2022 (available at https://www.gov.uk/government/statistics/police-workforce-england-and-wales-31-march-2021/police-workforce-england-and-wales-31-march-2021).

disproportionate use of the Regulation 13 procedure (removal from the force of unsuitable probationers).[10]

Furthermore, police officers who are women or from minority ethnic backgrounds may themselves be the target of abuse from their own colleagues. For example, the 'Operation Hotton' investigation undertaken by the Independent Office for Police Conduct (IOPC) found that Metropolitan Police officers had been involved in discriminatory and racist communication directed at their minority ethnic colleagues, coupled with bullying, aggressive and misogynistic behaviour and harassment.[11] The report also revealed that 'there was a reluctance to challenge inappropriate behaviour and misconduct'.[12]

In terms of using the civil courts to tackle 'institutional racism' or 'institutional sexism', the abuse of positions of power torts, as currently devised in common law, do not offer sufficient protection to claimants. Institutional racism was defined in the Macpherson report as:

> [t]he collective failure of an organisation to provide an appropriate and professional service to people because of their colour, culture, or ethnic origin. It can be seen or detected in processes, attitudes and behaviour which amount to discrimination through unwitting prejudice, ignorance, thoughtlessness and racist stereotyping which disadvantage minority ethnic people.[13]

While there is not a settled definition for 'institutional sexism', the National Police Chief's Council (NPCC) defines the abuse of position for sexual purposes as:

> [a]ny behaviour by a police officer or police staff member, whether on or off duty, that takes advantage of their position as a member of the police service to misuse their position, authority or powers in order to pursue a sexual improper emotional relationship with any member of the public.[14]

The abuse of position of power torts address civil wrongs from both a legal and moral lens, although it is arguable that the moral lens gives an opaque view because one must always ask the question 'whose morality'? Judges must

---

[10]   Analytical Report, The Baroness Casey Review, 2022, 20.

[11]   Operation Hotton: Learning Report, Independent Office for Police Conduct, 2022.

[12]   ibid., 13.

[13]   The Stephen Lawrence Inquiry: Report of an Inquiry by Sir William Macpherson of Cluny Cm 4262-1, 1999, 375. This report was commissioned to investigate allegations of major failings by the police in their investigation of the death of the Black teenager Stephen Lawrence who was murdered in an unprovoked racist attack on 22 April 1993.

[14]   See National Police Chiefs' Council, National Strategy to Address the Issue of Police Officers and Staff who Abuse their Position for a Sexual Purpose, 2017.

determine whether police officers have in fact acted in abuse of their powers. However, the definition of 'abuse' is often so interlinked with preconceived notions of the impeccability of police conduct that impeachment or challenge appears an incredulous step. An examination of the ownership of morality is necessary because there is a value judgment to be made about the political worth of agents of the state as against its subjects when it comes to litigation about abuse. This then informs decisions about if, when and how to correct injustices suffered by those subjects.

Hidden bias in the operation of the abuse of positions of power torts

The formulation of the abuse of position of power torts leads to their restrictive application by the courts. This is due to the existence of common law tests that constrain access to remedies, and in turn act to exclude legitimate claims arising from the abuse of police powers. This is largely because there exists a rigid dichotomy between the public interest in unmasking abuses of power, and the public policy of protecting office holders such as police officers.

One might ask why it should be the role of tort to provide specific remedies to rebalance the wrongs that disproportionately impact particular groups. John Goldberg and Benjamin Zipursky argue that tort is a law of civil recourse that sets standards of conduct and empowers victims to demand action to redress wrongs or injustices.[15] The theory places the victim as the agent and the state as merely a vehicle rather than an active responder. Martha Chamallas argues that Goldberg and Zipursky's so-called 'Civil Recourse Theory' fails to take account of the importance of group identity in the historical construction of right and wrong when framing remedies.[16] Chamallas considers this to be particularly important for theories that fall into the group that she describes as 'classical legal theory on legal consciousness'.[17] She argues that the state plays a crucial role and that there is a very public factor in tort law that must continue to play out for those victims who remain disempowered.[18] This is particularly true, Chamallas argues, for women and those from ethnic minorities, given that tort has a hidden bias.[19] Like Chamallas, Ronen Avraham and Kimberly Yuracko argue that tort law can be unintentionally biased based on the statistics it accepts.[20] For example, in

---

[15]   John C.P. Goldberg and Benjamin C. Zipursky, 'Torts as Wrongs' (2010) 88(5) *Texas Law Review* 917.

[16]   Martha Chamallas, 'Beneath the Surface of Civil Recourse Theory' (2013) 88(2) *Indiana Law Journal* 527.

[17]   ibid., 528.

[18]   ibid., 531.

[19]   Martha Chamallas and Jennifer B. Wriggins, *The Measure of Injury: Race, Gender and Tort Law* (New York University Press, 2010).

[20]   Ronen Avraham and Kimberley Yuracko, 'Torts and Discrimination' (2017) 78(3) *Ohio State Law Journal* 661.

personal injury cases the use of actuarial tables to determine compensation reflect an implicit bias in life expectancy, work expectancy and average wage because such tables aggregate data by 'race' and gender when the true reality is that life expectancy, work opportunities and average wages would be very different for these groups.

Tort law in England and Wales faces further dilemmas where microstructural factors arguably operate as a covert bias and where victims, far from being empowered agents, are disempowered. Though English tort law refers to 'claimants' rather than 'victims', this does not mean that the power balance is any more evenly distributed. Despite the UK courts openly embracing the theory of 'corrective justice' (reversal of wrongs),[21] the theory is often employed as a policy factor that results in the deviation from traditional tortious rules and tests to benefit an individual or class action group. For example, one could argue that the so-called 'floodgates argument', often used as a policy factor by courts to limit the number of claims by imposing a secondary test for certain groups of claimants, acts to favour the insurance industry or employers and businesses rather than individuals.[22] Policy factors are less often adopted specifically to correct embedded disadvantages for marginalised groups. For actionable torts for police misconduct, what we actually see operating is distributive justice (achieving fair and just outcomes by maximising benefits for the most disadvantaged), but the hands of equality are tied by considerations of proportionality and political worth. This leads to choices about whether to distribute justice in favour of the public interest or in favour of individual rights. Arguably, the abuse of position of power torts are easy to manipulate to achieve an outcome in favour of the status quo of authoritative control under the guise of the public interest.

The civil courts offer a route where compensation can be claimed for abuses of power, including by the police. In this context, the use of the abuse of position of power torts are important to ensure that the police remain accountable where other tortious routes are unavailable. However, to bring a civil claim for damages it is necessary to establish tortious wrongdoing. And, as we will see, these abuse of position of power torts are no less restricted by the operation of policy than other causes of action such as negligence.[23] No figures are collected for civil cases involving malicious prosecution or misfeasance in public office, which makes it difficult to assess the efficacy of the torts where police misconduct is concerned.[24]

---

[21] A theory thought to have first been formulated by Aristotle in his *Nicomachean Ethics*, Book V.

[22] See, for example, the 'floodgates argument' in cases such as *Leigh & Sullivan Ltd v Aliakmon Shipping Co Ltd ('The Aliakmon')* [1986] AC 785, 816 (Lord Brandon); *M v Newham London Borough Council* [1994] 4 All ER 602, 630 (Staughton LJ); *White v Chief Constable of South Yorkshire Police* [1999] 1 All ER 1, 6 (Lord Griffiths); *Rothwell v Chemical & Insulating Co Ltd* [2007] 4 All ER 1047.

[23] For detailed discussion of this area, see Godden-Rasul and Murray, Chapter 2, this volume.

[24] Note that His Majesty's Courts and Tribunals Service does not collect specific statistics on the number of claims brought for malicious prosecution or the tort of misfeasance in public office.

What is also concerning is the paucity of reported cases involving these two torts where the claims of women or minority ethnic claimants have been successful.

Even when discriminatory treatment has occurred, it may not be possible to use the civil courts, for example when legislation proscribes that a special Tribunal has jurisdiction. In *Wilson v The Commissioner of Police for the Metropolis and National Police Chiefs' Council*[25] (an abuse of position of power case involving a sexual misconduct allegation) the claims were initially brought in the civil courts and then came under the auspices of the Investigatory Powers Tribunal, a special judicial Tribunal reserved for use where there is an allegation of misuse of covert surveillance powers by the police. In this case, Katie Wilson alleged that an undercover police officer entered into a sexual relationship with her during a covert surveillance operation on an environmental group of which she was a member. The Tribunal held that the conduct of the police officer amounted to an infringement of her rights and was an abuse of police powers. Ms Wilson had settled her civil claim in the High Court against the defendant and the Tribunal was instead asked to focus on the human rights breaches. The Tribunal found that her rights under Articles 3, 8, 10, 11 and 14 of the European Convention on Human Rights (ECHR) 1950 were breached.

While the Police (Conduct) Regulations 2020 include a definition of 'misconduct' there is not a clear definition of 'misconduct' or 'abuse of power' to be found in the common law tests for the two torts. The 2020 Regulations definition of misconduct is conduct 'so serious as to justify disciplinary action'. However, it is clear from the case law that taking advantage of one's position to misuse the powers given would amount to a civil wrong as an abuse of position of power.[26] This by implication requires an imbalance of power between the claimant and the defendant.

As will be seen, both torts comprise microstructural barriers that place restrictions on their effectiveness. These barriers can be seen in the ill-defined terms that create vagueness in application of the law, the use of control tests with high thresholds that serve to constrain the utility of these torts for certain marginalised groups and the award of damages based on perceptions of morality of conduct.

The tort of malicious prosecution

The tort of malicious prosecution seeks to provide remedies to individuals who have been wrongfully prosecuted and where the decision to prosecute was made

---

[25] *Wilson v The Commissioner of Police for the Metropolis and National Police Chiefs' Council* [2021] UKIPTrib IPT _11_167_H.

[26] See, for example, the discussion in the false imprisonment tort case of *Lumba v Secretary of State for the Home Department* [2011] UKSC 12; *Mighty v Secretary of State for the Home Department* [2011] UKSC 12, 69–88.

maliciously and led to the individual suffering loss or damage. For a claimant to succeed in this tort s/he must prove five main elements. These are:

1. that the claimant was prosecuted by the defendant in criminal proceedings;
2. that the criminal prosecution failed and was decided in the claimant's favour;
3. that the criminal prosecution was without reasonable and probable cause;
4. that the criminal prosecution was malicious, and;
5. that the claimant suffered actionable damage.

If the claimant can establish all of these, the civil courts will award damages that arise from the above breaches if they are of the kind and type of loss that is foreseeable.[27]

Part of the difficulty with this tort is the construction and definition of words such as 'reasonable and probable cause' and 'malicious'. In *Hicks v Faulkner*[28] it was stated that 'reasonable and probable cause' is both a subjective and objective test. It requires the court to consider whether the defendant had an honest belief in the guilt of the claimant (subjective limb) based on the existence of circumstances that would lead an ordinary, prudent and cautious person to reasonably believe in that guilt (objective limb).[29] The test was summarised by Lord Devlin in *Glinski v McIver*[30] to be a question of whether the prosecutor actually believed, and reasonably believed, that s/he had cause for prosecution. Both the subjective and objective limbs must be satisfied for reasonable and probable cause to be established. *Moulton v Chief Constable of the West Midlands*[31] confirmed that as long as the judge made a finding based on the *Hicks v Faulkner* test, s/he would not need to specifically split the findings between the two limbs. The test is therefore a low threshold because where there is *some* evidence to justify arrest and subsequent prosecution this will be sufficient to show reasonable and probable cause. Conversely, this means that it is likely to be harder for claimants to prove to the necessary standard of proof that there was not reasonable and probable cause for the prosecution. This problem could be remedied by reversing the burden of proof onto the defendant through the operation of a rebuttable presumption. This presumption would operate once the claimant had shown that the prosecution had failed and that the criminal case was decided in favour of the claimant in the criminal courts. The defendant would then have to show that the prosecution was with reasonable cause rather than the claimant showing that it was not.

---

[27] *Overseas Tankship (UK) Ltd v Morts Dock & Engineering Co (The Wagon Mound No. 1)* [1961] AC 388.

[28] [1878] 8 QBD 167.

[29] For a critique of the 'reasonable person' standard (and similar framings) often relied on across tort law, see Abraham, Chapter 4, this volume.

[30] [1962] AC 726, 768.

[31] *Moulton v Chief Constable of the West Midlands* [2010] EWCA Civ 524, 24–25.

That said, 'malice' is perhaps the most difficult requirement to meet for this tort. *Glinski v McIver* provides a useful definition of malice as covering 'not only spite and ill-will but also any motive other than a desire to bring a criminal to justice',[32] but this is not an exhaustive definition. One could argue that where a finding is made that there is an absence of reasonable and probable cause, this should automatically lead to a finding that there is malice (if the definition of malice given in *Glinski* is to be accepted). However, claimants must prove both parts of the test and in separate stages.

It is notable that in *Moulton* it was argued that the court should lower the threshold requirement for malice in order to comply with Article 5 ECHR (right to liberty and security of person). This is because the burden of proving malice is placed on the claimant and it was argued that this is an onerous burden. Nevertheless, the court declined to lower the threshold. It was further argued that 'malice' does not allow for the fact that malicious prosecution may arise due to maladministration during the investigation or prosecution. Maladministration does not require illegal or unlawful behaviour or behaviour influenced by malice. In *R v Local Commissioner for Administration for the North and East Area of England ex parte Bradford Metropolitan City Council*,[33] Lord Denning stated that maladministration was a wide term that could include 'bias, neglect, inattention, delay, incompetence, ineptitude, perversity, turpitude, arbitrariness and so on'. This would not satisfy the common usage of the term 'malice', but the circumstances could still lead to a malicious prosecution taking place and therefore it arguably should be included within the common law test. Similarly, it is possible for a police officer to have wrongfully prosecuted due to inefficiency and dishonesty rather than actual malice, but knowing that a wrongful prosecution might occur. Under the present test this would not amount to malicious prosecution because malice remains the criterion. Dishonesty is not treated as synonymous with malice.

One only needs to consider the difficulties the definition of 'malice' has caused within criminal law to understand why its continued use in tort law might be problematic. Malice, as Bowen LJ observed in the criminal case of *R v Latimer*,[34] requires intention, yet as the criminal cases have shown, intention as a mental state is problematic. Bowen LJ stated: 'I use the word "malice" in the common sense of the term, viz., a person is deemed malicious when he does an act which he knows will injure either the person or the property of another'.[35] Intention in criminal law was found to have many meanings leading to an eventual distinction being drawn between direct intention and indirect intention.[36] Direct intention was given its common usage such as want, purpose,

---

[32] *Glinski v McIver* [1962] AC 726, 766.
[33] [1979] QB 287, 311.
[34] (1886) 17 QBD 359.
[35] ibid., [361].
[36] See, for example, *R v Moloney* [1985] AC 905 and *R v Woollin* [1999] AC 82.

desire. However, indirect intention is recognised through a common law test. If the consequences were virtually certain to occur and the defendant appreciated this then that would be sufficient for intentional malice (indirect intention).[37] If intention is the focus of what makes the act malicious, not only is it illogical to exclude intentional maladministration leading to wrongful prosecution, it is also illogical that the tort of malicious prosecution does not allow for the possibility of indirect intention through maladministration but instead juxtaposes malice only with direct intention, namely, spite, ill-will and motive. So far, there has been a reluctance to move the civil malice definition forward. While it is accepted that the *Glinski* definition of malice is not exhaustive – for example, *Willers v Joyce*[38] recognises that malice can involve deliberately misusing the court process – the interpretations in the common law still fall short of including the other elements of Lord Denning's partial definition of maladministration.

Another difficulty with the tort of malicious prosecution is in the identification of the so-called 'prosecutor'. There is a lack of a formal definition of 'prosecutor'. Lord Keith noted in *Martin v Watson*[39] that a defendant who is 'actively instrumental in setting the law in motion' against a claimant would be presumed to be a 'prosecutor', although merely starting the administrative process for a prosecution would not in itself make a defendant such.[40] The defendant's involvement must involve some special knowledge about the offence on their part. In short, they must have the necessary desire and intention that the claimant be prosecuted.[41]

The test therefore turns on the facts of each case. It could be more clearly and fairly defined to avoid uncertainty by becoming more closely associated with the so-called 'close connection' test found in the tortious principle of vicarious liability. This test arises where an employee has misused the position entrusted to the employee by the employer and injures a third party as a result. It considers whether the employee's tortious actions are so closely connected to his/her employment that it would be just to hold the employer liable.[42] The issue of whether one is a prosecutor goes beyond being merely an authorised representative and rests on a close connection with the defendant's special knowledge of the offence and their subsequent involvement in bringing about the prosecution. That close connection is then crucial to the defendant being designated as a prosecutor for the purposes of the tort of malicious prosecution. Attempts to recast the 'close connection' test as one of whether the employee is 'an authorised representative', in the sense that a reasonable observer would consider the employee to be acting in a representative capacity, were resisted in

---

[37] *R v Woollin* [1999] AC 82.
[38] [2016] UKSC 43, 55.
[39] [1996] 1 AC 74.
[40] ibid., [76].
[41] *AH(unt) v AB* [2009] EWCA Civ 1092.
[42] *Lister v Hesley Hall Ltd* [2002] 1 AC 215.

the case of *Mohamud v WM Morrisons Supermarkets PLC*[43] and should be similarly resisted in the tort of malicious prosecution.

The close connection test is arguably clearer than Lord Keith's 'setting the law in motion' test and could bring more clarity to the definition of a prosecutor. However, as currently particularised, the common law test relies on special knowledge, coupled with deliberate misstatement of the facts to the person making the decision to charge the claimant, and the intention that there should be a prosecution.[44]

The tort of misfeasance in public office

The tort of misfeasance in public office is intended to address a defendant's abuse of their position in public office through the unethical and immoral treatment of others. The tort has been described as 'exceptional in that it is necessary to prove the requisite subjective state of mind of the defendant in relation not only to his own conduct but also its effects on others'.[45] This tort does not require a prosecution against a defendant to have taken place but instead focuses on any abuse of power in public office. In addition, it does not matter whether the abuse is through exceeding powers or merely apparent in the way the powers are used.[46] In theory, this should make this a very useful tort for those who suffer from abuse of police (and other) power.

Unlike malicious prosecution that has 'malice' as its core, the tort of misfeasance relies on 'dishonesty' (although malice is still an aspect of the test). It is also intended to provide a remedy for maladministration where negligence cannot be used.[47] The focus is on whether the conduct is unlawful and the motive itself (unlike for malicious prosecution) is irrelevant. Thus, one would assume that this tort would provide a less restrictive alternative to a malicious prosecution claim. However, as we will see, it is also compounded by vague terminology and control tests.

The common law test for the tort of misfeasance in public office has six main elements, established in *Three Rivers District Council and Others v Governor and Company of the Bank of England*,[48] but its formulation is unnecessarily contortious:

---

43 [2016] EWCA Civ 116.
44 See *Rees and Others v Commissioner of Police for the Metropolis* [2017] EWHC 273 (QB), 144.
45 *Three Rivers District Council and Others v Governor and Company of the Bank of England* [2001] UKHL 16, 164 (Lord Hobhouse).
46 *Jones v Swansea City Council* [1990] 1 WLR 1453.
47 See the comments of Lord Steyn in *Three Rivers District Council and Others v Governor and Company of the Bank of England* [2001] UKHL 16; and *Calveley v Chief Constable of the Merseyside Police* [1989] AC 1228, 1238F.
48 [2000] UKHL 33, as reiterated by Lord Hope in *Three Rivers District Council and Others v Governor and Company of the Bank of England* [2001] UKHL 16, 42–6, and Lord Hutton, 121.

1. there must be evidence of an act or omission done or made in the exercise of power by a public officer AND;
2. the act or omission must constitute an abuse of power or authority by the public officer in the sense that it is unlawful AND;
3. that public officer must have either known they were abusing their public power or authority or be consciously reckless in the sense of going beyond the limits or restraints of their public power or authority AND;
4. the public officer must have acted (or omitted to act) EITHER with the intention of harming the claimant ('targeted malice') OR with the knowledge that the act or omission was beyond his/her powers and that it would cause harm/injury/loss to the claimant OR the public officer acted recklessly as to the probability of harm/injury/loss to the claimant by wilfully choosing to act although the public officer was aware there was a serious risk of harm/injury/loss but chose to disregard that risk ('untargeted malice');
5. the act or omission must have caused the claimant's harm/injury/loss;
6. the claimant must have legal standing to sue by having a sufficient interest in the alleged act or omission.

Like the tort of malicious prosecution, damages are recoverable using the usual rules of remoteness: where the type of damage is foreseeable then damages will be recoverable.[49]

The tort of misfeasance in public office is an intentional tort because regardless of the use of words such as 'recklessness' within the test, it is the act or omission that must be intentional, and it is the act or omission that carries the 'abuse of power' label. It is this that is sufficient to establish the 'bad faith' nature of the defendant's actions because the intentional abuse of power means that there is not an honest belief in the lawfulness of the conduct. It is true that the tort can be committed through subjective recklessness (the deliberate unlawful act or failure to act where the defendant is aware of a known risk of serious harm/injury/loss), but the act of abusing power must be intentional.

The requirement for intention therefore separates this tort from the tort of negligence (discussed later in this chapter). The advantage is also that the tort can involve a claim for pure economic loss without the constraints that have been imposed on pure economic loss in the tort of negligence. 'Malice' in the common law test for the tort of misfeasance in public office is given a more general meaning than in the tort of malicious prosecution. This is because misfeasance in public office recognises the possibility of indirect intention, as illustrated by the 'targeted' and 'untargeted' malice aspects of the test which are not recognised in the tort of malicious prosecution. Lord Millett observed: '[t]he element of knowledge which it involves is, in my opinion, a means of establishing

---

[49] *Overseas Tankship (UK) Ltd v Morts Dock & Engineering Co (The Wagon Mound No.1)* [1961] AC 388.

the necessary intention, not a substitute for it. But intention does not have to be proved by positive evidence. It can be inferred.'[50] As a result, this tort may be beneficial particularly to women bringing sex abuse claims based on abuse of position of power. His Majesty's Inspectorate of Constabulary and Fire and Rescue Services recognises that misogynistic and predatory behaviour by police officers amounts to prejudicial and improper behaviour.[51] Some sexual abuse within positions of power may therefore be caught by the wider definition of 'malice' for this tort. Another feature of the tort that makes it a potentially more desirable litigation route is that the claimant need not identify a prosecutor. It is only necessary to identify a public officer who has abused their public authority. As Mr Justice Mitting noted in the High Court decision of *Rees and Others v Commissioner of Police for the Metropolis*,[52] the exercise of power need not be common law or statutory and can be merely the exercise of a public function. Further, in *Darker v Chief Constable of the West Midlands Police*,[53] Lord Hope was prepared to accept that investigating crimes was a public function that could be covered by the definition of 'exercise of power' for the purposes of the tort of misfeasance in public office. While the police may enjoy a practical immunity from suit for the purposes of investigating crime,[54] this does not apply in situations where they commit an unlawful act without an honest belief that it is lawful. Further, the 'targeted malice' element of the tort can be committed by a police officer perverting the course of justice.

'Public office' remains undefined in the tort although the wrongful act must have been carried out by a public officer. Indeed, even when hearing submissions on the illogicality of developing an offence for public office holders when public duties are being increasingly carried out by private contractors, the court has declined the opportunity to define the term 'public office'.[55] The criminal offence of misconduct in public office is very similar to the tort of misfeasance and similarly lacks a definition of public office. However, the Law Commission in its 2016 consultation paper recommended a statutory definition based on status, duty, or performance or exercise of a public function including while under a duty to act in a particular way.[56] A similar tortious definition of public office would help to determine when a person merely holds office without the requisite powers and duties and where they have acted in that official capacity.

---

[50] *Three Rivers District Council and Others v Governor and Company of the Bank of England* [2000] UKHL 33 (Lord Millett).

[51] See An Inspection of Vetting, Misconduct, and Misogyny in the Police Service, His Majesty's Inspectorate of Constabulary and Fire and Rescue Services, 2022, 11.

[52] [2017] EWHC 273 (QB), 182.

[53] [2001] 1 AC 435, 446F.

[54] *Michael v Chief Constable of South Wales* [2015] UKSC 2. See further the discussion by Godden-Rasul and Murray, Chapter 2, this volume.

[55] *Attorney-General's Reference (No.3 of 2003)* [2004] EWCA Crim 868, 62.

[56] Law Commission, Reforming Misconduct in Public Office Cm No 229, 2016, para 4.23 and recommendations 4–8.

While the tort of misfeasance in public office has some features that would assist claimants, there is also a lack of clarity of terms that can hinder the correct application of the common law test. For example, there is not a universal acceptance and understanding of the meaning of 'bad faith' in tort. Lord Hutton said in *Three Rivers* that: '[b]ad faith is an essential element in the tort of misfeasance. In accordance with a well-established rule it is necessary that bad faith (or dishonesty – the term used in some authorities) should be clearly pleaded.'[57]

Yet one could argue that in law 'dishonesty' and 'bad faith' are different beasts. In *Ivey v Genting Casinos (UK) Ltd (t/a Crockfords)*, Lord Hughes stated that 'untruthfulness is often a powerful indicator of dishonesty'.[58] However, it is accepted that the definition of dishonesty has a wide spectrum that can also encompass a lack of integrity, use of illegitimate means or reprehensible or unconscionable behaviour generally.[59] In contrast, 'bad faith', as defined by Lord Burrows in *Pakistan International Airline Corporation v Times Travel (UK) Ltd*,[60] suggests that there exists a legal right and duty (whether contractual or otherwise) between the parties and that right or duty has been breached. He noted, in this case involving a claim for unlawful act economic duress, that:

> [w]ithout that tie to an existing legal right and duty, the 'bad faith demand' requirement loses its force as being underpinned by a workable standard of dishonesty: the bad faith demand is concerned with either a dishonest assertion of an existing right or the dishonest removal (by waiver) of an existing right.[61]

Therefore, very much like the principle of integrity,[62] bad faith is connected to, but is not the sole definition of, dishonesty.

Another difficulty is the application of causation. The act or omission that constituted the abuse of power must have caused the claimant harm or loss. The unfair effects of the operation of causation can be seen in the original High Court decision in *Rees and Others v Commissioner of Police for the Metropolis*.[63] In this case claims against the police were pleaded as both malicious prosecution

---

57 *Three Rivers District Council and Others v Governor and Company of the Bank of England* [2001] UKHL 16, 122.

58 [2017] UKSC 67, 75.

59 See, for example, *Hoodless and Another v Financial Services Authority* [2003] UKFTT 007 (FSM) and *Wingate and Evans v Solicitors Regulation Authority; Solicitors Regulation Authority v Malins* [2018] EWCA Civ 366.

60 [2021] UKSC 40.

61 ibid., [125].

62 See, for example, *Scott v Solicitors Regulation Authority* [2016] EWHC 1256, which considered the interplay between integrity and dishonesty for the purposes of disciplinary proceedings against solicitors.

63 *Rees and Others v Commissioner of Police for the Metropolis* [2017] EWHC 273 (QB).

and misfeasance in public office. Four claimants who were originally defendants in a criminal prosecution argued that police officers (in particular, the senior investigating officer DCS Cook) had been involved in misconduct in an effort to secure their conviction for a murder that happened some 30 years previously. This had allegedly involved pressuring at least three acquaintances of the defendants to give evidence against them, but in particular Eaton, a police informant.

In the High Court the misfeasance claims of three of the claimants (Jonathan Rees, Glenn Vian and Garry Vian) failed due to a lack of causation. Mitting J found the Crown Prosecution Service (CPS) should and could have sought to bring a prosecution against the defendants regardless of the evidence of the police informant (Eaton). Therefore, they had not suffered damage as a result of the police's conduct. The High Court was, however, prepared to accept that all elements were satisfied in relation to a fourth defendant (Fillery). Jonathan Rees and Glenn and Garry Vian appealed the High Court judge's findings to the Court of Appeal and were successful on the basis that the trial judge had not embarked on an investigation as to whether there was indeed a real chance of prosecution with Eaton's evidence.[64] Mitting J's conclusions that there had been reasonable prospect of conviction of the defendants without the crucial evidence of the police informant Eaton was criticised. The Court of Appeal argued this conclusion was not based on any available evidence before the trial judge as the CPS had not made the evidence available to the court. However, surprisingly the Court of Appeal then went on to decide the question of causation in favour of the claimants without the same crucial CPS evidence. It decided that there could not have been a reasonable prospect of conviction without Eaton's evidence. The Court of Appeal took the view that any other evidence in the case would have been tainted by the behaviour of the senior investigating officer DCS Cook, and as such no CPS counsel would have allowed the case to proceed. Yet this conclusion was also based on an absence of evidence from the CPS as the CPS claimed privilege in relation to the relevant parts of the investigation documents. The court made an assumption without knowing what other evidence the CPS held and whether in fact that evidence would indeed have been tainted by the behaviour of DCS Cook. It did not hear any evidence from the CPS or its counsel.

Therefore, both the original trial judge's decision and the Court of Appeal's decision were based on hypothesis. Mitting J based his hypothesis on the evidential test to be met for prosecution under the 5th edition of the CPS Code,[65] while the Appeal Court's decision was largely based on the abandonment of the prosecution by the CPS in 2011. However, it is notable that Mitting J's assessment of the reasonable prospect of conviction expressly states that it is based on the evidence that the CPS had at the time of charge, and this included evidence not just of the discredited witnesses Eaton and a second man Ward, but

---

[64] *Rees and Others v Commissioner of Police for the Metropolis* [2018] EWCA Civ 1587.

[65] See *Rees and Others v Commissioner of Police for the Metropolis* [2017] EWHC 273 (QB), 192; and 'The Code for Crown Prosecutors 2018'.

admissible evidence in relation to a witness Terry Jones.[66] One could therefore argue that the trial judge's original findings on causation were in fact based on firmer grounds than the Court of Appeal suggested. In any event, both courts based their conclusions on circumstantial evidence to satisfy causation. It was not possible to show whether or not the CPS would have prosecuted without the evidence of the informants because neither court had access to the CPS file and neither court heard conclusive evidence from the CPS as to what its prosecuting decision would have been.

This demonstrates how causation can be circumvented with an assumption. Although it is true that the standard of proof in civil proceedings is only on a balance of probabilities, the 'but for' test for causation requires a causal link between the decision to prosecute and the evidence of the informants and this could only be shown by evidence of what the actual prosecution decision would have been based on. This in turn would require evidence from the CPS file showing how it had applied the CPS Code. Therefore, *Rees* remains an unsatisfactory decision in the application of the two torts as far as causation is concerned. In the High Court decision of *Rees,* the court was invited to consider applying a varied causation test similar to the negligence test of material contribution to harm found in *Bailey v Ministry of Defence*,[67] but declined on the basis that no expert medical evidence is needed in misfeasance cases. The *Bailey* test examines cumulative causes and was summarised by Waller LJ as: '[i]n a case where medical science cannot establish the probability that "but for" an act of negligence the injury would not have happened but can establish that the contribution of the negligent cause was more than negligible, the "but for" test is modified, and the claimant will succeed.'[68]

It is important to note that when formulating the test Waller LJ did not see this 'material contribution' test as merely being confined to medical negligence cases,[69] and as such one could argue that there would not have been anything preventing its use in a misfeasance case.

Hidden bias in compensating misconduct and abuse

As Lord Woolf MR indicated in *Thompson and Hsu v Commissioner of Police for the Metropolis*,[70] courts normally only recognise two types of damages: ordinary damages (which are compensatory in nature) and aggravated damages (where there are aggravating features about the defendant's conduct – this can go beyond the underlying tort and involve considerations of the conduct during the litigation). Exemplary damages (sometimes called 'punitive damages') can

---

66   ibid., [58] and [192].
67   [2008] EWCA Civ 883.
68   ibid., [46].
69   ibid.
70   [1998] QB 498.

be awarded where the court considers that ordinary and aggravated damages alone would not be an adequate measure of the punishment to be made for the tort itself. Exemplary damages are therefore regarded as a windfall because they are awarded in addition to ordinary and aggravated damages. Guidance from *Thompson* suggests that the starting point for an award of exemplary damages should be £5,000.

Although misconduct through abuse of position might be thought of as oppressive and unconscionable behaviour justifying the award of exemplary damages, such damages are discretionary and left to be decided on a case-by-case basis. *Rookes v Barnard* identified three circumstances in which exemplary damages would be justified.[71] These include where there has been 'an arbitrary and outrageous use of executive power'[72] or 'unconstitutional action by servants of government'.[73] However, cases such as *AB v Southwest Water Services Ltd*[74] recognise that this head of damages is a remedy of last resort.

The guidelines from *Thompson* were used to reconfirm the exemplary damages awarded in *Rees*.[75] However, one should question whether the *Thompson* guidance on exemplary damages is still fit for purpose given that the reputation of the police is in an even more dire state than it was in 1998, with institutional corruption and institutional sexism added to the longstanding charge of institutional racism. For example, the final report of the 2023 Casey Review[76] of the MPS found that 'supervisors and senior officers look the other way, ignore their management responsibilities and actively engage in discrimination'.[77] The discrimination was found to be wilful. The starting point of £5,000 needs to be revised upwards significantly.

It is also argued that exemplary damages should not be regarded as a windfall but as an essential element of damages when the tort of malicious prosecution or misfeasance in public office has been established. The torts have a high threshold to cross to establish misconduct and it is perhaps egregious that a claimant should then have to meet a further high threshold to obtain exemplary damages. Such damages should become a mandatory element of the compensation to mark that an important right has been infringed against a subject of the state by an executive of the state or a public officer.

The common law has previously toyed with the idea of introducing a special head of damages known as 'vindicatory damages' as a mark of public outrage

---

[71]   [1964] AC 1129.

[72]   ibid., [1223].

[73]   ibid., [1226].

[74]   [1993] QB 507. See also *Kuddas v Chief Constable of Leicestershire Constabulary* [2002] 2 AC 122, 63 (Lord Nicholls).

[75]   *Rees v Commissioner of Police for the Metropolis* [2019] EWHC 2120 (Admin), 8-9 (confirmed in *Rees v Commissioner of Police for the Metropolis* [2021] EWCA Civ 49).

[76]   The Baroness Casey Review: Final Report. An Independent Review into the Standards of Behaviour and Internal Culture of the Metropolitan Police Service, 2023.

[77]   ibid., 330.

at the contravention of a constitutional right.[78] However, this head of damages was dismissed in the case of *Lumba v Secretary of State and Others* on the basis that vindicatory damages are closely aligned to punitive and exemplary damages in the English law and there was no need therefore to introduce a new head of damages.[79] However, the difficulty with this argument is that exemplary damages are restricted in use and scope. In 1997 the Law Commission recognised that exemplary damages play an important punitive role and should be an award that is left to a jury to decide rather than a judge.[80] This would move this head of damages from a stringent test to one based on the jury's view of the value of the breach that has taken place. The Law Commission recommended that exemplary damages should be available for all torts and renamed 'punitive damages' to reflect the serious nature of the award.[81] The Law Commission also proposed replacing the *Rookes v Barnard* categories with one single category where 'the defendant deliberately and outrageously disregarded the plaintiff's (sic) rights'.[82] This would align the purpose of exemplary damages more closely with vindicatory damages and also ensure that the award of compensation is more closely tied to the issue of the defendant's misconduct. Such reform would help to balance the court's ability to police the police.

Adjusting the hidden bias through formulation

The torts of malicious prosecution and misfeasance in public office have not adjusted to different value changes in society. Both torts are stifled by archaic foundations restricting their growth and evolution. For example, the tort of misfeasance in public office has its early origins in challenges to voting rights[83] and then through the use of controls such as licensing.[84] In *Dunlop v Woolahra Municipal Council*[85] it was declared that the tort was 'well established' by 1981.[86] The reality is it has rarely been used to tackle police misconduct or misconduct that affects the fundamental rights of citizens.

---

78   See the endorsement of this head of damages as legitimate additional compensation by the Privy Council in *Attorney General of Trinidad and Tobago v Ramanoop* [2005] UKPC 15 and the obiter endorsements in *Ashley v Chief Constable of Sussex Police* [2008] UKHL 25 (Lord Scott); and *Mosley v News Group Newspapers Ltd* [2008] EWHC 1777 (QB) (per Eady J).

79   *Lumba and others v Secretary of State for the Home Department* [2011] UKSC 12; *Mighty v Secretary of State for the Home Department* [2011] UKSC 12, 100.

80   Law Commission, Aggravated, Exemplary and Restitutionary Damages No 247, 1997, recommendation 1.3 (17).

81   ibid., recommendation 1.3 (16).

82   ibid., recommendation 1.3 (18).

83   See *Ashby v White* 1703 2 Ld Raym 938.

84   See *Bourgoin SA v Ministry of Agriculture, Fisheries and Food* [1986] QB 716.

85   [1982] AC 158.

86   ibid., [172F].

The law of tort has a rich history in making adjustments to common law tests to reflect policy changes and changes to societal attitudes. If we take the development of the common law test of causation as an example, we can see that it has been altered in several situations, including to reflect the move from paternalism to patient-centred care in medical law or to recognise new definitions of 'harm'. In medical negligence, *Chester v Afshar*[87] saw the courts remedy a previous reluctance to accept that doctors were bound by a doctrine of informed consent and impose a duty to reveal any material risks of an operation to a patient. The doctrine of informed consent had been accepted in the US since 1972 following the decision in *Canterbury v Spence*.[88] However, it was not until *Montgomery v Lanarkshire Health Board (Scotland)*[89] that the doctrine was formally recognised in the UK. In the interim, however, the judiciary, having grown tired of cases that continued to make patients the losers in medical negligence cases involving failure by doctors to disclose risk, simply made an adjustment to the common law test for medical negligence by circumventing the requirement to prove causation. In *Chester v Afshar*, Lord Steyn argued that medical paternalism stood in the way of progress and that patient autonomy should prevail in the area of consent to treatment. He suggested that rather than adopting traditionalist approaches to common law tests there should be a greater emphasis given to policy and corrective justice.[90] Therefore, despite the claimant being unable to prove a causal link between the failure by the surgeon to tell her of the risks that a back operation might lead to paralysis and the actual paralysis that resulted, her claim was still successful. Causation presented a problem because Ms Chester could not prove that if she had been told of the risks, she would not have had the operation at all. Instead, she could only agree that she might have changed the date of the operation by postponing it; this might still have led to the paralysis occurring.

Similar adjustments have been made in relation to industrial negligence. In *Fairchild v Glenhaven Funeral Services Ltd and Others*,[91] when the claimants were unable to establish on a balance of probabilities that they had inhaled harmful asbestos dust while working for different (negligent) employers, the court adjusted the standard of proof required. This is despite the fact that in order to attribute legal responsibility it is usually necessary to show who caused the claimant harm. The court adjusted the causation requirement to allow for a level of proof that recognised it was more probable than not that the named employer defendants had 'materially increased the risk' of the claimant contracting the inevitably fatal disease known as mesothelioma from inhaling the harmful asbestos dust in their negligent workplaces.

---

[87] [2004] UKHL 41.

[88] 464 F 2d 772 (DC) 1972.

[89] [2015] UKSC 11.

[90] *Chester v Afshar* [2004] UKHL 41, 21–4.

[91] [2003] 1 AC 32.

In *Dryden and Others v Johnson Matthey PLC*[92] the Supreme Court was willing to adjust the commonly held understanding of physical harm and widen it to include 'sensitisation' – the process whereby the body becomes sensitive to a product that may later cause them harm. On this basis, the claimants succeeded in their claim for 'Platinum Salt Sensitisation' that they alleged was caused by their exposure to platinum salt in the workplace. Though the condition itself was asymptomatic, it did cause allergies resulting in a running nose, skin problems and coughing. The Supreme Court disagreed with the previous assessment of the trial judge and the Court of Appeal that sensitisation was no more than economic loss because it did not lead to any meaningful or relevant harm. As sensitisation could lead to an immune system response that produced antibodies that in themselves could combine with antigens to provoke the release of histamines in the body, this process could be regarded as 'harm' because the histamines themselves caused an allergic reaction.

We see in such cases the operation of corrective justice (reversing wrongs) which is used as a policy tool to assist an individual claimant (for example, Ms Chester) or a group of claimants (such as mesothelioma and platinum salt sensitisation claimants). Despite this we also see a reluctance to adjust causation requirements in other areas of tort where other groups are affected, such as product liability cases where women have been harmed by defective products during reproductive care.[93] Similarly, causation adjustments have not been made to the abuse of positions of power torts despite their potential negative impact on women and ethnic minorities. This inconsistent approach to the 'deserving claimant' means that some torts remain unadjusted with continuing hidden bias(es).

Do suitable alternative remedies for marginalised groups exist?

Disciplinary proceedings are perhaps the obvious first remedy where police misconduct has occurred. Police officers are bound by a set of standards and expectations regarding professional behaviour which are set out in the Police (Conduct) Regulations 2020, underpinned by the College of Policing's Code of Ethics. As already noted, the 2020 Regulations define misconduct as a breach that is 'so serious as to justify disciplinary action'. While police misconduct can be

---

[92]   [2018] UKSC 18.

[93]   See, for example, cases such as *Multiple Claimants v Sanifo-Synthelabo* [2007] EWHC 1860, where a group of women failed in their claim to find a causal link between the epilepsy drug Epilem that they took during pregnancy and resultant birth defects in their children, and *XYZ and Others v Schering Health Care Ltd and Others* [2002] EWHC 1420 (QB) in relation to cardiovascular injuries following use of different brands of the oral contraceptive pill. For a full discussion of product liability and its gendered implications, especially in relation to medical devices, see Emily Jackson, Chapter 7, this volume.

punished internally through disciplinary proceedings[94] this is not always effective. Home Office data show that misconduct meetings were the most common disciplinary proceedings involving police officers (67 per cent).[95] Disciplinary proceedings can lead to sanctions such as dismissal and being barred from serving in police or other law enforcement roles.[96] The fact that most complainants are White men according to the IOPC[97] does not rule out the possibility that women and those from minority ethnic backgrounds are reluctant to file formal complaints. Only 13 per cent of complaints in 2020/21 led to formal investigations and only 18 of these led to a finding of evidence of misconduct or gross misconduct. The 2023 Casey Review found that the internal disciplinary processes of the Metropolitan Police Service took too long and that misconduct cases were often mishandled.[98]

In August 2022 the College of Policing issued new guidance on police misconduct sanctions with tighter procedural rules and recommendations about the types of misconduct that would reach the 'seriousness' threshold. This includes discrimination and violence against women by a serving police officer where dismissal would be considered appropriate.[99] It may be that future statistics will see a sharp increase in disciplinary proceedings leading to dismissals. This does seem to be the case in the wake of the conviction of PC David Carrick, following which he was dismissed without notice.[100] However, while disciplinary action may act as a deterrent to abuses of power, and may go some way to vindicating victims of police misconduct, it does not serve to satisfy compensation claims. Therefore, disciplinary proceedings or indeed criminal proceedings may not be a favoured route for an individual seeking compensation.

It is true that claimants can also use the torts of negligence and breach of statutory duty to address misconduct and abuses of power, however, a long run of cases culminating in *Michael v Chief Constable of South Wales*[101] has already established that the police do not owe a duty of care in negligence concerning their failure to investigate and protect an individual from the criminal actions of

---

[94] See the requirements for complaints handling in the Police Reform Act 2002.

[95] Home Office, Official Statistics Police Misconduct, England and Wales year ending 31 March 2022, 2023 (available at https://www.gov.uk/government/statistics/police-misconduct-engl and-and-wales-year-ending-31-march-2022/police-misconduct-england-and-wales-year-end ing-31-march-2022).

[96] See Police Barred List and Police Advisory List Regulations 2017.

[97] IOPC, Police Complaints: Statistics for England and Wales 2020/21, 2022, 8.

[98] The Baroness Casey Review, chapter 7.

[99] See College of Policing, *Guidance on Outcomes in Police Misconduct Proceedings* (College of Policing Ltd, 2022) – a response to the murder of Sarah Everard by a serving police officer.

[100] The record of PC David Carrick's misconduct hearing on 17 January 2023 and the subsequent outcome have since been deleted from the MPS website (Tristan Kirk, 'Details of serial rapist David Carrick wiped from Met Police website' *The Evening Standard* 26 March 2023). Nevertheless, Commissioner Sir Mark Rowley issued a statement on 25 January 2023 saying 'We must improve dramatically for London' (Martin Bentham, 'Two or three Met officers to face court a week' *The Evening Standard* 25 January 2023).

[101] [2015] UKSC 2.

a third party, unless they directly assumed responsibility to the victim. Therefore victims, witnesses or suspects must show that they have suffered harm from a failure by the police to act (where a positive duty to act exists based on an assumption of responsibility) before any claim in negligence will be successful.[102] In addition, policy factors are usually employed in negligence cases to provide the police with 'immunity' from civil suits to prevent 'defensive policing' occurring.

The criminal law provides an alternative route where there has been misconduct that involves abuse of position of power. The criminal law has created an offence for misconduct in public office that is similar in construction to its tort sibling misfeasance in public office. However, the burden of proof threshold is higher in criminal law as proof must be established beyond all reasonable doubt (often referred to as the 'sure test').[103] In civil proceedings a lower burden of proof will suffice: claims must be proved 'on the balance of probabilities' – that is, the claimant must show that the defendant's actions were 'more likely than not' the cause of their harm. The offence of misconduct is also much older than the tort of misfeasance as it can be traced back to the 1783 decision of *R v Bembridge*.[104] Indeed, in *R v Chapman and Others*[105] it was noted that 'an ancient common law offence is being used in circumstances where it has rarely before been applied'.[106]

According to *Attorney-General's Reference*[107] the criminal offence of misconduct in public office requires a wilful and intentional breach of duty by a public officer (whether by an act or omission). The duty must be one found in the common law or by statute. However, it requires the breach to fall seriously below the proper standards expected so that it amounts to serious misconduct before criminal liability can be established. The mens rea of 'wilful' and 'intention' denotes culpability that is deliberate rather than merely inadvertent.[108] Also, for the offence to be proved it is necessary to show harm is to the broader public interest, whereas a tortious claim merely needs to establish harm to the individual.

Both the tort and the criminal offence were created by common law rather than statute. The common law has developed tests which on first reading may appear detailed but in fact lack sufficient particularity. For example, unlike the tort of misfeasance, there is not a stringent test of 'bad faith' to be overcome for the criminal offence. Though it is true that both the tort and the offence require elements of bad faith and harm to the public interest, in the case of misconduct in public office, Pill LJ cautioned against the use of the term 'bad faith' in case it confused the jury.[109] By contrast, in the tort of misfeasance, bad faith

---

[102]   *Robinson v Chief Constable of West Yorkshire Police* [2018] UKSC 4.

[103]   See *R v Summers* (1952) 3 Cr App R 14 (Lord Goddard).

[104]   (1783) 3 Doug 327.

[105]   [2015] EWCA Crim 539.

[106]   ibid., [29].

[107]   *Attorney-General's Reference (No.3 of 2003)* [2004] EWCA Crim 868.

[108]   ibid., [46–59].

[109]   ibid., [63].

is key: Lord Steyn in *Three Rivers* referred to the 'unifying element of conduct amounting to an abuse of power accompanied by subjective bad faith' as being the 'raison d'etre of the tort'.[110] However, as stated, the focus of the misconduct is not on bad faith in the criminal cases. For example, in *R v Dytham*[111] Lord Widgery observed that the offence 'must be of such a degree that the misconduct impugned is calculated to injure the public interest so as to call for condemnation and punishment'.[112] In addition, for the criminal offence there must not be any justification or excuse for the abuse of power or authority or the failure to meet proper standards. However, as observed by Pill LJ in *Attorney-General's Reference*, the main difference between injury to the public interest when it occurs in the tort and the offence is that the civil tort of misfeasance involves a breach that is an affront to individual members of the public whereas the offence of misconduct in public office involves a breach that is an affront to the Crown.[113]

The Law Commission in its 2020 report noted that, as demonstrated by Home Office data, there was an almost fourfold increase in misconduct in public office claims between 2005 and 2018.[114] This included a notable number of prosecutions of police officers for corruption following 'Operation Elveden', which unmasked the receipt of unlawful payments made by journalists to police officers in return for the police providing classified information for their news stories.[115] While the offence of misconduct in public office appears to be used more often than reported cases of its sibling tort, a similar criminal offence of 'corrupt or other improper exercise of police powers and privileges',[116] which was introduced following the 2014 Stephen Lawrence Independent Review,[117] appears less accessible with only six convictions since its introduction in 2015.[118] Yet this is a much simpler offence in construction requiring only that the police officer knowingly exercises their powers and privileges improperly to achieve a benefit for himself/herself or a detriment to another.

The Law Commission proposed replacing both criminal offences and completely reforming the offence of misconduct in public office. The recommendations include replacing the offence of misconduct in public office with two new offences. This would involve removal of the existing common law test and replacement with two new statutory offences of 1) corruption in

---

[110] *Three Rivers District Council and Others v Governor and Company of the Bank of England* [2000] UKHL 33.
[111] [1979] 1 QB 723.
[112] ibid., 728.
[113] *Attorney-General's Reference (No.3 of 2003)* [2004] EWCA Crim 868, 48.
[114] Law Commission, Misconduct in Public Office Cm HC 1027 2020, para 2.20.
[115] Operation Elveden cost the taxpayer almost £15 million and led to the conviction of 34 police officers in 2016. See also Law Commission, ibid., para 2.28.
[116] Criminal Justice and Courts Act 2015, s 26.
[117] House of Commons, The Stephen Lawrence Independent Review HC 1094, 2014.
[118] Law Commission, Misconduct in Public Office Cm HC 1027 2020, para 2.87.

public office and 2) breach of duty in public office.[119] This is an interesting proposition as it recognises that abuse of process can be on the one hand far-reaching in the sense of damaging the wider public interest, and on the other hand individualistic in the sense of causing specific harm or loss to an individual. A similar separation by the creation of new torts would allow a clear route for negligence claims involving abuse of process as well as claims for malicious, corrupt or maladministration conduct. The Law Commission also proposes that in the creation of a replacement offence of breach of duty in public office there should be a reversal of the burden of proof on a defendant to show that their conduct was in the public interest.[120] A similar reversal of the burden of proof on a claimant for both torts would have the necessary effect of adjusting causation to make it easier to prove.

Another difference in use of criminal offences rather than tort is of course the question of remedy versus penalty. Misconduct in public office carries a maximum sentence of life imprisonment. The offence of corrupt or other improper exercise of police powers and privileges carries a maximum sentence of 14 years imprisonment and/or a fine. Tort carries a remedy that is monetary by imposing punishment through the use of exemplary damages. Creating subcategories of the torts would tackle the issue of whether such compensation is capable of truly reflecting the damage caused to an individual or group.

Conclusion

Obviously, better training, as well as improved internal disciplinary procedures, might go some way to preventing some police officers abusing their positions, especially in relation to marginalised or vulnerable groups. Or, as Freedland suggests in relation to the Metropolitan Police, we could start from scratch and totally rebuild the service.[121] Presumably this would or should entail a rebalancing of the composition of the service to include (at least) more officers who are women and from minority ethnic and other marginalised groups.

In terms of tort law, bringing clarity to bear for key terms within the common law tests for the abuse of positions of power torts would lead to a more consistent application of both torts as well as providing a more effective remedy for claimants from marginalised groups. The readjustment of the existing common law tests would also move the civil law back to a corrective justice agenda and empower

---

[119] For detailed discussions of the benefit of reforming the law of Misconduct in Public Office through new offences see Simon Parsons, 'Misconduct in Public Office: Should It Still Be Prosecuted?' (2012) 76(2) *Journal of Criminal Law* 179; Catarina Sjölin and Helen Edwards, 'When Misconduct in Public Office is Really a Sexual Offence' (2017) 81(4) *Journal of Criminal Law* 292; and Jeremy Horder, *Criminal Misconduct in Office* (Oxford University Press, 2018).

[120] Law Commission, Misconduct in Public Office Cm HC 1027 2020, recommendation 12, 176.

[121] Freedland, 'What to do with a Met police that harbours rapists and murderers? Scrap it and start again'.

those groups most impacted by abuse of power when police misconduct occurs – namely women and those from minority ethnic groups – especially given what is now known about the extent of institutional racism and sexism (even misogyny) within the police force.

Permitting mandatory exemplary damages would also serve to highlight to the public that true civil recourse has been achieved. The courts would then become active responders rather than passive gatekeepers of civil wrongs. Lessons can be drawn from the Law Commission's proposals for the reform of the criminal offences in this area, as these operate in the same sphere as the abuse of position of power torts. A revision of the causation principles and a reversed burden for aspects of these torts would also help to rebalance wrongs.

Homosexuality, Defamatory Meaning and Reputational Injury in English Law

Alexandros Antoniou and Dimitris Akrivos

This chapter was supported by the University of Essex's open access fund.

Introduction

In contrast to the law of negligence (which aims to compensate for injuries to the person and property) or the torts of wrongful arrest and false imprisonment (the purpose of which is to provide redress for the deprivation of personal liberty), the tort of defamation aims to deter and remedy unwarranted damage to a person's reputation during their life.[1] The action in defamation is designed to target falsehood.[2] If a defendant can establish the truth of the defamatory statement, they have a complete defence and their motive in publishing the offending words is irrelevant.[3] This long-standing principle of defamation law may be seen as tilting the balance in favour of publication in cases of uncomfortable, reputation-damaging truths, but this issue falls at the centre of the tort of misuse of private information. The structure of defamation does not seem to offer a place for it.[4] Although anyone can theoretically prevent

---

[1] There is no defamation of the dead in England and Wales. The position is the same in Scotland; *Broom v Ritchie & Co* (1904) 12 SLT 205. A deceased's relatives may have a claim if the words in question reflect badly on their reputations. Note that the European Court of Human Rights has held in several cases that an individual's Article 8 rights may be engaged by defamatory references to deceased members of that individual's family; see, for example, *Plon (Société) v France* (2006) 42 EHRR 36; *Genner v Austria* [2016] ECHR 36.

[2] See *McPherson v Daniels* (1829) 10 B&C 263, 272 (Littledale J): 'the law will not permit a man to recover damages in respect of an injury to a character which he does not or ought not to possess'.

[3] Note, however, the exception arising from sections 8 and 16(1)–(3) of the Rehabilitation of Offenders Act 1974 in cases where a person has a 'spent' conviction for a crime.

[4] Jenny Steele, *Tort Law* (5th edn, Oxford University Press, 2022), chapter 5.2.

the publication of (or recover damages for) untrue public statements that make other people think less of them, in reality, a significant number of cases in this area involve public figures,[5] including politicians, celebrities and multinational corporations, either because damaging remarks about them are more likely to reach a broader audience or because they enjoy wide visibility and may have a greater interest in what others think of them.

The chapter examines whether publications misidentifying an individual as homosexual should serve as the basis of a defamation suit. By contrast to other common law jurisdictions,[6] this question has not attracted sustained consideration within contemporary English law. To contextualise the issue, we begin by exploring the evolution of dominant societal norms, key events and pieces of legislation that shaped the trajectory of the LGBT movement in England and Wales. We then proceed to examine the law's treatment of false defamatory allegations imputing homosexuality. We conclude that, within the boundaries of the definitional elements of the tort of defamation, there are still some restrictions around falsely stating or implying that someone has engaged in homosexual conduct, despite the apparent shift in public attitudes towards gay individuals. We argue that in the current socio-political climate, in which echoes of the past stigma, discrimination and persistent stereotyping can still be heard in gay people's everyday lives, preventing them from achieving tangible equality with their heterosexual counterparts, the misidentification of someone as gay should never be treated as a legally recognisable reputational harm. Such recognition would endorse the undesirable idea that homophobia is worthy of law's respect.

Historical overview

To better understand the law's and courts' approach to false imputations of homosexuality, it is important to first consider the wider social context in which these are interpreted. Throughout history, there is ample evidence demonstrating

---

5   For example, a famous New Zealand cricketer won £90,000 in damages over statements on Twitter that he had been involved in match fixing. Such a very serious allegation about a professional sportsman was found to have gone to the core attributes of this personality and could 'entirely destroy his reputation for integrity'; see *Cairns v Modi* [2012] EWHC 756, para 121.

6   For instance, American and Australian jurisprudence is rich with cases and legal scholarship pertaining to defamation and homosexuality; see further Laurie Phillips, 'Libelous Language Post *Lawrence*: Accusations of Homosexuality as Defamation' (2012) 46(1) *Free Speech Yearbook* 55; Holly Miller, 'Homosexuality as Defamation: A Proposal for the Use of the "Right-Thinking Minds" Approach in the Development of Modern Jurisprudence' (2013) 18(3) *Communication Law and Policy* 349; Matthew Bunker, Drew Shenkman and Charles Tobin, 'Not That There's Anything Wrong With That: Imputations of Homosexuality and the Normative Structure of Defamation Law' (2011) 21(3) *Fordham Intellectual Property, Media and Entertainment Law Journal* 581; Theodore Bennett, 'Not So Straight-Talking: How Defamation Law Should Treat Imputations of Homosexuality' (2016) 35(2) *University of Queensland Law Journal* 313.

how the heteronormative foundations of the law, that is, its intrinsic mechanisms of constructing heterosexuality as natural and normal (for example, in the regulation of marriage, family life, labour, economic support and beyond),[7] favoured a view of gay people as 'deviant outsiders', contributing to their stigmatisation and marginalisation.[8]

The Buggery Act of 1533, the first legislation against sodomy in English criminal law, provided that the '*detestable* and *abominable* vice of buggery committed with mankind or beast' was punishable by death. More than three centuries later, the Offences Against the Person Act 1861 adopted a slightly more lenient approach, still recognising buggery as a criminal offence, but replacing the death penalty with a sentence of penal servitude for any term between ten years and life. In addition, the Criminal Law Amendment Act 1885 (also known as the Labouchere Amendment after the MP who proposed it) widened the net in the clampdown against homosexual acts and became known as 'The Blackmailer's Charter' as it rendered men who engaged in sexual activities with other men particularly vulnerable to extortion.[9] That Act introduced the offence of 'gross indecency', criminalising consensual sexual activity between men in public or private. This offence, which also became part of the statutes of Canada and other British colonies, carried a penalty of up to two years of imprisonment with or without hard labour. Due to the Act's ambiguous wording, 'gross indecency' was often used by the courts to punish sexual activity between men in cases where sodomy could not be proven.[10] It was under the 1885 Act that famous figures including author Oscar Wilde and mathematician Alan Turing were disgraced, convicted and punished for committing homosexual acts.[11]

What was largely regarded as a turning point in the state's treatment of homosexuals but, in actual fact, did little to tackle their dominant image as 'others', was the 1957 publication of the Report of the Departmental Committee on Homosexual Offences and Prostitution (known as the Wolfenden Report).[12] The committee, led by Sir John Wolfenden, recommended the decriminalisation of homosexual acts between consenting adults in private. This was, in principle, a positive development for gay rights, despite the committee making no attempt

---

7   Marcus Herz and Thomas Johansson, 'The Normativity of the Concept of Heteronormativity' (2015) 62(8) *Journal of Homosexuality* 1009, 1011.

8   Senthorun Raj and Peter Dunne, 'Queering Outside the (Legal) Box: LGBTIQ People in the UK' in Senthorun Raj and Peter Dunne (eds), *The Queer Outside in Law* (Springer, 2021) 4; Meredith Worthen, *Sexual Deviance and Society: A Sociological Examination* (Routledge, 2021) 132.

9   Kath Wilson, 'The Road to Equality: The Struggle of Gay Men and Lesbians to Achieve Equal Rights Before the Law' (2014) 12(3) *British Journal of Community Justice* 81, 81–2.

10   Hugh David, *On Queer Street: A Social History of British Homosexuality, 1895–1995* (HarperCollins, 1997) 17–18.

11   ibid., 5.

12   Home Office and Scottish Home Department, Report of the Committee on Homosexual Offences and Prostitution Cmnd 247, 1957 (The Wolfenden Report).

to challenge the view of homosexuality as immoral, but instead arguing solely that criminal law should only be concerned with homosexual acts taking place in public and that 'there must remain a realm of private morality and immorality which is, in brief and crude terms, not the law's business'.[13] Moreover, the committee drew a clear line between homosexual and heterosexual sexual acts, proposing that the age of consent for the former be set at 21 as opposed to 16 for the latter. The committee's proposals were met with great scepticism in the House of Commons at the time and it took another decade of continuous lobbying before they were passed into law with the Sexual Offences Act 1967.[14]

In the 1980s, section 28 of the Local Government Act 1988 cast a long and dark shadow over gay lives by legitimising anti-gay institutional discrimination and reinforcing the idea that homosexuality was shameful and a threat to children. The then prime minister, Margaret Thatcher, was quoted at the 1987 Conservative Party Conference as saying that, instead of teaching children to 'respect traditional moral values', schools allegedly taught them they 'had an inalienable right to be gay'.[15] In response to such concerns, 'Section 28', as it became known, was introduced a year later, prohibiting local councils from 'intentionally [promoting] homosexuality' or 'the teaching in any maintained school of the *acceptability of homosexuality as a pretended family relationship*'.[16] Section 28 provided an ineffectual basis for practical law enforcement as no one was entirely sure what 'promoting homosexuality' actually meant.[17] Nonetheless, this homophobic piece of legislation came at a time when gay men were being scapegoated for the AIDS epidemic[18] and further consolidated their vilification.[19] At the same time, however, it constituted a 'defining moment' in British gay and lesbian history – it contributed to the politicisation of a new generation of gay men and women,[20] inadvertently producing what it had aspired to hide

---

[13]   ibid., para 61; see also Charles Berg, 'The Wolfenden Report on Homosexual Offences' in Charles Berg (ed), *Fear, Punishment Anxiety and the Wolfenden Report* (Routledge, 2021) 15.

[14]   Matthew Waites, 'Sexual Citizens: Legislating the Age of Consent in Britain' in Terrell Carver and Véronique Mottier (eds), *Politics of Sexuality: Identity, Gender, Citizenship* (Routledge, 2005) 26.

[15]   Jeffrey Weeks, *Coming Out: Homosexual Politics in Britain from the Nineteenth Century to the Present* (Quartet Books, 1990) 231.

[16]   Local Government Act 1988, s 28 (our emphasis); see also Sue Wise, ' "New Right" or "Backlash"? Section 28, Moral Panic and "Promoting Homosexuality"' (2000) 5(1) *Sociological Research Online* 148.

[17]   David Evans, 'Section 28: Law, Myth and Paradox' (1989) 9(27) *Critical Social Policy* 73, 82; Stephen Engel, *The Unfinished Revolution: Social Movement Theory and The Gay and Lesbian Movement* (Cambridge University Press, 2001) 93.

[18]   Philip Thomas, 'The Nuclear Family, Ideology and AIDS in the Thatcher Years' (1993) 1(1) *Feminist Legal Studies* 23, 24.

[19]   Stuart Hall, *The Hard Road to Renewal: Thatcherism and the Crisis of the Left* (Verso, 1988) 282.

[20]   Anya Palmer, 'Lesbian and Gay Rights Campaigning: A Report from The Coalface' in Angelia Wilson (ed), *A Simple Matter of Justice: Theorizing Lesbian and Gay Politics* (Cassell, 1995) 35.

away, namely gay visibility in the public sphere.[21] After continuous efforts to repeal what it considered to be a fundamentally prejudiced piece of legislation, and despite strong opposition from the House of Lords, Tony Blair's Labour government finally succeeded in abolishing Section 28 in England and Wales in 2003.[22] In 2009, the then Conservative Prime Minister David Cameron (who had himself voted against the repeal of Section 28) publicly apologised for the distress the provision had caused to the gay community, stating that his party had 'got it wrong' on this 'emotional' issue and that he hoped gay people could forgive them.[23]

Beyond any attempts to mitigate the dark shadow of Section 28, enormous strides have been made in the 21st century in the fight for the destigmatisation of homosexuality and the legal recognition of gay rights through a wave of progressive legislations: the Sexual Offences (Amendment) Act 2000 lowered the age of consent for men engaging in same-sex sexual activities to 16, equalising it with the age of consent for heterosexual sexual activities. Moreover, several other Acts introduced in the early part of the century extended the definitions of family and marriage beyond the confines of heterosexual relationships. The Adoption and Children Act 2002 allowed unmarried people and same-sex couples in England and Wales to adopt children. The Civil Partnership Act 2004 permitted same-sex couples to form civil partnerships and, later, the Marriage (Same-Sex Couples) Act 2013 provided them with the same right to marry as opposite-sex couples. Importantly, the Equality Act 2010 created an overarching protective framework against discrimination, harassment and victimisation based on sexual orientation – albeit one which is not without limitations as the Act does not prohibit sexual orientation harassment in the context of provision of services, education, public functions and disposal and management of premises.[24] More recently, the government announced in the 2022 Queen's Speech plans to ban sexual orientation conversion therapy practices, stressing that these are 'abhorrent', ineffective and can cause extensive harm.[25]

Such legal developments have brought high visibility to gay people in the public sphere in recent years but, apart from raising the public's awareness over LGBT issues, they also increased the risks of gay people being targeted due to their sexual orientation.[26] Contemporary institutional approaches to LGBT issues

---

[21] Engel, *The Unfinished Revolution*, 93.

[22] Kirsty Milne, *Manufacturing Dissent: Single-Issue Protest, The Public and The Press* (Demos, 2005) 40.

[23] Andrew Pierce, 'Cameron says sorry to gays for 1980s Section 28 law' *The Daily Telegraph* 2 July 2009.

[24] Equality Act 2010, ss 29(8) and 33(6); see also Judicial College, *Equal Treatment Bench Book* (Courts and Tribunals Judiciary, 2021) 289.

[25] Prime Minister's Office and HRH The Prince of Wales, 'The Queen's Speech 2022' (2022) 128.

[26] Josh Milton, 'Anti-LGBTQ+ hate crime reports explode across UK, damning police figures confirm' *PinkNews* 15 August 2022.

may not be openly discriminatory like Section 28, but do not always go as far as they could to effectively address the LGBT community's concerns. The LGBT advisory panel that was set up as part of the government's plan to act upon the findings of its Equalities Office's 2018 LGBT Survey (one of the most notable government attempts to acquire an insight into the key issues non–heterosexual people in the UK are concerned about today)[27] was disbanded in 2021 with several of its members accusing the then Equalities Ministers Liz Truss and Kemi Badenoch of being 'ignorant' on key LGBT issues and ultimately creating a 'hostile environment' for LGBT people.[28] Almost a year later, several LGBT activists expressed disappointment at the government's failure to bring forward any concrete plans for establishing a 'replacement' LGBT panel.[29] Finally, 2022 presented gay people with new challenges: the ongoing discussions over the exclusion of 'consenting' adults from the proposed ban on conversion therapy,[30] or the stigmatising public discourse framing 'monkeypox' as a 'gay disease',[31] prove that the fight for gay equality is far from over and that any lessons from the past (such as in the case of monkeypox, the consequences of the demonisation of gay men during the AIDS epidemic)[32] cannot be taken for granted. The precariousness currently experienced by LGBT people in the UK is also reflected in the country's continuous drop in the International Lesbian, Gay, Bisexual, Trans and Intersex Association's (ILGA) annual rankings for LGBT rights across Europe: due to its 'ineffective and non-systematic work', the UK – which occupied first place back in 2015 – was the country with 'the most dramatic drop' in its score, falling from 10th place in 2021 to 14th in 2022 and 17th in 2023.[33]

With this contextual background in mind, we now proceed to look at the elements of the tort of defamation and examine how the courts have addressed

---

27 Government Equalities Office (GEO), National LGBT Survey: Summary Report, 2018.

28 Women and Equalities Committee (WEC), Oral Evidence: The LGBT Advisory Panel (House of Commons, 2021) HC 163 12. See also Aubrey Allegretti, 'Three UK government LGBT advisers quit with rebuke of "ignorant" ministers' *The Guardian* 11 March 2021.

29 Ashley Cowburn, 'Liz Truss faces criticism for failing to set up new LGBT+ advisory panel nine months after scrapping old one' *The Independent* 9 January 2022.

30 Adam Jowett, 'Does the government's plan to allow "consensual" conversion therapy undermine its proposed ban?' *The Conversation* 2 November 2021.

31 UNAIDS press release on monkeypox, 'UNAIDS warns that stigmatizing language on monkeypox jeopardises public health' Geneva, 22 May 2022 (available at https://www.una ids.org/en/resources/presscentre/pressreleaseandstatementarchive/2022/may/20220522_P R_Monkeypox).

32 Patricia Devine, Ashby Plant and Kristen Harrison, 'The Problem of "Us" Versus "Them" and AIDS Stigma' (1999) 42(7) *American Behavioral Scientist* 1212, 1215.

33 ILGA-Europe's Rainbow Map ranks all 49 European countries based on their legal and policy practices towards sexual minorities. For a breakdown of the criteria based on which countries are assessed and more information on the latest ranking, see ILGA-Europe, 'Rainbow Europe Map and Index 2023' (11 May 2023) (available at https://www.ilga-europe.org/report/rain bow-europe-2023/).

over the years the question of whether falsely calling someone gay adversely impacts an individual's reputation.

The elements of a claim generally

The primary function of the law of defamation is to protect individuals' interest in safeguarding and vindicating their reputation. The essence of the tort is the publication of words conveying a defamatory imputation. At common law, the claimant in a defamation action has needed to establish only that the defendant published a statement; with defamatory meaning; referring to the claimant. Liability is limited through several defences specific to defamation, including truth, absolute and qualified privilege,[34] honest opinion and publication on a matter of public interest. There are also special rules concerning website operators[35] and, in certain circumstances, the defendant may choose to apologise and make an offer of amends (rather than contest a case through the courts).[36]

Under English law, determining whether the words complained of are defamatory involves the examination of the following steps. As a starting point, a court must identify the meaning the words would convey to the 'ordinary reasonable' reader or viewer. Then, it must determine whether the meaning found meets the common law requirements for what is defamatory. It will do so if it satisfies what are being referred to as the 'consensus' and 'threshold of seriousness' requirements (discussed later). Finally, there is an additional statutory requirement under section 1 of the Defamation Act 2013, that is, the court must decide whether the claimant has established not only that the statement had a defamatory tendency but also that it did as a matter of fact cause them serious reputational harm (or that it was likely to do so), being harm of the kind represented by general damage, rather than special damage (such as pecuniary loss to interests other than reputation).[37]

This new element was born out of concerns raised over the past few years by campaign groups, academics and media organisations that the law of defamation had tipped the balance too far in favour of protecting claimants' rights and that its heavy-duty tools were used to suppress criticism with disquieting effect. Several of the tort's features, such as the complexity of costly proceedings, the absence of legal aid to support such claims, the reverse burden of proof on the defendant and the relatively limited defences, left the law open to misuse by powerful claimants, often intolerant of criticism. The law was eventually codified and placed on a

---

[34] For statutory privilege, see the provisions in the Defamation Act 1996, ss 14–15, and Schedule 1 (Parts 1 and 2). Note that there are some circumstances in which a defendant can benefit from privilege which exists in common law ('reply to attack').

[35] The Defamation (Operators of Websites) Regulations 2013.

[36] Defamation Act 1996, ss 2–4.

[37] *Lachaux v Independent Print Ltd & Anor* [2019] UKSC 27, para 15.

statutory footing by the reforms that led to the Defamation Act 2013.[38] The new Act intended to 'raise the bar'[39] for defamation claims so that only cases involving 'serious harm' to the claimant's reputation could proceed.[40] But how does the law of defamation (including its reformed version) react when a person is incorrectly and/or unwantedly described as gay?

Meaning

Defamation disputes often turn on meaning. This is a key issue, from which much follows. Determining meaning has a bearing on whether the 'serious harm' threshold has been met. It is also relevant to potential defences, for example if a publisher wants to defend a claim of corruption by relying on the defence of truth, they need to know what interpretation has to be proven 'substantially true'[41] to defeat that claim. The gravity of the allegation will also be considered in awarding damages. Prior to the 2013 reforms, the meaning of words in libel proceedings was pre-eminently determined by a jury (which represented a cross-section of society) as the tribunal of fact. A judge determined whether a publication was reasonably capable, as a matter of law, of being understood as defamatory and removed the case from the jury if it was not. However, the 2013 Act reversed the presumption in favour of a jury trial to enable better case management and reduce the costs of libel litigation.[42] Modern defamation practice now recognises that the determination of the meaning of the words complained of is a matter for judges to resolve at an early stage in the proceedings.[43]

A difficulty that often arises is that the words published may have multiple interpretations which may or may not have a defamatory meaning. A judge typically addresses the question of meaning by ascribing a single ('the one and only')[44] meaning – sometimes from a spectrum of possible meanings – to the words of an allegedly defamatory communication, that is, the meaning in which

---

[38] The Act came into effect on 1 January 2014. In July 2022, the UK government announced new proposals that would empower courts in England and Wales to dismiss at an early stage intimidatory legal actions by wealthy claimants to stifle free speech, known as Strategic Lawsuits Against Public Participation (SLAPPs). While the 2013 reform package seems to have worked reasonably effectively – on this point see The Lord Chancellor and Secretary of State for Justice, Post-Legislative Memorandum: The Defamation Act 2013 CP 180, 2019 – it was felt that it was not specifically designed to meet the new challenges presented by the growing threat of such tactics; see further Ministry of Justice (MoJ), Strategic Lawsuits Against Public Participation: Government Response to the Call for Evidence, 2022.

[39] Explanatory Notes to the Defamation Act 2013, para 11.

[40] Defamation Act (DA) 2013, s 1(1). If the claimant is a company, it faces an even higher threshold as it is required to establish actual or likely 'serious financial loss' under section 1(2) of the same.

[41] DA 2013, s 2.

[42] DA 2013, s 11.

[43] *Sharif v Associated Newspapers Ltd* [2021] EWHC 343, para 43.

[44] *Slim v Daily Telegraph* [1968] 2 QB 157, 173 (Diplock LJ).

'fair-minded',[45] reasonable people of ordinary intelligence, with the ordinary person's general knowledge and experience of worldly affairs, would be likely to understand them. The publisher's (writer's or speaker's) intention and knowledge are immaterial.[46] The standard practice followed at trials of meaning (without a jury) is that a judge reads the publication complained of in its original format and reaches some preliminary conclusions, but without being bound by the competing meanings contended for.[47] The judge places himself or herself as best as they can in the shoes of the hypothetical ordinary, reasonable reader (not any actual reader of the words),[48] having in mind the established legal principles of interpretation, developed in accumulated case law. These were distilled in the frequently cited judgment of Sir Anthony Clarke MR in *Jeynes*,[49] which was endorsed by the Supreme Court in *Stocker*[50] and more recently elaborated on by Nicklin J in *Koutsogiannis*.[51]

The hypothetical reasonable reader, viewer, listener (and so on) against whom a court is to judge whether the words have the meaning contended for, is admittedly an abstract concept, but there is a good reason why the common law approach excludes evidence of how individual readers actually understood the words. Among the actual audience of a defamatory publication there will normally be great variation in the way the words are understood. Evidence of reputational harm could include, for instance, receiving a torrent of abuse on social media or hateful mail and being called names (or even spat at) on the street. However, such evidence would do little to assist the court in choosing between competing meanings of words. Reasonable readers would not normally resort to such extreme behaviours so the current rule of interpretation introduces an element of fairness by limiting the speaker's responsibility to those meanings which a reasonable person would give the words.[52] The courts accept that the ordinary, reasonable reader is in essence 'a device to control liability and strike a balance between free speech and reputation'.[53]

Although it is not entirely clear what attributes the hypothetical reasonable reader carries, judges have recognised their potential weaknesses: they are unlikely

---

[45]   *Lewis v Daily Telegraph* [1964] AC 234, 260 (Lord Reid); *Charleston v News Group Newspapers Ltd* [1995] 2 AC 65, 71 (Lord Bridge). On the concept of the (queer) reasonable person, see further Haim Abraham, Chapter 4, this volume.

[46]   In practice, this means that it is not a defence for a publisher to claim that they did not mean to defame the claimant or did not realise what the words used implied.

[47]   See for instance *Lord Mohammed Sheikh v Associated Newspapers Limited* [2019] EWHC 2947, para 26; *Tinkler v Ferguson and Ors* [2019] EWCA Civ 819, para 9.

[48]   *Triplark Ltd v Northwood Hall (Freehold) Ltd* [2019] EWHC 3494, para 19.

[49]   *Jeynes v News Magazines Ltd* [2008] EWCA Civ 130, para 14.

[50]   *Stocker v Stocker* [2019] UKSC 17, para 35.

[51]   *Koutsogiannis v Random House Group Ltd* [2019] EWHC 48, para 12 (approved by the Court of Appeal in *Corbyn v Millett* [2021] EWCA Civ 567, para 8).

[52]   Paul Mitchell, *The Making of the Modern English Law of Defamation* (Hart Publishing, 2005) 39.

[53]   *Oduro v Time-Life Entertainment Group Ltd* [2003] EWHC 1787, para 10.

to engage in an over-elaborate analysis of text, particularly with respect to online communications on social media platforms.[54] They can read between the lines and pick up an implication. They are allowed a certain amount of loose thinking, without, however, being overly suspicious. On the one hand, a reader who always adopts a bad meaning where a less serious is available is not reasonable (they are avid for scandal). But, on the other, always adopting the less derogatory meaning would be naïve and thus unreasonable.[55] Moreover, ascertaining the meaning of a given statement is very much context-dependent;[56] for instance, the word 'mafia' may be understood in a certain context as a narrow exclusive circle held together by common interests or purposes in a metaphorical, rather than literal, sense. The views of the hypothetical reasonable person are also likely to change over time: 'words which 100 years ago did not import a slanderous sense may now; and so vice versa'.[57] It is thus the current general usage of the words that should be looked at when determining meaning. By way of example, the primary popular meaning of 'gay' is now homosexual, and perhaps not the stereotype of a bright and cheerful person, which would have been the case 60 years ago or so.[58]

As the next section discusses, the principal test to determine whether the meaning conveyed is defamatory makes 'right-thinking' persons in society the point of reference. While homosexuality imputations should not negatively affect people's views of the claimant, and in the minds of right-thinking people would not, it can hardly be discounted that unfortunately such imputation may often be considered damaging. Not all people are right-minded and even those who are may hold certain views by reason of their religious convictions which may lead them to see sexual interest in members of one's own sex as diminishing a person's standing. If the law deems a claim actionable in these circumstances, then at some level, it risks lending credence to societal prejudices (for example, that being gay is a negative attribute or that homophobia is right-thinking).[59] Judicial recognition of such claims has the potential to validate these perceptions and carry them forward. Does the tort of defamation provide any mechanisms to safeguard against this concern?

---

54   *Stocker v Stocker* [2019] UKSC 17, paras 41–6; see also Alexandros Antoniou, 'Libel, social media, and celebrity journalism in the WAG-gate' (2022) 27(4) *Communications Law* 177.

55   *Koutsogiannis v Random House Group Ltd* [2019] EWHC 48, para 12.

56   *Nevill v Fine Arts Co* [1897] AC 68, 72; *Charleston v News Group Newspapers Ltd* [1995] 2 AC 65; *Bukovsky v CPS* [2017] EWCA Civ 1529, para 13; *Stocker v Stocker* [2019] UKSC 17, para 40; *Brown v Bower and Anor* [2017] EWHC 2637, para 29.

57   *Harrison v Thornborough* (1713) 88 ER 691, 691–2.

58   Richard Parkes et al, *Gatley on Libel and Slander* (13th edn, Sweet & Maxwell, 2022) 3029.

59   See also Robert Post, 'The Social Foundations of Defamation Law: Reputation and the Constitution' (1986) 74(3) *California Law Review* 691, 737.

Defamatory imputations

Not every false statement about another person gives rise to a claim. Untrue imputations are only actionable in English law if they are defamatory. The English courts have not so far arrived at a single formulation of what amounts to a defamatory allegation but most courts holding false imputations of homosexuality to be defamatory per se would normally rely upon fitting the statements into one of the traditional common law categories of statements, namely that a publication tends to injure a claimant's reputation, first, by treating them as a figure of fun or an object of ridicule;[60] second, if it causes them to be shunned or avoided;[61] or third, if it 'tends to lower them in the estimation of the right-thinking members of society generally'.[62] These definitions are generally regarded as cumulative, so words falling within any of them are actionable. Although still influential, these distillations do not clearly differentiate between disparaging someone's reputation and wounding one's feelings and arguably offer little help in maintaining a distinction between protecting one's reputation from being impaired and protecting one's feelings or personal dignity. Though it was not suggested in parliament when the 2013 Act was passed that the common law tests for what amounts to a defamatory statement would be abandoned, it is questionable whether some of the old definitions (for example, ridicule) would survive under the new Act if read in the light of the new requirement of 'serious harm' to the claimant's reputation.

The present and dominant position under English law is that a meaning is defamatory and thus actionable if it meets two requirements. The first is known as the 'threshold of seriousness'. That is, to be defamatory, the imputation must be one that would tend to have a 'substantially adverse effect'[63] on the way people would treat the claimant. The second, which is often referred to as 'the consensus requirement',[64] is that the meaning must be one that 'tends to lower the claimant in the estimation of right-thinking people generally'.[65] A judge must determine whether the conduct or views the offending statement attributes to the claimant are contrary to 'common, shared values of our society'.[66]

The consensus requirement envisages that some standard of opinion must be set, and it is that of the 'right-thinking persons' generally. This is, however, questionable because it rests on the presumption of an unstated notion of a homogeneous community of 'right-thinking' people who would react in a uniform and foreseeable manner.[67] Much depends on how this judicial anthropomorphisation

---

[60]   *Parmiter v Coupland* (1840) 6 M & W 105, 108.

[61]   *Youssoupoff v Metro-Goldwyn-Mayer Pictures Ltd* (1934) 50 TLR 581, 587.

[62]   *Sim v Stretch* [1936] 2 All ER 1237, 1240.

[63]   *Thornton v Telegraph Media Group Ltd* [2010] EWHC 1414, para 98 (Tugendhat J).

[64]   *Corbyn v Millett* [2021] EWCA Civ 567 para 9 (Warby LJ).

[65]   ibid.; see also *Scott v Sampson* (1882) 8 QBD 491, 503 (Cave J).

[66]   *Monroe v Hopkins* [2017] EWHC 433, para 51.

[67]   Eric Barendt, 'What is the Point of Libel Law?' (1999) 52(1) *Current Legal Problems* 110, 120.

of a legal standard would react. Support for this construct that is conventionally used in shaping outcomes in defamation cases is not universal. In a case heard by the High Court of Australia, Kirby J candidly observed that: 'it would be preferable to drop this fiction altogether. Judges should not hide behind their pretended reliance on the fictitious reasonable recipient of the alleged defamatory material, attributing to such a person the outcome that the judges actually determine for themselves.'[68] In *Monroe v Hopkins*, Warby J (as he then was) summarised the 'right-thinking person' metaphor as referring to 'common standards', meaning that a statement is not defamatory if it would only tend to have an adverse effect on the attitudes to the claimant of a certain section of society.[69] The ordinary right-thinking person does not simply represent the 'majority'; it is a more abstract notion than that. The test sets a benchmark by which some views are excluded from consideration as being unacceptable.[70] Fogle argues that the 'right-mindedness' concept suggests that people whose attitudes directly contradict public policy are excluded and implicitly labels those who might entertain an adverse reaction to a person who had homosexual intercourse as 'wrong-thinking'.[71] These days, only 'wrong-thinking' people would harbour feelings of scorn, contempt or hostility toward gay people (a premise which is, however, susceptible to ever-swinging sociocultural pendulum shifts). From this perspective, if a particular group's attitudes conflict with laws or are at odds with public policy, a court is unlikely to recognise these.

The underlying rationale of Fogle's view is that laws furthering public policy are an external reflection of community attitudes to homosexuality generally. Despite the enactment of an increasing number of legislative provisions which influence a wide array of life facets (including same-sex relationships, rights to parenthood and parental responsibility, adoption, employment, immigration, inclusion in the armed forces and so on)[72] and seek to treat people equally regardless of their sexuality, it is still debatable (as we pointed out earlier in our historical overview) whether a sufficiently solid and consistent legislative regime has been achieved.[73] An implication of this is that gaps in or limits to anti–discrimination legislation could similarly be highlighted as indicators of community standards to be considered when determining the capacity to defame. So, while statutes

---

[68]   *Favell v Queensland Newspapers Pty Ltd* [2005] HCA 52, para 24.

[69]   *Monroe v Hopkins* [2017] EWHC 433, paras 50–1.

[70]   Some support for this proposition is found in *Monroe v Hopkins* [2017] EWHC 433, para 50, in which Warby J stated that this 'old phrase is … about people who think correctly'.

[71]   Randy Fogle, 'Is Calling Someone "Gay" Defamatory? The Meaning of Reputation, Community Mores, Gay Rights and Free Speech' (1993) 3 *Law and Sexuality* 165, 173.

[72]   Judicial College, Sexual Orientation, 2013 (available at https://www.judiciary.uk/wp-content/uploads/JCO/Documents/judicial-college/ETBB_SO+_finalised_.pdf); see also section 14 of the Armed Forces Act 2016, which repealed discriminatory laws enacted in the Criminal Justice and Public Order Act 1994 that enabled homosexual men and women to be sacked from the armed forces.

[73]   Judicial College, *Equal Treatment Bench Book* (Courts and Tribunals Judiciary, 2021).

might serve as an external foundation for legitimising judges' choices in rejecting a statement's capacity to defame, exclusively relying on them is not always a helpful and safe indicator of what standards should be applied by the courts.[74]

But, even if the courts seek to symbolically condemn homophobic attitudes as 'wrong-thinking', this does not eradicate the reality of prejudice,[75] which is amply demonstrated by the high levels of marginalisation and abuse gay people still face. Despite the progress made, homosexuality has not in effect been fully destigmatised and non-compliance with the heterosexual norm can still adversely impact on one's lived experiences: the UK government's 2018 LGBT Survey showed that respondents were less satisfied with their lives than the general UK population.[76] The survey highlighted various instances of inequality which negatively affected non-heterosexual people's quality of life.[77] Moreover, considering the alarming increase in homophobic hate crime figures in recent years, it would be erroneous and rather risky to assume that the road to gay equality is unidirectional. Official data show that police-recorded homophobic hate crime incidents in England and Wales almost doubled between 2016–17 and 2020–21.[78] While the authorities have claimed that this disconcerting trend might be due to a growing public awareness and improved identification of such offences, research indicating that non-heterosexual people remain reluctant to report their victimisation casts doubt over this explanation.[79] Such evidence shows a persistent – or, even more concerningly, widening – gap between legal efforts to promote gay equality and the discrimination, harassment and stigma that continue to constitute a distressing yet inevitable part of many gay people's lives.

---

[74] For a detailed critique of Fogle's argument, see Lawrence McNamara, *Reputation and Defamation* (Oxford University Press, 2007) 209–10.

[75] Robert Richards, 'Gay Labeling and Defamation Law: Have Attitudes Towards Homosexuality Changed Enough to Modify Reputational Torts?' (2009–10) 18(2) *CommLaw Conspectus: Journal of Communications Law and Technology Policy* 349, 369.

[76] That is, by a mean satisfaction score of 6.5 compared to 7.7 out of 10; see GEO, National LGBT Survey: Summary Report, 2018, 10.

[77] GEO, National LGBT Survey: Summary Report, 2018, 11–13: in particular, over 68 per cent of the respondents said they had avoided holding hands with their same-sex partner in public due to fear of a negative reaction from others; 65 per cent revealed they were not open about their sexual orientation in their workplace; 40 per cent had experienced an incident due to their sexual orientation (from verbal harassment and insults to disclosure of their LGBT status without permission, physical violence and so on) in the previous 12 months committed by someone they did not live with; finally, almost half of those who had decided to report such incidents to the police (45 per cent) were unsatisfied with the response they received.

[78] With 8,569 and 17,135 incidents, respectively: Home Office, Hate Crime: England and Wales 2020 to 2021, 2021 (available at https://www.gov.uk/government/statistics/hate-crime-engl and-and-wales-2020-to-2021/hate-crime-england-and-wales-2020-to-2021).

[79] Luke Hubbard, Hate Crime Report 2021: Supporting LGBT+ Victims of Hate Crime, Galop, 2021, 8: the LGBT anti-abuse organisation Galop found that only 13 per cent of respondents had reported incidents of violence or abuse to the police and even fewer to other agencies: local authorities (5 per cent), housing providers (4 per cent), medical services (7 per cent). Similarly, the aforementioned GEO LGBT Survey revealed that 94 per cent of the

Homosexuality as defamation

One consequence of the standard of opinion adopted is the variability of the defamatory nature of an imputation depending on time and the state of public opinion. As a result, it is not always easy to say that certain imputations are defamatory whereas others are not. Previous decisions can prove useful in determining whether particular words can convey a defamatory imputation, though it should be remembered that these were decided before the requirement that an allegation must meet the necessary threshold of gravity imported into the law in 2013. As a result, it is entirely possible that imputations once thought to be defamatory are now unlikely to be treated as such.

Imputations of homosexuality pre-2013

Early cases proceeded on the basis that imputations of homosexuality were inherently defamatory. The 1811 case of *Miss Marianne Woods and Miss Jane Pirie v Lady Helen Cumming Gordon*,[80] successfully appealed to the House of Lords in 1820, concerned two boarding school mistresses who were rumoured by a student to have indulged in a romantic affair. The allegation was incontrovertibly accepted as being defamatory, suggesting that romantic relationships between women were not greeted at the time with general societal approval. The judges were confronted with two equally (and evidently rather undesirable) controversial alternatives: whether the two well brought up, middle-class school mistresses had performed sexual acts together, or whether the half-Indian, half-Scottish schoolgirl from a good family had concocted a lurid tale about a rapturous relationship that would make any reader of that period blush. In words indicative of the heavy stigma attached at the time to any deviation from the heterosexual norm, Lord Justice-Clerk captured this dilemma: 'I never saw a cause so disgusting, view it in either light'.[81] Socio-legal analyses of this historical case recount how the subject matter of the proceedings, namely lesbianism, was shrouded with a veil of secrecy[82] and emphasise the judge's denial of the idea of female same-sex eroticism.[83]

---

most serious incidents against LGBT people went unreported if the perpetrator was someone the victim lived with; see GEO, National LGBT Survey: Summary Report, 2018, 13.

80   *Woods & Pirie v Cumming Gordon* (1820) (HL, unreported).

81   Geraldine Friedman, 'School for Scandal: Sexuality, Race, and National Vice and Virtue in Miss Marianne Woods and Miss Jane Pirie Against Lady Helen Cumming Gordon' (2005) 27(1) *Nineteenth Century Contexts* 53, 56.

82   Caroline Derry 'The "Legal" in Socio-legal History: *Woods and Pirie v Cumming Gordon*' (2022) 49(9) *Journal of Law and Society* 778, 792.

83   Lillian Faderman, *Scotch Verdict: Miss Pirie and Miss Woods v Dame Cumming Gordon* (William Morrow and Co, 1983) 148–9.

The issue reappeared in the early 20th century, when two draughtsmen in the employment of a Scottish engineering firm sued in 1917 over allegations they had participated in homosexual acts. Having observed that the two clerks had spent about ten minutes together in a water closet in the works with the door closed, the manager dismissed them summarily, refusing to hear any explanations. He addressed the staff the day after with the following strong language: 'Two of your number were dismissed yesterday at a moment's notice; they left without a shred of character; they are not men, they are beasts.'[84] Although it was accepted that the words were defamatory,[85] there is some debate on whether the harm to the clerks' reputation lay in the imputation of homosexuality per se,[86] or in the implication of criminality, given that homosexuality was at the time illegal in Scotland.[87] Little attempt was made to examine the nature of the imputations themselves. Instead, emphasis was placed on whether in the circumstances the communication was so violent as to afford evidence that it could not have been fairly and honestly made. It was ultimately held that the defendant's statement was privileged in respect of the interest and duty he had to inform the staff of the circumstances of the dismissal. No malice could be inferred either from the language he used or from the fact that he held no inquiry and demanded no explanations in accordance with fair employment procedures. Dismissing the claimants' actions, Lord Dundas stated:

> [i]t is to be regretted that the future careers of these two young men may be hampered by what has occurred. But it seems to me that, if this should be so, they have mainly themselves to blame. Their conduct, assuming the truth of their own averments, appears to have been amazingly foolish; they have augmented the publicity of the matter by raising these (as I think, ill-founded) actions.[88]

A similar approach seems to have been taken in the 1942 case *Kerr v Kennedy*,[89] in which the claimant complained that the defendant communicated to a common acquaintance of the parties that the former was a lesbian. This was found to bear a defamatory meaning on the basis that it implied unchastity within the meaning

---

[84]   *AB v XY* [1917] SC 15.

[85]   ibid., 21 (Lord Salvesen).

[86]   Lawrence McNamara, 'Bigotry, Community and the (In)Visibility of Moral Exclusion: Homosexuality and the Capacity to Defame' (2001) 6(4) *Media and Arts Law Review* 271, 293.

[87]   *Quilty v Windsor* (1999) SLT 346, 350K (Lord Kingarth OH).

[88]   *AB v XY* [1917] SC 15, 21.

[89]   *Kerr v Kennedy* [1942] 1 KB 409.

of that word in the Slander of Women Act 1891,[90] which included 'impurity' and 'lasciviousness'.[91]

In 'one of the most celebrated libel actions of the century',[92] the American entertainer Wladziu Valentino Liberace sued the *Daily Mirror* gossip columnist William Connor (who wrote under the name 'Cassandra') over two publications in September and October 1956. The first of those referred to the famous pianist with the following words:

> He is the summit of sex – the pinnacle of Masculine, Feminine and Neuter. Everything that He, She or It can ever want. I spoke to sad but kindly men on this newspaper who have met every celebrity arriving from the United States for the past thirty years. They say that this deadly, winking, sniggering, snuggling, chromium-plated, scent-impregnated, luminous, quivering, giggling, fruit-flavoured, mincing, ice-covered, heap of motherlove has had the biggest reception and impact on London since Charlie Chaplin arrived at the same station, Waterloo, on September 12, 1921. ... There must be something wrong with us that our teenagers longing for sex and our middle-aged matrons fed up with sex, alike should fall for such a sugary mountain of jingling claptrap wrapped up in such a preposterous clown.[93]

The piece, pejorative and judgmental in its tone, manifestly exposed Liberace to ridicule and contempt. The litigation was about the meaning of these words, and particularly whether they could convey an imputation that the claimant was homosexual. One of the critical words in this passage was 'fruit-flavoured', which in America was slang for being gay. This was not apparently the meaning that the author of the article had attached to it; rather, it was used to bolster the impression of confectionary Liberace conveyed to him (that is, 'over-sweetened, over-flavoured, over-luscious and just sickening').[94] This was, however, immaterial, as the meaning of the statement is derived from an objective assessment to be determined by 'right-thinking members of society'. Liberace, a devout Catholic who considered his meeting with Pope Pius XII as one of the highlights of his life, took the stand in a seven-day hearing and passionately denied he was gay. Being asked in the witness box how the article affected him, the artist

---

90   Section 1 of the 1891 Act read: '[w]ords spoken and published after the passing of this Act which impute unchastity or adultery to any woman or girl shall not require special damage to render them actionable.'

91   *Kerr v Kennedy* [1942] 1 KB 409, 413 (Asquith J).

92   Obituary of Lord Salmon *Daily Telegraph* 9 November 1991.

93   'How about refund? Tabloid says of Liberace libel award' *Los Angeles Times* 11 February 1987. See also *Liberace v Daily Mirror Newspapers, The Times,* June 17, 18, 1959.

94   Hugh Cudlipp, 'Laughter in Court' (1992) 3(2) *British Journalism Review* 20, 27. Lord Cudlipp was at the time editorial director of the *Daily Mirror* and recounts the story behind the *Liberace v Cassandra* libel action with reference to hearing transcripts.

replied: '[m]y feelings are the same as anyone else's. I am against the practice because it offends convention and offends society.'[95] The defendant newspaper submitted that, in so far as the words were factual statements, they were true, and to the extent that they consisted of expressions of opinion, they were fair comment. The jury was not, however, persuaded and found that the words meant Liberace was a homosexual, that without that meaning the statements complained of were neither true nor fair comment as expressions of opinion. They awarded £8,000 damages, with £2,000 attributable to the imputation of homosexuality (plus £27,000 in legal costs). Liberace's case makes clear that in the late 1950s, 'right-thinking' people generally would think less well of a person by virtue of their homosexuality.

A closer examination of more modern cases reveals a slightly more complex picture. The courts' initial response to bare assertions of homosexuality appears to have progressed to a more reflective approach. The issue was next raised over three decades later in a highly publicised libel action. Singer and actor Jason Donovan (who initially achieved fame alongside Kylie Minogue in the Australian TV series *Neighbours*) sued music magazine *The Face* in 1992 after it published a doctored photo of a T-shirt imprinted with the artist's face and the words 'Queer as fuck', seemingly doubting the singer's heterosexuality.[96] Rather than pleading an imputation that the publisher had claimed he was gay, Donovan argued that the sting of the libel lay in hypocrisy, namely that the magazine suggested he was deceitful about his sexuality. The case did not, therefore, put to the test the question of whether it is defamatory merely to say someone is gay. The jury was satisfied the publication was defamatory and Donovan was awarded the substantial sum of £200,000. This was subsequently reduced by agreement to £98,000, after the magazine announced that it would have to cease business. Apart from attacking a fashionable magazine, another implication of this lawsuit was that Donovan himself invited accusations of homophobia, despite creatively framing his claim around dishonesty. Although he won, the adverse publicity had a negative impact on his career, with the singer considering the decision to sue *The Face* 'the biggest mistake of his life'.[97]

The dilemma of allowing a false claim of homosexuality to remain unchallenged or rushing to court to set the record straight was once again posed a few years later in the star-studded case of *Cruise and Anor v Express Newspapers Plc and Anor*.[98] In 1999, Hollywood actors Nicole Kidman and Tom Cruise brought libel proceedings in respect of an article which appeared in the magazine section of the

[95]   ibid., 26.
[96]   Unreported, but see Julie Scott-Bayfield, 'Libel: Bonanza or Burst Bubble?' (1993) 137 *Solicitors' Journal* 29, 45; and Vincent Graff, 'Gay? Not gay? So, what! Why should it be a matter for the libel lawyers?' *The Independent on Sunday* 11 December 2005.
[97]   Emine Saner, 'Jason Donovan on Kylie, coolness, and cocaine: "I'm a survivor and I've made mistakes"' *The Guardian* 4 October 2021.
[98]   [1999] QB 931; [1998] EMLR 780; [1998] EWCA Civ 1269.

Express on Sunday and contained several defamatory meanings which provided good reasons to regard the couple as 'hypocrites, frauds and liars',[99] including that they had entered a bogus marriage in a cynical business arrangement which was a cover for their homosexuality. The Court of Appeal seemed to have uncritically accepted Popplewell J's judgment that an imputation of homosexuality was capable of having a defamatory meaning.[100] By contrast, the Court of Session (Scotland's supreme civil court) held in the same year in *Quilty v Windsor* that an imputation of homosexuality was incapable of defaming a person.[101] The dispute involved a letter written by an inmate about a prison officer and alleged, among other things, that the latter was homosexual. Lord Kingarth said that he was 'inclined to agree with counsel for the first defender that merely to refer to a person as being homosexual would not now generally at least be regarded—if it ever was—as defamatory per se'.[102]

In an action remarkably reminiscent of Donovan's some thirteen years earlier, *The People* newspaper, along with Northern & Shell's *Star* magazine and OK!'s *Hot Stars* supplement, had £200,000 in damages awarded against them for wrongly alleging that pop star Robbie Williams was about to deceive the public with the publication of a forthcoming authorised biography which did not include details of a sexual encounter he had had with another man in the toilets of a Manchester nightclub.[103] Williams, whose counsel emphatically stated at trial that his client was not and never had been homosexual,[104] did not frame his case on the grounds that people would think less well of him because he was gay. Instead, his counsel argued that the printed articles meant that Williams, by omitting details of the Manchester episode, 'pretended' that his only sexual relations had been with women, though 'in reality he was a homosexual who had engaged in casual and sordid homosexual encounters with strangers'.[105]

The extent to which the perspective of homosexuality materially affects the defamatory meaning of the imputation may however be questioned. In the cases of Donovan, Cruise and Williams, for instance, the presence or absence of homosexuality arguably played little role in determining whether the meanings of the publications were defamatory. For instance, what gave rise to a defamatory meaning in *Cruise* was the underlying perfidiousness about the true state of the couple's marriage. Likewise, for Robbie Williams, it was the allegation of public

---

[99]   [1999] QB 931, 938; [1998] EMLR 780, 786.
[100] [1999] QB 931, 939; [1998] EMLR 780, 787.
[101] *Quilty v Windsor* (1999) SLT 346.
[102] ibid., 355.
[103] Graff, 'Gay? Not gay? So, what!'.
[104] Duncan Gardham, 'Robbie Williams wins "gay" libel fight' *The Telegraph* 7 December 2005.
[105] *Robert Peter Williams v Northern and Shell Plc* (Statement in High Court, 6 December 2005). The case is unreported, but we have drawn on media reports, including for example: Mark Honigsbaum, 'Robbie Williams wins damages over "secret homosexual" claims' *The Guardian* 7 December 2005; Gerard Jasper, 'Robbie's libel pay-out can only harm gay rights' *Sunday Times* 11 December 2005.

deception and the implication of a dishonest attempt to conceal a string of sexual encounters with men he did not otherwise know. And, for Jason Donovan, it was the alleged insincere outward façade the claimant had maintained toward his fan base. However, individuals can be hypocrites or liars without being homosexuals. In these cases, the imputations of homosexuality were purely a conduit through which defamatory allegations were expressed and as such they can be seen as tangential. Nevertheless, their centrality in legal pleadings and considerations served, albeit perhaps unwittingly, to reinforce the erroneous idea of a 'damaged' heterosexual and effectively bolster a dubious and unhelpful hierarchy of sexualities.

Imputations of homosexuality post-2013

In the broader sphere of sexuality and sexual conduct, today's standards have arguably changed more than in any other field. There are therefore certain imputations which would now most likely not lower an individual in the estimation of 'right-minded' members of society. In *CC v AB*, Eady J observed, albeit in the areas of breach of confidence and misuse of private information:

> [a]t one time, when there was, or was perceived to be, a commonly accepted standard in such matters as sexual morality, it may have been acceptable for the courts to give effect to that standard in exercising discretion or in interpreting legal rights and obligations. Now, however, there is a strong argument for not holding forth about adultery or attaching greater inherent worth to a relationship which has been formalised by marriage than to any other relationship.[106]

So, for example, unmarried cohabitation is no longer looked upon as discreditable and having been sexually assaulted or seduced[107] are unlikely to (and obviously should not) lower someone's standing. Likewise, public attitudes towards homosexuality have changed drastically in recent years. We saw earlier the shift towards more inclusive legal initiatives that reflect to some degree societal changes in the ways homosexuality is made sense of in today's Britain. Recent public opinion research suggests that the social stigma attached to homosexuality is gradually but promisingly subsiding. For instance, King's College London's Policy Institute found that the percentage of the British public who viewed homosexual relationships between consenting adults as morally wrong in the past three decades significantly dropped from 40 per cent in 1989 to only 13 per cent in 2019.[108] Similarly, Stonewall's 2022 survey showed that the public sentiment

---

[106] [2006] EWHC 3083, para 25.

[107] Compare with *Youssoupoff v Metro-Goldwyn-Mayer Pictures Ltd* (1934) 50 TLR 581.

[108] The Policy Institute, *How British Moral Attitudes Have Changed in the Last 30 Years* (King's College London, 2019) 5.

towards gay people in the UK today is much more likely to be one of respect (37 per cent) and admiration (19 per cent) rather than of disgust (9 per cent), fear (4 per cent) or resentment (3 per cent).[109]

The issue of whether statements falsely imputing homosexuality could be defamatory remained dormant for several years until arising again in 2017 in *Brown v Bower and Anor*,[110] a preliminary issues trial of meaning. The case is a more recent example of the constantly moving goal posts of social attitudes and their potential to influence what is defamatory and what is not. Here, the claim was brought by Nick Brown, MP for Newcastle upon Tyne East, against investigative historian Tom Bower and his publisher Faber & Faber over an extract in Mr Bower's book *Broken Vows—Tony Blair, the Tragedy of Power* which concerned the time in 1998 when the *News of the World* outed the claimant as gay. Nicklin J found that the words complained of meant that there were grounds to suspect that Mr Brown engaged in a commercial transaction with young male prostitutes to subject him to 'rough sex' (in the sense of consensually violent intercourse). Although the court ruled on meaning, it was not asked to offer a view on whether that meaning was defamatory, as the defendants made concessions on that point.[111] Both parties agreed that an allegation that the claimant was gay (or that he had had sex with men) was *not* defamatory.[112] It should, however, be emphasised that this issue was not adjudicated upon by the court itself as a matter of law. Whether a judge would today find that an imputation, without more, that someone was a practising homosexual is defamatory must be doubtful. In fact, things have changed so much that a statement imputing antipathy or intolerant attitudes towards sexuality, for example, homophobia, is more likely to be found damaging and thus defamatory.[113] An article describing the appellant's tweet as homophobic and, by inference, that he held homophobic views, was recently held by the Court of Session in Scotland to be defamatory in principle and an award of substantial damages would have been appropriate, in light of the acknowledgement that 'an accusation of homophobia [is] a serious one in contemporary society'.[114]

---

[109] Stonewall, Take Pride Report: Public Sentiment Towards Lesbian, Gay, Bi and Trans People in the UK, 2022, 3–4.

[110] *Brown v Bower and Anor* [2017] EWHC 2637.

[111] Although born out of expediency, the parties' agreement attracted Nicklin J's criticism because their concessions had the effect of keeping the action alive, adding to the courts' workload. On balance, the judge decided not to determine the issue of whether the meaning he had found was defamatory, as ruling on the matter could risk a wasteful expenditure of costs and court resources on an appeal; ibid., paras 57–61.

[112] ibid., para 50.

[113] Parkes et al, *Gatley on Libel and Slander*, 2025.

[114] *Campbell v Dugdale* [2020] CSIH 27, para 47. Note, however, that the defence of fair comment was made out in this case.

Serious harm

Section 1(1) of the Defamation Act 2013 brought about a significant change to the meaning of what is defamatory under English law. A detailed consideration of the consequences of the enactment of section 1(1) is beyond the scope of this chapter,[115] but for present purposes, it suffices to say that section 1(1) builds on the consideration previously given by the courts on what is sufficient to establish that a statement is defamatory[116] and adds to the common law requirements. 'Serious' is not a defined term in the Act. However, in *Lachaux*,[117] the leading authority that considered how the serious harm test should be interpreted and operate in practice, the Supreme Court held that section 1 raises the threshold of seriousness *above* the tendency of defamatory words to cause damage to reputation and focuses on the actual *impact* of the publication.[118] Simply arguing that the words complained of have the tendency substantially to damage the claimant's reputation is no longer sufficient to ground a cause of action.[119] The application of the serious harm test must be determined by reference to the actual facts and not just the meaning of the words. Notably, the causation element features very prominently in the language used in section 1(1). A claimant must establish a causal link between the effect of each specific statement they complain about and serious harm to their reputation (actual or likely). If they cannot show serious reputational harm by a false imputation of homosexuality, the claim is now likely to fail.

Importantly, the new test also makes clear – if it wasn't already – that the (likely) harm must be 'to reputation'. While a person who has been misidentified as a homosexual may claim to have suffered anxiety or have become upset because of the publication, evidence of injury to their feelings, however grave, is not evidence of harm to reputation. A defamation action is concerned with what people think of the claimant and how they judge his or her worth. It is for damage to reputation that a person can sue, and not for damage to their own sense of inner worth or disposition. Section 1(1) is thus a helpful reminder of the distinction between the terms 'reputation' and 'character', which are sometimes used interchangeably. An individual's character is what they in fact are (their actual attributes), whereas their reputation is what other people think they are (others' perception of that person).[120] A reputation is enjoyed when an individual

---

[115] But see Charlie Sewell, 'More Serious Harm Than Good? An Empirical Observation and Analysis of the Effects of the Serious Harm Requirement in Section 1(1) of the Defamation Act 2013' (2020) 12(1) *Journal of Media Law* 47.

[116] Explanatory Notes to the Defamation Act 2013, paras 10 and 11; *Lachaux v Independent Print Ltd & Anor* [2019] UKSC 27, para 12; *Thornton v Telegraph Media Group Ltd* [2010] EWHC 1414.

[117] *Lachaux v Independent Print Ltd & Anor* [2019] UKSC 27.

[118] ibid., paras 12–14; see also *Turley v UNITE the Union & Anor* [2019] EWHC 3547, para 107.

[119] *Lachaux v Independent Print Ltd & Anor* [2019] UKSC 27, paras 13–17.

[120] *Scott v Sampson* (1882) 8 QBD 491.

regularly interacts with others as a member of a community; hence, the law of defamation is about community and social attitudes. The separation between the two becomes even more pronounced by the new statutory test. Defamation law should not be used to remedy wounded feelings and a loss of self-esteem caused by false statements that an individual is gay, when there is no indication that any harm to reputation has occurred.[121] Such an approach would not reflect the harm caused to the interaction and engagement with others[122] and would shift the concern of the law away from how other people evaluate the claimant.

Moreover, under the new statutory test, the existence (and seriousness) of reputational harm are factual questions, and there is no presumption of serious harm. A complainant must demonstrate *as a fact* that the publication of a statement has caused/is likely to cause harm to their reputation that is serious.[123] The relevant facts may be established by evidencing specific instances of serious consequences inflicted on a claimant because of reputational harm. For instance, comments posted online by those who have read, heard or watched the relevant publication can be evidence of reputation harm, 'to the extent they can be said to be a natural and probable consequence of the publication complained of'.[124] Evidence that the claimant has become unemployable or has been excluded from the community of others might also in principle be admissible. Harm to reputation may also manifest itself financially, for example through the loss of an employment opportunity.

However, even though the statutory qualifier 'serious' harm has the effect of raising the bar in terms of the requisite degree of harm to reputation from where it was previously set,[125] a claimant's case will not necessarily fail for want of such evidence.[126] The test may also be satisfied by general *inferences* of fact as to the seriousness of harm, drawn from the evidence as a whole, that is, the combination of the meaning of the words, the claimant's situation as well as the scale and circumstances surrounding the publication.[127] A court will in principle avoid considering the issue of serious harm 'in blinkers'; 'directly relevant background

---

[121] Barendt, 'What is the Point of Libel Law?', 117.

[122] David Howarth, 'Libel: Its Purpose and Reform' (2011) 74(6) *Modern Law Review* 845, 853.

[123] *Lachaux v Independent Print Ltd & Anor* [2019] UKSC 27, paras 12–16 (Lord Sumption).

[124] *Economou v De Freitas* [2016] EWHC 1853, para 129 (Warby J).

[125] *Thornton v Telegraph Media Group Ltd* [2010] EWHC 1414; see also *George v Cannell* [2021] EWHC 2988, para 117 (Saini J).

[126] *Lachaux v Independent Print Ltd & Anor* [2019] UKSC 27, para 21 (Lord Sumption).

[127] Generally, the potential of a defamatory statement to cause harm is greater if it is published to the world at large and repeatedly, than if it has been published to a single person on one occasion. But note that the assessment of reputational harm is not purely 'a numbers game; it needs only one well-directed arrow to hit the bull's eye of reputation' in certain circumstances; *King v Grundon* [2012] EWHC 2719, para 40 (Sharp LJ). So, serious harm can be caused by publication to a small number of publishees. In appropriate cases, a claimant can also rely on the 'grapevine effect' of defamatory publications (that is, a metaphor used to recognise the propensity of defamatory material to percolate beyond their immediate audience), which has been 'immeasurably enhanced' with the advent of modern methods of communications and the opportunity they afford for damaging allegations to 'go viral' more quickly and more

facts'[128] which explain the context in which the defamatory publication came to be made may have some bearing on whether the test is met. So, although the new statutory requirement creates a significant hurdle for potential claimants, this is not insurmountable. The shift in public sentiment towards understanding homosexuality does not necessarily mean the lack of a common societal standard in respect of *any* sexual conduct between consenting adults. Public opinion has in fact become less permissive towards some forms of exploitative sexual conduct over recent years.[129] Defamation law could create restrictions with respect to untrue allegations of homosexuality linked to further imputations of favouritism, for example when homosexuality interferes with a prison officer's work, affecting their fitness to hold office in the prison service, particularly in relation to their dealings with young offenders. False statements of homosexuality potentially also hold a seriously defamatory meaning when they impute infidelity or breach of trust at an intimately personal level by suggesting, for instance, that an individual has concealed from their partner a central aspect of their personal identity affecting the very nature of their relationship. Therefore, as section 1(1) creates a multifactorial model of evaluating harm to reputation, it remains possible that contextual factors might clothe the words in further defamatory meaning likely to cross the necessary seriousness threshold.

Understood in this manner, the approach of defamation law to false imputations of homosexuality does not appear to have changed significantly since the 1990s. It is notable for example that the courts' decision-making in *Donovan*, *Cruise* and *Williams* arguably reflects a tacit recognition that allegations of homosexuality have the capacity to defame but only contingently and instrumentally connected to the claimant's circumstances, personality and traits. Their approach suggests a subtle shift in favour of accepting that such allegations can give birth to correlative defamatory imputations implying lying, dishonesty or hypocrisy. In other words, the determination of whether a statement that an adult was consensually involved in a private homosexual relationship or activity with another adult could carry defamatory meaning was not to be made in an abstract vacuum but instead required a broader understanding and scrutiny of additional contextual factors present in a particular case. Likewise, in the post-2013 defamation landscape, the misidentification of someone as gay could lend defamatory import to the words in question through a secondary or extended defamatory meaning which is understood by publishees with knowledge of certain extrinsic matters relating to the claimant (also known as 'true' or 'legal' innuendo).

---

widely than ever before; see *Slipper v BBC* [1991] 1 QB 283, 300; *Cairns v Modi* [2012] EWHC 756, para 27; *Monir v Wood* [2018] EWHC 3525, para 123.

[128] *Burstein v Times Newspapers Ltd* [2000] EWCA Civ 338, para 42 (May LJ); *Umeyor v Ibe* [2016] EWHC 862, para 79 (Warby J).

[129] See, for example, *AVB v TDD* [2014] EWHC 1442, in which Tugendhat J highlighted the aspects of exploitation involved in the prostitution industry.

Damages

An interesting yet comparatively neglected aspect of the debate is the award of damages to a claimant who is presumably heterosexual and has successfully sued under English law for being falsely labelled gay. A successful claimant would be awarded compensatory (general) damages to vindicate their reputation but also remedy their mental distress and any loss flowing from the loss of social standing that is said to come with being incorrectly publicly identified as homosexual. When determining the level of damages, a court usually considers the gravity of the libel, the injury to the claimant's feelings for being thought of or treated like a homosexual, the extent of the publication and perhaps any mitigating (or aggravating) factors.[130] However, the idea that a social status change from heterosexual to homosexual is a legally compensable harm endorses a hierarchical structure which sustains an overarching heteronormative schematism[131] and constructs homosexual people as citizens who qualify as less deserving, 'partial members' of society,[132] reserving full membership for heterosexuals. In this way, defamation law would effectively shield 'damaged' heterosexual people from negative societal attitudes and be complicit in marginalising individuals who are frequently exposed to prejudicial beliefs held by the homophobic parts of society.

If it is accepted that the expressive and symbolic value of the law requires that an imputation of homosexuality (even if shaped by certain contextual factors or related to true innuendo) should no longer be treated as having the capacity to defame, does this mean that a heterosexual claimant who might have suffered serious harm to their reputation or a serious loss as a result of being wrongly identified as a homosexual is left without legal recourse? Not entirely. Reliance on the tort of malicious falsehood, which protects against a defendant's falsehood that causes harm to a claimant's economic (not merely commercial) interests,[133] provides a reasonable alternative.[134] The essentials of this action were defined in *Kaye v Robertson* as being: 'that the defendant has published about the claimant words which are false, that they were published maliciously and that special damage has followed as the direct and natural result of their publication'.[135]

---

[130] Compensatory damages can include special damages for actual pecuniary loss (for example, the loss of a potentially lucrative contract or a loss of profit caused by the impact of the publication and so on) and additional damages reflecting the harm caused by the defendant's conduct in case any aggravating circumstances are present (for example, failure to publish an adequate apology). See further Alexandros Antoniou, 'When the Litigation Winner Becomes the Loser: Undeserving Claimants and Mitigation of Damages in Libel Claims' (2018) 10(2) *The Journal of Media Law* 128, 131–9.

[131] See also Haven Ward, 'I'm Not Gay, M'Kay? Should Falsely Calling Someone a Homosexual Be Defamatory?' (2010) 44(3) *Georgia Law Review* 739, 761.

[132] Roy Baker, *Defamation Law and Social Attitudes: Ordinary Unreasonable People* (Edward Elgar, 2011) 54.

[133] *Joyce v Sengupta* [1993] 1 WLR 337 (CA).

[134] Bennett, 'Not So Straight-Talking', 325.

[135] *Kaye v Robertson* [1991] FSR 62, 67 (Glidewell LJ).

The requirements to prove either actual loss or a statement calculated to cause pecuniary damage and malice[136] severely limit the tort,[137] but they are seen as control devices to preserve legitimate free speech.[138] By contrast to defamation, the tort of malicious falsehood does not rely on the test of 'right-thinking' persons and social attitudes about homosexuality. The requirement to prove special damage,[139] typically understood as actual loss outlined in monetary terms, allows for compensation for actual harm caused to a heterosexual claimant while avoiding likely endorsement of any negative attitudes towards homosexuality. Another potential legal avenue is the tort of intentional infliction of physical harm or distress, provided that a claimant can prove actual psychological harm (such as clinical depression as a result of the defendant's statement) under the criteria established by the Supreme Court in *Rhodes v OPO & Anor.*[140] The action, to which Lord Neuberger referred as 'the tort of making distressing statements',[141] is 'sufficiently contained'[142] by the combination of the conduct element requiring words or conduct directed at the claimant for which there is no justification or excuse; the mental element requiring an intention to cause at least severe mental or emotional distress (recklessness is not sufficient); and the consequence element requiring physical harm or a recognised psychiatric illness.

Conclusion

Disparagement of reputation is the essence of an action of defamation. The harm at the core of this tort relates to how an individual is seen in the eyes of others. This chapter first looked at the evolution of legal and societal attitudes towards homosexuality over time. Society's increasing acceptance of homosexuality suggests that its right-thinking members would not today estimate the inherent worth of gay people to be less than that of heterosexual people. This shift is also evident in external indicators like legislative developments which reflect improvements in community sentiment and speak strongly to changes in societal values concerning homosexuality. Nevertheless, we argue that the English defamation law still retains restrictions with respect to publications carrying a false imputation that a person is gay.

A line of relatively recent cases (albeit prior to the 2013 legislation) recognised that such an assessment needs to be made on a case-by-case basis. This slightly

---

136 Malice is understood here to involve known falsehoods or improper and impermissible motives in the sense of aiming to injure rather than further someone's own interests; Andrew Tettenborn (ed), *Clerk & Lindsell on Torts* (23rd edn, Sweet & Maxwell, 2022) 22-13.

137 See *Quinton v Peirce & Another* [2009] EWHC 912 (QB), para 83, in which Eady J emphasised the 'high hurdle' of establishing malice.

138 *Ajinomoto Sweeteners Europe SAS v Asda Stores Ltd* [2009] EWHC 1717.

139 Except for those cases falling within section 3 of the Defamation Act 1952.

140 [2015] UKSC 32.

141 ibid., paras 101 and 119.

142 ibid., para 88 (Baroness Hale and Lord Toulson).

altered contemporary form marks a departure from the earlier historical position that a bare imputation of homosexuality is inherently defamatory and can be seen as a gradual evolution of the construction of defamatory words rather than an abrupt change. However, homosexuality appears to have been mainly used as a vehicle to accentuate imputations that are already defamatory (such as disloyalty, hypocrisy, exploitation and so on), adding little, if anything, to determining defamatory meaning. The lack of a contemporary firm judicial pronouncement in English law on whether imputations of homosexuality bear a defamatory meaning somewhat muddles the position. Some legal scholars express the unequivocal view that an allegation would not now be regarded as defamatory if it amounted to no more than that a same-sex couple were in a sexual relationship.[143] In other words, it seems no longer possible to contend that the shared societal standards with which the ordinary reasonable member of the community is imbued include that of holding those who engage in gay sex in lesser regard on account of that fact alone.

We believe however that this proposition is narrowly formulated and qualified in that falsely calling someone gay could raise more complex defamatory imputations, denting someone's image so deeply that 'serious harm' is at stake. Even after the 2013 reforms, which make it less likely to sustain a viable claim than was the case at common law, whether an imputation of homosexuality is capable of being defamatory depends on associating that imputation to extrinsic, contextual factors that can endow otherwise innocent words with defamatory meanings through general inferences of fact. Statements misidentifying someone as homosexual cannot thus always be held to be void of defamatory meaning, unless the importance of inferences in this context is relegated.

This is very worrying as it can result in a dangerous connotative interplay between homosexuality and other conduct like dishonesty or exploitation, which risks perpetuating the stereotypical image of gay people as deceitful and untrustworthy.[144] Although it would be unfair not to recognise how much contemporary British society has moved away from the homophobic legacy of 'The Blackmailer's Charter' or Section 28, the shadows of the past loom over any such implicit association between homosexuality and hypocrisy to the point that it becomes difficult, even for 'right-thinking members of society', not to see the two as intrinsically linked. Imputations of homosexuality should not be treated as defamatory in any situation. Recognising that false imputations of homosexuality can function, even under certain circumstances, as the basis for a legal harm worthy of remedy indirectly endorses and perpetuates a heteronormative culture that treats homosexuality as inherently negative.

---

[143] Parkes et al, *Gatley on Libel and Slander*, 2025.

[144] Elizabeth Peel, Sonja Ellis and Damien Riggs, 'Lesbian, Gay, Bisexual and Transgender People: Prejudice, Stereotyping, Discrimination and Social Change' in Cristian Tileagă, Martha Augoustinos and Kevin Durrheim (eds), *The Routledge International Handbook of Discrimination, Prejudice and Stereotyping* (Routledge, 2021) 109.

10

Rethinking 'Negligence' in 'Medical Negligence': Can Trespass to the Person Torts Help Protect Autonomy?

Eliza Bond and Jodi Gardner

Introduction

Responding effectively to interferences with autonomy has been an ongoing challenge for tort law, particularly in the context of medical negligence.[1] These challenges have meant that some claimants who have clearly suffered harm have been denied relief,[2] some have been provided compensation on a questionable basis[3] and some have seen standard concepts of negligence stretched to fit challenging, unique situations.[4] While this may not, at first blush, appear to be too concerning, it has important ramifications for the coherence and consistency of the law of tort as a whole.

This chapter examines the extent to which the tort of negligence is an inherently inadequate vehicle for the protection of autonomy interests in the medical context, and, if this is the case, whether the trespass to the person torts can provide a solution.[5] In relation to the trespass torts, this chapter will explore their historical origin, the nature of liability imposed and the extent to which such torts have become less relevant in the medical context. It will then examine the problems that negligence has faced in responding to situations where a patient has been the victim of a wrong, but the harm that they experience does not fit within the ordinary tortious definition of 'damage'. Drawing these threads

---

[1] See McCandless and Horsey, Chapter 5, this volume, for analysis of how autonomy violations in 'reproductive torts' have and should be dealt with.

[2] *McFarlane v Tayside Health Board* [2000] 2 AC 59.

[3] *Rees v Darlington Memorial Hospital NHS Trust* [2003] UKHL 52.

[4] *Chester v Afshar* [2004] UKHL 41.

[5] Henceforth, 'the trespass torts'.

together, this chapter questions whether the trespass torts can or should assume a new prominence in the medical context.

This question is important to ask because there is a tendency to think of negligence as the primary vehicle for justice in tort law. Tony Weir, one of the prominent tort lawyers of his generation, famously spoke of the 'staggering march of negligence'.[6] Elsewhere, he suggested that it was 'dining out on the other torts, eating them up, and waxing dangerously fat'.[7] We should therefore question the extent to which this bloating is a problem and if it disadvantages any particular subsets of claimants. It is important to ask this question because, as this chapter shows, an analysis of the trespass torts shows that their purpose is to vindicate the claimant's right to be free from interference with an interest highly regarded at law. This contrasts with negligence, where damage is the gist of the action.[8] The trespass torts may therefore be a much more effective and appropriate vehicle for protecting autonomy in the medical context, where patients experience harm which does not fit within the orthodox definition of damage.

The trespass to the person torts

The historical basis and nature of liability

Generally speaking, there are three torts that involve trespass to the person: assault, battery and false imprisonment.[9] These are sometimes called 'intentional torts', since Lord Denning in *Letang v Cooper* ostensibly confined trespass to intentional acts:

> If one man intentionally applies force directly to another, the [claimant] has a cause of action for assault and battery, or, if you so please to describe it, in trespass to the person ... If he does not inflict injury intentionally but only unintentionally, the [claimant] has no cause of action today in trespass. His only cause of action is in negligence, and then only proof of want of reasonable care.[10]

However, Allan Beever has persuasively shown that relying on this passage to support the view that the trespass torts *must* be intentional oversimplifies the

---

6   Tony Weir, 'The Staggering March of Negligence' in Peter Cane and Jane Stapleton (eds), *The Law of Obligations: Essays in Honour of John Fleming* (Oxford University Press, 1998) 97.

7   Tony Weir, 'Tort, Contract and Bailment' (1965) 23 *Cambridge Law Journal* 186, 190.

8   *Gregg v Scott* [2005] 2 AC 176, 217.

9   For a useful tabular summary of the trespass to the person torts, as well as other intentional torts, see Sarah Green and Jodi Gardner, *Tort Law* (Macmillan Education UK, 2021) 262–3.

10 *Letang v Cooper* [1965] QB 232, 239.

position.[11] In his view, all the judges accepted in *Letang v Cooper* was that there was no cause of action for negligent trespass, not that there was a particular fault standard for trespass generally. Therefore, notwithstanding the fact that some commentators commend the evolution from strict to fault-based liability,[12] it cannot be said with certainty that the trespass to the person torts are truly 'intentional', and it may be that liability is strict. We will therefore call these torts the trespass torts to avoid this terminological confusion.

The historical origin of these torts – in particular, assault, battery and false imprisonment – dates back to the medieval writ system in the 13th century. Under this system, in order to obtain a writ of trespass from the court, the claimant had to show that the wrong done to them was 'the immediate result of the force originally applied by the defendant'.[13] It was the very act of engaging in conduct which directly interfered with the personal security of the claimant which was sufficient to attract liability.[14] In other words, the focus was on *what* the defendant did, rather than on *how* the defendant did it and the circumstances in which the interference occurred.[15] In medieval law, running parallel to the action of trespass was the 'action on the case', where liability was based on a notion of fault. These actions coexisted harmoniously until the 18th century.[16] With the abolition of the writ system in the Supreme Court of the Judicature Acts in 1873 and 1875, judges began to develop the boundaries of the substantive law of trespass. However, in the 20th century, these developments were dwarfed by the judicial innovation which led to the modern law of negligence and the development of Lord Atkin's 'neighbourhood principle' in *Donoghue v Stevenson*.[17]

Understanding this history is important to contextualising the role of trespass in tort law. The fact that the focus was centred around both the wrong done to the claimant and on what the defendant did is in fact reflected in the modern understanding of these torts. The best view is that they seek to vindicate the claimant's right to be free from interference with an interest highly regarded at law. This is frequently cited by the courts as justification for the torts being actionable per se,[18] which means

---

[11] Allan Beever, 'The Form of Liability in the Tort of Trespass' (2011) 40(4) *Common Law World Review* 378.

[12] Anthony Gray, *The Evolution from Strict Liability to Fault in the Law of Torts* (Hart Publishing, 2021).

[13] *Leame v Bray* (1803) 5 East 593; 102 ER 724.

[14] Christine Beuermann, 'Are the Torts of Trespass to the Person Obsolete? Part 2: Continued Evolution' (2018) 26(1) *Tort Law Review* 6.

[15] Christine Beuermann, 'Are the Torts of Trespass to the Person Obsolete? Part 1: Historical Development' (2017) 25(3) *Tort Law Review* 103.

[16] David Ibbetson, *A Historical Introduction to the Law of Obligations* (Oxford University Press, 1999) 156 chapter 8.

[17] [1932] AC 562.

[18] *John Lewis and Co v Tims* [1952] AC 672. There is, however, debate as to whether it is the importance of the rights protected that result in the tort being actionable per se: see John Murphy, 'Tort's Hierarchy of Protected Interests' (2022) 81(2) *Cambridge Law Journal* 356.

that provided claimants can prove the elements of the tort, there is no separate requirement to prove damage. The consequence of this is that when a designated interest is compromised, this generates a secondary obligation to pay damages to vindicate the claimant's right to be free from interference. The torts are therefore fundamentally concerned with secondary obligations generated by the infringement of a primary right.

This is why the Supreme Court decision in *Lumba v Secretary of State for the Home Department* is so troubling.[19] There, a majority of Supreme Court Justices consisting of Lords Philips, Rodger, Brown, Collins, Kerr and Dyson held that the victim of false imprisonment was only entitled to nominal damages because, even if the Home Department had followed the correct policy, the claimant would have been detained anyway. By contrast, the minority, consisting of Lords Hope and Walker and Lady Hale, considered that where a claimant's right to be free from interference has been compromised, they should be entitled to more than nominal damages. Commenting on *Lumba*, Sandy Steel suggested that it would have been consistent with developing authority, and would have accorded adequate recognition of our most important rights, to allow for the possibility of vindicatory damages in the context of tortious protection of rights to bodily autonomy, personality and liberty.[20]

Even if authority precludes the possibility of vindicatory damages being granted for these interferences, that does not detract from the fact that trespass protects interests that are highly regarded at law. However, this simply begs the question of how we determine *which* interests are so regarded. The best view is that of Robert Stevens: whether a wrong is classified as actionable per se depends on whether or not the right in question is, as a question of social fact, sufficiently important to be considered deserving of protection.[21] The implication is that the importance of the right justifies relieving the claimant of the burden of proving actionable damage.

Such an exposition accords with the interests which the three main trespass torts protect: battery protects the physical integrity of a claimant, assault protects a claimant's psychological integrity when they anticipate physical harm and false imprisonment protects a claimant's liberty. These are all interests which, as a matter of social fact, are regarded as highly important. Not only this, but the protection of these interests in other areas of law is inherently precarious. There is no clearer example of this latter point than in the area of abortion. Until 2022 in the US, unduly restrictive state regulation of abortion was unconstitutional under the principle derived from *Roe v Wade*.[22] However, the Supreme Court decision in *Dobbs v Jackson Women's Health Organization* reversed this, eliminating

---

[19] [2011] UKSC 12.

[20] Sandy Steel, 'False Imprisonment and the Fetch of the Hypothetical Warrant' (2011) 127(Oct) *Law Quarterly Review* 527, 531.

[21] Robert Stevens, 'Rights and Other Things' in Donal Nolan and Andrew Robertson (eds), *Rights and Private Law* (Hart Publishing, 2012) 135.

[22] 410 US 113 (1973).

the federal constitutional right to abortion.[23] This shows that even in the presence of constitutional protection, rights that protect autonomy can so easily be taken away. Although tort law cannot be a substitute for public law protection of autonomy interests, it certainly has the potential to safeguard these interests in other ways.

Trespass in the medical context

Given that the trespass torts protect interests highly regarded at law, we may think that they are a useful vehicle for providing redress to claimants in the medical context, where there are often interferences with a person's bodily integrity. However, recent experience shows a reluctance to use the trespass torts to protect this interest, with the courts instead preferring to utilise the law of negligence. This is most clear in the context of 'informed consent'.

It is a general principle of the trespass torts that the interference occurs without the consent of the claimant. In *Appleton v Garrett*, a dentist carried out extensive and unnecessary treatment such that it vitiated the consent of the patient. This therefore amounted to battery, and Dyson J awarded aggravated damages for the interference.[24] Similarly, in *Hamilton v Birmingham Regional Hospital Board*, a doctor carried out a sterilisation operation without consent, and the patient brought a successful claim.[25] Finally, in *Potts v North West Regional Health Authority*, a patient gave her consent to receiving what she thought was a routine postnatal vaccination. In fact, this was a long-acting contraceptive. In an unreported decision, the judge awarded the claimant damages for battery because the patient had never been given the opportunity to accept or refuse the particular treatment given to her. This was a violation of her 'basic human right to do with her body as she wishes'.[26] This trio of cases show that it is possible to use the trespass torts to protect a patient's interest in bodily integrity through ensuring that they consent to a procedure.

However, there are limits to this approach. Indeed, in *Chatterson v Gerson*, the court emphasised that provided a patient is informed of the nature of the procedure in broad terms, their consent will be valid, further adding that it is only in cases of administrative error or fraud where trespass is likely to be the appropriate cause of action.[27] For consent to be valid, the law of battery therefore does not require that this consent is 'informed' in the sense that the patient knows of the risks inherent in the treatment.[28] The consequence of this principle is that

---

23   No. 19-1392, 597 US (2022); 142 S. Ct. 2228 (2022).
24   [1996] PIQR P1 QB.
25   [1969] 2 BMJ 456.
26   *Potts v North West Regional Health Authority, The Guardian*, 23 July 1983.
27   (1981) 1 All ER 257.
28   Caterina Milo, 'Informed Consent: An Empty Promise? A Comparative Analysis Between Italy and England, Wales, and Scotland' (2022) 22(2) *Medical Law International* 147, 154.

in cases where 'informed consent' is at issue, a patient may only resort to the law of negligence. As the Supreme Court confirmed in *Montgomery v Lanarkshire Health Board*, in this context, 'the issue is not whether enough information was given to ensure consent to the procedure, but whether enough information was given so that the doctor was not acting negligently and giving due protection to the patient's autonomy'.[29]

This case study on informed consent supports the suggestion of Percy Winfield and Arthur Goodhart that the tort of negligence has 'driven the action of trespass for personal injuries into the shade'.[30] It also raises the important normative question of whether information non-disclosure, and the issue of informed consent, *should* be dealt with under the tort of battery or negligence.[31] This is a topic which has prompted fierce academic debate.

Tan Keng Feng made a persuasive argument that battery should assume a greater role in this context as 'trespass, not negligence, is the most appropriate vehicle to protect the patient's exclusive non-clinical right to self-determination'.[32] This links back to the theoretical basis of the trespass torts themselves: they are designed to protect interests highly regarded in law. Similarly, other commentators have also suggested that issues surrounding informed consent should be dealt with under the trespass torts, as this would ensure that the focus is on the infringement of rights, rather than on the fault of the doctor.[33] Alasdair Maclean objects to this, however, stating that negligence gives courts greater control over the scope of tortious liability by virtue of the *Bolam* principle,[34] and enables a more nuanced evaluation of whether or not the doctor was acting reasonably.[35] Others, such as Margaret Brazier, suggest that the historical association between the tort of battery and the criminal law means that negligence may be a more appropriate vehicle.[36] However, this last point may slightly overstate the position. In *Ms B v An NHS [National Health Service] Hospital Trust*,[37] in holding that the continuation of invasive ventilation treatment to a person of capacity who had withdrawn her consent amounted to a battery, Dame Butler-Sloss P nevertheless praised

---

[29]   *Montgomery v Lanarkshire Health Board (Scotland)* [2015] UKSC 11, 108, citing Jonathan Herring, *Medical Law and Ethics* (4th edn, Oxford University Press, 2012) 170.

[30]   Percy H. Winfield and Arthur L. Goodhart 'Trespass and Negligence' (1933) 49(3) *Law Quarterly Review* 359, 377.

[31]   See Emily Jackson, 'Informed Consent and the Impotence of Tort' in Shelia Maclean (ed), *First Do No Harm: Ethics and Healthcare* (Ashgate Publishing, 2006).

[32]   Tan Keng Feng, 'Failure of Medical Advice: Trespass or Negligence?' (1987) 7(2) *Legal Studies* 149, 164.

[33]   Allan Beever, 'Trespass in General' in *A Theory of Tort Liability* (Hart Publishing, 2018).

[34]   *Bolam v Friern Hospital Management Committee* [1957] 1 WLR 583.

[35]   Alasdair Maclean, *Autonomy, Informed Consent and Medical Law: A Relational Challenge* (Cambridge University Press, 2009) 192.

[36]   Margaret Brazier, 'Patient Autonomy and Consent to Treatment: The Role of the Law' (1987) 7(2) *Legal Studies* 169, 178.

[37]   [2002] EWHC 429 (Fam).

the actions of the doctor, strongly suggesting that there is no longer a 'criminal stigma' surrounding trespass in a medical context. Overall, it is clear that the law of negligence is swallowing up battery in this context, and is therefore having to respond to an interference with a patient's *interest* – namely autonomy – *rather* than responding to a tangible form of *harm*. It is negligence's relationship with autonomy protection to which we now turn.

Negligence and autonomy rights

Does negligence protect autonomy in the medical context?

Is the tort of negligence up to the challenge of protecting patient autonomy? The recent Court of Appeal decision in *Shaw v Kovac* would suggest it is not.[38] In that case, Mr Ewan was advised to undergo a transcatheter aortic valve implantation procedure (TAVI), but was not advised on the alternatives of open-heart surgery or conservative treatment. Mr Ewan underwent the TAVI procedure, and sadly died due to aortic bleeding. His daughter, on behalf of the estate, successfully claimed £15,000 at first instance, but in the Court of Appeal, claimed she was entitled to an additional sum for Mr Ewan's 'loss of personal autonomy'. The Court of Appeal decisively rejected this claim, with Davis LJ stating that it would have 'very real, even if unquantifiable, financial, [and] practical' implications.[39]

Similar remarks were made by Leggatt LJ in *Duce v Worcestershire Acute Hospitals NHS Trust*.[40] Mrs Duce underwent a total abdominal hysterectomy and bilateral salpingo-oopherectomy to treat painful and heavy menstrual periods. Although the operation was performed non-negligently, she developed a condition called chronic post-surgical pain (CPSP) owing to nerve damage. Mrs Duce submitted that, because this injury was 'intimately involved with the duty to warn', that duty was owed by the doctor who performed the surgery to which the patient had consented, and since the injury was the very product of the very risk that the patient should have been warned about when they gave their consent, causation could be made out. However, the Court of Appeal dismissed the appeal. Leggatt LJ stated the following: 'The right to make an informed choice is not a right that is traditionally protected by the tort of negligence. Rather, the purpose of the tort is to protect a person from being exposed to injury through the carelessness of another.'[41] At face value, therefore, the law of negligence does not protect autonomy in its own right. This is ostensibly in keeping with the theoretical foundations of the tort, as rooted in the tenet that damage is the gist of the action. The main purpose of the law of negligence is to compensate claimants

---

[38] [2017] 1 WLR 4773.
[39] ibid., [82].
[40] [2018] EWCA Civ 1307.
[41] ibid., [88].

for loss and place them in the position they would have been had the tort not occurred. Although we could define the 'loss', 'damage' or 'harm' as 'diminished autonomy', it is much more linguistically sensible to think of self-determination as a 'right'. Indeed, as Donal Nolan suggests, claimants who want their rights to autonomy to be vindicated should use the more appropriate vehicle of the trespass torts.[42]

How, then, do we explain *Rees v Darlington* and *Chester v Afshar*? In *Rees*, Mrs Rees had a visual disability which led to her decision to be sterilised. That sterilisation was performed negligently. Mrs Rees became pregnant, and eventually gave birth to a healthy son. The House of Lords unanimously affirmed the principle in *McFarlane* that Mrs Rees could recover damages for her physical injury during the involuntary pregnancy but could not recover damages for raising the child. However, a bare majority also held that Mrs Rees could recover a conventional award of £15,000 as a recognition that she had been denied the opportunity to live her life in a way that she had wished and planned. Lord Bingham explicitly stated that this award was not compensatory, and was rather a recognition of the wrong done.[43] Similarly, Lord Millett said that the award reflected the denial of the parents' 'right to limit the size of their family'.[44] Does *Rees* therefore amount to the law of negligence protecting autonomy as a standalone right, contrary to what was said in *Shaw* and *Duce*?

This is unlikely. Notwithstanding some rights-based vindicatory language, the majority in *Rees* clearly conceived of the conventional sum as compensatory, and the most that can be extracted from the case is a narrow recognition that diminished autonomy can, in very particular circumstances, be a form of actionable damage.[45] It is useful to note that although many subsequent decisions refer to the *Rees* award,[46] there is not a single reported case which actually grants the award to a claimant. The implication of this point is that the law of negligence struggles to protect autonomy in a comprehensive way, even where the violation of autonomy has 'long-lasting and ever-present consequences' in the context of reproductive torts.[47] It is also interesting to compare the quantum of the award in *Rees* with the case of *Yearworth v North Bristol NHS Trust*.[48] In the context of the tort of conversion, it was held that Mr Yearworth could recover damages for mental distress upon learning that his sperm had been wrongly destroyed by the

---

42 Donal Nolan, 'New Forms of Damage in Negligence' (2007) 70(1) *Modern Law Review* 59, 79.

43 *Rees v Darlington Memorial Hospital NHS Trust* [2003] UKHL 52, 8.

44 ibid., [123].

45 Nolan, 'New Forms of Damage in Negligence', 79–80.

46 The most recent reported case to refer to the conventional award was in 2018: *ARB v IVF Hammersmith Ltd and Anor* [2018] EWCA Civ 2803.

47 Tsachi Keren-Paz, 'Gender Injustice in Compensating Injury to Autonomy in English and Singaporean Negligence Law' (2019) 27(1) *Feminist Legal Studies* 33, 45.

48 [2009] QB 1.

NHS Trust. As Tsachi Keren-Paz points out, the fact that the award in *Yearworth* is likely to far exceed the £15,000 figure in *Rees* is problematic in terms of gender equality.[49]

At first glance, *Chester v Afshar* seems to amount to the law of negligence protecting autonomy in its own right.[50] Dr Afshar told Miss Chester that surgery was a solution to her lower back pain but did not inform her of the 2 per cent risk of complications. There was no negligence in the performance of the surgery, but Miss Chester suffered the complication of cauda equina syndrome. It was found as a matter of fact that had Miss Chester been warned of the risk of complications, she would have still had the operation, but would not have undergone the procedure *at that particular time*. In light of this, a bare majority consisting of Lord Steyn, Lord Hope and Lord Walker held that the 'but for' test was satisfied, because but for Dr Afshar's failure to inform her of the risks, Miss Chester would not have undergone the specific surgery performed. This was so even though the failure to inform Miss Chester of the risk in no way increased the chance that the cauda equina syndrome would materialise.

Jane Stapleton disagrees with this last point.[51] In her view, the cauda equina syndrome was not coincidental, since a negligent failure to warn would increase the number of patients undergoing a particular procedure because they would not be aware of the risks involved, which in turn would increase the total number of instances of cauda equina syndrome. Therefore, she believes that *Chester* can be explained on orthodox principles. However, the majority of commentators disagree with this analysis and regard the decision as an exceptional case where damages were given for depriving a patient of the right to make an informed choice.[52]

As Craig Purshouse has persuasively argued, while it is perfectly orthodox to use the law of negligence to protect *aspects* of autonomy, *Chester* takes this a step further in awarding damages for the diminished autonomy itself.[53] The unorthodoxy of *Chester* is also explored by Sarah Green, who, in criticising the majority decision, states that:

> their findings in favour of liability are explained in terms of the need for a patient's autonomy and right to choose to be vindicated; a need that is difficult to deny. Such denial is not necessary, however, in order to adhere to established principles of causation. A patient's dignity

---

[49]   Keren-Paz, 'Gender Injustice in Compensating Injury to Autonomy', 47.

[50]   [2004] UKHL 41.

[51]   Jane Stapleton, 'Occam's Razor Reveals an Orthodox Basis for *Chester v Afshar*' (2006) 122 *Law Quarterly Review* 426.

[52]   See Tamsyn Clark and Donal Nolan, 'A Critique of *Chester v Afshar*' (2014) 34(4) *Oxford Journal of Legal Studies* 659.

[53]   Craig Purshouse, 'Liability for Lost Autonomy in Negligence: Undermining the Coherence of Tort Law?' (2015) 22(3) *Torts Law Journal* 226.

and right to decide is protected by the law of tort's recognition that a doctor has a duty to warn, not by the readiness to override causal considerations in the claimant's favour. If a breach of that duty to warn causes the patient no loss, then a finding of no liability does not violate that right. It merely serves as an acknowledgement that the patient's inability to exercise that right did not, on this occasion, cause him any harm.[54]

However, like *Rees*, *Chester* has proved something of a damp squib. In *Correia v University Hospital of North Staffordshire NHS Trust*, Simon LJ, on behalf of the Court of Appeal, refused Ms Correia's claim to disapply the ordinary principles of causation in favour of the 'exceptional principle of causation' from *Chester*.[55] This was on the basis that she had not asserted that she would have either refused the operation or deferred it had she been informed of its risks.[56] More significantly, in *Diamond v Royal Devon and Exeter NHS Foundation Trust*, although Ms Diamond initially argued that the cumulative effect of *Chester* and *Montgomery* was that there was a freestanding right to claim damages for denial of a patient's autonomy right to choose a particular form of treatment, this argument was abandoned on appeal.[57] These cases, along with the decisions in *Shaw* and *Duce* considered earlier, cast significant doubt on the proposition that autonomy is an interest which the law of negligence protects in its own right.[58]

Should negligence protect autonomy in the medical context?

The recent cases show that the relationship between negligence and autonomy is complex. Although *Chester* and *Rees* amount to attempts to protect autonomy as a right, neither of these cases have transformed the law of negligence into a tort which is actionable per se.

The justifications for this position are set out most clearly by the Court of Appeal in Singapore (SCA) in *ACB v Thomson Medical Pte Ltd*.[59] In this case, ACB and her husband approached Thomson Medical to receive in vitro fertilisation (IVF). However, an administrative error meant that ACB's egg was fertilised with the sperm of another male, not ACB's husband. ACB gave birth to a healthy baby, but it became clear that the baby was not conceived using ACB's husband's sperm: the baby's ethnicity was a mix of Chinese and Indian, whereas

---

54   Sarah Green, 'Coherence of Medical Negligence Cases: A Game of Doctors and Purses' (2006) 14(1) *Medical Law Review* 1, 9–10.

55   [2017] EWCA Civ 356, 28.

56   ibid., [40].

57   [2019] EWCA Civ 585.

58   See Joanna M. Manning, 'Oh What an Unholy Mesh! *Diamond v Royal Devon & Exeter NHS Foundation Trust* [2019] EWCA Civ 585' (2019) 27(3) *Medical Law Review* 519.

59   [2017] SGCA 20.

the couple were Chinese and Caucasian. ACB brought an action against the clinic for breach of contract and in negligence for the cost of raising the child, but this failed at first instance on the basis of causation. When the case came before the SCA, the judges rejected the first instance conclusion on causation, but upheld the outcome that no damages were recoverable for raising the child on the basis of public policy, as in *McFarlane*. However, the SCA did award damages for 'loss of genetic affinity', which was quantified at 30 per cent of the cost of raising that child.

In the course of its decision, the SCA decisively rejected the view that loss of autonomy could, without more, amount to an actionable injury in its own right. The SCA gave three reasons for this conclusion. The first was that the concept of autonomy was too nebulous and too contested to ground a claim.[60] The SCA noted that while autonomy is chiefly defined in 'thin' terms, and understood as the *liberty* to live one's life free from external interferences or control,[61] there are also those who would espouse a 'thicker' version of autonomy that seeks to give effect to not only current desires of the decision maker, but also a person's long-term desires and values. The SCA also identified that others would argue that both of these accounts do not adequately factor in the socially embedded nature of human relations, and therefore fail to support a more substantive and communitarian view of autonomy.[62]

The second reason for rejecting autonomy as an actionable head of damage in its own right was that the notion of autonomy does not comport with the concept of damage in the tort of negligence.[63] The common law has traditionally understood damage in terms of 'objective detriment', in that in order to make out a cause of action, it is necessary for a claimant to show that they are more than minimally worse off than they would otherwise be. Most interferences with autonomy would, in the SCA's view, fall far short of this standard. Further still, the notion of an action for 'loss of autonomy' was more compatible with a rights-based vindicatory model of tort law, which would pose a fundamental challenge to negligence principles which are primarily concerned with granting remedies for *harms*.[64]

The third and final reason for rejecting autonomy as a head of damage was that it would undermine the existing control mechanisms which keep recovery in the tort of negligence within sensible bounds.[65] The problem is that any form of damage can be reconceptualised in terms of damage to autonomy. In particular,

---

[60] ibid., [116]–[119].

[61] *Airedale NHS Trust v Bland* [1993] 2 WLR 316, 351F; *Re T (Adult: Refusal of Treatment)* [1992] 3 WLR 782, 796–797A.

[62] Craig Purshouse, 'How Should Autonomy be Defined in Medical Negligence Cases?' (2015) 10(4) *Clinical Ethics* 107.

[63] *ACB v Thomson Medical Pte Ltd* [2017] SGCA 20, 120–2.

[64] *Kingdom of Spain v Christie, Manson & Woods Ltd and Another* [1986] 1 WLR 1120, 1129D.

[65] *ACB v Thomson Medical Pte Ltd* [2017] SGCA 20, 123–4.

this would undermine existing restrictions on recovery for negligently caused psychiatric harm.[66] The SCA also justified its conclusion by drawing an analogy with the rejection of a claim for loss of a chance in *Gregg v Scott*.[67] In this case, Dr Scott negligently misdiagnosed a lump in Mr Gregg's armpit as a benign tumour, when in fact it was non-Hodgkin's lymphoma. It was agreed that but for the negligent delay in misdiagnosing the tumour, Mr Gregg would have had a 42 per cent chance of surviving for ten years, but the current prognosis placed that value at 25 per cent. Mr Gregg brought a claim on the basis that Dr Scott's negligence had reduced his chance of survival by 17 per cent. The House of Lords, relying on *Hotson v East Berkshire Area Health Authority*,[68] refused to recognise a percentage reduction in the prospect of a favourable outcome as a head of damage. The SCA drew attention to the remarks of Baroness Hale, who explained that recognising such a head of claim would have substantial implications since almost any claim for loss of an outcome could conceivably be reformulated as a claim for loss of a chance of that outcome.[69]

Although we do not believe that difficulties in defining autonomy should necessarily prevent recovery in negligence, we do believe that the second and third reasons are persuasive. As Sarah Fulham-McQuillan has recently argued, 'infringement of autonomy as damage in medical negligence would require altering the theoretical framework' of negligence itself,[70] since damage is the gist of the action.[71] There is also the related problem of how recognising damages for loss of autonomy would interact with other, more conventional forms of personal injury. For example, consider *McFarlane v Tayside Health Board*.[72] In that case, following a vasectomy operation conducted on Mr McFarlane, the McFarlanes were advised that contraception was unnecessary. Relying on this advice, the couple dispensed with contraceptives, but Mrs McFarlane became pregnant and gave birth to a healthy child. The McFarlanes sued the health board responsible for the negligent advice, claiming damages in respect of the physical discomfort caused by the pregnancy and birth and the financial costs of raising the child. The House of Lords held that Mrs McFarlane was entitled to damages in respect of the physical discomfort, but was not entitled to damages for raising the child. If loss of autonomy was recognised as a generalised head of damage, then not only would the McFarlanes recover for the autonomy loss associated with raising a healthy child, but presumably Mrs McFarlane would *also* recover for the loss of autonomy associated with the pregnancy and birth. However, given that this

---

66   *Alcock v Chief Constable of South Yorkshire Police* [1992] 1 AC 310.
67   *Gregg v Scott* [2005] 2 AC 176.
68   [1987] AC 750.
69   *Gregg v Scott* [2005] 2 AC 176, 224–6.
70   Sarah Fulham-McQuillan, 'Infringement of Autonomy as Damage in Medical Negligence' (2023) 139 *Law Quarterly Review* 126, 126.
71   Jane Stapleton, 'The Gist of Negligence' (1988) 104 *Law Quarterly Review* 213, 213.
72   [2000] 2 AC 59, discussed further by Horsey and McCandless, Chapter 5, this volume.

is likely to amount to double recovery, the court would have to undertake the complicated exercise of separating the autonomy interference from the remainder of the loss.[73]

How does Montgomery fit into this?

As we mentioned earlier, information non–disclosure is more commonly dealt with under the tort of negligence, rather than the trespass torts. The key case here is *Montgomery v Lanarkshire Health Board*,[74] which marked a shift away from medical paternalism and the *Bolam* test. Mrs Montgomery both suffered from diabetes and had a small physical frame. This increased the risk that her baby's shoulders would get stuck in the birth canal, which is known as shoulder dystocia. Sadly, this risk became a reality, and her son suffered serious injuries during birth. Mrs Montgomery had not asked the doctor about the specific risks associated with shoulder dystocia but had raised concerns about the size of her baby. The doctor's decision not to disclose the risk of shoulder dystocia was on the basis that had Mrs Montgomery known of this risk, she would have elected for a caesarean section, which, in the doctor's view, was not in her overall interest. However, it was found as a matter of fact that had Mrs Montgomery known of the risk, she would have had a caesarean section, and therefore, on the balance of probabilities, the injuries to her son would not have occurred.

The Lord Ordinary initially held that, in accordance with *Sidaway v Board of Governors of the Bethlem Royal Hospital*,[75] whether a doctor's omission to warn a patient of certain risks constitutes a breach of duty was to be determined by the application of the *Bolam* test. In other words, the question is whether the omission was accepted as proper by a responsible body of medical opinion. On the facts, the Lord Ordinary found that the omission was justified. The Inner House of Session refused Mrs Montgomery's appeal. However, the Supreme Court overruled *Sidaway*, and held that although the *Bolam* test applies to diagnosis and treatment, it does not apply in relation to advising patients about the risks involved in undertaking a certain treatment. Instead, Lord Kerr and Lord Reed said the following:

> An adult person of sound mind is entitled to decide which, if any, of the available forms of treatment to undergo, and her consent must be obtained before the treatment interfering with her bodily integrity is undertaken. The doctor is therefore under a duty to take reasonable care to ensure that the patient is aware of any material

---

[73] Donal Nolan, 'Negligence and Autonomy' (2022) 2022(2) *Singapore Journal of Legal Studies* 356, 366.

[74] *Montgomery v Lanarkshire Health Board (Scotland)* [2015] UKSC 11.

[75] *Sidaway v Board of Governors of the Bethlem Royal Hospital and the Maudsley Hospital* [1985] AC 871.

risk involved in any recommended treatment, and of any reasonable alternative or variant treatments. The test of materiality is whether, in the circumstances of the particular case, a reasonable person in the patient's position would be likely to attach significance to the risk, or the doctor should reasonably be aware that the particular patient would be likely to attach significance to it.[76]

A doctor is only entitled to withhold information about risk if they reasonably believe that disclosure would be seriously detrimental to the patient's health, or in circumstances of necessity.[77] *Montgomery* undoubtedly moves the law of negligence away from the paternalistic approach inherent in the *Bolam* test.[78] Praising the decision, Colm McGrath suggested that the basis for disclosure is 'the patient's right to be put in a position where they can fully exercise their decisional autonomy'.[79] However, this reference to 'decisional autonomy' reveals an awkward question about *Montgomery*: is the case consistent with a traditional negligence analysis?

Donal Nolan has recently considered this question.[80] In his view, 'by adopting a patient-centred material risk test, rather than simply defaulting to a generic "reasonable doctor" test, the Supreme Court arguably abandoned negligence analysis altogether', in that for liability to arise it may no longer be necessary to show that the defendant acted in an unreasonable way.[81] He acknowledges that while the actual test laid down by the court appears to be one of negligence, since the duty is to take *reasonable steps* to make disclosure of material risks, there is 'no shortage of evidence that *Montgomery* has been treated as laying down a straightforward outcome-based test of "material risk" disclosure, shorn of the subtleties involved in a reasonable conduct standard'.[82] Finally, he concludes by stating that *if* this outcome-based approach is adopted:

> there may be circumstances where a doctor has reasonably failed to disclose such a risk (so that her conduct cannot be characterised as negligent) but where liability is nevertheless imposed. *Were this to happen, then the link between medical non-disclosure and negligence would have been broken and this area of law would more appropriately be*

---

76   *Montgomery v Lanarkshire Health Board (Scotland)* [2015] UKSC 11, 87.
77   ibid., [88].
78   For an interesting argument that *Bolam* should be completely relegated to history, see John-Paul Swoboda, '*Bolam*: Going, Going ... Gone' (2018) 1 *Journal of Personal Injury Litigation* 9.
79   Colm McGrath, '"Trust Me, I'm a Patient ..."': Disclosure Standards and the Patient's Right to Decide' (2015) 74(2) *Cambridge Law Journal* 211, 214.
80   Nolan, 'Negligence and Autonomy'.
81   ibid., 378.
82   ibid., 380.

classified as a sui generis *head of liability, falling somewhere between battery and negligence.*[83]

This raises fundamental questions about tort law: can we, and should we, allow distinct actionable per se torts to develop in order to protect autonomy? Could this provide a better doctrinal explanation for cases such as *Chester, Rees* and *Montgomery*? Is the law of trespass, with its theoretical foundation rooted in the protection of fundamental interests, a more suitable basis for developing such torts?

Can the trespass torts help us protect autonomy?

The case for developing specific torts

The expansion of negligence, and its corresponding displacement of other torts, 'has not always been treated with approbation'.[84] One commentator has noted that having one 'über-tort of negligence cutting across the rest' creates inevitable overlaps.[85] We also believe that the case law explored earlier shows that the loss-based paradigm of negligence invariably means that when the courts attempt to protect autonomy in cases such as *Rees, Chester* and *Montgomery*, it is at the expense of the coherence of the tort.

The cases of *Diamond, Shaw* and *Duce* also show a sustained effort on the part of claimants to alter the boundaries of negligence, particularly in the clinical context. In *Khan v Meadows*, a recent Supreme Court decision on wrongful conception, Ms Meadows submitted that the 'imbalance of knowledge and power between the clinician and the patient' demands a somewhat different approach to the law of negligence.[86] Although this argument was rejected by the Supreme Court,[87] the patient–doctor relationship is characterised by a vulnerability not replicated in other legal relationships.[88] Should we use specific actionable per se torts to respond to this vulnerability and, by doing so, would we be able to protect autonomy?

Use of specific torts to protect autonomy is not unprecedented. The most notable example is the development of the protection of privacy rights. *Campbell v Mirror Group Newspapers Ltd* suggested that following the Human Rights Act 1998 there had been a shift in the 'centre of gravity' of the (equitable) action for breach of confidence.[89] Although this did not result in the creation of a new tort,

---

83   ibid., 381 (emphasis added).
84   Ken Oliphant, 'Rationalising Tort Law for the Twenty-First Century' in Kit Barker, Karen Fairweather and Ross Grantham (eds), *Private Law in the 21st Century* (Hart Publishing, 2017) 51.
85   Robert Stevens, *Torts and Rights* (Oxford University Press, 2007) 295.
86   [2021] UKSC 21, 21.
87   ibid., [62] (Lords Hodge and Sales); [90] (Lord Leggatt).
88   For an argument that vulnerability is a central theme in tort law, see Jane Stapleton, 'The Golden Thread at the Heart of Tort Law: Protection of the Vulnerable' (2003) 24(2) *Australian Bar Review* 135.
89   [2004] UKHL 22, 51.

in *OBG Ltd v Allan*, Lord Nicholls stated that 'as the law has developed, breach of confidence, or misuse of confidential information, now covers two distinct causes of action protecting two different interests: privacy and secret ("confidential") information' and that it was 'important to keep these two distinct'.[90] Another example, in the specific context of the trespass torts, is the tort in *Wilkinson v Downton*.[91] Under this principle, a claimant has a cause of action when the defendant intentionally does an act calculated to cause physical harm or severe mental or emotional distress to the claimant, and has thereby in fact caused physical harm or a recognised psychiatric illness.[92] As with the protection of privacy rights under *Campbell*, the tort in *Wilkinson* protects an individual from 'intrusive and invasive conduct jeopardising legal rights to personal safety, dignity, autonomy and mental wellbeing'.[93]

Writing about the relationship between trespass and negligence, Gerald Dworkin argued that 'the desire for complete individuality of different torts will only be acceptable if the courts are always prepared to create a new tort' in response to specific situations.[94] Although we do not believe that every situation involving an actual or potential loss of autonomy justifies the creation of a new tort to respond to this interference, we do believe that there is a justification for the *specific* torts to respond to information non-disclosure and wrongful conception, as there is clear judicial recognition – through *Chester* and *Rees* respectively – that the victim of information non-disclosure and wrongful conception has suffered a legal wrong. We also believe that this is justified on the basis of the nature of the loss of autonomy in these cases.

In the information non-disclosure context, as Lord Bingham stated in *Chester*, the duty to warn of risks exists to 'enable adult patients of sound mind to make for themselves decisions intimately affecting their own lives and bodies', that is, to protect their autonomy.[95] If this duty is not adhered to, this is in itself an infringement on the patient's autonomy, and undermines the very basis of the patient–doctor relationship. However, there is also a second autonomy infringement which arises where that very risk eventuates: in *Chester*, this was the cauda equina syndrome, whereas in *Montgomery*, this was the shoulder dystocia.

---

90   [2007] UKHL 21, 255.
91   *Wilkinson v Downton* [1897] 2 QB 57. Note, however, that Lord Hoffmann suggested in *Wainwright v Home Office* [2004] 2 AC 406 that the tort in *Wilkinson v Downton* 'has nothing to do with trespass to the person' (at 426).
92   *Rhodes v OPO & Anor* [2015] UKSC 32.
93   Pita Roycroft, '*Wilkinson v Downton* after *Rhodes* and its Future Viability in New Zealand' (2017) 48(1) *Victoria University of Wellington Law Review* 107.
94   Gerald Dworkin, 'Trespass and Negligence – A Further Attempt to Bury the Forms of Action' (1965) 28(1) *Modern Law Review* 92, 96.
95   *Chester v Afshar* [2004] UKHL 41, 5.

In relation to wrongful conception, the clearest description of the reduction of autonomy upon the birth of the child is found in the judgment of Hale LJ in *Parkinson v St James and Seacroft University Hospital NHS Trust*:

> Parental responsibility is not simply or even primarily a financial responsibility .... The primary responsibility is to care for the child. The labour does not stop when the child is born. Bringing up children is hard work. ... The obligation to provide or make acceptable and safe arrangements for the child's care and supervision lasts for 24 hours a day, seven days a week, all year round, until the child becomes old enough to take care of himself.[96]

The desire to protect autonomy in these contexts must, of course, be balanced against the concern that the concept is itself malleable, and therefore liability is potentially indeterminate. This concern is particularly acute at a time where the NHS is under immense pressure, and the cost of clinical negligence cases continues to rise.[97]

Can this work in practice?

We think that the best way forward is to try to develop specific torts to protect autonomy in these situations. This would be akin to the trespass torts in that they respond to an interference with an interest highly regarded at law. They would also be like the trespass torts in that they would be actionable per se: that is, actionable without proof of damage or injury.

In the case of wrongful conception, this would be based on the award in *Rees*, but would not be fixed. This is because, as Nicolette Priaulx suggests, a fixed award assumes all victims of unsolicited parenthood are impacted in the same way,[98] when loss of reproductive autonomy is an inherently subjective process and each individual requires specific consideration.[99] The concerns about distributive justice which prevented the House of Lords from allowing Mrs McFarlane's claim for maintenance costs in that case would not apply here,[100] as the amount of damages would be determined by the interference with autonomy rather than according to the cost of upkeep. We would caution against calculating damages as a percentage or ratio of the compensatory loss suffered by the claimant, like

---

[96]   [2001] EWCA Civ 530, 70–1.

[97]   Alexander Carter, Elias Mossialos, Julian Redhead and Vassilios Papalois, 'Clinical Negligence Cases in the English NHS: Uncertainty in Evidence as a Driver of Settlement Costs and Societal Outcomes' (2022) 17(3) *Health Economic Policy and Law* 266.

[98]   Nicolette Priaulx, *The Harm Paradox: Tort Law and the Unwanted Child in an Era of Choice* (Routledge-Cavendish, 2006)

[99]   *Parkinson v St James and Seacroft University Hospital NHS Trust* [2001] EWCA Civ 530, 85.

[100]   *McFarlane v Tayside Health Board* [2000] 2 AC 59, 82.

the position adopted by the SCA in *ACB v Thomson Medical*, as this could further blur the distinction between actionable per se torts and negligence. Given that the action would be based on the trespass torts, it would also be possible to grant nominal damages.

A similar model would be adopted for information non-disclosure. As with *Rees*, the law already provides a model for structuring a new tort if we take a broad understanding of *Montgomery* combined with *Chester*. As we explored earlier, one way to read *Montgomery* is that in adopting a patient-centric view of material risk, the Supreme Court to some extent severed the link between medical non-disclosure and negligence.[101] Much of the justification for adopting this test was based on the idea that medical paternalism no longer reigned. This seems to amount to the court recognising an actionable per se tort, on the basis that a patient's right has been interfered with. It would be more honest for the law to call it as such. Once we take medical non-disclosure outside the negligence paradigm, as with wrongful conception, it would be necessary to quantify damages according to the extent to which the right has been interfered with, rather than the extent to which loss has been suffered. This would quell some of the criticisms surrounding the potential scope of *Chester*.

As discussed before, the torts of trespass are sometimes described as intentional torts.[102] We do not, however, think this is a problem for our model. This is because, as we discussed at the beginning of this chapter, this label is misleading. In any event, we are simply modelling actionable per se torts based on an analogy with the law of trespass, and they do not therefore need to fit within existing categories of liability.

What are the benefits of developing new torts?

Developing new torts to respond to autonomy infringements in the situations explored earlier would encourage courts to engage in a process of decentralisation from the tort of negligence. Although the trespass torts have been described as 'obsolete',[103] we believe that using the *principles* derived from those torts can provide the courts with a more sensitive tool to respond to interferences with a patient's autonomy. There are five key benefits of doing so.

First, it would provide more consistency than the current approach. Under that approach, general principles of negligence operate to preclude recovery, with cases such as *Chester* and *Rees* constituting exceptional principles applied in an exceptional manner. By implementing new torts based on the fundamental idea behind the trespass to the person torts, tort law could more appropriately

---

[101] Nolan, 'Negligence and Autonomy', 378.

[102] Francis A Trindade, 'Intentional Torts: Some Thoughts on Assault and Battery' (1982) 2(2) *Oxford Journal of Legal Studies*, 211.

[103] Beuermann, 'Are the Torts of Trespass to the Person Obsolete? Part 1: Historical Development' and 'Are the Torts of Trespass to the Person Obsolete? Part 2: Continued Evolution'.

respond to any pre-existing disadvantages and inequalities which may exist in these contexts as opposed to exacerbating them. Second, our model would place the infringement of the patient's right, as opposed to the fault of the doctor, at the centre of the court's enquiry.[104] Although *Montgomery* shows that negligence can focus on the autonomy interests of the claimant,[105] its foundation on the concepts of actionable loss and fault means that it is ultimately ill-suited to this task.

Third, moving towards specific torts could also quell distributional concerns. Think about *McFarlane* for example. You will remember that many of the judges in the House of Lords were reluctant to provide damages for the full cost of raising a child on the basis that the 'ordinary man on the Underground' would find it objectionable.[106] However, if damages were quantified according to the diminution of the right, these concerns may fall away, as the interference with the right is not necessarily correlated to the level of loss. It is true that any rights-based award must not be so low that it is derisory, as was clearly the case in *Rees*. However, moving to specific torts could provide a more nuanced assessment of damages, as compared with the current all-or-nothing approach.

Fourth, it would allow adequate damages to be awarded without the need to go through the complex and rarely successful routes of punitive or vindicatory damages, or a requirement for the courts to engage with damages under the Human Rights Act 1998. There are substantive and procedural difficulties associated with any of these courses of action, and the discretionary nature creates a lack of certainty and predictability for the claimants who have experienced interferences with their autonomy. We therefore believe that developing a specific tort with clearly defined elements would provide much needed certainty, not just for the victims but also for potential tortfeasors.

Finally, and most fundamentally, analysing factual scenarios in this way could precipitate a more nuanced discussion about the proper scope of the tort of negligence. For too long has negligence been allowed to expand into new areas without proper justification, which has inevitably led to calls for the abrogation of the whole system of tort law. We argue that total abrogation is not necessary,[107] but that it is essential to develop a system where negligence is not viewed as the only tortious cause of action.

Conclusion

Protecting patient choice should be at the heart of healthcare. Among other things, the emergence of the contraceptive pill, the development of IVF and the

---

[104] See Beever, 'Trespass in General'.

[105] Gemma Turton, 'Informed Consent to Medical Treatment Post-*Montgomery*: Causation and Coincidence' (2019) 27(1) *Medical Law Review* 108.

[106] *McFarlane v Tayside Health Board* [2000] 2 AC 59, 82.

[107] See Jonathan Morgan, 'Abolishing Personal Injuries Law? A Reply to Lord Sumption' (2018) 34 *Professional Negligence* 122 for an interesting article on this debate.

partial liberalisation of abortion under the Abortion Act 1967 further this choice. However, although our society views medical decisional autonomy as a central aspect of our independence, a series of cases have highlighted that the law of negligence is inadequate in responding to autonomy interferences. This chapter has highlighted that the approach in this area is theoretically messy, often resulting in unfair outcomes, and therefore it may be time for a new approach. We have suggested that the trespass torts could provide a solution to this, owing to their historical underpinning and ability to respond to private law rights violations. Overall, we should be sceptical about the ability of the tort of negligence to provide a solution for all tortious problems,[108] and be willing to flexibly consider the other mechanisms available in the tort law toolbox.

Acknowledgements

We acknowledge the very helpful comments on earlier drafts from Kirsty Horsey, John Murphy, Craig Purshouse and the anonymous reviewers. The usual caveat applies.

---

[108] See Jenny Steele, 'Scepticism and the Law of Negligence' (1993) 52(3) *Cambridge Law Journal* 437.

11

Image-based Sexual Abuse and Gendered Conceptions of Harm in Tort

Aislinn O'Connell

Introduction

Image-based sexual abuse, intimate image abuse, image-based abuse, or non-consensual pornography are terms referring to a spectrum of behaviours centred around the non-consensual making, taking and sharing of photos/videos of intimate, sexual and/or private circumstances, including creating 'deepfake' videos or images.[1] This is not a new cultural practice – taking, making or sharing images of people without their knowledge or consent has a long history – but it is one which has become more prevalent in an increasingly digital word. Image-based sexual abuse (IBSA) has a range of negative consequences on victim-survivors, including on reputation, mental health and wellbeing.[2] This chapter explores the definition of IBSA and the harms which can result from this form of abuse. It then moves on to examine the potential tortious claims which could feasibly be used to ground a claim for relief of the harms suffered as a result of instances of IBSA. It builds on

---

1   Anne Pechenik Gieseke, ' "The New Weapon of Choice": Law's Current Inability to Properly Address Deepfake Pornography' (2020) 73(5) *Vanderbilt Law Review* 1479. For convenience, throughout the remainder of this chapter, we will use the term image-based sexual abuse (IBSA).
2   Erika Rackley, Clare McGlynn, Kelly Johnson, Nicola Henry, Nicola Gavey, Asher Flynn and Anastasia Powell, 'Seeking Justice and Redress for Victim-Survivors of Image-Based Sexual Abuse' (2021) 29 *Feminist Legal Studies* 293; Clare McGlynn, Kelly Johnson, Erika Rackley, Nicola Henry, Nicola Gavey, Anastasia Powell and Asher Flynn, ' "It's Torture for the Soul": The Harms of Image-Based Sexual Abuse' (2020) 30(4) *Social & Legal Studies* 541.

existing work in this area and joins with previous publications in calling for the development of a tort specific to IBSA.[3]

Four separate tortious areas with potential for the redress of the harms caused by IBSA are explored – intentional interference with the person (the 'trespass torts'), intentional infliction of emotional distress, negligence resulting in freestanding (or 'pure') psychiatric injury and misuse of private information. The chapter concedes that none of these tortious actions provide a suitable remedy for victims of IBSA, concluding that the gendered nature of IBSA has worked to mask the lacuna into which it falls, despite the very real harms suffered by victims of this spectrum of behaviours, and thus strengthens the call for a tort based on existing state obligations.[4]

Image-based sexual abuse – definitions and examples

Image-based sexual abuse (IBSA) is a term coined by Clare McGlynn and Erika Rackley in their groundbreaking work on the phenomenon.[5] It is an umbrella term that refers to a spectrum of behaviours around the making, taking and sharing of intimate images. McGlynn and Rackley explain the term as the 'non-consensual creation and/or distribution of private sexual images',[6] and suggest that the term itself avoids many of the difficulties with problematic language which has become embedded in the vernacular to refer to the range of behaviours that the spectrum encompasses.[7] It also has the advantage of characterising IBSA as a form of sexual abuse,[8] which is in keeping with the experience of victim-survivors, and builds on the continuum of sexual violence theory identified by Liz Kelly to allow responses to be formed within the spectrum of sexual violence and violence against women and girls, taking into account gendered phenomena

---

3   Kirsty Horsey and Erika Rackley, 'Tort Law' in Rosemary Auchmuty (ed), *Great Debates in Gender and Law* (Palgrave, 2018) 13. As will be discussed later, the obligations placed on state bodies by Article 8 of the European Convention on Human Rights (ECHR) necessitate acting in a way which is consistent with protecting the right to a private and family life.

4   Horsey and Rackley, in Auchmuty (ibid.).

5   Clare McGlynn and Erika Rackley, 'Image-Based Sexual Abuse' (2017) 37(3) *Oxford Journal of Legal Studies* 534.

6   ibid., 536.

7   For example, the commonly accepted phrase 'revenge porn' fails to encompass the spectrum of IBSA for several reasons – it frames intimate images which the subject did not intend to be public as pornographic, when pornography is specifically made for public consumption. It further suggests that 'revenge' is a suitable motive for sharing intimate images, or the only motive for sharing images, when in fact there are myriad motives, and it encompasses only one type of IBSA – non-consensual public image disclosure – when the spectrum is much wider than this. For more detailed discussion, see Alex Dymock and Charlotte Van der Westhuizen, 'A Dish Served Cold: Targeting Revenge in Revenge Pornography' (2019) 39(3) *Legal Studies* 361; and Clare McGlynn and Erika Rackley, 'Not "revenge porn", but abuse: Let's call it image-based sexual abuse' *Inherently Human* 15 February 2016.

8   McGlynn and Rackley, 'Image-Based Sexual Abuse', 537.

such as victim blaming.[9] Using the term allows us to conceptualise a range of seemingly discrete behaviours as part of the same system of power, control and sexism, and brings together a range of behaviours under a single umbrella to allow us to more closely assess the suitability of tortious regimes for seeking redress for harms suffered. Although some of the behaviours discussed in this section are criminalised and some are not, bringing them together as elements of the same general practice of behaviour allows the formation of a single tortious response.[10] As will be seen in the next section, the harms of the various behaviours that IBSA encompasses are similar, meaning that grouping them together from a tort perspective brings a broad sense of similarity and allows for a single tortious action for the range of harms suffered.

Private sexual images

The definition given by McGlynn and Rackley, quoted earlier, refers to 'private sexual images', that is, images which are both private and sexual in nature. They go on to discuss that 'sexual' should be defined in a way that is both broad and flexible, taking into account the context in which an image could be exploited, but specifying that there must be a sexual element to it.[11] They ground this in an understanding that the harm of IBSA lies in 'the exploitation of a victim-survivor's sexual identity, and harm to their sexual dignity and autonomy'.[12] They further qualify the 'sexual' requirement with a requirement that the image is also 'private', and discuss in some detail how to define this, specifically rejecting the 'ordinarily seen in public'[13] test which is set out in the disclosure offence which criminalises some forms of so-called 'revenge porn'. They recommend instead that an understanding of 'private' should be led by the intentions and expectations of the person depicted in the image.[14]

This can be contrasted with the definition adopted by the Law Commission in its 2022 review of the law around the taking, making and sharing of intimate

---

[9] ibid., citing Liz Kelly, *Surviving Sexual Violence* (Polity Press, 1987).

[10] Criminal law, however effective, serves a different purpose from tort law. As with assault, battery, sexual violence and voyeurism, the combination of tortious and criminal law remedies is required for an effectively functioning legal system. For more, see Horsey and Rackley, 'Tort Law', 15.

[11] McGlynn and Rackley, 'Image-Based Sexual Abuse', gives an example of an image of feet which, although could be used in a sexual context, is not inherently sexual, and so would not fall under the definition of a private sexual image. The definition of 'private sexual images' is used to fall in line with the criminal offence established in the Criminal Justice and Courts Act 2015, c 2 (CJCA), which refers to the disclosure of a private sexual image.

[12] ibid., 541.

[13] CJCA, s 35(2), defining the offence set out in s 33.

[14] McGlynn and Rackley, 'Image-Based Sexual Abuse', 542. This is similar to the standard set out in misuse of private information tort cases – information in which one has a 'reasonable expectation of privacy' – *Campbell v Mirror Group Newspapers Ltd* [2004] UKHL 22.

images without consent.[15] In its final report, following a two-year consultation on the criminal elements of image sharing, the Commission suggested a definition of 'intimate images' as 'sexual, nude, partially-nude and toileting'.[16] This is both broader (in that it includes toileting images) and narrower (in that it takes an objective, rather than subjective, view of what amounts to intimate) than the definition offered by McGlynn and Rackley. The government signaled its intention to implement those provisions as part of the Online Safety Bill in November 2022,[17] with the amendments due to be included in the Lords' debate.[18] For the purposes of this chapter, we will use the term 'private sexual images', but with an understanding that it includes toileting images. For toileting images we will use the definition suggested by the Law Commission – 'an image of a person in the act of defecation or urination, or an image of personal care associated with genital or anal discharge, defecation or urination'.[19] This gives us a definition which encompasses that which is considered sexual by the person depicted in the image, but expands it to include extremely private personal care which might not otherwise fall within the definition.

The reason for preferring the McGlynn and Rackley definition over that of the Law Commission is due to the differing nature of the context in which the definition is considered. While the Law Commission focuses on the wrongful conduct of the perpetrator, the tortious claims which we will discuss in this chapter focus on the harms suffered by the victim-survivor. Thus, a definition which focuses on the victim-survivor, rather than the perpetrator, is more in keeping with the aims of tort law remedies.

Non-consensual image taking

There are several forms of taking images which infringe on the bodily autonomy and sexual privacy and dignity of individuals. What follows next is discussion of some examples of behaviours that have been highlighted as forming part of the spectrum of IBSA (although this is by no means a comprehensive list).

Covert or non-consensual recording

Voyeurism is defined in the Sexual Offences Act 2003. This outlines the requirements of the offence of voyeurism, that is, recording a person doing

---

[15] Law Commission, Intimate Image Abuse: A Final Report Law Com No 407 HC 326, 2022.

[16] ibid., 36.

[17] Ministry of Justice and The Rt Hon Dominic Raab MP, 'New laws to better protect victims from abuse of intimate images' Gov.uk 25 November 2022.

[18] Communications and Digital Committee, 'Uncorrected oral evidence: Online Safety Bill', Tuesday 6 December 2022.

[19] Law Commission, Intimate Image Abuse, 48.

a private act with the intention that the image will be viewed (by the person filming or a third person) for the purpose of obtaining sexual gratification, and they know that the person depicted does not consent to the recording of the act with that intention.[20] Voyeurism is a criminal and sexual offence, which is historically and stereotypically understood to be the action of a 'peeping Tom', who sets up equipment to view activities which are private through windows or in rented bedrooms. However, the advent of the Internet of Things (IoT) means that there are myriad avenues for covert image taking which were not envisioned at the time of drafting the law, and multiple circumstances which have confounded the law as it stands.[21] The span of voyeurism has been expanded in recent years to include recording where the victim has consented to sexual activity. In 2020, the Court of Appeal confirmed that a man who covertly filmed sexual encounters where the other party had explicitly not consented to the recording had committed two counts of voyeurism, despite the consent of the women involved to sexual activity.[22] This was then used to inform a campaign by Emily Hunt.

In May 2015, Emily Hunt woke up in a hotel room with a man she did not recall meeting. Over a year later, she discovered that the man – Christopher Killick – had taken a 62-second video of her, unconscious and naked. Despite police investigations, Killick was not charged with sexual assault, and the Crown Prosecution Service (CPS) declined to prosecute on voyeurism grounds, arguing that consent to a sexual encounter was implicit consent to being recorded.[23] Following the decision in *R v Richards* in 2020, Killick was arrested and sentenced for voyeurism, expanding the understanding of voyeurism to include situations where a consenting sexual partner is not aware that they are being filmed.[24] Further examples of non-consensual recording include covert bathroom cameras,[25] recordings of sexual assaults[26] and rapes,[27] incidents captured on

---

20   Sexual Offences Act 2003, c 42, s 67.

21   Puneet Kaur, Amandeep Dhir, Anushree Tandon, Ebtesam A. Alzeiby and Abeer Ahmed, 'A Systematic Literature Review on Cyberstalking. An Analysis of Past Achievements and Future Promises' (2021) 163 *Technological Forecasting and Social Change* 120426; Eileen Guo, 'A Roomba recorded a woman on the toilet. How did screenshots end up on Facebook?' *MIT Technology Review* 19 December 2022.

22   *R v Richards* [2020] EWCA Crim 95.

23   Emine Saner, 'Emily Hunt: Why she fought to make sure no woman is filmed naked without consent' *The Guardian* 21 July 2021.

24   Kerry Grumka, 'The flawed justice system of the United Kingdom: The case of Christopher Killick' *St Andrews Law Review* 9 February 2021.

25   Clare Dyer, 'Doctor Who Secretly Filmed Women With Hidden Cameras is Struck Off' (2022) *British Medical Journal* 378.

26   Connor Simpson, 'The Steubenville victim tells her story' *The Atlantic* 26 March 2013.

27   Megha Mohan, 'I was raped at 14, and the video ended up on a porn site' *BBC News* 10 February 2020.

CCTV,[28] upskirting and downblousing – both of which I discuss in slightly more detail next.

Upskirting and downblousing

Upskirting refers to the practice of taking images under someone's clothing without their knowledge, generally for the intention of viewing their genitals or buttocks, whether with or without underwear.[29] It is a criminal offence, enacted after the campaign spearheaded by Gina Martin,[30] under the Voyeurism (Offences) Act 2019, and is now covered by the Sexual Offences Act 2003.[31]

A similar practice to upskirting, downblousing refers to taking images or videos down a person's top, with the intention of viewing their breasts or chest area.[32] It is currently not a criminal offence – although it could potentially be prosecuted under the offence of outraging public decency.[33] The Law Commission, in its 2022 report, recommended that downblousing be included in the range of offences proposed[34] and the government agreed to include it in the Online Safety Bill as it made its way through the House of Lords in 2023.[35] Downblousing is already a criminal offence in Northern Ireland.[36]

Non-consensual image making

The spectrum of non-consensual image recording is broad and covers a range of scenarios. Not all of these are covered by criminal offences, and even fewer are adequately redressed in tort law, as this chapter will explore. Alongside the variety of scenarios in which an image or video can be taken which displays something intimate, there are also a variety of scenarios in which images can be created depicting the victim in an intimate or sexual context. Author and poet

---

28 Annabel Rackham, 'Stephen Bear: Revenge porn conviction "sets a precedent"' *BBC News* 14 December 2022.

29 Ministry of Justice and The Rt Hon Lucy Frazer KC MP, 'Upskirting: Know your rights' *Gov.uk* 11 February 2019.

30 Ministry of Justice, 'How one woman made upskirting illegal: Gina Martin's story' *YouTube.com* 12 February 2019.

31 2003 c 42; s 67A.

32 The Sexual Offences Act 2003 does criminalise taking images or making images for sexual gratification or humiliation, distress or alarm where the individual depicted is breastfeeding, but the offence does not specifically refer to the image being of breasts or chests – just that the individual is breastfeeding, is about to breastfeed or has just finished breastfeeding (s 67A 2A-3B).

33 As was the case in *R v Hamilton* [2007] EWCA Crim 2062.

34 Shiona McCallum, 'Calls for downblousing to be made a criminal offence in England and Wales' *BBC News* 7 July 2022, citing Law Commission, Intimate Image Abuse.

35 Ministry of Justice and Raab, 'New laws to better protect victims'.

36 Justice (Sexual Offences and Trafficking Victims) Act (Northern Ireland) 2022 c 19 s 1.

Helen Mort was the victim of 'deepfake pornography', where images of her were uploaded to a site and users invited to create pornographic, explicit and violent images with her face on them.[37] The term deepfake refers to an image or video created by artificial intelligence (AI) (deep learning) which merges the face or voice of one individual with another, creating near-seamless images and videos which are difficult if not impossible to differentiate from reality. While the possibilities of deepfake technology are endless,[38] in reality there is one overwhelming application – pornography.[39] The creation and distribution of faked images and videos depicting individuals in sexual, private and explicit scenarios is by far the most common use of deepfake technology. Creation of synthetic media does not necessarily even require a deepfake AI – sufficient time and effort with an image editing program, such as Photoshop, can also produce realistic and convincing explicit imagery.

Non-consensual image distribution (including 'revenge porn')

The sharing of intimate images in a relationship is a relatively common practice – not just among teens,[40] but also in committed relationships[41] and in a majority of adults aged 18 to 32.[42] However, images and videos shared in the context of an intimate connection come with a distribution restriction – there is a generally understood expectation that those images are not for further distribution. While some have disagreed with this conception – Hunter Moore, the 'most hated man on the internet'[43] and founder of revenge porn site IsAnyoneUp.com suggested that by sending an intimate image, the sender was transferring all rights to the recipient[44] – in legal terms, sending an image or video to a specific individual is not consent to its wider distribution. However, there are multiple instances of

---

37   Sara Royle, 'Deepfake porn images still give me nightmares' *BBC News* 6 January 2021.

38   In 2022, BBC television drama *The Capture* explored the possibilities of deepfakes on news broadcasts: BBC, 'Security Minister gets deepfaked on Newsnight | The Capture Series 2 – BBC' *YouTube.com* 30 August 2022.

39   See Henry Adjer, Giorgio Patrini, Francesco Cavalli and Laurence Cullen, 'The State of Deepfakes' (2019) (available at https://regmedia.co.uk/2019/10/08/deepfake_report.pdf).

40   Sheri Madigan and others, 'Prevalence of Multiple Forms of Sexting Behavior Among Youth: A Systemic Review and Meta-Analysis' (2018) 172(4) *Journal of the American Medical Association of Pediatrics* 327.

41   Elle Hunt, 'Sexting: Do men and women do it differently?' *The Guardian* 14 November 2019, citing Rob Weisskirch et al, 'Abstaining and Engaging in Sexting Behaviors among Late Adolescents: Attitudes, Personality, and Attachment' (2020), presented at Society for Research on Adolescence.

42   Emily Stasko and Pamela Geller, 'Reframing Sexting as a Positive Relationship Behavior' (2018) (available at https://www.apa.org/news/press/releases/2015/08/reframing-sexting.pdf).

43   Alex Morris, 'Hunter Moore: The most hated man on the internet' *Rolling Stone* 11 October 2012.

44   Bob Garfield, 'Revenge porn's latest frontier' *On the Media* 6 December 2013.

this implicit permission being ignored – hackings,[45] ex-partners[46] and 'collector culture'[47] all contribute to the sharing of images online, and the criminal offence as it stands in England and Wales has large gaps in its effectiveness.[48] The sharing of intimate images online can take many forms, from posting on social media sites[49] to dedicated revenge porn sites[50] to mainstream pornography sites,[51] and can even take such malicious forms as specifically sending images or videos to families, employers, coworkers or the person depicted.[52] Only some of these sharing behaviours are criminal, although the harms caused are various, and tend to depend on the consequences of the sharing, rather than the intention of the perpetrator.

Threats to do any of the above

The threat of taking, making or sharing intimate images can have serious consequences, and can lead to victims feeling trapped in situations where they have little power.[53] While threats to distribute (in accordance with section 33 of the CJCA) are criminalised,[54] this suffers from the same weaknesses and lacunae as the disclosure offence, with motivations and types of images limited by the Act in the same way.[55]

There are a range of other activities which could conceptually fall within the spectrum of IBSA, or more broadly technology-based violence, including cyberflashing,[56]

---

[45] Jason Murdock and James Lillywhite, 'What is the Fappening? A guide to the nude photo scandal that shook the celebrity world' *International Business Times* 16 March 2017.

[46] Emily Reynolds, 'Why there's no "silver bullet" for ridding the web of revenge porn' *Wired UK* 16 March 2017.

[47] Anna Moore, '"I have moments of shame I can't control": The lives ruined by explicit "collector culture"' *The Guardian* 6 January 2022.

[48] Dymock and Van der Westhuizen, 'A Dish Served Cold'.

[49] Alexandra Ryan, 'The truth about my "sex tape"' *Goss.ie* 28 December 2020.

[50] Morris, 'Hunter Moore'.

[51] Mohan, 'I was raped at 14'.

[52] In England and Wales, this was the case in *ABK v KDT & FGH* [2013] EWHC 1192 (QB), where images of the claimant were sent to her spouse, her friends and her spouse's friends, in order to inflict maximum damage on the claimant; DeGregory, 'US weatherman fired after his nude photos were sent to boss' *news.com.au* 20 September 2022; Jennifer Smith, 'Teacher, 25, who was fired after topless selfie she sent to an ex-boyfriend was leaked to students three years later says the principal confronted her by showing her the picture on his computer screen' *Daily Mail* 5 April 2019; Aussa Lorens, 'My ex sent my nude pictures to my coworkers' *Cosmopolitan* 2 September 2014.

[53] Jennifer Savin and Natasha Saunders, 'My abusive ex threatened to post my intimate photos online – and it's still not a crime' *Cosmopolitan* 16 July 2020.

[54] As enacted by s 69 of the Domestic Abuse Act 2021, c 17.

[55] Dymock and Van der Westhuizen, 'A Dish Served Cold'.

[56] Clare McGlynn and Kelly Johnson, *Cyberflashing: Recognising Harms, Reforming Laws* (Bristol University Press, 2021).

cyberstalking,[57] online harassment and misogynistic abuse online. This chapter focuses on a range of scenarios where intimate images are taken or created of the victim-survivor, which necessarily excludes a range of scenarios such as unwanted pictures of genitalia,[58] 'tributing'[59] and other misogynistic and harassing behaviour.[60]

Image-based sexual abuse – harms and consequences

The examples already highlighted demonstrate the breadth of possibilities for IBSA, which centres around the violation of the bodily integrity, sexual autonomy and sexual privacy of the person depicted in the image. The actions of sharing, making and taking are varied, and are covered by a variety of criminal offences. The criminal regime, however, serves a different purpose to that of tort. Torts, as Jenny Steele suggests: 'are "wrongs". To be slightly more precise, torts are civil wrongs for which law will provide a remedy. This remedy will be enforceable against one party, to the benefit of the other, and it will reflect (and perhaps correct) the wrong committed.'[61] A remedy in tort is meant to address the harm which has been suffered – damages will compensate for the harm, but more importantly, an injunction can enforce the removal or deletion of images or videos. In order to argue that there should be a tortious remedy for the varied spectrum of IBSA, however, it is necessary to demonstrate that some wrong has been committed.

From a sexual autonomy, bodily privacy and feminist perspective, the wrong of IBSA is clear. The privacy and dignity of the individual has been violated, and that is something which ought to be protected – and in fact is protected by Article 8 of the European Convention on Human Rights (ECHR). This has been successfully applied in misuse of private information cases,[62] and means that a breach of this right should be actionable per se. To further bolster the argument, however, there are real harms which come as a consequence of IBSA and I offer here a few non-exhaustive examples of the far-ranging consequences of various types of this abuse.

---

[57] Michael Pittaro, 'Cyber Stalking: An Analysis of Online Harassment and Intimidation' (2007) 1(2) *International Journal of Cyber Criminology* 180.

[58] McGlynn and Johnson, *Cyberflashing*.

[59] Law Commission, Intimate Image Abuse, 9–10.

[60] This may be better addressed by comprehensive approaches to tackling violence against women and girls (VAWG) online, as suggested by the VAWG code of practice recommended for inclusion in the Online Safety Bill: Clare McGlynn and Lorna Woods, 'Violence Against Women and Girls (VAWG) Code of Practice' (available at https://bills.parliament.uk/publications/46668/documents/1880).

[61] Jenny Steele, *Tort Law: Text, Cases and Materials* (5th edn, Oxford University Press, 2022) 4.

[62] *ABK v KDT & FGH* [2013] EWHC 1192 (QB), and *Contostavlos v Mendahun* [2012] EWHC 850 (QB).

Victim-survivors of image-based abuse recount nightmares,[63] job losses,[64] online abuse[65] and emotional distress.[66] The psychological impact of image-based abuse is not dissimilar to that of sexual assault or rape.[67] Social backlash[68] and mental distress[69] are among the consequences documented from intimate images being shared. Further, not all those whose images are shared survive. There are numerous reports of individuals taking their own lives after images and videos of them in personal situations were shared.[70]

The consequences of image sharing are broad and varied. In their 2017 article, McGlynn and Rackley state: '[a]longside a coherent criminal law response, it is vital that victim-survivors of image-based sexual abuse are able to harness the civil law when seeking redress.'[71] In this chapter, I explore the potential avenues that victims can use to do so.[72] I also outline the civil remedies which are potentially available to victims of IBSA in England and Wales, and contemplate some potential reasons behind the near-impossibility of finding an adequate remedy for an entire spectrum of behaviours and abuses.

Tortious remedies for image-based sexual abuse

To successfully sue in tort for the harms suffered as a result of IBSA, a suitable tort needs to be identified. There are several questions to be asked here, and the order in which they can be asked is not fixed. This chapter will seek to outline the requirements of several torts and examine whether any of them provide a suitable remedy for IBSA. It will consider first the actions of the tortfeasor – first in looking to the intentional torts, and whether any of these can apply to IBSA, and then in looking to whether negligently inflicted harm would provide a suitable remedy. The discussion will then move on to the protection of personal

---

63   Royle, 'Deepfake porn images still give me nightmares'.
64   DeGregory, 'US weatherman fired'; and Smith, 'Teacher, 25, who was fired after topless selfie'.
65   Ryan, 'The truth about my "sex tape"'.
66   McGlynn et al, '"It's Torture for the Soul"'.
67   Samantha Bates, 'Revenge Porn and Mental Health: A Qualitative Analysis of the Mental Health Effects of Revenge Porn on Female Survivors' (2016) 12(1) *Feminist Criminology* 22, 38.
68   Hugo Gye, '"Distraught" girl, 17, faces humiliation on the web after explicit pictures of her performing sex acts at Eminem gig go viral on Twitter and Instagram' *Daily Mail* 20 August 2013.
69   Caroline Linton, '#SlaneGirl: Teenager hospitalized after oral sex photo goes viral' *Daily Beast* 22 August 2013; Ryan, 'The truth about my "sex tape"'; Lorens 'My ex sent my nude pictures to my coworkers'.
70   Examples include Sam Tranum, 'Family "bitterly disappointed" Garda likely to avoid criminal prosecution for Dara Quigley filming' *Dublin InQuirer* 8 August 2018; Elizabeth Chiu, 'The legacy of Rehtaeh Parsons' *CBC News* 6 April 2018; Ed Pilkington, 'Tyler Clementi, student outed as gay on internet, jumps to his death' *The Guardian* 30 September 2010; BBC News, 'Two arrested in Egypt after teenage girl's suicide sparks outrage' *BBC News* 4 January 2022.
71   McGlynn and Rackley, 'Image-Based Sexual Abuse', 557.
72   Rackley et al, 'Seeking Justice and Redress'.

interests, in the form of reputation and privacy protection, concluding that there are serious weaknesses with any of the tortious regimes as they currently stand in England and Wales.

Intentional torts

The first class of tort which will be discussed are the 'intentional' torts. These loosely grouped torts share a common feature of intention on the part of the tortfeasor. Referred to as 'intentional invasions of interests in the person and property',[73] and 'torts of intention',[74] the classification is not closed or agreed. In Kirsty Horsey and Erika Rackley's *Tort Law*, the classification given is 'the personal torts',[75] which groups trespass to the person with defamation and misuse of private information and separates out the land-based torts. Christian Witting, in *Street on Torts*, classifies trespass to land and goods as 'intentional invasions of interests in the person and property'.[76] Very briefly, trespass to land is of little use in IBSA situations because there is no land-based interest triggered. Although it may be possible to seek an action in trespass to land for some cases of voyeurism, peeping Toms or installing equipment to record images or videos, the action would not necessarily cover the resulting images or videos, only the trespass required to capture them. Similarly, as laid out in *Hunter*,[77] overturning *Khorasandjian*,[78] private nuisance attaches to a property interest, rather than a personal interest, so it would be unsuitable for similar situations. Further, nuisance requires a continuous activity or state of affairs,[79] so is unsuitable for a single incidence of taking images, although it may apply if distribution of the images later occurs.[80] Trespass to goods and the tort of conversion are similarly limited, in that they attach only to physical goods, and the intangible aspects of images and videos are not covered.[81] Thus, we move on to consider other intentional torts.

---

[73]   Christian Witting, *Street on Torts* (16th edn, Oxford University Press, 2021) 257.

[74]   Steele, *Tort Law: Text, Cases and Materials*, 33.

[75]   Horsey and Rackley, 'Tort Law'.

[76]   Witting, *Street on Torts*, 245.

[77]   *Hunter v Canary Wharf* [1997] UKHL 14.

[78]   *Khorasandjian v Bush* [1993] EWCA Civ 18.

[79]   *Bamford v Turnley* [1862] EWHC Exch J63.

[80]   It is potentially arguable that the consequences of images being shared – their being available online – is a continuous state of affairs, but it is difficult to see how that would be argued specifically against the person who took the images. It could perhaps be argued under *Law Society v Kordowski* [2011] EWHC 3182 (QB), 64.

[81]   *OBG Ltd v Allan* [2007] UKHL 21. Whether this is a preferable interpretation is debatable, but it is the law as it stands.

Intentional interference with the person

Witting outlines four distinct elements of trespass to the person and related torts.[82] I will discuss three of these – battery, assault and harassment.[83] The first two relate to physical interference with the person, while the third is a more nebulous consideration. Although creation, taking or distribution of images of an individual are undoubtedly a violation of their bodily integrity, this violation sits uneasily with the requirements of any of the three torts mentioned.

Battery and assault

Briefly, '[b]attery requires an act of the defendant which directly and intentionally brings about contact with the body of the claimant, where the contact exceeds what is lawful'.[84] There is no suggestion, in most situations of IBSA, of physical contact with the body, making this cause of action non-applicable. The target of *physical contact*[85] as the intentional element[86] renders this useless for situations relating to images.

Secondly, assault. Steele defines this as 'a direct threat by the defendant which intentionally places the claimant in reasonable apprehension of an imminent battery'.[87] Although assault is a 'secondary tort', the same barrier arises, in that there is an element of direct physical contact in the apprehension of the plaintiff. Again, with a lack of physical contact in IBSA, this is inapplicable in our situation.

Harassment

Finally for this section, we look to the tortious rights granted by the Protection from Harassment Act 1997. This Act specifically creates a right to sue in tort for an actual or apprehended breach of section 1(1), that is, a course of conduct which amounts to harassment, and grants a remedy in damages for, inter alia, anxiety and financial loss resulting from the harassment.[88] In theory, this is a very suitable remedy for cases of IBSA. However, in diving deeper into the Act and what amounts to harassment, several weaknesses become clear. Harassment requires a 'course of conduct',[89] meaning that there must be at least two instances of the

---

[82] Witting, *Street on Torts*, 260.

[83] The fourth element of this is false imprisonment, which is not directly relevant to the issues discussed in this chapter.

[84] Steele, *Tort Law: Text, Cases and Materials*, 37.

[85] ibid., 38.

[86] F.A. Trindade, 'Intentional Torts: Some Thoughts on Assault and Battery' (1982) 2 *Oxford Journal of Legal Studies* 211, 220.

[87] Steele, *Tort Law: Text, Cases and Materials*, 39.

[88] Protection from Harassment Act (PHA) 1997, c 40, ss 3(1)-(2).

[89] ibid., s 1(1).

behaviour to fall within this provision.[90] This means that a serial downblouse photographer would be able to continue their course of action unhindered by the prohibition, provided they never photographed the same woman more than once. While there is a provision in the Act about a course of conduct relating to multiple individuals,[91] it has limitations which place it outside of the specific example we have given.[92]

Beyond the 'course of conduct' restriction, while the definition of harassment given in the statute is relatively sparse,[93] there is ample case law defining what amounts to harassment. This is 'well understood', according to Lord Sumption in *Hayes v Willoughby*, as 'a persistent and deliberate course of unreasonable and oppressive conduct, targeted at another person, which is calculated to and does cause that person alarm, fear or distress'.[94] However, the characteristics of IBSA will not always sit easily within these parameters. While a vengeful former partner sharing images to deliberately inflict distress on their former lover would fall within this definition, and would satisfy the knowledge component,[95] hackings are not necessarily 'targeted at another person'.[96] The test for liability under the 1997 Act is an objective one, meaning that motivations of sharing 'for a laugh' or without thought for the impact on the plaintiff will still be captured, if constructive knowledge can be applied.[97] Nonetheless, this is not a perfect remedy. It leaves gaps where images are shared or created by multiple individuals,[98] where there is a single instance against multiple victims,[99] and leaves no injunctive relief against bodies corporate, such as websites or website operators, where images are allowed to circulate, causing further distress to the victim. Finally, while the 1997 Act does specify that injunctive remedies are available in civil suits of this nature,[100] they are injunctions restricting the named parties from further acts of harassment.[101] While this provides the victim with an enforceable cause of action against the individual harassing them, there is no solution granting them an ability to force websites to remove instances of images or videos from online, nor to prevent further uploads from being redistributed. Therefore, while this is a helpful cause of action in certain, specific circumstances,

---

[90] ibid., s 7(3)(a): though it can potentially be argued that repeated viewings online amount to a course of conduct, as indicated by *Law Society v Kordowski* [2011] EWHC 3182 (QB), 64.

[91] PHA 1997 s 1A.

[92] ibid., s 1A(c).

[93] That is, 'alarming the person or causing the person distress' (s 7(2)).

[94] [2013] 1 WLR 935, 1.

[95] PHA 1997 s 1(2). This is an objective test only: *Banks v Ablex Ltd* [2005] ICR 819, 20.

[96] *Hayes v Willoughby* [2013] 1 WLR 935, 1.

[97] *Levi v Bates* [2015] EWCA Civ 206 [35].

[98] Royle, 'Deepfake porn images still give me nightmares'.

[99] Our hypothetical downblouser, see text to note 90.

[100] PHA 1997 s 3A.

[101] ibid., s 3A(2).

it fails to encompass the full spectrum of interferences with the personality and privacy of the individual depicted.

Intentional infliction of emotional distress

The tort in *Wilkinson v Downton*[102] is a much discussed but rarely applied[103] tort which occurs where a defendant has 'wilfully done an act calculated to cause physical harm to the plaintiff'.[104] In the case itself, the plaintiff suffered from various physical reactions to an extreme nervous shock.[105] Although usually referred to as 'the tort in *Wilkinson v Downton*', it was also named as the tort of wilful infringement of the claimant's right to personal safety in *Rhodes v OPO & Anor*,[106] the tort of 'outrage' in the US,[107] 'intentional infliction of harm'[108] or, as named in this section header, intentional infliction of emotional distress.

In the American Restatement (Third) of Torts: Liability for Physical and Emotional Harm (2012), the commentary to the description of the tort states: '[t]he outrage tort originated as a catchall to permit recovery in the narrow instance when an actor's conduct exceeded all permissible bounds of a civilized society but an existing tort claim was unavailable.'[109] This sounds ideal for our circumstances. Taking private photos, sharing private photos or creating intimate and sexual images is very clearly outside the permissible bounds of a civilized society, but as we have seen already, tortious remedies for trespass to the person seem inapplicable. Thus, hopefully this tort can provide some elements of redress, although as our discussion will show, it may be more effective as a response to some kinds of IBSA than others.

As laid out in *Rhodes*, the modern version of the tort 'has three elements: a conduct element, a mental element, and a consequence element'.[110] The judgment goes on to state in the following paragraph that 'the conduct element requires words or conduct directed towards the claimant for which there is no justification or reasonable excuse, and the burden of proof is on the claimant'.[111]

---

[102] [1897] 2 QB 57.

[103] Arden LJ described it as 'the well-known but seldom used principle in *Wilkinson v Downton*' in *OPO v MLA* [2014] EWCA Civ 1277, 30.

[104] *Wilkinson v Downton* [1897] 2 QB 57, 58–9 (Wright J).

[105] Including 'producing vomiting and other more serious and permanent physical consequences at one time threatening her reason, and entailing weeks of suffering and incapacity to her …' (ibid).

[106] [2015] UKSC 32, 81.

[107] Russell Fraker, 'Reformulating Outrage: A Critical Analysis of the Problematic Tort of IIED' (2008) 61(3) *Vanderbilt Law Review* 983.

[108] Witting, *Street on Torts*, 268.

[109] Cited in *Rhodes v OPO & Anor* [2015] UKSC 32, 69.

[110] ibid., [73].

[111] ibid., [74].

However, the subsequent paragraphs present a troubling discussion which creates a difficulty likely to make this tort less impactful than it otherwise might have been. In *Rhodes*, the question was whether the book concerned was addressed to the claimant, a young child (the son of the author), and whether there was a justification for its publication. But the Supreme Court argued that the book was addressed to a wide audience, and thus the question of justification must be considered by reference to the entire audience.[112] This presents several issues for a hypothetical IBSA scenario. The previously mentioned downblouse photographer's actions are not necessarily directed at the people photographed. For people sharing images or videos online (whether artificially created or not), it is entirely possible that the individual depicted was not part of the intended audience, and so although the images or videos may be *of* the claimant, they may not necessarily be directed *towards* the claimant. Thus, despite the conduct violating the integrity or privacy of the person depicted, it may well not fall within the conduct element of the tort of intentional infliction of emotional distress.

Moving beyond the conduct element to the mental element, the question of intention arises. In *Rhodes*,[113] the Supreme Court discussed the requirements for the mental element at length, concluding that the proper formulation of the test was that the defendant must have 'intended to cause severe distress',[114] and held that recklessness was not sufficient for liability to arise. This is also troubling for our circumstances, both because it places a burden on the plaintiff to prove an intention to cause severe distress, and because there are many circumstances of image sharing which do in fact cause severe distress, even where that was not the intention.[115]

There are two cases which may prove helpful in applying *Rhodes* to the context of IBSA. In *ABC v WH & Whillock*,[116] a successful claim was brought under *Rhodes* for a course of conduct which involved grooming, encouraging the sending of explicit images and sexual contact between a vulnerable sixth form pupil and a schoolteacher. The judgment points out that '[i]t was obvious that the illicit relationship would in the end cause nothing but harm to the vulnerable Claimant some 39 years younger than her groomer and those consequences must have been entirely clear and obvious to Mr Whillock', basing this on the statement from *Rhodes* that '[t]here are statements (and indeed actions) whose consequences or potential consequences are so obvious that the perpetrator cannot realistically say that those consequences were unintended'.[117] The other

---

[112] ibid., [74]–[75].

[113] ibid., [83]–[87].

[114] ibid., [83].

[115] McGlynn et al, '"It's Torture for the Soul"'.

[116] [2015] EWHC 2687 (QB).

[117] ibid., [112]. The harms of IBSA are perhaps more well-known now in a post-#metoo world, but are arguably not yet entirely obvious or clear. The 2020 leak of thousands of non-consensual nude and sexual images from an Irish discord server indicates that more than 500 users downloaded images, and the prevalence of 'collector culture' indicates that there is, as

relevant case, which ultimately failed on vicarious liability grounds, was *MXX v A Secondary School*,[118] where a student in year 8 (aged 13/14) was groomed and assaulted by a former student who was on the school premises for a work experience placement. The judgment in *MXX* is clear that the elements of *Rhodes* are made out by the former pupil – the issue is when, and whether, the school is vicariously liable.[119] Where both of these cases fail to provide clear guidance, however, is in circumstances where there is not a relationship of grooming, or no physical contact: both *ABC* and *MXX* escalated to physical assault. Thus, while an abusive or grooming relationship can then be assumed to meet the requirements of *Rhodes,* there are nuances still to be discovered in many circumstances of IBSA.[120]

The third element of this tort is the consequence element. This, in line with the freestanding psychiatric injury discussed later, requires more than 'mere emotional distress', but rather a specific 'recognisable psychiatric illness with or without psychosomatic symptoms'.[121] This requires the harm suffered through the sharing or taking of images to meet a certain threshold – that of a recognisable psychiatric injury. This limitation, or minimum standard of harm, is distinct from other elements of intentional interference torts – assault and battery, for example, require only contact, and not necessarily that any harm results from that contact. It is a feature of trespass torts that there is no requirement for proof of damage.[122] While intentional infliction of emotional distress can be characterised as a tort of intention, it is undesirable in that it places additional requirements on the individual to show that they have suffered harm as a result of the tort. Thus, an individual who has their skirt lifted in public to allow a momentary glimpse of their underwear, buttocks or genitals would have an actionable case without proof of damage, but an individual who had a photograph taken under their clothes, allowing the perpetrator to view the image at their leisure, not only must prove consequent harm, but also that the harm amounts to a psychiatric illness – as mentioned earlier, mere emotional distress is not enough. Both the foregoing examples are interferences with the person – one much longer-lasting than the

---

yet, no generalised understanding of the very real harms that image sharing inflicts on victim-survivors. See Aoife Moore, ' "Collector culture": Thousands of non-consensual images of Irish women still being traded online' *Irish Examiner* 19 February 2021; Alexa Dodge, 'Trading Nudes Like Hockey Cards: Exploring the Diversity of 'Revenge Porn' Cases Responded to in Law' (2021) 30(3) *Social & Legal Studies* 448.

[118] [2022] EWHC 2207 (QB).

[119] ibid., [155].

[120] This is discussed in Horsey and Rackley's 'Tort Law' as being significant for cases of sexual abuse and grooming – although it does require a certain level of interaction between the claimant and defendant which many IBSA examples – hacking, trading nudes, upskirting, downblousing – do not tend to include.

[121] *Khorasandjian v Bush* [1993] EWCA Civ 18, 736 (Dillon LJ).

[122] Steele, *Tort Law: Text, Cases and Materials*, 40.

other – yet the momentary interference is the harm with the more accessible tortious remedy.

Overall, while the tort of intentional infliction of emotional distress is helpful in some circumstances of IBSA, it is limited in its applicability by virtue of the strict criteria required to successfully bring an action. Thus, while it provides a suitable remedy in circumstances where the IBSA is directly targeted at the victim and causes severe emotional distress, which the proponent intended to cause, this is only a sub-section of the spectrum of IBSA, leaving many victims unable to rely on intentional infliction of emotional distress to provide a remedy. It is a tort designed to protect a slightly different interest – freedom from emotional distress – from that which IBSA infringes – the right to privacy and dignity. Thus, it is not quite correct for our purposes.

Negligence: freestanding psychiatric injury

Many of the intentional examples discussed in the previous section fail to provide a remedy based on the same element – that there must be an intention to cause distress or upset to the victim. Perhaps, then, given the distinction between intentional torts and negligence,[123] an action in negligence would perhaps provide a suitable remedy.

Negligence has three basic components – the defendant must owe the claimant a duty of care, they must breach that duty and harm must arise as a result of that breach. In terms of duty of care, we can go back to the original formulation of the neighbour principle from *Donoghue v Stevenson*,[124] in which Lord Atkin states that you 'must take reasonable care to avoid acts or omissions which you can reasonably foresee would be likely to injure your neighbour'. Lord Atkin further goes on to define one's neighbour as 'persons who are so closely and directly affected by my act that I ought reasonably to have them in contemplation as being so affected when I am directing my mind to the acts or omissions which are called in question'.[125]

The duty of care has undergone multiple formulations and revisions since *Donoghue*, but the test as it stands since *Robinson*,[126] (re)outlining the incremental approach to be followed in novel factual situations, would do little to deter the conviction that when sharing an intimate image, the person depicted in the image is likely to be within the contemplation of a reasonable person when acting around that image or video. However, where the damage suffered by an

---

123   *Letang v Cooper* [1965] QB 232: 'If he does not inflict injury intentionally, but only unintentionally, the plaintiff has no cause of action to-day in trespass. His only cause of action is in negligence, and then only on proof of want of reasonable care' (Denning MR).

124   [1932] AC 562.

125   ibid., 578–83.

126   *Robinson v Chief Constable of West Yorkshire Police* [2018] UKSC 4.

individual is purely psychiatric, additional restrictions are put in place before the claimant can bring a case for negligent breach of duty of care.

Negligence requires firstly that the harm suffered by the claimant is 'compensable' harm.[127] In these circumstances, compensable harm requires something more than mere grief or anxiety, but must amount to a 'medically recognised condition of a sustained nature that disturbs the normal functioning of the mind'.[128] This is the same issue as discussed previously – while the interference with the physical body is actionable without proof of harm, the interference with the privacy of individuals through image sharing requires a higher threshold before it becomes actionable.

Further, there are more stringent standards required for psychiatric harm in the absence of physical harm, or the danger of physical harm. A series of cases covering freestanding psychiatric injury have created two categories of victim in psychiatric injury cases – primary victims[129] and secondary victims.[130] A primary victim is generally someone who was in the 'zone of physical danger',[131] but in circumstances of IBSA, there is no physical danger. There are several control devices which limit recovery for negligently inflicted psychiatric injury, but they are not all applied in primary victim scenarios. The first control device is that of a 'sudden shock'; cases concerning secondary victims require the victims to have been witness to some kind of shocking event.[132] The second control device, which has three elements, is the question 'Would it be foreseeable that a person of "ordinary fortitude" might suffer psychiatric injury, in the circumstances as they occurred?'[133] This is a departure in many respects from the normal approach to foreseeability in negligence, with actual physical perception required,[134] and the injury needing to be reasonably foreseeable[135] in a person of ordinary fortitude[136] – a distinction from the 'egg shell skull' rule that is usual in tort law, meaning that an egg-shell personality is not accounted for. The element of foreseeability is also assessed with hindsight – specific foreseeability, rather than foreseeability in the practical sense.[137]

---

[127] *White v Chief Constable of South Yorkshire Police* [1999] 2 AC 455, 491.

[128] Witting, *Street on Torts*, 72.

[129] *Page v Smith* [1995] UKHL 7.

[130] *Alcock v Chief Constable of South Yorkshire Police* [1992] 1 AC 310.

[131] *Page v Smith* [1995] UKHL 7.

[132] *McLoughlin v O'Brian* [1993] 1 AC 410.

[133] Steele, *Tort Law: Text, Cases and Materials*, 204.

[134] *Jaensch v Coffey* (1984) 155 CLR 549, 566–7 (Brennan J): 'a psychiatric illness induced by mere knowledge of a distressing fact is not compensable; perception by the plaintiff of the distressing phenomenon is essential'.

[135] *King v Phillips* [1953] 1 QB, 440.

[136] *McLoughlin v Jones* [2001] EWCA Civ 1743.

[137] Steele, *Tort Law: Text, Cases and Materials*, 205.

An important question which arises, then, is whether a claimant – who suffers a recognised psychiatric injury through the sudden shock of discovering their images have been shared online – would be a primary or secondary victim. Thus, we must look to circumstances where there has been no physical danger imposed on the claimant, but they have suffered psychiatric injury. Perhaps the closest analogy would be 'stress at work' cases, such as *Walker v Northumberland County Council*,[138] in which the claimant was permitted to recover through breach of duty for the nervous breakdown they had suffered as a result of their case load at work. This was confirmed in the Court of Appeal in *Hatton v Sutherland; Barber v Somerset CC*,[139] where Hale LJ (as she was then) outlined the 'threshold question' as whether the 'kind of harm to the particular employee was (or ought to have been) reasonably foreseeable'.[140] Stress at work is, thus far, the only circumstance in which a negligently inflicted psychiatric injury has been recoverable outside of an event which created, or purported to create, a physical danger. Thus, although it is theoretically possible to conceive of a situation in which a duty of care could be established between a perpetrator and a victim of image sharing,[141] it would be groundbreaking, and would require a level of argument which is outside of the scope of this chapter to explore. As the law in England and Wales stands at present, negligently inflicted psychiatric injury is unlikely to be a suitable cause of action. A further note – though damages can be a powerful remedy, injunctive relief is rarely granted in cases of negligence, which would leave the victim-survivor with little recourse to control the further spread of images or videos, making this also a less than ideal avenue for redress.

Personal interests

The final category of torts which are worth inspecting for potential remedies for IBSA are the personal torts – torts which protect personal interests such as reputation and privacy. These torts are well-placed to act in circumstances of IBSA because they already protect intangible assets and interests. Reputation and right to a private and family life are hugely important, but they are incorporeal interests. Thus, torts which already revolve around this area of interest provide a natural avenue for exploration of appropriate remedies.

---

[138] [1994] EWHC QB 2.

[139] [2002] EWCA Civ 76.

[140] And later confirmed and approved by the House of Lords in *Barber v Somerset CC* [2004] UKHL 13; Horsey and Rackley 'Tort Law', 141.

[141] And it may well be a work situation which leads to the expansion of this tort, as a circumstance where a supervisor or boss is the abuser would bridge the gap between circumstances, but this has yet to come before the courts.

Defamation

The tort of defamation is regulated by the Defamation Act 2013, which adopts previous common law rules of defamation. The requirements for a defamation action are:

- the defendant has published a statement;
- the statement has defamatory meaning;
- the statement refers to the claimant;[142]
- the statement has caused or is likely to cause serious harm to the reputation of the claimant.

The fourth of these elements was added by the 2013 Act.[143] Defamatory meaning is explored in *Sim v Stretch*,[144] where Lord Atkin suggests that the question to be asked is 'would the words tend to lower the plaintiff in the estimation of right-thinking members of society generally?' Defamation also has a complete defence in the form of truth.[145] This presents three major difficulties for victim-survivors of IBSA.

The first difficulty is that defamation requires publication of information.[146] Thus, it is not applicable for any scenarios of voyeurism, upskirting, downblousing, filming of sexual assaults or filming of intercourse where the images or videos are not subsequently circulated – even if the images or videos are then shared with the person depicted in them. *Sim v Stretch* outlines that at least one other individual needs to see the communication – even if that is only the telegraph clerk. The second difficulty presented is that there is a requirement, to successfully claim in defamation, to argue that a photograph or video of an individual in a sexual context would lower the plaintiff in the estimation of right-thinking members of society. This is an ideological position which may not be supported by many victim-survivors of IBSA – particularly those who have willingly expressed their sexuality through images and videos or who have engaged in sex work. There is nothing inherently wrong with expressing one's sexuality, and the free circulation of images or videos depicting that is not inherently wrong either – provided it occurs with the consent of the person depicted. Successfully claiming in defamation would require the claimant to show that there is something inherently degrading or negative about sharing images and videos which are private and/or sexual – an ideological position that may not be applicable for all victim-survivors. Third, as already briefly mentioned, truth

---

[142] Steele, *Tort Law: Text, Cases and Materials*, 793.
[143] s 1(1).
[144] [1936] 2 All ER 1237.
[145] Defamation Act, s 2(1).
[146] *Sim v Stretch* [1936] 2 All ER 1237; *Huth v Huth* [1915] 3 KB 32.

is a complete defence to defamation. Thus, where the images or videos shared are true images – not manipulated or synthesised – the defendant need only show that the images are entirely truthful, and they will be able to rely on the complete defence of truth to avoid a defamation claim. This is an unsatisfactory consequence of trying to fit the violation of one's bodily integrity into the tort of damage to reputation.

Finally, defamation can also be used as a weapon by abusers against their victims – if someone speaks up about the abuse they have suffered, defamation is a tool that can be used by the abuser against the victim-survivor. This can be seen in the much-publicised cases between actors Johnny Depp and Amber Heard in the UK and the US in 2020 and 2022.[147] In the UK action, although Depp did not sue Heard personally, she was called as a witness and forced to relive the turbulent relationship through seven witness statements and oral examination, which can work to silence victim-survivors of abuse. In the US action, Depp sued Heard, who countersued, and both were successful in some claims, but not all of them. The case was televised, lengthy and distressing for both parties, but Heard by far received the larger backlash, and ultimately was more severely punished by the jury for a statement that did not name Depp, nor did it make specific allegations of abuse.[148]

Defamation does have one strength as a cause of action – a successful action in defamation empowers the court to also make an order to websites or republishers to remove or cease publishing the defamatory statement.[149] This civil remedy to cease distribution of material is a powerful asset in the arsenal of someone unwillingly displayed online.

Misuse of private information

The final tortious action this chapter examines is misuse of private information.[150] This Human Rights Act (HRA)-influenced tort developed from the historical equitable doctrine of breach of confidence,[151] building on the obligations of the HRA 1998 to create a new tort which allows for a remedy where information which falls within the bounds of one's private and family life is circulated without justification or permission. The tort rests on the implementation of Articles of the

---

[147]   In the UK, *Depp v News Group Newspapers Ltd* [2020] EWHC 2911 (QB); in the US, *John C. Depp, II v Amber Laura Heard* (Unreported, Fairfax County Circuit Court 1 July 2022). See Holly Honderich, 'Amber Heard settles defamation case against Johnny Depp' *BBC News* 19 December 2022.

[148]   The piece in question was a 2018 opinion piece in *The Washington Post*: Amber Heard, 'Amber Heard: I spoke up against sexual violence – and faced our culture's wrath. That has to change' *The Washington Post* 18 December 2018. See also Moira Donegan, 'The Amber Heard-Johnny Depp trial was an orgy of misogyny' *The Guardian* 1 June 2022.

[149]   Defamation Act 2013, s 13(1)(a)-(b).

[150]   *Campbell v Mirror Group Newspapers Ltd* [2004] UKHL 22.

[151]   *Coco v AN Clark (Engineers) Ltd* [1969] RPC 41.

ECHR via the HRA, imposing an obligation on public bodies to act in a way in keeping with Convention obligations.[152] It requires a balancing between the Article 8 right to a private and family life and the Article 10 right to freedom of expression and right of a free press.[153] Where the right to a private and family life is deemed to override the right to freedom of expression, the court is empowered to order an injunction to prevent the publication or further publication of the information concerned in the case, and/or make an order for damages.

This is, it must be said, the most applicable tort to the spectrum of IBSA. Misuse of private information has been successfully used to sue for malicious distribution of intimate images,[154] so it is settled law that it is valid and applicable for some areas of IBSA. It provides injunctive relief which can be exercised against multiple defendants,[155] who need not specifically be named, and can allow for interim injunctions pending settlement of a full case. However, misuse of private information is not a perfect tort for the full spectrum of IBSA, for several reasons, many of which have already been discussed.[156]

First, misuse of private information only applies to circumstances where information is distributed, not where it is created or taken without permission, and not further circulated. This means that it does not apply to situations of upskirting or downblousing, photographs taken by voyeurs or peeping Toms, the non-consensual retention (without further distribution) of images or videos sent as part of a relationship, or other, similar circumstances. Without the distribution of the photographs, or threat thereof, there is no remedy forcing the perpetrator to delete or destroy the images or videos concerned, only the possibility of ordering them not to distribute the material further, which is an unsatisfactory situation. Second, misuse of private information, although it can be used against multiple defendants, is in practice difficult to use to force websites to remove content, even where that content has been the subject of a judgment. Finally, the cost of an action in misuse of private information is, or can be, prohibitive. YouTube star Chrissy Chambers, who sued her former partner for uploading videos and images of them to commercial porn websites, incurred legal costs in excess of £20,000.[157] This is, for many individuals, an insurmountable obstacle, preventing access to justice for those without recourse to such funds, even in the limited circumstances where misuse of private information is a viable course of action.

Misuse of private information need not necessarily be taken as a sole course of action – in *FGX v Gaunt*[158] the claimant was successful in claims for both

---

[152] *Campbell v Mirror Group Newspapers Ltd* [2004] UKHL 22, 16–17.

[153] *Re S (FC) (a child)* [2004] UKHL 47; Human Rights Act 1998, s 12(4).

[154] *ABK v KDT & FGH* [2013] EWHC 1192 (QB).

[155] As was the case in *Contostavlos v Mendahun* [2012] EWHC 850 (QB).

[156] Horsey and Rackley, 'Tort Law'.

[157] Jenny Kleeman, 'The YouTube star who fought back against revenge porn – and won' *The Guardian* 18 January 2018.

[158] [2023] EWHC 419 (KB).

misuse of private information and the intentional infliction of injury, citing *ABC v WH & Whillock*, and the judgment gives a useful summation of the principles for assessing the quantum of damages, relying on a number of earlier cases to amass a metric for assessment of special damages in image-based abuse cases.[159]

Conclusion

IBSA is a spectrum of behaviours which prey on individuals' bodily integrity, privacy, sexual dignity and ability to control the distribution and depiction of their own image. While there are a variety of torts which deal with invasion of privacy, bodily integrity and harassment, in many situations of IBSA, none of these torts are applicable, leaving claimants with no remedy. This is particularly noteworthy in circumstances of taking or making explicit images of individuals without further distributing them. The tortious remedies which do exist and are specifically targeted at invasion of privacy only suffice as a remedy where there is distribution of the image or video. The very fact of the existence of an image or video, regardless of how it was obtained, such as upskirting or downblousing, peeping Toms, hidden cameras or videos or images of sexual assault or rapes, is not sufficient to reach the threshold for a tortious remedy, either to compensate for the harms this can cause, or to force the delivery up or destruction of the images or videos.

The patchwork of tortious actions available to potential claimants in IBSA is unsatisfactory, and the gaps in the regime hinge on the gendered nature of IBSA.[160] Margaret Atwood once said that 'Men are afraid women will laugh at them. Women are afraid men will kill them.'[161] For a male–centred world view, the existence of explicit images and videos is not the issue – their distribution is. A violation of the body is not a violation unless there is physical touching. And a single violation of privacy, integrity or feelings of safety is not enough to allow for a tortious remedy in harassment – despite that violation potentially leaving the person concerned to fear for their safety on an ongoing basis.

Victim-survivors of IBSA are predominantly female,[162] with 75 per cent of calls to the Revenge Porn Helpline being made by women.[163] This further ties

---

[159] [2015] EWHC 2687 (QB). It further emphasises the importance of using appropriate terminology, referring to the sharing of intimate images as 'image-based abuse' and rejecting the term 'revenge porn'.

[160] The phrase of 'patchwork' is common to many elements of discussion around IBSA – see the Law Commission's Intimate Image Abuse final report, which refers to 'the patchwork of laws and intimate image threats'. Although referring to the criminal law, the same approach of piecing together the appropriate tortious solution inhibits access to justice for victim-survivors. Similar arguments are made by Horsey and Rackley, 'Tort Law'.

[161] As quoted in Jennifer Wright, 'Women are afraid men will murder them' *Harper's Bazaar* 17 January 2018.

[162] Victims' Commissioner, The Impact of Online Abuse: Hearing the Victim's Voice, 2022, 27.

[163] Revenge Porn Helpline, 'RPH cases and trends of 2021' (2022).

into cultures of sexuality and shame. In Ireland in 2013, an image circulated on social media of a male-female couple engaging in fellatio. The picture went viral and the female participant – dubbed #Slanegirl – was shamed and criticised; despite both parties engaging in a sexual act together, and the female participant being fully dressed, while the male participant was half-naked, with his genitalia exposed.[164] The consequences of circulation of intimate images are more severe for women than for men. Thus, a justice system and a tort structure which is largely made by men and interpreted by men is unlikely to take into account the devastating consequences of IBSA in all its forms. IBSA is a serious and growing issue causing harm to and violating the rights of men, women and non-binary people, young and old, with serious, often life-changing or life-ending consequences. The failure of tort law to consider these multiple harms is a consequence of its short-sighted limitations in categorising torts into individual causes of action which fail to properly encompass the trauma and harms which can result from the various activities on the spectrum of IBSA. For these reasons, I add my voice to the existing calls[165] for a new, specific tort, a tort which is future-proofed[166] and acknowledges the nuanced impacts that IBSA has on people from different backgrounds, protecting the sexual privacy of individuals and providing remedies in the form of both damages and injunctions for those whose privacy has been violated by the myriad forms of IBSA.

---

[164] Gye, ' "Distraught" girl, 17, faces humiliation on the web'; Linton, '#SlaneGirl: Teenager hospitalized'.

[165] Horsey and Rackley, 'Tort Law'; McGlynn and Rackley, 'Image-Based Sexual Abuse'; Rackley et al, 'Seeking Justice and Redress', 314–17.

[166] The word 'deepfake' was only coined in 2017, but is now a pervasive form of IBSA.

Index

The letter 'n' indicates a footnote.